WHO KNOWS TOMORROW?

Uncertainty in North-Eastern Sudan

Sandra Calkins

berghahn
NEW YORK · OXFORD
www.berghahnbooks.com

Published in 2016 by
Berghahn Books
www.berghahnbooks.com

Library of Congress Cataloging-in-Publication Data
A cip record for this book is available from the Library of Congress.

British Library Cataloguing in Publication Data
A catalogue record for this book is available from the British Library

ISBN 978-1-78533-015-5 (hardback)
ISBN 978-1-78533-016-2 (ebook)

CONTENTS

ILLUSTRATIONS

Acknowledgements

Many people have encouraged this project in different ways. I therefore want to thank all who have supported me over the past years spent doing my research and writing this manuscript. My greatest thanks go out to the many Rashaida who shared their life with me, particularly Hamda and her daughters, who took me into their home. I thank them especially for their hospitality and for enduring my intrusive presence in difficult circumstances.

I want to thank Ursula Rao for critically reading various drafts of the chapters; this work owes much to her thoughtful criticism. Special thanks also goes to Richard Rottenburg, who encouraged this work intellectually. I am grateful to him for inviting me to join the Law, Organization, Science and Technology (LOST) group. Working in the field between anthropology and STS inspired the theoretical outlook for this book, and the new approach advanced for Sudan ethnography and anthropology is closely connected to debates taking place in LOST.

I further want to thank Susan Reynolds Whyte for her intense and critical reading of this manuscript, and for offering much cherished advice. Thanks to members of the LOST group who have read and commented astutely on various draft chapters and helped me to improve them. I want to thank Enrico Ille for his ethnographic commentary and for providing useful suggestions. I want to give my special thanks also to Guma Kunda Komey for many insightful conversations on Sudan. Thanks are also due to my colleagues Janka Linke and David Kreuer for their friendship and stimulating exchanges.

I want to express my gratitude to Jörg Gertel, who invited me to join an interdisciplinary research programme, funded by the German Research Foundation (DFG), where I secured a position and money for field research. I would also like to thank Günther Schlee for arranging for me to be associated to his department at the Max Planck Institute for Social Anthropology. This provided me with an excellent infrastructure within which to read and compose the manuscript. Thanks are due to the University of Khartoum, but in particular Musa Abdul-Jalil for his long-standing intellectual and administrative support in Sudan.

I thank Lea Bauer for preparing the maps and figures and am grateful to Paul Tyler for proofreading chapters. Many thanks also to Molly Mosher and Charlotte Mosedale at Berghahn. Any remaining errors are my responsibility. Finally, I thank Marco and Hannah for their patience.

Notes on Transliteration

I value readability for a non-Arabist audience more than exact scientific transliteration and thus have introduced a number of compromises as well as idiosyncrasies. The transliteration of Arabic is generally done according to the transliteration guide of the *International Journal of Middle Eastern Studies* (IJMES, www8.georgetown.edu/departments/history/ijmes/index.html), which is a modification of the transliteration system of the *Encyclopedia of Islam*. Accordingly, to enable easier reading, diacritical marks and italics are only used for technical terms and not for personal, group or place names (apart from ʿayn and *hamza* in names). For example, *dār* as a technical term bears the diacritical mark, but it is not used in the place name Darfur. I use technical terms sparingly. For the sake of clarity I cite only the standard Arabic transliteration of technical terms, which corresponds to the written form of words (*miskīn* instead of *misčīn*), and do not follow the Rashidi dialect, which has a strong Gulf inflection (instead of *k*, Rashaida often say *č*). Words in the *Webster's Collegiate Dictionary*, such as jihad or sheikh, are not considered technical terms. I refrain from transliterating technical and administrative terms (*nazir/nazarah* instead of *nāẓir/naẓāra, omda/omodiya* instead of *ʿumda/ʿumudīya*) introduced by the British colonizers, as these are commonly known to readers of Sudanist literatures. I use accepted English spelling for names and places; when there are no common or preferred English spellings, merely ʿayn and *hamza* are added. However, I do not commonly use ʿayn in personal or place names with the letter A (not ʿAli but merely Ali, although I do use it with the letters U and I, i.e. ʿUbeid or ʿId).

LIST OF ABBREVIATIONS AND GLOSSARY

'awlād ʿamm (Ar.; sg. *wad ʿamm*): father's brother's sons

bayt (Ar.): house; also nuclear household

CPA: Comprehensive Peace Agreement

dār (Ar.): circle, territory; also extended household

dhuwī (Ar. *ḏuwī*): literally 'those of' (to be followed by senior man's name); extended household

DUP: Democratic Unionist Party

feddan (Ar.): measurement unit for land: one *feddan* equals 0.420 hectares

GRAS: Geological Research Authority of the Sudan

karāma (Ar.): value and norm of generosity; also grace and nobleness (opposite of *taḥaššud*)

khor (Ar.): seasonal watercourse

marḍ/marḍān (Ar.): sickness/sick

Native Administration: system of indirect rule through local headmen, established under British colonial rule

Nazarah (Ar.): territory of a Native Administration

Nazir (Ar.): head of a Native Administration

NCP: National Congress Party, the present ruling party in Sudan (which emerged out of the National Islamic Front)

NGOs: Non-Governmental Organizations

rakūba (Ar.): tent-like hut of wood and cloth

ruṭal: a standard weight, 449.28g

RFL: Rashaida Free Lions; ethnically oriented political party mainly of eastern Sudan

SDG: Sudanese pound, former currency in Sudan, which replaced the Sudanese dinar in 2007, and was in turn replaced by the new Sudanese pound in July 2011 *šawāl/ǧawāl* (Ar.): a hollow measure of volume that fits into a standard sack of grain or sugar

sorghum: a grain; the main subsistence crop of north-eastern Sudan

SPLM/A: Sudan People's Liberation Movement/Army

STS: Science and Technology Studies

taḥaššud (Ar.): bashfulness (esp. of poverty) which constrains acting

UN: United Nations

INTRODUCTION

Taming Unknowns in Sudan

> Man who lives in a world of hazards is compelled to seek
> for security. ... The quest for certainty is a quest for a
> peace which is assured, an object which is unqualified
> by risk and the shadow of fear which action casts. For it
> is not uncertainty per se which men dislike, but the fact
> that uncertainty involves perils of evil.
>
> John Dewey (1929: 3, 6)

'We have no dinner tonight', Hamda tells her children quietly. When her
twelve-year-old son complains bitterly, she replies in a low, sharp voice, 'We
are avoiding eating' (lit. avoiding the food, *nataǧannab al-'akl*). Hamda's food
reserves are running low. To 'avoid eating' means eating less, and skipping
some meals to delay the complete exhaustion of food supplies. It is a strategy
of rationing that people such as Hamda, who usually have food, employ. It
thus differs from hunger (*ǧūʿ*), which is a constant companion of the poor.
Hamda does not know whether her supplies will run out completely this
time. If God wills, they will eat. Now they are forgoing a meal. For how long
they must do so is unknown. What next? How long can this situation last
before the consequences become serious?

Anxiety increases as staples decrease. Running out of food is an existential
situation experienced by many Rashaida women in a small settlement in
the Lower Atbara area of north-eastern Sudan. In 2009 and 2010, the main
period covered by this book, men were often absent due to labour migration

or gold mining in nearby wadis. What should a woman do as her flour stock runs low? Will her husband return from gold mining soon and, most importantly, will he return with money? Or will he return empty-handed, and perhaps even with debts? How do women deal with such uncertainties? And how do they provide food for their children?

Uncertainty is a universal phenomenon, a lived experience, an unease about acting in view of an unpredictable future. Uncertainty is a rendering of realities, which can lead to innovations and creative solutions, but also can debilitate people through fear or unease, impairing their ability to act. Conceived broadly, uncertainty is logically an element of all action, because outcomes are always unknown and indeterminate. While uncertainty is inextricably present in all human enterprises, plans and aspirations, it is not evenly distributed across time and space. It is not a uniform property of action; rather, how it is perceived, experienced and dealt with varies.

This treatise had its genesis in my observation that the daily affairs of Rashaida in Sudan occur within a strikingly limited range of predictability. I often sensed an enormous uncertainty about what was going to happen next, a pervasive anxiety about the future. Perhaps this made a particular impression on me because I had come from Germany, where people often take for granted that the outcomes of actions are more or less predictable, and where state institutions still to a large extent produce a sense of security by issuing relatively reliable prognoses and insuring people against misfortunes such as unemployment, disability or debilitating old age.[1]

This study examines how Rashaida in a marginal area of Sudan experienced various unknowns and how they dealt with such situations. Reference to 'Rashaida' in the Sudanese discourse denotes pastoral people who migrated to north-eastern Sudan in the mid-nineteenth century from the Gulf States and were classified by colonial administrators as a landless settler tribe (MacMichael 1922: 345; W. Young 1996: 101–6; Bushra 2005: 277–78; Pantuliano 2005: 12). In view of their difficulty in accessing not only grazing land but also land for rain-fed farming and settlement, and their reliance on agreements with landowning groups (Pantuliano 2005: 15, 16; W. Young 2008), settlement is still a fairly recent phenomenon among Rashaida in Sudan. It gained impetus as from the 1970s and 1980s many gradually began to move away from a pastoral economy to other sources of income, such as farming, labour migration to the Gulf, trade and, most recently, gold mining.

In the Lower Atbara area of north-eastern Sudan, the overall circumstances of Rashaida appear dismal and precarious. Many Rashaida have more or less settled there in the past decade. They mostly live in tents or newly erected huts or adobe houses on the parched hinterlands, the fruitful agricultural land near the river Atbara already occupied by sedentary farming communities. Resources are scarce, infrastructure (electricity, roads, deep wells, etc.) and public services are lacking. While artisanal gold mining offers new income opportunities and some have literally found a gold vein, it also exposes people to new uncertainties about their livelihoods. Drawing on my fieldwork among Rashaida in the Lower Atbara area in the northern River Nile State and the observed limited predictability of daily life, this study analyses different kinds of uncertainty and how they relate to agency.

Uncertainty refers to the limited ability to predict even the immediate future – that is, to engage it prudently and with foresight in a more calculative mode and to enact certain visions of what will happen. I show that the degree of reflexive enquiry with which people in Sudan act is decisive for the perception and management of situational unknowns. Reflexivity here denotes critical probing about premises and grounds of interpretations and actions. It involves self-awareness when attention shifts from doing something to the conditions under which it is done. It concerns how people conceive of and evaluate relationships between objects out there (reality) and representations (images). For example, reflexivity may be low when people view the representation of something as faithful to their own experience, but they may also stumble upon a distance between representations and their experience, triggering increased reflexivity. I do not see reflexivity as solely constituting an irritating problem for knowledge claims but also as an opportunity, a way of engaging with the world that enables one to refine what is known and generates new forms of knowledge (Woolgar 1988).

Differentiating between engagements with varying degrees of reflexivity thus allows me to qualify subtypes of uncertainty – from a situation where uncertainty is bracketed and the existence of a reality is taken for granted without sceptical examination, to one where there is radical uncertainty about all entrenched things. Relevant questions for the discussion thus arise. What allows people to take social norms or organizational forms for granted most of the time as a common basis for interactions? When do they become aware that what recently was accepted as a given is no longer so, and begin to question the validity of social arrangements and associated mores?

The short vignette that opened this chapter provides a glimpse into this complex field by highlighting a source of existential uncertainty and pointing to seemingly converging but also contradictory ways of engaging it. In the above situation, Hamda avoids preparing some meals in order to conserve the flour stock for as long as possible. It is a pressing problem and she does not question its premises reflexively. She invokes ideas of a divine will and preordination, which delegate responsibility for events to an all-knowing, inscrutable Islamic God. At the same time, Hamda actively, self-reliantly and pragmatically engages the uncertainty through reciprocal exchanges with other women in the settlement (see chapter 4). Sometimes she also consults a fortune-teller, who lays out cowrie shells to predict when Hamda's husband will send money from Kuwait or whether one of her sons-in-law will return with money from the gold mines – a practice that her brother-in-law, the sheik and local imam, condemns as spiritistic and backward. This indicates that uncertainties are not always passively endured – Hamda and other Rashaida actively and versatilely engage and process daily unknowns so typical of life in rural Sudan.

In this book I explore how people experience incertitudes – from gruelling everyday uncertainties to life-threatening dangers – and how this relates to situational needs to cooperate and survive. I use the ethnographic data presented in my four empirical chapters to qualify (sub)types of uncertainty and the ways in which individual people manage them. As a contribution to an anthropology of uncertainty, I theorize how lacking knowledge about the present and the future is processed in relation to different degrees of confidence in reality and varying needs for action. To that end, I examine situations and the configuring relationships between uncertainty, reflexivity and forms (i.e., rules, conventions, lists, agreements, norms, etc.), the latter utilized as supports for action and coordination. The stability of forms – their ability to hold together – hinges on how they are invoked, used and taken for granted, or doubted, critiqued and challenged in interaction.

Mary Douglas's work on the perception of dangers/risks is a good starting point for conceptualizing an anthropology of uncertainty. Thinking along these lines means elaborating various everyday practices, methods and non-/probabilistic techniques through which people address and seek to exert control over the uncertainties of life – individually and collectively. It also means outlining those things which ordinary people take for granted in their management of everyday unknowns and those moments in which once self-evident things are critically appraised to renegotiate a broader range of options. A basic assumption is that uncertainties need to be processed and that people thereby 'invest in forms' (Thévenot 1984): they seek to establish certain elements as binding orientations for actions, that is, as something they can refer to when interacting and when disputes arise. In my theoretical discussion below, I show that all forms are to some extent selective and arbitrary, which makes them vulnerable to denunciation. The indeterminacy of being cannot be tamed entirely. Yet, extreme kinds of uncertainty, where all epistemic foundations are lost or distrusted, can be translated into something more manageable, such as insecurities or risks, where at least some points of reference are assumed to be stable.

To provide the reader with an overview of how this book addresses gaps in knowledge and the establishment of forms, or the more established theoretical terms of contingency and agency, this introductory chapter first presents an overview of the different types of uncertainty and forms encountered in the ensuing empirical chapters. Then, I present the contexts that situate and qualify the experience of existential unknowns in Sudan.

The Argument

This study focuses on the creation, confirmation or critique of forms as semantic devices to deal with uncertainties. I am inspired by the pragmatist philosopher John Dewey and his approach to problems and problem-solving through experimentation. In his famous 1896 text, 'The Reflex Arc Concept in Psychology', Dewey criticized those psychologists of his day who conceived of action mechanistically – that is, as a series of separate events. He provided a typical example of such compartmentalization of action: a child sees a bright candle, reaches for it with a hand, feels the pain caused by the hot flame, and consequently withdraws the hand. Dewey argued that the differentiation of different phases of action can only result from exercising reflexivity after the act, because people lack a complete conception of the end until they have a complete grasp of the course of action that will take them there. In other words, when people experience something as problematic, they are already outlining what is problematic and thus are beginning to articulate a path to a solution. Applying this to my study means that uncertainty cannot be disassociated from the forms developed to address it nor from the ends in view, because as people test whether forms work, they are simultaneously enquiring whether an action can clear up the uncertainty or whether the problem itself, or some of its aspects, have to be reformulated, whether new questions have to be posed and whether new scenarios have to be developed.

Conceiving of action as testing and experimenting as Dewey did means accounting for the principal openness of outcomes; I adopt such a point of departure for this study of how uncertainties are managed. I have not only adopted a pragmatist paradigm from which I argue but also have devised a special form for the book, which I hope the reader will find at least suggestive and somewhat innovative for what could otherwise have been a classical anthropological study. My method of presentation is one of progressive contextualization: context is not behind or beyond a situation, but is in the situation itself. Although I do set the stage and prepare an argument about marginalization and uncertainty in Sudan, I purposely do not primarily provide the cultural context to explain how people live elsewhere, nor do I describe who Rashaida are, what they believe, what their institutions, organizational structures and norms are, and what their history is. Rather, in this account of uncertainty, I delve into practices in various situations and then untangle what was taken for granted in actions and to which institutions or moral understandings people deferred. I try to give only as much background as is needed to understand what is happening in the situations under scrutiny, to avoid the impression that certain effects were caused directly by this or that factor. This enables me to retain some uncertainty in the text.

I begin by analysing a delimited event that occurred on a single day (chapter 2), then move on to an income-generating activity (chapter 3), and then to broader concerns of everyday life – hunger and sickness (chapters 4 and 5). I consider various kinds of forms and explore how people mobilize and reflect on them, and thereby I intend to create a novel kind of ethnography, an ethnography of experience and uncertainty that gradually takes its shape as readers follow along through different situations and contexts that comprise people's lives in this part of the world.

Overall, this book articulates its concern over how uncertainties are processed in a situation marked by scarcity, transformations and ruptures in Sudan in seven chapters: an introduction, a theoretical road map, four empirical chapters and concluding reflections. The empirical chapters cover disparate spatial and temporal horizons and focus on the relationships between the main actors: to wit, a charity, the sheikhs and the entire settlement, gold miners and detector users, neighbouring women, and sick family members and their extended kin. The focus on how the various main actors manage indeterminacies also draws attention to other principles of sociality in the different chapters: interactions at a communal level between sheikh and villagers (chapter 2), patron–client and other professional relationships among male gold miners working outside the settlement (chapter 3), reciprocity in the immediate neighbourhood among women, and normative expectations of kin solidarity in caring for the sick (chapters 4 and 5). The chapters are organized to give a topical overview of existential unknowns typical of daily life in this part of Sudan – health and illness, food supply and hunger, uncertainties of income, and a controversy about the distribution of incoming aid – and to outline people's means of managing them. However, I have selected the concrete situations and occurrences – the ethnographic core of each empirical chapter – based on a method of theoretical sampling: they relate and respond to my theoretical propositions concerning the relationships between uncertainty, reflexivity and the stability of forms.

This book should therefore perhaps not be judged as a conventional ethnography. It neither aims at a systematic presentation of the lives, social forms and historical circumstances of Rashaida in the Lower Atbara area of north-eastern Sudan, nor is it primarily a contribution to regional studies, working out the hidden logics and peculiar dynamics of certain remote places in Sudan. This book is about a problem, and it is rooted in the problem, not in the people or the place. To some extent I am writing within a long-established tradition of anthropological scholarship by focusing on a 'small place' – that is, a small settlement and its surroundings in the hinterlands of the Lower Atbara area of north-eastern Sudan – but the ongoing concern at the heart of my investigation is a fundamental issue: a universal dimension of the human condition, namely, the uncertainty of human existence. While I locate this at a specific site and at a historical moment, the topic resonates and articulates with comparable sites where people are struggling with hunger, poverty, disease and insecurity at the margins of dysfunctional states without working welfare structures; it serves as a reminder of human vulnerability and a common humanity. My main contribution thus is to the social study of uncertainty by way of an ethnographic study in Sudan.

This approach seeks to capture a broad spectrum of situations – between a situation where vexing qualms about priorities and values emerge, which can mount a challenge to existing orders, and a situation where uncertainty is bracketed and actions presume a shared interpretation of reality. I contend that the degree of reflexive enquiry is relevant in interpreting and acting upon situational unknowns. Subtypes of uncertainty and the responses they elicit can be differentiated based upon the degree of reflexivity with which the knowledge in the situation itself is questioned. The burden of my argument is to demonstrate the way in which a focus on how forms are engaged in situations, whether they are reflexively interrogated or taken as unquestioned elements of reality, makes things visible that other theoretical approaches and propositions may take for granted.

Figure 0.1 depicts an abstract relational model to capture, approximately, these connections. The array consists of two axes: the Y-axis stands for reflexivity, the X-axis for uncertainty. Moving up the axes means increasing either uncertainty or reflexivity. The diagonal from bottom left to top right indicates the stability of forms and represents an ideal typical correlation between uncertainty and reflexivity: when both are high, forms are very unstable, whereas low or zero uncertainty and reflexivity imply a high stability of forms. The diagonal extends between a bracketing of uncertainties and a consensus on knowing one version of reality at the lower left, and controversies, that is, people's realization that their interpretations of reality differ, at the upper right. These connections are explored in this study. Radical uncertainty in this model denotes that differences and doubts are allowed to surface to such an extent that they destabilize and deconstruct 'reality' and its sense of objectivity and open up a situation to renegotiation. Here is where we can locate a revolutionary potential.

I must introduce a caveat here. Examining the figure may imply that uncertainty and reflexivity can be measured or are in a necessary correlation. This, of course, is not the case. With this visualization I do not present a mathematical model that can measure the intensity of the experience of uncertainty; rather, my thinking is relational. My goal is to draw attention to the relationship between uncertainty, reflexivity and the stability of forms.

The four large circles in the figures highlight specific configurations of these three analytical categories and explore their ability to confirm or challenge orders; investigating these connections is at the heart of the different empirical chapters. However, the location on the figure is not meant to suggest that certain phenomena inflict more or less stress upon people. When a risk is understood as life-threatening, most Rashaida would find it more vexing than a radical unknown. Extreme uncertainty due to the lack of knowledge about what is actually at stake produces disorientiation, whereas conceiving something as existential danger produces orientation for actions.

Figure 0.2 situates the empirical chapters of the book (chapters 2–5) in the relational model. Chapter 2 (charity) covers the emergence of the most radical – that is, revolutionary – forms of uncertainty in the book. Suddenly, during a distribution of aid by a charity, villagers cease to cooperate with

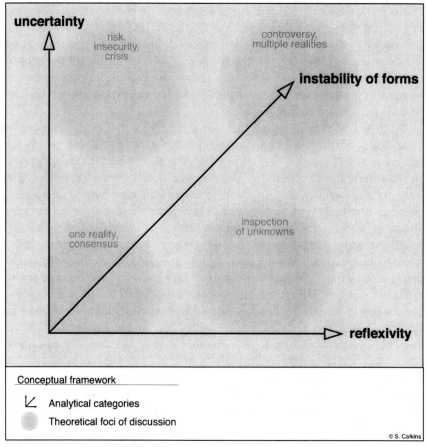

Figure 0.1 Uncertainty, reflexivity and forms: a relational model

the sheikhs and reflexively question forms (social categories, lists, rules of distribution, etc.), openly criticizing what is taking place. This shift from lower to higher reflexivity and uncertainty in the ethnographic narrative is marked by an arrow in the figure; and an increasing fussiness and instability of the form. The situation results in chaos and a challenge to the established order. In contrast to the controversies dealt with in chapter 2, chapter 3, on gold mining, deals with agreement. It details how multiple existential uncertainties in gold mining are limited and pushed aside by an insistence on consensus and the rightness of forms. Reflexivity is low and established organizational forms (shifts, rules of revenue distribution, etc.), and the orders they support, are confirmed as miners focus on the tasks at hand.

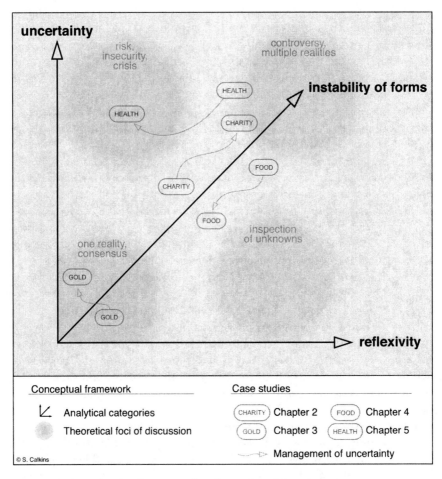

Figure 0.2 Situating the chapters in the relational model

The other empirical chapters do not fit into the neat correlation between reflexivity and uncertainty, but they allow us to explore other important dimensions of the relationship between reflexivity, instability and forms. Chapter 4 (food) details how existential unknowns are processed with regard to the mundane, though no less serious, problems of daily life. It deals with the gnawing uncertainty of running out of food supplies. I investigate how this existential incertitude is displaced through the establishment of a certain form – standards of exchange – to increase predictability in exchanges and guarantee equivalence; here in Figure 0.2 the form gains stability. The circle at the top left implies that different types of uncertainty have already been given a form, namely, as risk, insecurity or crisis, and along with this definition, ways of dealing with them are being outlined: reflexivity is low and uncertainty is high but limited by knowledge that the forms embody. Chapter 5 (health) explores troubling uncertainties of ill health and how these are managed by investing in forms (serious sickness, crisis, etc.). As ill health is translated into sickness, the proper course of action is more circumscribed and reflexivity about epistemic foundations and premises is reduced and must be subordinated to the necessity of preserving lives.

One circle in the model is empty. None of the empirical chapters addresses this way of managing uncertainty and there is a good reason for this. Rashaida, as far as I was able to observe, engage uncertainties pragmatically, making ends meet, doing something with what is at hand in the situation. According to the figure, in the empty circle reflexivity is high, while uncertainty is comparatively low and forms are fairly stable. An example for this would be intellectualizing serious problems of life, addressing them by means of reason and reflection without great fear or anxiety. I would suggest that this rational management of uncertainties, especially the preoccupation with calculating futures and making them predictable, is characteristic of 'modern' government, a type of government linked to a loss of metaphysical foundations: 'the discovery that the world is not deterministic' and the invention of statistical laws (Hacking 1990: 1). Modern government in this sense has not been fully institutionalized in Sudan.

Theorist Michel Foucault studied the historical rise of modern institutions in Europe from the sixteenth century.[2] A crucial feature of a modern configuration is a concern with rendering futures readable and predictable. According to Foucault, a shift to modern government came about when both new dangers and new possibilities to accumulate wealth arose. Security was problematized and techniques of security developed, linked to the emergence of 'population' as a new subject to be managed in nineteenth-century Europe; normalcy was invented as 'society became statistical' (Hacking 1990: 1, 4; Lemke 2011: 42, 43). The government of life and its calculation were novelties, enabled by a liberal conception of freedom and anchored onto an indeterminate future, which is a prerequisite for all attempts at engineering certain outcomes (O'Malley 2004: 173). The Foucaultian term 'biopolitics' designates state politics, the administration and regulation of population and of the material conditions of its existence, for instance, by implementing programmes for education, health, sanitation and so on.[3] The identification of statistical regularities is a key feature of such a modern figuration and enabled a new obsession, expressed in an avalanche of numbers: 'the taming of chance' through the invention of numerical and classificatory technologies, which contribute to 'making up people' (Hacking 1990: 2, 3).

Effective biopolitics depends upon an intricately developed art of governance, including fully-fledged statistical and calculative apparatuses, which generate knowledge, anticipate futures, identify dangers and calculate risks in order to regulate, secure and control the population. This results in a situation, as is the case in European welfare states, in which life is seen as something that individuals and collectives rationally organize and seek to improve. Today, most areas of EuroAmerica at least appear to be governed by risk-based routines for which 'great bodies of data are turned into predictive formulae … to make objective, standardized and exact predictions to replace subjective expectations based on such non-quantitative modes of calculation as rules of thumb, experience, foresight, estimation and professional judgment' (O'Malley 2004: 1), i.e., preventive diagnostic testing, dietary and exercise regimes.

Foucault's argument about security and the calculative tasks of government is helpful when engaging with uncertainty and the in/stability of forms. The practice of biopolitics presupposes and creates a high stability of forms. To enable calculations, systems of classification need to be invented and institutionalized, a number of uncertainties have to be translated into quantifiable probabilities, and regularities have to be discovered and explained. Emerging numbers, statistics and categorizations not only describe a reality but actually make it, forming the epistemic basis for biopolitical interventions such as legal acts, regulations or disciplinary measures, but also for how individuals make sense of the world. The absence, or rather very selective practice, of biopolitics in Sudan is part of the problem and explains why uncertainties can reach such an existential level. The prevalence of pragmatics in managing uncertainties in the Lower Atbara area of Sudan from this perspective points to the absence of strong central institutions to secure the population against the greatest harms.

Political Practices and Uncertainty in Sudan

Uncertainty is a universal phenomenon, something which is constitutive of human experience and life. It permeates all actions to some extent. Nonetheless, there are significant differences in one's experience of uncertainty depending on where one lives. We can hardly claim that the uncertainties experienced daily by Rashaida in north-eastern Sudan are the same uncertainties that people experience elsewhere when engaging in highly risky activities, for instance, at the London Stock Exchange. Rashaida I got to know have to process unknowns in a precarious setting where actions may have life-and-death consequences. Unknowns and the limited predictability of everyday life are existential matters.

The specific quality of uncertainty experienced by Rashaida in the hinterlands of the Lower Atbara area is framed by processes of marginalization on various scales. The state is controlled by an elite, who have translated global patterns of in/exclusion into national politics that marginalize communities religiously, culturally and economically. This section discusses some aspects of how this affects the situation of Rashaida in the Lower Atbara area. Furthermore, I explore how incertitudes in Sudan may be enmeshed with what many observers have described as an emerging global social order and mechanisms of in/exclusion. Attention then is shifted to state practices, but I view them from the perspective of the marginalized. I contend that discourses on marginalization raise normative expectations among people of what a state should do. This understanding is linked to a model of the state that is circulating but unrealized. This affects how people make sense of the unpredictability of being and leads to dissatisfaction with governmental practices.

Margins and Marginalization

But what does the metaphor of the margins mean? Margins are not geographical, anchored in Euclidean space; rather, they are always relational concepts.[4] Margins refer to a centre, and to an unfavourable or extreme position with respect to the centre. In the social sciences, margins and the making of margins, that is, marginalization, are often applied to state–society relations, referring to a voluntary or enforced distancing of groups from the state's reach and means of security.[5] Reflecting on margins and the state, Das and Poole (2004: 4) argue that 'margins are a necessary entailment of the state, much as the exception is a necessary component of the rule'. They further posit that while margins may be territorial, 'they are also, and perhaps more importantly, sites of practice on which law and other state practices are colonized by other forms of regulation that emanate from the pressing needs of populations to secure political and economic survival' (ibid.: 8). Understanding margins as a site of practice is useful when attempting to make sense of Sudan, where state institutions are exploited by a narrowly focused ruling party and fail to redistribute resources to the peripheries. People thus mainly have to secure their survival through their own efforts and to negotiate their own norms for coordination, which partially disregard and violate state law.

In Sudan the concept of marginalization is articulated on various levels with different connotations. Firstly, it is used as a heuristic by scholars dealing with Sudan, such as in the present attempt to situate my work within Sudan ethnography. Secondly, on the ground in Sudan, it is above all a political claim and refers to a lack of socio-economic and political recognition by the central governmental. Marginalization is a concept that is used by armed opposition groups to justify their resistance to the government – and is also used by Rashaida. Thirdly, this discourse has circulated and become a common language for everyday actors to describe their position vis-à-vis the state.

In scholarly analyses, the term 'marginalization' refers to interlinking socio-economic and sociocultural processes, to wit, how elites have monopolized the state apparatus in postcolonial Sudan (Rottenburg 2002: 10–12), enriching themselves and enshrining their power while delivering 'tangible development benefits for key constituencies' only (Jok 2007: 275–76; Large and Patey 2011: 181). Lesch (1998: 15) summarizes the situation: 'Muslim Arabs from the Nile Valley have dominated the political, economic, and cultural life of Sudan. They hold the main government posts in the capital city, the majority of seats in all the parliaments, and the senior positions in the armed forces. They lead the educational institutions, trade unions, industries, and businesses'. This discriminatory distribution of resources between the centre and peripheries is also backed by a number of developmental statistics. To give one example from a multitude of reports and NGO papers, the calculated national poverty rate of 46.2 per cent shows broad regional disparities, such as 26 per cent in Khartoum and 60 per cent in peripheral states including the Red Sea, South Kordofan and North Darfur (World Bank 2013).

Heather Sharkey (2008: 33–37) analysed the historical background against which the marginalization of vast areas and populations has unfolded. She points to the problematic processes of nation building after independence (1956), which replaced British colonial rule with an internal colonialism: the hegemonic rule of a small number of northern riverine Arabs over the rest of the vast country. This has produced peripheries in the south, east and west, and 'a post-colonial political and economic culture of Arabs-take-all' (ibid.: 42). Arabization and Islamization are the pillars of national unification programmes, but this compulsive politics of homogenization marginalizes communities on religious and cultural grounds (for instance, Hutchinson 1996: 4; Holt and Daly 2000: 153–54, 187–89; Johnson 2003: 138; Jok 2007: 212–14, 221; Komey 2010: 90–93). Echoing Mamdani's influential work, one scholar noted with regard to the discriminatory Sudanese politics that 'those who are considered Arabs by the racialized state are treated as citizens, … and those who are perceived as non-Arabs are treated as subjects' (Idris, in Sharkey 2008: 42).

But what does this mean for Rashaida in north-eastern Sudan? They are in a paradoxical situation. As Muslims with an uncontested Arab pedigree, many Rashaida nonetheless articulated a sense of being both socioculturally and economically marginalized by the very government that championed Arabization and Islamization policies. This relates to other axes of marginalization. The neglect of rural communities in governmental economic planning, especially via a rural-urban divide and an occupational marginalization, is an established scholarly theme. Postcolonial nationalization policies in Sudan promoted the marginalization of rural communities by disbanding customary land tenure and abolishing the Native Administration in the early 1970s. The Unregistered Land Act notoriously converted all non-registered land into government land, annulling customary communal claims to land and enabling urban capitalist farmers to expand their businesses (Kibreab 2002: 456). This enabled the encroachment of mechanized, export-oriented agriculture on former pasture and rain-fed farming land – an ongoing process that has recently accelerated with the financialization of agribusiness as well as the financial and food crises (Gertel et al. 2014; cf. Tetzlaff and Wohlmuth 1980; O'Brien 1986).[6] This increasing competition for land has affected rural populations across Sudan. Along with other factors, it has contributed to a demise of pastoral production among Rashaida in the Lower Atbara area and their impoverishment since the 1980s (Calkins 2014).

The marginalization of Rashaida can also be linked to their occupation. Even if Rashaida from the Lower Atbara area barely engage in pastoral production anymore, but rather depend heavily on labour migration to the Gulf and artisanal gold mining, they still are classified as herders and thus suffer the consequences of marginalization. The prejudice that nomadic pastoralists are prone to excessive and irrational behaviour – overexploiting pastures and resisting change – was and still appears to be widespread among government officials in Sudan (Ahmed 1980: 39, 49; Manger 1996: 26; cf. Rao and Casimir 2002). In spite of their important contributions to the economy, pastoral nomads in Sudan and those with a background in livestock herding 'are enduring multiple marginalization processes, exacerbated by strict land laws and misguided development plans promulgated by the state' (Casciarri and Ahmed 2009: 11, 12).[7]

Different kinds of marginalization also intersect. Guma Kunda Komey (2010: 73–77) described how the postcolonial state in Sudan has systematically excluded Nuba populations from their own land allegedly for national economic interests and has marginalized them socioculturally, all the while promoting large-scale mechanized farming in South Kordofan. Similar to Sharkey, Komey (2010: 2–6) sees marginalization as a sort of continuity from British colonial rule, which divided the country into a core centre, where economic and sociocultural development occurs, and underdeveloped peripheries, where resources are extracted.[8]

In political claims margins and marginalization (Ar. *taḥmīš*) also feature prominently. These claims are commonly connected to demands of socio-economic and political recognition by the central government and the elite along the Nile.[9] Jok (2007: 14, 15) connects the rise of political discourses of marginalization to John Garang, a leader of the SPLA, who interpreted the second civil war (1983–2005) 'as being more about cultural, economic, and political marginalization of the peripheries than race and religion', from where the discourse travelled to Darfur and other peripheries, such as Abyei, Blue Nile and South Kordofan. John Young (2007a: 11) indicates a longer historical trajectory, namely, that marginalization as a term was already employed during the political rallying for the Beja Congress since its foundation in 1958. 'Marginalization' and 'marginalized areas' reverberate in the political programmes of opposition parties, such as the Beja Congress, the Justice and Equality Movement and the Rashaida Free Lions (RFL).[10] It has been a main justification for taking up arms. Many Rashaida with whom I talked in the Lower Atbara area have been sympathetic with the political goals of the RFL for a long time, even if few actually joined the armed insurgency in eastern Sudan.

Eastern Sudan is often characterized as one of Sudan's most marginalized regions (Pantuliano 2005; J. Young 2007a), referring mainly to the poverty of its inhabitants. In this context, Leif Manger (1996) speaks of a 'marginal environment', that is, an environment marked by scarcity of resources and 'human adaptations' in the form of pastoral production, rain-fed farming, lumbering and charcoal production. People in eastern Sudan have not received a share of the oil wealth, even though the pipelines cut across the area to transport the oil to Port Sudan. Benefits have been siphoned off elsewhere. Young (2007a: 11) writes that marginalization in eastern Sudan meant and 'continues to mean the overwhelming poverty of the region, the government in Khartoum refusing to pursue development, or even provide basic services such as health and education in the east, and the government undermining local economies and traditional authorities'.[11] This regional setting of scarcity is important to understand the existential aspects of uncertainty that weigh upon Rashaida in the Lower Atbara area.

In eastern Sudan, Rashaida had already rallied against their marginalization in the 1990s. As nomadic pastoralists, many felt disadvantaged by Sudanese land laws, which continue to be based on colonial classifications of groups, conferring upon them a status as landless newcomer tribe. This had profound political implications: Rashaida lacked settlement land and were administratively subjected to a rival group, namely Hadendowa, a customary landowning group with its own tribal territory (*dār*) and an independent Native Administration. After a severe drought had decimated livestock, strict anti-smuggling measures in eastern Sudan in the 1990s curtailed cross-border trade with Eritrea, a lucrative source of income for many (Pantuliano 2005: 15, 16; J. Young 2007a: 21). Some began to organize resistance to the Sudanese government. They accused the government of launching hostilities aimed at undermining the livelihoods of Rashaida. Mabrouk Mubarak Salim, a former DUP member and wealthy trader, enrolled people in opposition to the marginalization of the Rashaida, and founded the Rashaida Free Lions political party in the late 1990s (J. Young 2007a: 21; Calkins 2014: 194–95).[12] A considerable number of young men were mobilized and joined the armed opposition in eastern Sudan and Eritrea (mid-1990s–2006). Hence, overall, the Rashaida Free Lions developed the same goals as the Beja Congress (BC),[13] the long-standing ethnic opposition party of eastern Sudan, namely, to bring an end to their marginalization.

The Lower Atbara area was somewhat disconnected from these developments, however. Only three men who were living in Um Futeima in 2010 had joined the fighting in Eritrea, although many more people expressed their disdain of the government that did nothing for them and continually praised Mabrouk for his courage and manliness.[14] Yet, like their kinsmen in eastern Sudan, Rashaida in the Lower Atbara area are classified as landless nomadic herders, although few own stock today. Pastoral production in this area has been in decline since the great drought of the mid-1980s, but customary ownership of land is still firmly in the hands of Bishariyn and Ja'aliyn. Gaining access to land for settlement – something that Rashaida in different parts of Sudan increasingly desire – and rain-fed cultivation thus depend significantly on personal relationships with local landowning groups, to the dismay of many (Calkins 2014).

Political claims of marginalization, therefore, are not only made within the national political sphere and mirrored by scholarly discourses, but have entered everyday discourses in Sudan. Rashaida in the rural Lower Atbara area where I conducted my study often articulated a sense of being neglected and marginalized by the central government. In light of people's disgruntled attitude towards the government, the state is viewed as remote and disinterested, and yet still potentially threatening to people inhabiting this area. Individuals complained about the lack of access to health and veterinary services, education, electricity and a permanent water source, but also cited sociocultural marginalization.[15] Some sheikhs and clan leaders reinforced the ongoing process of marginalization by referring to their constituency's *taḥalluf* as nomadic pastoralists – that is, being backward, slow-witted and filthy ('we are dirty') – when compared with the more urban, riverine and purportedly purer Islamic lifestyle among settled people along the Nile. In Um Futeima, the settlement where I spent most of my time, settling down was seen as an important step in catching up and becoming civilized, modern and educated in a purer Islam. The settlement's first building was a mosque, and soon afterwards the imam started teaching the Quran to children. A school was soon to follow; however, neither school nor mosque was funded by the government but instead by charities after certain individuals had expended much time and energy to mobilize funds. People often maintained that this was necessary, since Rashaida were uneducated, sitting in the desert and running after camels, but that their children should become doctors in order to help their communities and have better lives.

This feeling of inferiority, caused by their pastoral and 'unclean' background, was the explicit reason why some sheikhs in Um Futeima, where I carried out most of my research, felt they had to hold closely to orthodox Islamic interpretations. During my stay, the urban educated sheikh and imam in the settlement worked hard to eradicate 'false' folk-Islamic practices among fellow Rashaida, such as divination, the wearing of amulets and other lucky charms, and fortune-telling, which were more widespread among mobile Rashaida I encountered in Kassala. He preached against such practices and condemned them as un-Islamic, demanding a turn to a purer Islam as found among the Arabs along the Nile. The Arab–Muslim identity project thus affected how my interlocutors engaged with the lack of assurance concerning the future and seems to have marginalized certain practices as un-Islamic. This is relevant for how people process uncertainties and may explain why such practices have declined or at least have become less acceptable in public.

Margins can also refer to a territorial dimension, as can be seen when viewing the relative distance of my field site in the Lower Atbara area of north-eastern Sudan from the nation's centre around Khartoum (see Map 1). The Lower Atbara area appears to be so marginal and uninteresting that it is even peripheral to Sudan's conflicts – in stark contrast to South Kordofan, for instance, an area rich in agricultural land and oil reserves. Whereas parts of South Kordofan, Blue Nile State and Darfur reinstigated war against the government in 2011, the Lower Atbara area has remained peaceful. As a longtime pastoral region, it has seen no strategic governmental investments in agriculture, oil or other industries, and hardly any infrastructural services have been established for its rural settlements. The region's marginality, however, may soon be over. Concession agreements with foreign investors for gold mining were signed in 2010, for an area which included the artisanal mines in the Lower Atbara area (Calkins and Ille 2014).[16] The area has suddenly been mapped as worthy of exploitation but without the concomitant promise of

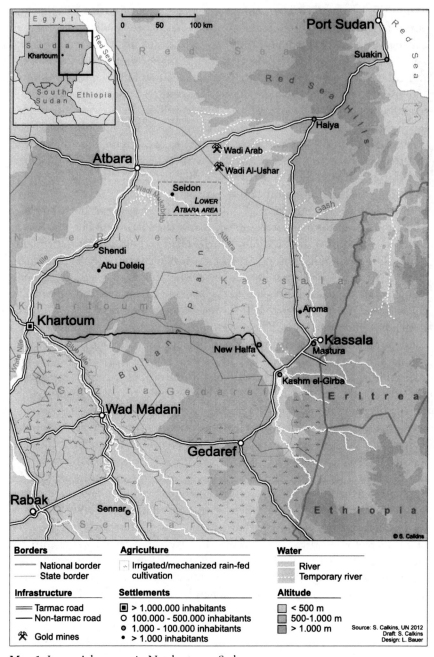

Map 1 Lower Atbara area in North-eastern Sudan

tangible benefits for the inhabitants. Margins are multidimensional: centres of resource extraction for some and a site of exclusion for others.

To sum up, ideas of margins, marginality and marginalization situate this study. They are notions to describe how people in Sudan experience their position vis-à-vis the Sudanese government and make sense of their exclusion from essential resources. They express the understanding that the government is not living up to expectations of what a good government should do, namely, to protect its citizens from the most threatening perils of existence. The ongoing discussions about marginalization indicate that people in the study area perceive themselves as being at the margins of the state's distribution of resources and its strategic interests. This shapes people's understandings of *al-ḥukūma* (the government), its intentions and their opinions concerning what to expect – if anything – from such a distant, detached state apparatus: certainly, nothing good. This ethnography details the disorienting effects of interlacing processes of marginalization, the unpredictability of the future and the way in which situations are experienced where survival is at stake. It shows how people deal with the constant uncertainties that overshadow their lives when the state does not provide security but rather evokes feelings of being ignored.

Global Ordering and In/Exclusion

The notion of the margins is trickier in international relations, where a clear centre is missing. The historian Ali A. Mazrui in 1968 referred to Sudan's position vis-à-vis both the Middle East and Africa as 'multiple marginality' (Sharkey et al. 2015: 2). And when we follow Manuel Castell's (2004) assertion that a new global social structure has arisen – the network society, which connects places through technically mediated flows of information and communication, enhancing people's communicative and interactive options – then Sudan would certainly qualify as a country situated at the margins of these global communication networks, perhaps best known instead for its devastating wars in Darfur and South Kordofan and for having the first ruling president to be indicted by the International Criminal Court. Otherwise it is little reported on, except when it makes the news with ever fresh examples of sickening cruelty, which generate moral sentiments in the recipients, a type of 'distant suffering' (Boltanski 1999). The crucial point for this discussion is that the uncertainties with which Rashaida grapple in Sudan do not result from an inherent backwardness or their delayed arrival in modernity. Rather, I draw on authors who enable me to argue that the marginal position of many in Sudan and in the world relates to contemporary neoliberal processes of ordering, which systematically produce excluded populations – that is, 'black holes' – in global society, while tightly integrating small productive and extractive enclaves (Stichweh 2005: 59). Developing this argument is important because I will discuss below theorists for whom risks are markers of modernity. They would not classify Sudan as modern, but would assent to an unproblematic link between uncertainty/ premodernity and risk/modernity, a view I seek to undercut. Rather, I assert that the particular uncertainties Rashaida experience are strongly linked with contemporary globalizing orders.

In view of the superabundance of literature, I need to limit the discussion to a few central aspects for my argument. Since the 1980s studies have proliferated that theorize novel transnational processes. The acceleration of information and communication technologies, new forms of global connectivity, the deregulation – or rather, neoliberal regulation – of markets, the devolution of state powers, commodification and privatization, new mobilities and new experiences of space-time compressions, are often subsumed by buzzwords that imply an increasing streamlining of life worlds, such as neoliberalization or globalization (Castells 2004; Harvey 2005; see Knöbl 2007). The new and the global seem to go hand in hand. Wallerstein (1974) had already posited a connection between modernity and global systemic integration. A similar point that anthropologists like to stress is that small places can no longer be understood without paying attention to the large issues (Eriksen 2001), the dynamics of integration into globalizing economics, politics, arts, media and legal structures.[17] Furthermore, in Sudan selected economic sectors – above all the resource extractive industries – are strongly integrated into transnational flows of capital and knowledge. Sudan has been a source of foreign resource exploitation for a long time, dating back to ancient pharaonic invasions to plunder gold, and in the ninth century, Arab invaders' quest for gold, ivory and slaves (Ḥasan 2005: 56). Mineral extraction and export-oriented large-scale agriculture were initiated under colonial Anglo-Egyptian rule and have drawn major investors from Western states, the Gulf States and most recently Asian countries (Large and Patey 2011; Verhoeven 2012; Linke 2014; Umbadda 2014). But this integration concentrates on small extractive or productive enclaves, which bypass most people in Sudan and do not deliver any benefits to them; these enterprises instead often figure as a source of insecurity that drives rural people from their land (Komey 2010).

Every inclusion entails exclusion. Rudolf Stichweh's notion of world society and Manuell Castells's global information network both work with the metaphor of black holes (see Rottenburg 2002).[18] Stichweh (2005: 59) argues that black holes – as the impenetrable gaps that suck up everything which comes near them and from where hardly anything can ever extricate itself – are a fitting physical analogy for the chaotic, obscure margins in the unfolding global tapestry. Apart from the included islands of global capitalist extraction, Sudan can be seen as a marginal country, or black hole, in the world society. This is an arresting point when compared to earlier Sudan ethnography. A number of studies had highlighted the gradual breakdown of 'barriers of exchange' and the involvement of local communities in more global economic exchange, their appropriation and mixing of capitalistic practices with socially established ideas of morality, and the emergence of an indigenous 'peripheral capitalism' (Duffield 1981; Omer 1985; Rottenburg 1991; see Barth 1967 for spheres of exchange). One might suggest that the near-complete marginalization and exclusion of many Sudanese livelihoods marks a gradual shift away from a colonial and postcolonial process of integration into a globalizing social and economic order, from exploitation to total exclusion. Today global integration concentrates on productive enclaves – typically in terms of mineral extraction (Ferguson 2006: 194).[19]

Many scholars aver that there is a novel quality about how people relate to each other and to things, whereby 'the global' is often seen the main marker of a new modern period. I follow Latour's (1993) thesis, *We Have Never Been Modern*, as it resolves the problem of 'othering' that inevitably accompanies the occidental periodization of modernity (Rottenburg 2008a: 405). Based on a clear divide between nature and culture, Latour argues that the modern person is deceived and believes herself to be different from other cultures.[20] This represents an important contrast to authors who inspired my conceptualization of uncertainty, such as Foucault, Luhmann, Beck and Boltanski. They all agree that there is modern/premodern, based on the rise and differentiation of central institutions (science, medicine and so on) since the eighteenth century, which secure, organize and regulate populations against anticipated harms. From these perspectives Sudan – distinct from Europe – is not modern and never has been. In contrast, when modernity is defined as self-deception as Latour would have it, nobody has ever been modern, but this does not rule out the existence of substantial differences among various places.

James Ferguson (2006: 185) maintains that the coevalness of African societies, their alternative modernities, is out of sync with how many Africans – still inspired by the dreams that modernization theory holds out, the promise of a brighter future, of catching up through development – think about modernity. Nonetheless, the disbanding of modernity as a uniform cultural object has been an important contribution of theorists who do not venture from the assumption of one modernity, but plural, alternative or entangled ones.[21] This also implied a break with an evolutionist understanding of history as progress. There are many ways of being modern; many paths lead to modernity but they do so in different ways. Modernities therefore should always be considered in the plural (Knöbl 2007: 60). But what then are the common criteria that justify calling them modern? And what do we get if we assume that Sudan is in fact modern but only differently so? Ferguson has drawn attention to a blind spot of such approaches, particularly prevalent among anthropologists, who often mistake deplorable circumstances for happy bricolages, creative adaptations and syncretisms. This runs the danger of 'evading the question of a rapidly worsening global inequality ... the enduring axis of hierarchy, exclusion, and abjection, and the pressing political struggle for recognition and membership in the emerging social reality we call "the global"' (Ferguson 2006: 192–93).

But a non-modern stance is equally unable to address power asymmetries between different places and institutional contexts (Rottenburg 2008a: 422). Being modern/non-modern does not present itself simply as a choice. While the moderns may take off their distorting spectacles to glance at modernity as a type of reality construction, the non-moderns may have no comparable way of becoming modern. Rashaida in Sudan would probably prefer the security of being modern because it implies not only self-deception but also the existence of strong institutions that can provide secure references for acting and achieving a noticeable predictability. If I assert that no one has ever been modern – in the end, so what? The important point is that moderns managed to create a situation of predictability, regularity and security that is fundamentally different from the existential uncertainty experienced on a daily basis by Rashaida in north-eastern Sudan.

Having confined modernity to a specific, powerful reality construction – certainly underwritten with relatively stable material-semiotic arrangements to which many Africans aspire (Ferguson 2006) and which feed imaginations of good life as well as expectations and critiques of government – I can connect modernity to real circumstances in Sudan without promulgating the latter's alterity or their participation in a different modernity. Rather, it is the circulation of modern ideas in the sway of neoliberal processes that allows people in Africa to notice gaps between 'sweet dreams ... [and] an insomnia full of nightmares of "being left behind" – of missing the train, or falling out of the window of a fast accelerating vehicle' (Bauman 2007: 11; see also Comaroff and Comaroff 2001; Mbembe 2002). In combining the insights of Stichweh and Castells, the production of black holes appears as an inevitable characteristic of globalizing social orders, patterned by discursive and material mechanisms of in/exclusion. The selective economic inclusion of productive and extractive enclaves means more generalized exclusion. Rottenburg (2002) argues that Sudan's exclusion from global society is translated into an exclusionary discourse of Arab-Islamic autochthony, which is used to violently suppress non-Arab, non-Islamic communities. Following this argument allows directly linking processes of marginalization and the acuteness of survival in Sudan to the emergence of black holes. In Sudan, most of the population tends to fall into black holes, struggling for survival on the margins, whereas crucial resources (oil, gold, etc.) are extracted through globally integrated and foreign-dominated enterprises, which are largely disconnected from national political and social developments in Sudan. Global patterns of in/exclusion thus at least co-produce multiple processes of marginalization in Sudan and, together with the lack of governmental securing mechanisms, produce a situation where survival is at stake for many.

Biopolitical Projects in Sudan

Marginalization is an effect of political practices in Sudan, and it is reflected in the understanding of some people with regard to what the government is failing to provide for them and is thus at the root of opposition to the government in Sudan. There have been intermittent violent conflicts between governments and citizens since independence. Civil wars between north and south shook the country from 1955 to 1972 and from 1983 to 2005, and during the 1980s and 1990s conflicts also flared between the government of Sudan and other armed groups in South Kordofan, Blue Nile State, Eastern Sudan and Darfur (Johnson 2003). In 2011 war escalated again in South Kordofan, Blue Nile State and Darfur, as many had predicted in light of unresolved political grievances (Komey 2010; Rottenburg et al. 2011). What I wish to stress in this section is that the quality of uncertainty in the north-eastern Sudanese hinterlands is entangled with Sudanese politics, which is not devoted to regulating and securing the entire citizenry but rather pursues discriminatory and assimilationist policies.

Many Sudanese live in abject poverty, with infrastructural services such as clean water, sanitation, roads, hospitals and schools lacking. Disease and hunger are endemic. Yet Sudan experienced some of the highest rates of economic growth on the African continent since the onset of oil production in 1999 and has received significant direct foreign investment (Large and Patey 2011). This paradox between high revenues from oil and the persistence of hunger and poverty raises troubling questions about the state and stateness in Sudan. Recent scholarship has highlighted that the state should not be taken for granted as an entity existing above and separate from society, wielding power over citizens; rather, the pertinent analysis is to demonstrate how a situation arises in which a state is represented as a unified and cohesive entity (Gupta 2012). In anthropology there has been an impetus to investigate how 'the state' is being produced through mundane bureaucratic practices in institutions, locales, offices, bureaus and so on (see, for example, Ferguson and Gupta 2005: 118, 105; Gupta 2012: 46; Bierschenk and De Sardan 2013). Or, similarly, a call has been issued to study sovereignty not only through the legal texts and norms but also as a practised 'right over life (to protect or to kill with impunity)' (Hansen and Stepputat 2006: 296).

Drawing inspiration from such scholarship, the relevant questions become: how it is that Rashaida experience the state as a marginalizing entity, as something that is up there, and potentially hostile, distant and uncaring? What practices construct these images and ideas of the state and how do they affect the experience of uncertainty?

Practices of government are brought to bear on Rashaida in the Lower Atbara area in ways that marginalize them, especially economically and socioculturally. Ruling elites in Sudan have used their political power for private accumulation and self-preservation, while ignoring most of the populace. For most people the state is a source of insecurity, something that needs to be coped with rather than relied upon (Hutchinson 1996). There seems to be scholarly consensus that the development of modern institutions, which can protect citizens from harm and formulate common goods, failed in Sudan (Lesch 1996; Battahani 2000; Rottenburg 2008b).[22] But based on what conception of modern institutions does this evaluation of failure often occur? What are these modern institutions?

Debates on modernity and the state are wide ranging, and attempting to do them justice lies beyond my attempt to understand how political practices in Sudan are intertwined with uncertainty. I stand on the shoulder of a giant, namely, Michel Foucault.[23] Although pertaining to historical dynamics in Europe since the sixteenth century, Foucault's work can be utilized to make sense of the situation in Sudan. He provided crucial impetus to debates about modern government, control and power by linking the historical rise of modern institutions to a new need for security and to the emergence of population as a new object of government. Risks to population and its subgroups had to be identified and managed, and knowledge about population had to be generated. This led to the creation of statistics, which would define regularities and calculate probabilities. Soon statistical regularities started to define what is normal and what deviates from it. The task of government is accordingly to normalize the most deviant cases, to regulate them by devising measures and policies that push the deviant closer to the normal curve (Foucault 2007: 62, 63). In this type of governance, futures became manageable based on statistical predictions.

The absence of such an inclusive biopolitics was experienced as a deficiency by some of my interlocutors, as is perhaps more frequently the case in African countries: 'Biopolitics calls here forth not threat and loathing, but nostalgia and desire' (Geissler et. al. 2012: 13). This point is supported by historical research on care, which has criticized the fact that the coziness of kin-based care is often overestimated in scholarly analyses, while the merits of public welfare systems tend to be underestimated (Horden and Smith 2009: 1, 2). Rashaida in the rural Lower Atbara area have expectations of what a state government should be and of the various redistributive and securing functions it should assume. A model of statehood or modern state institutions, quite similar to that which Foucault saw rising in the late eighteenth century, has long been disseminated. It raises expectations of good governance centred on the welfare of the population, which are by no means met by the present Sudanese government.

Biopolitics in Sudan is practised in an exclusionary way; it is more accurate to speak of biopolitical projects of limited range and duration. These are not oriented towards securing the population and discovering risks but rather seek to mould citizens of a certain cultural, economic and religious kind – Arab-Muslim – and thereby produce considerable margins, and furthermore ignore the people inhabiting them. The contours of a Foucaultian concern for the well-being, security and health of a population can be retraced mainly among a spatially limited constituency along the Nile. Diagnoses of the state of affairs often point to this missed chance of building institutions after national independence that could arbitrate between competing and often conflicting interests with a view of the welfare of all citizens (Rottenburg 2008b: viii, ix; Calkins et al. 2015a; Calkins et al. 2015b). The lack of socio-economic development and infrastructure (roads, electricity, schools, health facilities, etc.), together with widespread poverty, hunger and the spread of diseases are problems that either people are left to struggle with on their own or are delegated to NGOs.

An important critique of the analytical concept of biopolitics is that it takes the nation-state as its basis and assumes a unified, centralized and purposeful state apparatus (Gupta 2012: 44–46). It has long been emphasized that various transnational processes reconfigure the sovereign power of the nation-state, delegating some state functions to international organizations and agencies. In order to integrate into the global economy, governments are pressed to adopt neoliberal norms and practices at least partially in their management of population. Modes of government through foreign-imposed disciplinary and regulatory measures, such as structural adjustment programmes promoted by the International Monetary Fund, can be understood as a sort of 'transnational governmentality' (Ferguson and Gupta 2005: 115). Development aid in particular has been interpreted as a crucial liberal technology in an unfolding global system of governance, assembling donors, NGOs, companies, military organizations and UN agencies (Duffield 2002: 1050), which has led to an outsourcing of state functions. Biopolitics in Sudan – the care for population, its health and well-being – has likewise to a large extent been handed over to international NGOs and UN organizations (ibid.: 8–10). Often the government offices have been reduced to offering a platform for coordination among international NGOs and allotting them areas in which to work, while complicating or barring their access to other areas (FMOH 2004).

The present government in Sudan (1989–today and preceding ones as well) does not organize a population-wide redistribution of wealth and resources, but rather translates global patterns of in/exclusion religiously and socioculturally. Biopolitics in Sudan is pursued through a discriminatory vision of society: the ruling National Congress Party (NCP) has a hegemonic and narrow vision of who constitutes the nation and defines Arab-Muslim identity as its basic building block, ruling out multiculturalism and religious diversity (Lesch 1998: 21). After its coup, the ruling party (first the National Islamic Front, then the NCP) has called itself a salvation regime (*'inqāḏ*) and refers to its ideological identity project as a civilization project (*mašrū' ḥaḍarī*). The management and regulation of population was thoroughly influenced by transnational Islamist discourses, mainly the Muslim Brotherhood. The explicit goal was to restore society to its Islamic roots, to reinstate Islamic law and to save the country from its corruption by a Western-educated elite, 'to "depose and remove" those "infidel rulers" who had allowed the destruction of Islamic traditional laws, customs and institutions' (Burr and Collins 2003: 4, 5).

A central figure in formulating this Islamist ideology was Hassan al-Turabi, an intellectual and religious adviser, who has close ties to the Muslim Brotherhood. He promoted the pan-Islamic idea of uniting all Muslims with God in a divine community (*'umma*) based on the Quran and sharia (Turabi 1987: 2, 3; Burr and Collins 2003: 6). Biopolitics, as pursued in Sudan, was therefore aimed at producing an Islamic nation. To that end, it converted the administrative and educational apparatus across Sudan into Arabic (Lesch 1998: 22). It further introduced an Islamic system of law (Warburg 1988: 155 ff). These measures coerced people to either adhere to Islamic ideas of proper behaviour or be excluded or even punished. The educational apparatus enforced the idea that people have to learn Arabic in order to be included in society and to regard themselves as citizens. Among the most significant biopolitical projects in Sudan were orchestrated attempts to produce a uniform population – religiously, legally and morally – one that claims to be part of an Arab-Muslim civilization. This homogenizing project was halted temporarily by the Comprehensive Peace Agreement, signed on 9 January 2005. However, the short transitory phase during which multiculturalism and religious diversity were recognized ended with the secession of South Sudan in July 2011. Since the succession, Bashir and other party leaders have endorsed, in a number of public speeches, a return to a strict Islamic path. This governmental blueprint fails to accommodate the dreams and aspirations of a significant portion of the populace. It tends to promote the instability of forms and the unpredictability of futures in Sudan.

Arabization and Islamization should not be mistaken for a return to an Islamic premodernity or Stone Age. Rather, the ruling elite seeks to push Sudan into a new era of prosperity. Narratives of development and modernization have influenced policies. Since the inception of the Gezira Scheme (among the world's largest irrigation projects) under Anglo-Egyptian colonial rule, one idea has persisted, namely, that agricultural export production was the only possible path to develop Sudan's rural potential – at times this was represented as the only way forward for the entire country (Barnett 1977). Plans for agricultural intensification were launched in unison with hydro-dam projects. Verhoeven (2012) refers to the latter as 'new modernist temples', signifiers of progress and development. These ideas were revived in the framework of the so-called breadbasket strategies of the 1970s, which depicted Sudan as a granary for investors from the Gulf States (Tetzlaff and Wohlmuth 1980). The plan was to turn Sudan into a food-exporting country – not an importer – by initiating capital-intensive agricultural production, financed by investors from the Gulf States. According to the theoretical assumptions of the time – firmly rooted in modernization theory – this should have led to a trickle-down effect on other economic sectors. But these grand developmental schemes failed. Nonetheless, a modernist vision for the agriculture-based development of Sudan survived and was imbued with new vigour in the context of the recent Sudanese Agricultural Revival Programme (for further details, see Verhoeven 2011, 2012).

Foreign investments in Sudan's agricultural land have soared recently (Umbadda 2014). They form part of the desperate measures undertaken to gain foreign currency after the recession related to the loss of most oil resources to South Sudan in mid-2011. This modernist economic vision, which builds on capital-intensive mechanized agriculture to achieve self-sufficiency in food supply, is bolstered by legislation in support of capitalist enterprises and transnational corporations. It marginalizes certain occupations and customary types of land usage. Small farmers and pastoralists have been evicted from their territories, as these have been reserved for dam construction, mining, or zones for intensive agriculture (Gertel et al. 2014). Governmental practices have been unable to resolve such conflicts peacefully and to protect common goods in Sudan.

This discussion has highlighted certain dynamics of governance, which affect the means by which people in marginalized areas of Sudan can deal with uncertainties. I argue that the limited scope and vision of biopolitical projects in Sudan shapes economic, political and sociocultural/religious margins and marginalized people. Important aspects of care for the population are outsourced to NGOs and UN agencies, which are compartmentalized into specific areas and tend to focus on specific services and priority groups. There is no comprehensive system in place to provide health care and economic security for the entire population. In the Lower Atbara area, a pastoral hinterland, uncertainty about the future is enormous. Achieving security appears to be an unattainable goal, as people have to fend for their survival; they seem focused instead on increasing the daily range of predictability for their actions. Before I enter into anthropological debates on uncertainty, I will next outline my methodology, present the challenges of doing research on uncertainty, and discuss some of the settings and dynamics that moulded my research topic and interest.

Methodological Reflections

Choosing uncertainty as my object of analysis necessarily entails reflexivity, a questioning of premises and foundations, and this needs to include my own. In his classic essay on objectivity, Max Weber (1922) posited that there can be no empirical observation without value judgements; the choices regarding what to study and the selection and definition of the study's object are always connected to what the researcher holds dear. As Niklas Luhmann (1984) pointed out, there is no way around this, no grounds from which to claim objectivity. Every observation has its blind spot and needs subsequent observation to pinpoint the blind spot, which again produces a new blind spot. Haraway (1991) made a related point by stressing that all knowledge is situated, positioned and partial. The implications of practising a reflexive approach to social science are far-reaching and cannot be condensed into a few remarks in a methods section (Burawoy 1998). Rather, it affects the way in which ethnography is written. For me it means writing in such a way that the positional and partial perspective of observation forms part of the narrative flow. I show in every chapter how my position and my methodology situated me and try to show how this qualifies the emerging piece of knowledge. Therefore this section is rather brief, but nonetheless raises important issues that help the reader to situate the ethnographic findings in this book and show how the methodology therein is intertwined with my research experience, observations and conclusions, and even with my selection of the theoretical framework of uncertainty.

Studying Existential Situations

This section discusses the notion of survival and its applicability to existential situations in Sudan as well as three theoretical approaches formulated in development studies on poverty. In the Lower Atbara area of north-eastern Sudan, poverty and uncertainties quickly take on an existential flavour, literally becoming matters of life and death.[24] While survival is an analytical term, I see it as being close to the ways in which many Rashaida understand their precarious situations: avoiding eating, being hungry, exhausted, often on the verge of wasting away or actually dying. In north-eastern Sudan, in a settlement of mainly Rashaida where I did my fieldwork, food supplies ran short and meals were often skipped. Sicknesses often went untreated, leading to death, especially among infants and children, in nearly every family. Condolence visits to mourning parents and kin were common. Thus, I was doing research in a challenging existential settting, in which such basic human needs as food, (clean) water, clothing and medication were inadequately met and often required urgent action.[25]

Survival is hopeful.[26] This notion focuses on the goal of continuing to live in spite of adversity and bleak prospects. It has gained currency as an analytical term in the past decades and seems to have gradually crowded out the notion of living (Schmieder 2012). The French, Spanish and German terms *survivre*, *sobrevivir* and *überleben* literally denote something more than or beyond (*sur-*, *sobre-* or *über-*) merely living. Survival is a strange and paradoxical word because it 'implies that an entity, which is dead or should be dead, is still alive' (Lyotard 1994, in Schmieder 2012: 15, my translation). As Schmieder (2012: 15) suggests, the notion of survival denotes a caesura, an existential danger or encounter with death, and a continuity of the past in the present, which preconditions the caesura. The notion of survival conjures up people who should be dead, near-dead, or the living dead. It is therefore no surprise that the terms survival and survivor abound in the literature on the Shoah, referring to the devastating psychological and cultural consequences of Nazi wartime crimes, particularly the experience of surviving concentration and extermination camps.

Das and Poole (2004) connect survival to the margins of the state: sovereignty not only concerns territories but life and death, being ultimately exercised over bodies. This is most apparent in the conflict-ridden regions of Sudan, where atrocities of various sorts threaten the survival of certain population categories, particularly those who resist the dominant Arab-Muslim identity project (cf. Hutchinson 1996; Rottenburg 2002; James 2007; Mamadani 2009).[27] This study, however, does not encompass such extreme devastation and the havoc of war, instead having been carried out in a peaceful rural area of north-eastern Sudan. Survival in this book therefore refers to the daily struggle of getting by when little is at hand to actually make a living and receive one's bread.

Three theoretical approaches formulated in the past offered conceptual tools to study the activities of people with such uncertain livelihoods: survival economies, vulnerability[28] and sustainable livelihoods. These three approaches provided a valuable foil against which I developed my research. What unites them is their realist understanding of risks or dangers, which are diagnosed by researchers, attributed to people, possibly translated into developmental programmes, and may result in concrete interventions. People who are considered vulnerable are portrayed as mostly rational agents in pursuit of a single goal – securing their livelihoods. I saw this as a limitation, because people's everyday understandings of uncertainty and their ways of dealing with it were largely irrelevant to such programmes.

Nonetheless, I am sympathetic to the survival economy approach, which emerged by way of Hans-Dieter Evers in the 1980s, concerning how people manage to cooperate, particularly in urgent situations.[29] This approach criticized economic models that assumed that people's primary interest lay in the maximization of profits; such models ignored the fact that the so-called group of the insecure need first and foremost to secure their livelihoods and that therefore households opt to spread risks rather than maximize profits, developing new mechanisms of solidarity and building strong personal networks (Elwert et al. 1983; Evers 1986). While I support in principle the direction of this critique, the approach supplanted a rationality of economic maximization and replaced it with another rationality – safety first.

A focus on sustainability has been an important contribution of the sustainable livelihoods framework that also informs this study: it is about anticipating the future and security of livelihoods.[30] At the heart of the livelihoods approach is the analysis of the scopes of action according to which people secure their livelihoods, based on their entitlement to livelihood assets, resources or capital. In this view, a livelihood is sustainable when it devises strategies to cope with and recover from shocks and stresses without damaging its assets or its natural resources (Chambers and Conway 1991: 6; Carney 1998: 4). I share the concern for the concrete ways in which people secure or fail to secure their incomes, but with an important extension: the role of social institutions in organizing livelihoods has been too long neglected. SL approaches focused on how resources combine to allow strategies to be pursued and different outcomes to be achieved, concentrating solely on easily measurable economic variables (Scoones 1998: 11, 12; Gertel 2007: 18).[31]

The gap in the developmentalist literature regarding institutional mediation was a starting point for my research, which I first carried out in a project on livelihood security among pastoralists. The guiding question posed for that field research concerned people's institutional coverage in the context of a war-torn state such as Sudan. I took to the field on the lookout for institutions and institutional regulation, to an extent taking their existence and a certain stability of orders for granted. But staying with people in their homes and sharing their lives in a setting of scarce resources, I quickly began to feel disconcerted and puzzled by what I experienced as an impression of emergence, instability, manifold fragile agreements and very limited predictability. I was a party to situations in which people adjusted with surprising speed to new exigencies, drawing elements and arguments in support of their convictions from various sources or inventing ways of cooperating and sharing, whereby what they took for granted and what they questioned seemed negotiable. I slowly began to see through their eyes, noticing their momentary bewilderment about the fleeting nature of arrangements that were taken for granted yesterday, about new promises of prosperity and new uncertainties, as well as the obvious onslaught of social change that transformed a pastoral into a mining economy with unpredictable outcomes. I challenged my own assumptions. The focus on institutions alone laid too much emphasis on the permanence of orders and appeared too static and restrictive to capture the ongoing situational negotiation of norms of cooperation. My interest thus shifted to a level that was sociologically deeper, preceding that of institutional regulation, namely, to the fundamental uncertainty of coordination and the problem of how to produce commonality in situations that appear open and indeterminate, especially in view of their often existential character.

Entering the Field

Here I show how the location of 'the field' and my own biography are entangled with the discussion of uncertainty.[32] I did nearly a year of ethnographic research in north-eastern Sudan, in several shorter periods between December 2007 and May 2010. I mainly stayed with Rashaida in the hinterlands of the rural Lower Atbara area in the River Nile State.[33] I visited the area for the first time in December 2007 when most people I later met again in the village were still living in tents and had some small stock, moving in a small annual radius between the river in the dry season and the higher grounds in the rainy season. These first visits to the region and encounters with people were important. I doubt whether the rapid transformations that occurred between 2007 and 2009 would have struck me as much if I had not witnessed them but only learned about them through hearsay. When I returned for further research in early 2009, many people had meanwhile settled and were building houses. What had been a tiny hamlet of a few houses around a mosque in the nomadic hinterlands had turned into a settlement of more than two hundred people with a school, a (inoperative) small health centre, clay houses, huts and tents. The most dramatic transformation, however, concerned people's sources of livelihood.

Upon my return in autumn 2009, most people had deserted pastoralism or small farming to become artisanal gold miners. Gold was discovered in a wadi some dozens of kilometres from the settlement. The discovery drew thousands of people into the region, some of them into the village, spawning new building activity. It also led to traffic of water tankers and public transport through the settlement. A new branch of gold mining elicited much excitement during my stay – work with metal detectors. In view of the novelty of gold mining, the indeterminate absence of men due to this new work, and more permanent settlement as well as the influx of people from different areas, things seemed to be very much in flux with few stable references for action. This situates the discussed ethnographic material – it is about dealing with the wobbliness of orientations and foundations. Being able to track some of the rapid transformations from one visit to the next provided me with a deeper context to interpret my findings, particularly those obtained during the last nearly nine months of research in 2009 and 2010.

My fieldwork occurred during the so-called interim period (2005–2011) after the Comprehensive Peace Agreement (CPA) of 2005, which was signed by the National Congress Party and the Sudan People's Liberation Army/Movement (SPLA/M), and more importantly the Eastern Sudan Peace Agreement (ESPA) of 2006, where Rashaida Free Lions as members of the Eastern Front were a signatory party, ending their political marginalization at least in eastern Sudan (Kassala, Gedarf, Red Sea State) (Calkins 2014). This time of peace, hope and suspense stirred anticipation that a new era of sociocultural diversity and the development of marginal areas had dawned.

This period was decisive for colleagues working ethnographically in former war zones, such as South Kordofan, Darfur and Blue Nile State, as these regions were plunged into war once again in 2011 and the fighting is still ongoing at the time of writing. This book, in contrast, deals with a region that appears so marginal that it is even marginal to Sudan's conflicts. Between 2007 and 2010, when I did my study, the Lower Atbara area was barely connected to the political processes in other parts of the country. In contrast to other regions of Sudan, there were virtually no security hurdles that had to be passed to do research in this area. The state was largely uninterested in or unsuspicious of activities in this marginal area.[34] Most people in the Lower Atbara area were struggling to meet their daily needs through subsistence rain-fed cultivation, herding and most recently various activities in and around gold mining. In the hinterlands, where new pastoral settlements had begun to emerge, there was no electricity, the coverage of telecommunications was weak and faltering, there were only dirt tracks, no paved roads, and poverty was abject; I have no reason to assume that the situation is much different today. Food supplies were scarce and the lack of ritual hospitality, which I had experienced while travelling in other areas of Sudan, especially among Rashaida, was striking. I became interested in how people in this part of the world experience existential situations and master them. Working in a peripheral region of Sudan thus strongly situated my fieldwork. I conducted participant observation of mundane daily life and its challenges, not of grandiose and memorable events, political acts or specific rituals. The hardships and uncertainties of life in this area of the world were important topics of conversation as Rashaida sought to increase the predictability of everyday life in rural north-eastern Sudan. They became a central concern of this work.

It is important to stress what enabled my awareness of unpredictability: I came from a different background, having a different experience of the past in Germany. I also came to Sudan with more or less fixed plans for the immediate and more distant future: finishing fieldwork, writing my thesis, getting a degree (PhD) that would enable me to find a good job in order to grant me a comfortable life, having a baby at some later point and so on. My interlocutors did not think like this about their futures; they did not have such a long horizon of expectation. People in the home where I stayed, with whom I was most intimately acquainted, often talked about changes, what the past as nomadic pastoralists used to be like, how life had been easier, food more readily available. It seemed that many – especially the older people – were confused because their past experience no longer offered secure orientations for how to act under new circumstances.

A further factor that situates my results in important ways is my gender. Arriving alone as a woman in rural north-eastern Sudan, I was integrated into a Rashaida household. My host mother was Hamda, whose husband was on labour migration in Kuwait. Hamda lived in a separate one-room adobe house and an attached wood and straw hut with her son (12), her unmarried daughters (15 and 7), her married daughter (19), her toddling grandson and her granddaughter (4). Two other married daughters lived in adjacent houses with their husbands and children. I participated in the daily activities of the women and children. Part of a woman's day was spent in the sizzling heat of their wood and straw huts, sitting next to the smoke and fire of the hearth, making coffee and tea or baking bread for breakfast and lunch, sending children out on errands, getting water from the wells or firewood (usually the task of girls). Another part was reserved for relaxing with neighbouring women, lying around, dozing, chatting, laying out cowrie shells for entertainment, sewing, working on embroidery, joking and story-telling. By being in the midst of their conversations, I learned much about the joys and worries, affection and friendship among neighbouring women but also about quarrels and falling outs, which I allude to in several chapters.

Sharing the lives and houses of people in Um Futeima meant an absence of privacy for my hosts and myself. Women went through my belongings, unpacking my backpack. They told me what is appropriate for a woman and what not, correcting where I was allowed to sit and where not, how to go to the toilet and how not, even trying to influence who I should talk to and who not. I learned that the radius of female activities is largely confined to their houses and those of neighbouring women. Women depend on male providers. Men only dropped by houses occasionally, for meals or to sleep.

Most came and went to the gold mines. When they were in the settlement, they met friends and sat in the shade in front of the mosque, a room built for men, or one of the shops in the settlement. In view of this intimate acquaintance with women, particularly Hamda, her daughters and their associates, my account tends to privilege the perspectives of women.

Uncertainties of Exploring Uncertainty

Uncertainty is not the sole object of my study, since investigating how people deal with uncertainties is itself rife with uncertainties of various kinds. Not least of these is relating to how such volatile things can be studied – experiences that perhaps cannot be fully enunciated, indeterminacies, qualms about acting that are dealt with differently, lived through, entangled with affectivity, anticipation and the plethora of ways of grappling with such experiences and making sense of them.

My main method of knowing and producing knowledge was ethnography, a research method that privileges experience.[35] Uncertainties as lived experiences can be empirically investigated by following situations of controversy when, for instance, the very definition of the situation and its stakes are in question. The expression of uncertainty – particularly its subtler kinds – can be verbal, but it need not lead to utterances at all. The focus on experience makes the problematic of ethnographic knowledge production all the more visible, namely, that its goal is revealing social relations and formations while relying on them as a medium of investigation, turning research into a critical, inexact and open-ended process. It stimulates reflection, uncertainty. This has been addressed in a large body of literature in anthropology, especially since the 1980s, which problematized the distinctively anthropological modes of knowledge production, the writing of ethnographies, and the way in which the relationship between anthropologist and others had often been effaced from earlier ethnographic accounts.[36]

Still, when I think of what method should do I agree with Haraway (1991: 187) that it should enable us to tell at least somewhat 'faithful accounts of a "real" world' while acknowledging the situatedness and partiality of all knowledge. This implies ongoing reflexive and critical reviewing of 'own "semiotic technologies" for making meanings' (ibid.: 187).[37] Participant observation means producing knowledge through long-term intimate personal experiences and serendipity, the success of which cannot be measured solely in time or by a certain research methodology. Fieldwork is vulnerable to charges of impropriety or violation of research ethics – it is unpredictable and duly bound up with uncertainty. But does the source of uncertainty lie with the analyst or in the research participants?

Here lies the crux of the matter. Uncertainty as defined above is a part of all actions to different degrees, depending upon the extent of reflexivity with which a situation is engaged. It is thus part of doing research. At the same time it is the experience of Rashaida in this area of Sudan, an experience that I came to share with them, turning fieldwork itself into a lived experience. Thus I was using my own experiences of uncertainty concerning the situation in which I was involved to try to understand the uncertainties that other people experience. This is a difficult task. Uncertainty is multiplied.

I often thought longingly about the time I could leave this place of poverty and sickness again and wondered how people deal with these enormous hardships when they have no way of exiting, not even a means of knowing whether current dire straits will end. This sensitized me to the experiences of other people and drew my attention to the uncertainties of existence. I therefore stress not only the role of knowing uncertainty by observing how other people deal with it, but also highlight participatory, empathetic aspects related to my own engagements. This implies letting my reader know how I came to know uncertainty by experiencing situations together with other people, feeling sensations, talking about them: heat, dust, the lack of water to clean, the dullness of food, its pollution with dirt, its scarcity, and hunger; the fighting among members of the household for scarce food; what it means to be sick in this rural hinterland; the anxiety, discomfort and hardships of travelling to town with fever and in pain; what being a woman can mean in this part of the world, when children need care or supplies run out. This enabled the observations and analyses of how individuals engage with 'what is', their ways of creating some coherence, some predictability for their lives.

Taking uncertainty seriously also means acknowledging that the production of ethnographic texts is never a passive and neutral process that can be accurately presented and contextualized. Rather, it means letting reflexivity be the ethnographer of the text (Woolgar 1988: 29), interrogating concepts and categories while furnishing representations of field events. Some uncertainty should be sustained and recovered in the final account. But how to do this practically?

An important critique of anthropology issued in the 1980s concerned temporality and periodization in ethnographic writings. Fabian (1983) contended that anthropologists tend to be in the here and now, while locking their interlocutors in the 'there and then' through their texts, constructing and relegating the other to a time that is not coeval with the anthropologist. The so-called ethnographic present was particularly problematized, as it suggested that research findings are immutable timeless truths, which ignores the fact that they arise from a dialogue between researcher and research participants. Anna Tsing (1993: xiv) has beautifully summarized some of the dilemmas involved in taking this insight into account and still writing about a marginal place: 'The use of the "ethnographic present" is tied to a conceptualization of culture as a coherent and persistent whole ... turning ethnographic subjects into exotic creatures (Fabian 1983); their time is not the time of civilized history'. Nonetheless, she chose to switch back and forth between past and present tense, because she also sensed a danger in the tendency of many anthropologists to switch to a past tense in order to avoid the issue altogether: 'Yet, here too, there are problems in describing an out-of-the-way place. ... To many readers, using the past tense about an out-of-the-way place suggests not that people "have" history but that they *are* history in the colloquial sense' (Tsing 1993: xiv, xv).

This also applies to my study. I do not want to suggest that my interlocutors are history and I am facing a particular challenge: I am dealing with uncertainty and with how people jointly develop orientations and anchors for acting in situations of low predictability. Putting this into the past tense might create the impression that in the time that has elapsed since the event the uncertainty has been overcome, or perhaps the reader will feel assured by the writer's calm narration of past events and begin to doubt whether there was any uncertainty at all. I am thus re-creating an uncertainty and openness of outcomes by using the ethnographic present sometimes, because I do not know what became of many of my interlocutors. I also move back and forth between present and past tenses because I am not making a claim about Rashaida in Sudan or uncertainties in general; rather, I am writing about a specific time and a specific place. This account could and would be different at a different time and place; it even would be different at the same place at a different time.

Since Weber's groundbreaking insight into the impossibility of a value-free social science, researchers have stressed that the construction of interests, objects and questions is inextricably linked to political and historical contexts. This short section aimed to underscore how my topic began to emerge: by engaging in earlier scholarship, taking up a funding opportunity for research in Sudan based on certain assumptions about institutional social security mechanisms, and by undergoing experiences in the Lower Atbara area of Sudan. When and where I did my study has substantially affected what I studied. I focus neither on urban middle classes nor urban squatters in Khartoum, nor on survival issues in Sudan's war-torn areas. Rather, my study explores the more subtle gruelling uncertainties of everyday life in a rural area of north-eastern Sudan, such as the lack of food, clean water and health services – situations that result from the discriminatory resource politics of the central government but that receive little or no scholarly or media attention. My own situatedness has also affected my discussion of uncertainty by drawing my attention predominantly to the experiences of women and to the struggle of achieving some predictability, of having something that holds together to which future action can refer. This I will explore in the following chapters.

The Chapters

My investigation is concerned with how the experience of uncertainty, reflexivity in acting and stability of forms are articulated in actual practices; this is the red thread running through the various chapters. They trace how Rashaida in a newly settled community of north-eastern Sudan establish forms situationally to manage uncertainties, as well as how old and new elements are interwoven in this form-giving process. Four empirical chapters substantiate my theoretical argument.

Chapter 2 deals with a situation in a small nomadic settlement in the Lower Atbara area. On a day in March 2010, a Kuwaiti welfare organization arrived to distribute goods to the poor and a controversy emerged in the settlement. It was about how people who suffer a dearth of resources make sense of a distribution's fairness. In the situation doubts were raised about what is, what counts and how one can be sure about what one knows. People based their claims on various forms, in this case specifically established organizational elements such as rules, lists and procedures, and social categories such as 'the poor', 'the sheiks', 'the migrants'. The situation resulted in a chaotic scramble for the meat of a slaughtered camel, followed by accusations of unfair seizure, pertaining mainly to one of the sheiks. These ethnographic insights are used to theorize connections between cooperation and uncertainty and outline a code-switch from a practical to a reflexive moment. To cooperate in practical moments, people have to be oriented towards specific goals and assume one 'metacode' that captures reality, which enables the passing over of divergent interpretations of reality to a certain degree and limiting themselves to a number of questions (Rottenburg 2005a). In reflexive moments, people become aware of their divergent interpretations and contractions. In the above situation this ushered in a radical uncertainty, in which the fairness of resource allocations and therewith the representation of reality was questioned.

Cooperation is likewise essential in order to participate in a new livelihood activity. Chapter 3 portrays a dramatic livelihood configuration in northern Sudan – the burgeoning of artisanal (illegal) gold prospecting. It analyses the management of uncertainties in this male social world. I qualify how artisanal gold miners from the settlement experienced four types of uncertainty (with the terminology I develop below): economic uncertainty, the insecurity of governmental suppression, the threat of crimes, and health problems. My main focus, however, is on economic uncertainty. I discuss how a novel extractive technology was introduced to deal with this uncertainty – metal detectors that electromagnetically prospect the terrain according to the ability to distinguish metal from non-metal. Inscribed with various functions and programmes, metal detectors were 'de-scripted' and associated with an overarching imaginary of a divine ordination that dictated success or failure with regard to gold finds. This translation of the technology to Sudan reinforced an unequal distribution of resources and wealth in society. Instead of raising doubts about the fairness of what was going on, miners passed over uncertainties by confirming fixed organizational forms, such as existing rules, procedures, modes of cooperation and distributive orders. This rhetorical insistence on forms pushed aside elements that would have led to a reflexive enquiry, which might disrupt much needed cooperation in extracting the precious metal; it thus can be connected to the substantial fears with which men live while searching for gold.

Chapter 4 continues the debate concerning how to act in desperate situations, focusing on the mundane need for food. How do women deal with the exhaustion of food supplies? The perpetual interruptions in the food supply related to the burgeoning of artisanal gold mining in the northern Sudanese desert. Thousands of men streamed to the gold mines, leaving their families behind for indeterminate periods. Here uncertainty appears from a novel angle, pertaining to the everyday, the mundane, and women had to digest it. They did so by building cooperative relationships with neighbours to whom they could lend and from whom they could borrow food when supplies ran out. The chapter connects to debates on contingency/agency by showing how women sought to establish standards of exchange – the main form encountered – and to produce knowledge about the exchange by employing simple techniques of measurement. Two exchange circles among Rashaida women in the settlement are identified and associated with disparate principles of coordination: staples and cooked food. The food exchanges were not means of supporting the poor, whose food supplies were always precarious, but rather were used to fill in supply gaps among women in a similar situation. Women sought predictability through standards concerning their most vital food needs, while relegating generosity and the social ties it engenders to a less essential kind of food exchange.

Finally I address situations that turn desperate; that is, when the normal is momentarily suspended by the fear of death. Here collective agency is mobilized to procure treatment for serious sicknesses. Chapter 5 traces how Rashaida go about determining whether something is a sickness. How do they know that it needs treatment? How do they represent this knowledge to others? And, conversely, when is ill health ignored as an unpleasant but minor thorn in one's side, an ailment that poor people simply have to endure? I dwell upon the uncertainty of qualifying ill health, the uncertainty of others' evaluations, uncertain boundaries between chronic and urgent cases, and the bracketing of uncertainty when something is established as a crisis. The chapter thus focuses on situations in which there is an urgency about action but uncertainty regarding the proper course of action. How is acting possible in the face of a lack of knowledge about one's condition, the severity of ill health and the dread of deadly outcomes? Rashaida distinguished between different types of health-related uncertainty, namely everyday infirmities, chronic illness and acute health crises, which entailed different obligations of carers and kin. I suggest a link between a family's material situation and the moment when sickness was established as a form to generate curative actions: the poorer the family, the later the category of 'sickness' was applied. Death needed to be lurking for others to act. The more exceptional and surprising the health problem, the more likely it was to move people to donate money. 'Sickness' in this understanding emerged as any physical ailment worth treating, but what and who is worthy of treatment was negotiated according to asymmetrical relationships between people and to situational dynamics. Nagging uncertainties of ill health among poor people were often unnoticed, muted and ignored.

Preceding the empirical heart of this study, chapter 1 provides a dense theoretical roadmap for the exploration of uncertainty. It discusses anthropological approaches to uncertainty and develops a theoretical argument from two disparate bodies of literature – a more developmental literature on poverty and livelihoods, and risk theories with recourse to pragmatist thought, particularly Dewey and Boltanski. The final section of chapter 1 deals with the processing of uncertainty: inspired by Simmel and Thévenot, it proposes forms as an appropriate analytical tool to straddle the relationship between contingency and agency.

Notes

1. But theorists such as Ulrich Beck et al. (2003) have emphasized people's increasing awareness that complete control and predictability of actions is no more than a chimera—a characteristic of what he calls 'reflexive modernization'.
2. Foucault (2007) relates the beginning of these processes to the emergence of market towns and an increased circulation of goods from the sixteenth century onwards. A new configuration of power then manifested itself by the end of 'the eighteenth century from an art of government to political science, from a regime dominated by structures of sovereignty to one ruled by techniques of government' (Foucault 1991: 101).
3. Foucault (1980: 139) calls the power exerted over human beings 'biopower', meaning both the discipline applied to individual bodies and the regulation of population.

Governmentality is seen as a type of power exercised in and through 'the conduct of conduct', that is, all attempts to align behaviour with norms and rationalities (Dean 1999: 10, 11). Lemke (2011: 20) notes that 'government refers to more or less systematized, regulated, and reflected modes of power (a "technology") that go beyond the spontaneous exercise of power over others, following a specific forms of reasoning (a "rationality") that defines the objective ("telos") of action and the adequate means to achieve it'. Among them are state agencies, who seek to govern the population. The population is thereby at once constituted and administered, giving way to new social realities and new subjectivities. Governmentality as the mentality of government to govern the mentality of population is also called biopolitics. Biopolitics is exercised through "security dispositifs" conceived as heterogeneous assemblage of techniques, mechanisms, institutions, discourses and so on, used to define reality and to govern, defend and secure populations, their welfare and health (Foucault 1991: 101–103; 2007: 59, 60; cf. Deleuze 1991; Hubig 2000). Security dispositifs imply a difference in the ways in which power is yielded, when compared to the Westphalian model of state politics, which surmises that sovereignty denotes a bounded territory and a particular sovereign actor that is able to control and administer territory and resources independently of others (Elden 2005: 8). A concern for the safety of the sovereign was replaced with a concern for the security of the population: 'We see the emergence of a completely different problem that is no longer that of fixing and demarcating the territory, but of allowing circulations to take place, of controlling them, sifting the good and the bad, ensuring that things are always in movement, constantly moving around, continually going from one point to another, but in such a way that the inherent dangers of this circulation are canceled out' (Foucault 2007: 65).

4. See Massey 2005 for a general discussion on space.
5. With regard to pastoralists, see Azarya 1996.
6. This development contributed to overgrazing, competition for land, famines, and the eruption of farmer–herder conflicts as well as a gradual reintroduction of Native Administration in the 1990s (cf. Duffield 1990; De Waal 1997; Kibreab 2002; C. Miller 2005).
7. See also Ahmed (1980: 40, 41) and Osman and Schlee (2014) for cases from the Blue Nile, and Azarya (1996) for a more general case.
8. Ille's study (2013) underscores the deep structural roots of this inequality in South Kordofan. Based on an example of water supply systems, his study shows how recent development projects undertaken during the short period of peace (2005–2011) reinforced these patterns of marginalization.
9. This has promoted the application of the centre–periphery model to the analysis of state–citizen relations in Sudan, according to which exploitative state institutions have extracted resources from the periphery and monopolized them around Khartoum (cf. Harir and Tvedt 1994; C. Miller 2005).
10. In addition, a nationwide opposition movement was temporarily formed under the name Union of the Marginalized Majority (Flint and De Waal 2005: 94; Pantuliano 2005: 14, 15).
11. In addition to land access and counter-smuggling measures, the formation of Rashaida tribal politics was fuelled by other political developments: the National Islamic Front (NIF) takeover in 1989, and its subsequent promotion of a single Arabic culture and its fundamentalist version of Islam, resulted in the consolidation of diverse Sudanese opposition groups, uniting under the umbrella of the National Democratic Alliance (NDA) in Asmara in 1991. From its inception, the NDA was nurtured by the Eritrean and Ethiopian governments and soon embraced the SPLM/A; in 1993 the Beja Congress

joined the NDA (J. Young 2007b: 27–29). The front in eastern Sudan never turned into a fully-fledged war, like the wars in Southern Sudan, the Nuba Mountains or the southern Blue Nile. Rather, military operations in eastern Sudan took the form of a low-level insurgency with occasional strikes on oil pipelines, roads and mechanized farming schemes (Johnson 2003: 138; J. Young 2007a: 39, 44, 45). The defeat of the Eritrean army in the Eritrean–Ethiopian war (1998–2000) led to the loss of bases and material supplies in Eritrea, weakening the NDA, which further disintegrated with the SPLA/M's withdrawal after the Comprehensive Peace Agreement of 2005, leaving eastern Sudanese groups alone in their struggle (Johnson 2003: 138–39). Consequently, the Beja Congress abandoned an ethnic rationale in favour of a regional one, allying diverse local opposition groups, above all the Rashaida Free Lions and the Beni Amer, to form the Eastern Front in early 2005 (J. Young 2007a: 11, 12).

12. The Rashaida Free Lions work closely with an ethnically oriented charity (the Kuwaiti welfare organization for Rashaida), which in some localities has provided critical public services for communities and distributed goods to disadvantaged groups.

13. The Beja Congress has been dominated by the Hadendowa, the largest group that identify as Beja, who are traditionally linked to the Ansar order. Other Beja groups are said to follow the Khatmiyya Sufi order. Morton (1989: 63, 70) points out that the allegiance to an order tends to coincide with identity issues.

14. Overlooked by these comments was the fact that the Rashaida Free Lions had meanwhile allied itself with the government.

15. This type of marginalization was, of course, even more central to north–south dimensions of the conflict in Sudan. See earlier complaints of Nuer in Hutchinson (1996: 33).

16. This is based on interviews with officials and on concession maps I was shown at the Ministry of Energy in Mining in May 2010.

17. In systems theory, for instance, functional differentiation of society at some point is thought of as becoming world-encompassing, ignoring national borders (Knöbl 2007: 45). In his later work, Luhmann recognizes that there is an area of exclusion from functional differentiation (Knöbl 2007: 46).

18. See Knöbl (2007) for a detailed and differentiated analysis of various attempts to frame modernities. He remarks that Stichweh's world society is based on the Luhmannian premise that communication implies order, which forecloses some of the more interesting sociological questions. He suggests that Luhmann is too quick to deduce the existence of order from acts of communication and thus fails to see how different forms of order emerge at various levels with different degrees of stability (Knöbl 2007: 49, 50).

19. Zgymunt Bauman (2007: 29, 30) refers to people excluded from neoliberal processes of globalization as 'wasted humans' – that is, humans who are classified as useless to the emerging global social disorder.

20. Latour (1993) argues that the Western separation between political and scientific representations is based on their fundamental mixing in translation practices and what he calls a move of purification, which obscures and denies this heterogeneity. He traces this back to the compartmentalization of domains between science and politics and the attribution of responsibility for non-humans/humans respectively.

21. For more on multiple modernities, see Eisenstadt 2002; for alternative modernities, see Gaonkar 2001; for entangled modernities, see Conrad and Randeria 2002.

22. The case of the contested oil-rich border region now between Sudan and South Sudan is a well-known example. According to the CPA of 2005, a referendum among the people of Abyei should decide its destiny – whether it should remain in Sudan or become part of South Sudan (Johnson 2010, 2011). The Sudanese government obstructed and

postponed the referendum time and again, and the question of who will have the right to vote is still an issue of fierce contention. The government has also subverted attempts at arbitration through its tactics of postponement and the simultaneous creation of new facts on the ground through violent displacements of the local Dinka population (Johnson 2007; 2010: 10, 11; Calkins and Komey 2011: 30–32). In early 2011 the Sudanese Armed Forces occupied the region (Johnson 2011: 1–5). Instead of concerning itself with different population categories, their modes of production and the dangers they face, regulating and insuring them, the Sudanese government focused only on the control of territory and the right to confer contractual legality upon foreign investors, thereby making the land amenable for oil extraction (Linke 2014; Johnson 2010: 10).

23. I draw upon ideas presented in Foucault's lecture series from 1978 and 1979 at the Collège de France, published in English as *Security, Territory, Population* (2007) and *The Birth of Biopolitics* (2008).

24. Offering an inspiring account of uncertainty and its management, Jenkins, Jessen and Steffen (2005: 9) write: 'Matters of life and death are self-evidently at the heart of human existence. When [something] calls into question that existence we are confronted with the uncertainties of life'. I nonetheless contend that the above expression 'confront' is misguided. Uncertainties are nothing reified, outside of the human body and isolated from human action; rather, they are an inseparable part of all human endeavours, they are experienced and felt; of course, this is what Jenkins et al. also mean to denote with 'managing uncertainty'. I thus talk of how Rashaida process, manage or directly deal with uncertainties.

25. In chapters 2 and 4 I show how this survival setting also led to tensions between research participants and myself.

26. Referring to a similar situation in the Red Sea Hills of Sudan, Leif Manger (1996) talks of 'survival on meagre resources'. In a somewhat similar situation of scarcity, Gerd Spittler (1989: 198) describes the consciousness of camel and goat herders from Niger as existing close to death: 'the living are those who have escaped from death ... to live is a treasure' (my translation).

27. For instance, Wendy James's (2007) recent ethnography of Uduk, who survived the civil war, documents the ravages of war and suffering.

28. One notable contribution to studying poverty was made by Chambers and others at the Institute of Development Studies (IDS) in Sussex. They proposed a distinction between vulnerability and poverty, explicitly addressing the exposure of different groups to possible adversities. The IDS school criticized the fact that poverty had become a catch-all, void of analytical value and applied to a smorgasbord of situations, treating the poor as an unclassifiable, homogeneous mass. Their studies emphasized that the poorest people are not necessarily the same as those who are the most vulnerable to certain shocks and stresses. Vulnerability was understood as a condition that resulted from diverse layers of deprivation and that impaired the ability to cope with crises; while vulnerability was a category used by experts, it took no account of the affected people's own understandings of their situations.

29. The survival economy approach focused on the informal sector, the interconnectedness of market and subsistence production and the income activities in developmental contexts. It was premised upon the contention that underdevelopment results from the incorporation of Third World countries into the capitalistic world system (Bierschenk 2002).

30. The sustainable livelihoods (SL) approach/framework was elaborated by scholars and development practitioners from IDS and the Department for International Development

(DFID) in the 1990s (see Chambers and Conway 1991; Scoones 1998; Carney 1998, 2002).

31. To address this lacuna, some have suggested being more reflexive about epistemological assumptions and methods by shifting attention to institutions as the locus of mediation and negotiation (Scoones 1998: 12; Prowse 2010).

32. In recent decades, debates in anthropology have revolved around the whatness and whereabouts of 'the field', disbanding entrenched methodological commitments of studies localized in small-scale communities. Suggestions include tracking issues through various sites, along multiple strands, or extending cases on variant spatial and temporal scales (see Marcus 1995; Gupta and Ferguson 1997; Comaroff and Comaroff 2003).

33. A prior consideration for my research was linguistic. I was intent on working with Arabic-speaking people, because I was fluent in Arabic after four years of Arabic classes at the University of Leipzig and studying Arabic for seven months at the University of Damascus.

34. In contrast, when I planned to start my research in the thriving pastoral area and market town of Kassala, on the border with Eritrea, the state was very much present. The Sudanese security service did not allow me to travel and work in this border zone. The state's lack of interest in the Lower Atbara area is matched by scholarly disinterest. Apart from a baseline study by Hassan Abdel Ati (1985) and a few consultancy papers, there is no literature on this area.

35. To gain a better understanding of the tapestry of conditions of life in this region, I visited my hosts' and friends' relatives and kin for certain occasions, such as mourning periods, weddings or name-giving feasts for newborns, in the broader surroundings of the river Atbara. I also conducted a range of interviews when I felt that I needed to gain information that I could not gather through participant observation: semi-structured interviews with gold miners from Um Futeima; with officials in the locality's administration in Edamer, where I was shown a number of maps and statistics, indicating governmental knowledge of the region; with representatives of the Kuwaiti charity in Edamer, which transferred various goods and services to Um Futeima; with tribal representatives in Khartoum and Kassala; and with officials and geologists at the Ministry of Energy and Mining (now Ministry of Mining) in Khartoum.

36. There is an ocean of reflexive literature on anthropological knowledge production. I here merely refer the reader to some influential works, which have critically interrogated the anthropologist's texts, person, voice and position (Asad 1973; Fabian 1983; Clifford and Marcus 1986; cf. Latour 2005: 39). However, the more forthright challenge to claims of scientific objectivity came from the field of science studies, which studied the fabrication, selection and political agendas in scientific practices, raising questions about the legitimacy and authority of researchers and their 'unavoidable complicity in reality-making' (Law 2004: 153; cf. Haraway 1991; Harding 1993; Clarke and Star 2008).

37. Powdermaker (1966) considered the anthropologist as a 'human instrument' in studying other human beings, subverting scientistic ideas about methods in anthropology and drawing attention to the particularity of encounters in the field. As Rottenburg (2005b: 44) points out, there is a tension between the aim to produce knowledge that is at least somewhat robust and 'the anthropologist's intimate participation in the research process, … [which] by definition possesses no definitively verifiable criteria'. A similar approach was propounded in scholarship highlighting the role of doubt in the research process, and how doubt serves as 'engine of abductions' in the Peircian sense, opening up the work of theorizing to the imaginative, the unanticipated and surprising (Locke et al. 2008).

Chapter 1

TOWARDS AN ANTHROPOLOGY
OF UNCERTAINTY

Uncertainty is important. It is an integral part of human doings, 'a generic feature … of the human condition in general' (Jenkins et al. 2005: 12). It can concern life and death. At the same time, uncertainty is an elusive notion. It has generated a prolific literature in various disciplines, particularly in philosophy and sociology, and to some extent also in economics and recent management studies (see, for example, Dewey 1929; Parsons 1991 [1951]; Beck 1986; Luhmann 2005, 2011: 277ff; Bauman 2007; Renn 2008). However, in spite of the relevance of the notion with regard to human activity and these extensive theorizations, uncertainty has long received insufficient, ambivalent attention in anthropological scholarship.

In recent years, a heterogeneous literature on uncertainty has emerged. Some ethnographic studies have devoted themselves to exploring the sensory, making more room for the felt indeterminacies of being. These studies paid attention primarily to how ordinary people deal with uncertainty. Studies in this scholarly tradition tended to concentrate on the phenomenology of suffering, body politics and individual ways of engaging uncertainty (Whyte 1997, 2005; Steffen et al. 2005; Geissler and Prince 2010). The experience of suffering has been the object of studies, which have taken affliction as the moment where moral ideas, meanings and the quality of relationship are revealed (Kleinman 1999: 29; see Kleinman et al. 2003). The experience of sufferers can be used to caution against a tendency in anthropology 'to interpret contingency as "a problem" for humanity; that is, as an experience to be avoided at all costs' (Honkasalo 2006: 30). To gain a fuller understanding of risk and daily sufferings, uncertainty should, according to this view, be treated as an experience of openness and indeterminacy without valuations. Accordingly, this study emphasizes an uncertainty that is lived, experienced, felt – at times debilitating, at other times liberating.

More recent literature in medical anthropology often places at centre stage the perspectives of experts – health practitioners, organizations and governments with their therapeutic regimes and ideas of health management. The focus of such work ranges from investigating issues such as the entanglements between anticipated harms and their management through traditional healers to the introduction of new high-tech diagnostic technologies, therapeutic experimentation, risks in epidemiology and other security technologies at the state level (Janzen 1978; Geissler 2005; Rottenburg 2009b; Nguyen 2010; Livingstone 2012; Samimian-Darash 2013). Work in STS has often observed the growth of uncertainty in connection with scientific and technological developments, the rise of socio-technical controversies, such as genetic modification or nuclear power, and a tendency of policy makers and scientists to depict public mistrust as irrational and emotional, underestimating the intellectual substance of public concerns while authorizing different forms of expert knowledge to deal with unknowns (Wynne 2001; Callon et al. 2009).

There is an older body of anthropological work that in various ways prepared the ground for the study of uncertainty. Scholars mostly working with a structural functionalist paradigm that endorsed stability, solidarity and equilibrium relegated uncertainty to a marginal position as a sort of residual of social experience (Radcliffe-Brown 1971a; Gluckman 1968). While often not discussing uncertainty directly, important scholarship in anthropology dealt with witchcraft and magic as a means of enquiring about unknowns and of devising ways of dealing with them. This literature highlighted the rationality of these institutions of knowledge production and their role in preserving a society's social order; it also explained cultural patterns of perception and interpretation of misfortune and danger (see, for instance, Evans-Pritchard 1968 [1937]; Lienhardt 1954; Douglas 1966, 1990). Early Sudan ethnography, especially Evans-Pritchard's work on Zande witchcraft, made an original contribution to debates about knowledge production and institutions. These debates migrated to other disciplines, such as philosophy and the social studies of science, where new insights were made but somehow failed to find their way back into modern Sudan ethnography. I attempt to reintegrate these insights into Sudan scholarship and anthropology but seek to give them a new twist by reconceiving what classical sociology/anthropology termed 'institution' in light of recent pragmatist revisions. These revisions explore the links between uncertainty and order, that is, how predictability, which is central to social ordering, is established through various investments of forms. This approach allows for a focus on practices through which forms with different ranges and on different scales of ordering are un/made and gain in/stability; it can render the notion of institutions or 'invested forms' useful for empirical work, and also for ethnographic analyses outside of Europe and North America.

Approaching Unknowns

In a work that has proven influential in the fields of anthropology, philosophy and the social studies of science, Edward E. Evans-Pritchard analysed Zande witchcraft and magic as institutions that produce knowledge, which in turn enables people to act. This knowledge concerns the causes, motives and supernatural interventions that lie behind a particular misfortune, a knowledge otherwise not readily available. It provides an opportunity to assess social relationships, assign moral responsibility and determine appropriate courses of action.

While a Zande wondered why a misfortune has affected her ('why me?'), a Nyole in Uganda was more preoccupied with the question of why someone else has caused her a problem ('why you?') (Whyte 1997: 30–32). Susan Reynolds Whyte (1997) dealt with misfortunes and the actions that Nyole in Uganda took to address and manage them.[1] She asserted that Nyole are pragmatic and that their interest is on doing, on deliberating problems and dealing with them, on achieving security, not abstract and unattainable certainty (Whyte 1997: 3, 14). Yet, both the experience of being struck by misfortune and the ways in which it is managed involve uncertainty: a characteristic of eschewing misfortune is the generation of new uncertainties (ibid.: 19; Lock 1998: 7).

Both Azande and Nyole, according to these ethnographers, sought to explore who or what is behind a misfortune, that is, they sought post-hoc explanations of adversities. Similarly, I witnessed situations in which Rashaida referred to the evil eye as a causal force of misfortune, but these attributions were rare and only occurred after critical moments had passed. Exploring causes and motives was not of primary importance to my interlocutors. I am not claiming that Rashaida I met did not ask causal questions or theorize about misfortune, but instead that I could not discern a clear connection between these practices and the troublesome, disorienting circumstances when action had to be taken. The present study thus addresses primarily the experience of the principal openness of a situation and the lack of assured outcomes before such causal questions are raised, before adversity strikes, whereby its sting is the possibility of harm or 'the perils of evil' (Dewey 1929: 6).

For Evans-Pritchard (1968: 63) witchcraft offered security for acting but one founded on false beliefs; he claimed that 'Witches, as Azande conceive them, cannot exist'. This is inconsistent with an otherwise strong ethos of rehabilitating 'primitive societies' from the accusation of irrationality. In this view, Zande witchcraft – while based on false presumptions – was congruent with Western conceptions of causality but reached beyond them, providing additional moral valuations.[2]

Evans-Pritchard explored what he perceived to be a logical error in the reasoning of Azande: being a witch is an inherited trait that manifests itself through a substance in the belly, namely, witchcraft-substance. Women inherit it from their mothers, men from their fathers. Post-mortem examinations of the opened belly can establish whether the substance is there and thus whether someone was a witch or not. Following the logical implications of this examination would either lead to entire clans being identified as witch clans or would establish that there are no witches at all. But this was not the case: Evans-Pritchard (1968: 24, 25) contended that Azande did not explore this logical contradiction – in fact they did not perceive any contradiction at all – because they had no theoretical interest in the issue at hand. More importantly, they would not have been able to bear the consequences of this insight – the collapse of the institution of witchcraft, which in his view was central to the maintenance of social order. Thus, they had blinded themselves to the logical error, ensnared within their institution: 'in this web of belief every strand depends on every other strand, and a Zande cannot get outside its meshes because this is the only world he knows. The web is not an external structure in which he is enclosed. It is the texture of his thought and he cannot think that his thought is wrong' (ibid.: 194–95).[3]

On the subject of whether Azande essentially had been hoodwinked by their institutions, Peter Winch (1997), a philosopher of science, suggested that Evans-Pritchard's focus on the contradictions of witchcraft was misleading. He argued that the issue was not whether all Azande were witches or none of them were – Azande took it for granted that entire clans could not be witches. What is real according to this logic is rooted in languages of representation, which structure the experience of the world (Winch 1997: 326). Thus, instead of being a part of the whole as Evans-Pritchard suggested, Azande witchcraft was guided by its own logic, distinct from Western logic. Similar to Evans-Pritchard, Winch refrained from conceiving of Azande as irrational and refuted the accusation of irrationality by drawing a difference between them/us and their/our logic, which, however, turned out to be just as fallacious: while Azande were locked within the iron cage of their institutions, the outsiders – Evans-Pritchard and Winch – appeared to be endowed with a neutral and objective view, a view unqualified by history and location, a view from nowhere (Rottenburg 2013: 63).

But the ascribed distinction between true and false beliefs in this specific case was not problematized until a later intervention, which dissolved the difference. David Bloor (1991) confronted both Evans-Pritchard's and Winch's arguments with the demand that all knowledge be analysed symmetrically, without a priori distinctions concerning their truth or falsehood. He concurred that there is no contradiction at all between identifying someone as a witch and knowing that not all clan members can possibly be witches. Rather, such allegedly challenging logical contradictions could effortlessly be dissolved: 'All that is needed is that a few cunning distinctions be drawn' (Bloor 1991: 141). Bloor averred that Evans-Pritchard missed the opportunity to capitalize on Zande distinctions between hot and cold witches: hot witches were actual practising witches, while other clan members, the cold witches, bore an unrealized potential in them. He concluded: 'logic poses no threat to the institution of witchcraft, for one piece of logic can always be met by another' (ibid.).

Bloor (1991: 142–43) masterfully exhibited this by inviting an alien anthropologist to analyse Western metaphysical distinctions and reasoning. The alien anthropologist states:

> [I]n your culture a murderer is someone who deliberately kills someone else. Bomber pilots deliberately kill people. Therefore they are murderers. We can no doubt see the point of this inference but would no doubt resist the conclusion. Our grounds would be that the alien observer did not really understand what a murderer was. He could not see the difference between the two cases he had conflated. Bomber pilots are performing a duty, and this duty is specifically sanctioned by governments.
>
> [...]
>
> The anthropologists might then ply us with more questions about (civilian) car-drivers who kill people. No doubt he would be fascinated by the intricate way in which the concepts of accident, manslaughter, chance, responsibility, mistake and intention have proliferated in our culture. The anthropologist might even conclude that we see the point of his arguments but attempt to evade their logical force by an 'ad hoc' and shifting tangle of metaphysical distinctions. In that culture, he would perhaps say, they have no practical interest in logical conclusions. They prefer their metaphysical jungle because otherwise their whole institution of punishment would be threatened.

The invention of subtle distinctions is not about protecting institutions from denunciation and critique; rather, the institutions remain stable as we perpetually adjust our reasoning, because we take the activities of bomber pilots and drivers for granted (Bloor 1991: 143). In other words, Bloor refutes the idea of a separate Zande logic: logic does not differ, institutions do (ibid.: 145; see Rottenburg 2013).

Older approaches used the concept of institution to explain how 'false' systems of belief perpetuated themselves as timeless regulative constructs, in spite of contradictions, due to their social functions in maintaining order. The capacity to fully understand the role of institutions and to critique them was regarded as the ethnographer's privilege. Newer approaches, such as the French pragmatic sociology of critique, propose that the capacity to test and critically interrogate reality constructions is an inalienable part of all institutions. Institutions are understood as being based on a dialectic between confirmation and critique: the main task of institutions is to qualify and certify 'what is'; this work of confirming things constantly anticipates critique, which explores the differential between the institutional qualifications of 'what is' and understandings of 'what should be' (Boltanski 2011). Without the threat of critique, there would be no need to confirm institutional orders.

The conceptual framework of the French pragmatic sociology of critique offers a useful toolbox to study and theorize the notion of uncertainty in anthropology. Taking uncertainty and the fragility of reality as starting points directs attention to the hard work needed to create a sense of predictability and stability in social life and to the crucial role of institutions in certifying realities (Wagner 1993: 466–67; Bogusz 2010: 35; Boltanski 2011). When what is unknown and what is real are engaged reflexively and critically, this allows for the conceptualizing of how people test and de/stabilize social arrangement. Thus, this approach opens up a space of possibility where actors – including people such as Rashaida at the margins of a dysfunctional and corrupt state – are no longer seen as trapped in their immutable, traditional institutions; rather, it exposes their arbitrary and coercive properties, which can change them and their situation because their institutions always entail the probability of critique. But they do not always criticize their institutions just because they can. My main emphasis here is on how dealing with uncertainties demands engaging them in some way, either denying indeterminacies or pushing them aside in order to act, translating radical uncertainties into something more calculable where at least some bases for action are posited as being stable; or using uncertainty about a state of affairs in order to imagine other possibilities and outcomes, to rally others behind a differential between what is and what should be, to critique the established order of things and extant normativities, and possibly to seize the moment of uncertainty as an opportunity to eke out fairer social arrangements in cumbersome negotiations.

Not surprisingly then, a particular emphasis of this work is on uncertainty with regard to action, that is, what people do in processing different kinds of uncertainty – from gruelling everyday uncertainties to the fear of exceptional harm. Jenkins et al. (2005: 10, 11) aver 'that most people, most of the time, obstinately create and find some continuity in their lives, in the face of hostile circumstances and their own vulnerability, is perhaps the most significant story'. My findings agree with the thrust of this argument. Even in the most dismal conditions, people seem to be groping for something to hold on to, some cognitive and/or material supports to help identify stakes in the present situation – often creating these supports themselves or together with others – and to influence outcomes. But I tend to be cautious, not too quick to assume continuities as a given, as necessary for social life; rather, I investigate the techniques through which an impression of continuity or rather stability is created, which enables acting in spite of uncertainty.

Johnson-Hanks (2005) asserted that in view of uncertainty women in Cameroon forfeited planning their reproductive futures intentionally, preferring to let the future decide. Women were not depicted as devising ends but rather as seizing opportunities that presented themselves via the means at hand. But if we assume a wobbliness of foundations, how does a women know when an opportunity has arisen? An opportunity is something that a woman engages because she believes this will render a positive outcome for her. This does not imply uncertainty but requires much knowledge about the situation in order to engage it in a calculative manner, anticipating favourable results. Johnson-Hanks thus tends to downplay the enormous difficulties of interpreting a situation, what is at stake, what conditions are necessary to understand something as an option in the first place; the proposed approach to uncertainty is better at capturing this.

I draw on broader literatures developed in the social sciences (particularly Dewey, Douglas, Beck, Foucault, Luhmann and Boltanski) to analyse and theorize the processing of uncertainties. I seek to sensitize the reader to different qualities of uncertainty phenomena that are enacted in practice and to some extent also begin to mobilize actions. To reiterate, my proposition is that various types of uncertainty, while always overlapping and fluid, can be analytically differentiated based on their relation to reality, that is, between the epistemological questioning of reality as arbitrary construction and taking it for granted as the basis for calculations. Uncertainty is explored as a lived experience with semantic, deontic and epistemological dimensions. It refers to anticipated outcomes, harms and benefits, and is manifested as a disconcertment that can arise from a plurality of ways of dealing with a present situation. I conceive the processing of uncertainties through forms as a type of anticipatory knowledge production, a type of testing which forms can hold and which are fragile – a practice which allows one to know, organize and govern the future and to make it more calculable. With Boltanski, I take seriously the uncertainty about what is, what counts, and how one can know what one knows, and the problems that this constitutive uncertainty poses to action and coordination. Thus my analysis is slower to dismiss the quandaries about acting in view of the indeterminacy both of the present and what is desired as to the future. I seek to show how Rashaida experience different unknowns, how they interpret and process them, and to add subtle qualifications of what so often appears as a rather uniform and black-boxed notion of uncertainty.

To situate my argument, I will review theoretical approaches to risk and danger that have inspired this work and which it seeks to extend conceptually. Against this backdrop I will situate my own approach, which draws upon neopragmatism – especially Boltanski's work on institutions and Thévenot's notion of 'investments of forms' – and seeks to reinsert debates about knowledge and institutions into the corpus of Sudan ethnography and anthropology.

Theories of Risk, Danger and Uncertainty

I have just described how I intend to extend the development studies debates by framing this study in terms of the relationship between contingency and the conditions of agency. Next, I draw upon well-known approaches to danger, risk and uncertainty, namely those of Dewey, Douglas, Beck, Foucault, Luhmann and Boltanski – the four in the middle being typical representatives of different risk theories, the cultural theory of risk perception, risk society, governmentality and systems theory.[4] I develop an argument from these theoretical propositions and use some of their conceptual tools to clarify what I mean by uncertainty, risk and insecurity and why I find it useful to distinguish between these notions in spite of their bleeding into one another.

While the notion of risk is well established and conceptualized, there is much fuzziness and inconsistency concerning the notions of insecurity and uncertainty. They are often used interchangeably in scholarly literature, especially in anthropology. I do not endorse drawing overly rigid analytical boundaries, i.e., between risk/uncertainty or calculable/incalculable risk, but rather suggest that concentrating on reflexivity and the stability of forms can help to focus the analysis. This sensitizes us to different realities and different understandings as to what should be.

I begin and end this brief and, in view of the immense available literature, necessarily selective journey with theoretical approaches in a pragmatist tradition. These are attentive to people's situational, experimental engagements with realities to contribute to what some have recently outlined as an anthropology of uncertainty (Whyte 1997; Boholm 2003;

Samimian-Darash 2013). I suggest that the degree of reflexivity with which people engage in a situation is crucial. Do they radically challenge all knowledge embodied in the situation? This could debilitate acting. Or do they take for granted certain elements – e.g., social categories, qualifications about the situation (this is a crisis, the risk is…), statements about rules of behaviour, normative principles – as stable orientations against which to act? I hold that the degree of reflexivity with which ordinary people make sense of and cope with indeterminacies and hazards in a situation is a yardstick to gauge the links between uncertainties and ways of processing them. The higher the reflexivity, the more extreme the uncertainty may turn out to be. The lower the reflexivity and the more elements are taken for granted, the less uncertain the foundations for acting.

In his influential book *The Quest for Certainty* (1929), John Dewey criticized the disassociation of knowledge and action, theory and practice, and the preference given to the former, which has moulded philosophical reasoning since Greek antiquity. His pragmatist position associates this exaltation of pure knowledge or thinking with the human endeavour to find an unshakeable certainty, whereas action is always overshadowed by uncertainty, because it occurs in unique circumstances where 'no complete assurance is possible' (Dewey 1929: 6). Hence, 'doing is always subject to peril, to the danger of frustration' (ibid.: 32, 33). In view of these uncertainties and the individual's fear about the outcomes of one's own actions and those of others, an imagined sphere of pure, unaltered thought was long conceived as the only abode of perfect certitude. Truth and reality were situated in this realm and were juxtaposed with an ever-changing and inferior realm of practical experience. The division of knowledge and practice corresponds to the distinction between knowledge and belief: the former is sure, necessary, perfect and incorruptible by change; the latter is imperfect, particular and empirical, inextricably uncertain and contingent, the work of opinion and probability (ibid.: 18–20).

Dewey (1929: 17) contended that this division has led to an essentialist conception of knowledge, diverting attention from a theory of knowledge that could address practical problems and enable coping with 'the vicissitudes of existence'. The quest for cognitive certainty, the denial or transcendence of uncertainty, figures as an inferior way of dealing with the lack of assurance. It results from a need for security in acting and thus should be substituted with a practical quest for security concerning which values should guide actions (ibid.: 24, 25, 33–39). To that end, he proposed that actors must concentrate on the 'methods of action', that is, modes of knowing through doing or experimentalization (ibid.: 36). Through his distinction between the cognitive properties of un/certainty and the action-oriented aspects of in/security, Dewey dismissed the possibility of absolute cognitive certitude as mere idealism. He argued that the practical security concerning the values imbricated in the situation are not only vital, but also partially attainable by means of directing or controlling practical involvements in the world.

The possibility of achieving practical security for acting appears too elusive a goal for more recent authors, most notably Zygmunt Bauman (2007). He asserted that a new phase of modernity has dawned, with a shift from solid to liquid modernity, propelled by unfathomable processes of globalization and individualization that have occurred during recent decades. Liquid modernity refers to the fluidity and instability of social forms which no longer manage to solidify into regular patterns. Bauman (2007: 1–4) related this to the unravelling of institutionalized insurance and state welfare, the breakdown of communal forms of solidarity, the nesting of power in global market forces and its divorce from politics, the abandoning of long-term thinking, and global changes that are unpredictable and uncontrollable. As a result, individuals are increasingly vulnerable to 'the vagaries of the market' and are isolated from prior social bonds and mechanisms of security (ibid.: 13). This loss of collective foundations and safe references for acting instills fear and uncertainty. Uncertainty in this influential argument is the hallmark of the unruly contemporary, a new global disorder.

A quite different contribution to theorizing human attempts to master the unknown was made by Mary Douglas, whose life project was 'understanding the relation between forms of association and the forms of moral judgment that ratify the former' (Fardon 1987: 4). While I do not lean on Douglas's structuralist interpretation, I am inspired by her attempt to explain perceptions of risk and danger in similar terms, without using risk to construct a discontinuity with the past. She argued: 'the ideal order of society is guarded by dangers which threaten transgressors. The whole universe is harnessed to men's attempt to force one another into good citizenship' (Douglas 1966: 3). The danger of transgressing taboos was seen as a means to encourage desirable behaviours, and thereby taboos served as technologies aimed at ordering society. Douglas and Wildavsky (1982) extended this argument to modern industrialized societies, suggesting that risks likewise enable instigating a moral discourse because risks connect damages to some breach of social norms. Modern secular societies have therefore translated danger into risk, cancelling out the divine and replacing it with ideas of scientific objectivity, and thus should be seen as 'sanitized' functional equivalents to misfortune (based on sin) in other societies (Douglas 1990: 5–7). Risk, now located in the realm of individual responsibility, is turned into a 'forensic resource' to hold individuals accountable for their actions and for moving beyond the limits of acceptable risk.

Douglas also drew attention to the role of social context for perception. Her thinking was particularly indebted to Ludwig Fleck's styles of thought, which are conceived of as preconditioning cognition, that is, the perception of reality and judgements about rationality and truth (Douglas 1986: 12, 13, 17).[5] The cultural theory of risk perception emphasizes that what is sifted out and perceived as a risk is an inherently cultural process: the form of and values enmeshed in social organization shape how people select, perceive, and manage risks (Douglas and Wildavsky 1982: 7).[6] Whereas Douglas established the cultural situatedness of risk selection, perception and management, she took the objectivity of her own analysis for granted (Tulloch 2008: 169), in a marked contrast to more recent analyses that problematize the situatedness of all knowledge.[7]

One name immediately comes to mind in connection with risk. Ulrich Beck was probably the most well-known, politically relevant but possibly also the most controversial risk theorist. With the ambition of formulating a comprehensive theory, Beck was interested in discovering the logics and structures governing the contemporary era. In contrast to Douglas, who refused to see a serious rupture between pre-modern danger and modern risk, he diagnosed a new periodization, namely, reflexive modernity: science and technology, once deployed to make the world calculable and predictable, are increasingly understood as risky. They systematically co-produce greater, uncontrollable and often invisible risks that can only be perceived by the very means that brought them forth, to wit science and technology (i.e., global warming, human genetic manipulations, pesticide pollution of food and water, etc.). Risks in Beck's theory are simultaneously real and unreal.[8] Beck's risks anticipate catastrophes and project dangers into the future, endowing the future with a fictive causal agency that has real consequences in orienting present actions, displacing the past as the horizon for orientation in the present (Beck 1986: 44). Risks are viewed as the main world-making force and the hallmark of modernity; they are what uncertainty is for Baumann. Beck suggested a qualitative difference between risks in former days, which were faced personally and where the lack of adequate technologies led to risks for people, and what he called the global risks of reflexive modernity, incalculable large-scale hazards, which endanger life on the whole planet. Global risks are seen as the collaterals of industrial progress, and the oversaturation and massive expansion of science and technology (ibid.: 28, 29).

Zinn (2008b: 177) noted that Beck, in his later *World Risk Society*, referred to risk as simultaneously real and constructed, drawing on Latour's critique of nature/culture distinctions. Proponents of the global risk society approach have proposed that the differentiation between natural and cultural must be critically interrogated to make room for and capture the heterogeneity of what is designated as 'natural' (Beck et al. 2003: 17, 18). But they also applied this same reasoning to dissolve other dichotomies such as global/local, international/national, work/non-work, fiction/reality and so on. The distinction between real and perceived risks can be qualified as a modern invention, equally as artificial as the distinction between nature and culture. Risks then are seen as man-made hybrids of real events, human interpretations, and calculations assembled in a network of associations (Beck 1999: 146).

However, this attempt to justify the position on risks as both real and constructed is not consistently presented. Bruno Latour (2003: 40, 41) observed that, in the end, risks for Beck always tended to refer to something 'happening out there' and in a 'society out there', implying that he was able to render an accurate description of real events from an all-seeing perspective. He contrasted Beck's theory of a change in 'substance' between modernity and reflexive modernity to an actor–network approach according to which change only concerns interpretations; society is bracketed and can only be 'locally achieved' by a multitude of interpretations of what holds things together (ibid.: 41). Furthermore, in contrast to Latour, who deconstructed the discontinuity between pre-modern and modern societies by claiming *We Have Never Been Modern* (1993), Beck (1999: 151) continued to provide a single narrative of modernization to construe a divide between a first modernity and a risk society.[9] Through his totalizing theory, Beck sought to explain the underlying structure of an entire era, dismissing the intricate logics that guide everyday practices. Instead of such a macro-approach, which may be more relevant for the management of uncertainties at this level of government, this analysis is attentive to the specific ways in which people understand, represent and engage the unknowable, often menacing future in north-eastern Sudan.

A third perspective, following the focus on the structure of danger/risks (Douglas) and risk as the driving force of modernity (Beck), frames risk as a governmental technology. In governmentality approaches, already introduced above, risk is understood not as an observable or real phenomenon but as an instrument in the hands of power (O'Malley 2008: 68). Risk is a part of the overarching technology of governing and controlling populations and thus is mainly in the hands of powerful actors, i.e., governments or organizations. As a calculative practice, risks involve the classification of events, people and things, which then serves as a basis for probabilistic predictions; in this view, the individual is treated only as a member of a population category (ibid.: 57, 66). Studies in the governmentality tradition have focused mainly on how uncertainty is managed through science and technology, particularly by means of statistical and probabilistic procedures, how risk is a technology of insurance (Ewald 1991), how uncertainty itself is a means of governing futures (O'Malley 2004), and how this is strategically employed to produce social realities and new subjectivities (Zinn 2008a: 7).

Crucial to this theoretical perspective is the fact that risk as a rationale of government cannot refer to real harm or danger itself. As Zinn (2008b: 174) pointed out, 'harm or danger just happens'. Risks emerge when certain assemblages of perceptions, discourses, techniques, practices and classifications are deployed in calculating uncertainties and managing threats by attributing them to categories of the population, through which governments define certain behaviours as ir/rational, un/desirable or un/safe (O'Malley 2008: 63). Given that biopolitics in Sudan is concerned mostly with enforcing assimilationist policies and not with calculating risks and securing the population, I shift the focus to ordinary actors and their daily micro-assessments of uncertainty and risk, a step others have also advocated (O'Malley 2004; Jenkins et al. 2005; Honkasalo 2006; Van Dongen 2008).

While my main interest is on how people in Sudan process uncertainties, Niklas Luhmann was disinterested in the acting subject. He proposed that self-referential communicative acts are key to the emergence of social systems and their functional differentiation (Luhmann 2011: 306). Luhmann asserted, similar to Beck, that risk is a distinctly modern phenomenon. But for him its appearance is linked to a functional differentiation of modern society, not directly to the rise of science and technology (Japp and Kusche 2008: 77–79). Notwithstanding that Luhmann sought to make sense of how modern society works as a whole, while I explore how individuals process uncertainties, I find the conceptual distinctions he elaborated useful for my own analysis. Risk for him cannot be empirically observed. Rather, it is an observation of other observations, something that abstracts from the empirical, what Luhmann called a second-order observation. Every second-order observation has its blind spot – it cannot reflect upon the position from where its own observations were made. Therefore further observations are needed which, however, also have their own blind spots. This understanding implies that when something is posited as a risk, it cannot reflect upon its own foundations. This is crucial to my argument about the connections between uncertainty, forms and reflexivity: risk denotes an assessment of an empirical observation, which is unable to reflect upon its own premises and grounds.

A second point related to Luhmann's work is relevant to this discussion. In a famous essay on risk and danger, Luhmann criticized the conventional juxtaposition of risk and security/safety (*Sicherheit*). He argued that this distinction seems to imply that safety is achievable, when – confirming Dewey's point – there simply can be no certitude concerning the future. Given that the 'future is and continues to be a horizon of uncertainty', safety is an unattainable ideal, an orientation for actions and decision-making (Luhmann 2005: 128, my translation). Uncertainty thus always concerns the difference between present future and future present (ibid.: 138). To account for contingency at the heart of social life, Luhmann proposes replacing the opposition security/risk with an analytical distinction between risk and danger.[10] Risk and danger both pertain to possible damages in the future, and their occurrence is uncertain, but risk denotes a more active engagement, contemplating decisions with respect to the future, a deliberating of options and possible averting of damage (ibid.: 131). Thus there is a difference in the attribution of harm: risks mean that future damages are attributed to a present decision. Therefore, risk is ascribed to a conscious calculation and action, whereas danger is attributed to potential damages and external harms that appear beyond personal influence and control (ibid.: 141). For example, cancer is a risk for smokers; for people exposed to the smoke it is a danger (ibid.: 140). In the same vein, one could argue that life in Sudan is more dangerous than life in Western Europe, but that does not make it necessarily riskier.

Thus, for Luhmann the distinction between risk and danger corresponds to the distinction between decision-makers and affected people. This distinction orients my analysis but with an important difference. For Luhmann meaning is bound to communication. His theory therefore purposely ignores the subject who takes a decision to attend to how whole systems emerged. In contrast, the concrete ways in which my Rashaida hosts in Sudan manage uncertainties are my main interest. I use the term risk to refer to something that people create through their interpretations and deliberations and that they engage through purposeful actions and decisions, and use the term dangers when things appear beyond people's immediate control and everyday means of prediction. I am inspired by Luhmann's disconcerting theory, which highlights that things could always be otherwise. It places contingency – the principal openness and indeterminacy of things – at the centre of analysis. Only in the context of contingency can there be any talk of decisions at all. In line with Dewey's assertion that 'doing is always subject to peril and frustration', decision-making for Luhmann is always uncertain and risky, as there are no permanent and safe references for the future (Japp and Kusche 2008: 80). From this unsettling perspective, Luhmann emphasized that uncertainty may debilitate communication. It may instill fear in people, freezing their ability to act and select options.

There appears to be much more certainty concerning what a risk is than what the experience of uncertainty is. The latter is largely taken for granted, treated as a poor cousin to risk, as O'Malley (2008: 73) remarked. A theoretical programme that, similar to Luhmann's contingency, places the unknown and unknowable future at the heart of social life is the pragmatic sociology of critique. To provide a different view on uncertainty and its constitutive role for social life, Luc Boltanski extends the concept of uncertainty. What was once a phenomenon marginalized by systems, structures, institutions, dispositifs and so on, has been unleashed. Uncertainty is seen everywhere at all times. It is constitutive of social existence, only varying in the degrees of intensity through which it is perceived. I follow Boltanski's conceptual broadening, which is useful in breaking the deadlock in debates on agency and contingency and can help to rethink what is un/specific about uncertainty and the ways in which it engages and is engaged.

In Boltanski's (2011) argument about the need to extend the concept of uncertainty, he refers to his discomfort with the plethora of sociological and anthropological theories that resort to some kind of shared meaning which miraculously emerges from interaction or a purportedly self-evident need to cooperate, where the prevalence of order is posited as the normal case and agreement is taken for granted. Critiquing this 'absolutism of agreement' in social analysis and the speed with which it dismisses uncertainty and unease was the starting point for Boltanski and Laurent Thévenot (2006), who elaborated a theoretical framework to accommodate dispute and agreement and the various forms in between. For Boltanski (2011: 55) uncertainty is radical and poses a problem for coordination. This uncertainty is at once semantic and deontic: it concerns the 'whatness of what is' and what matters or should matter in a situation (ibid.: 56, 57). This uncertainty cannot be dispelled or tamed by means of techniques, predictions or calculations; it is a fundamental part of social life. At times it is latent and does not come to the fore as people pragmatically cooperate and seem to agree on what is happening; at other times uncertainty leads to unease and fear or explodes into conflict.

The idea of uncertainty can be further qualified by considering a crucial differentiation that Boltanski makes – namely, reality and world. Reality is that which holds together and which is oriented towards stability and permanence; it is the state of affairs that institutions present as real, official, authentic and true, and that they continually reproduce in their everyday work. This product of institutional confirmation is supported by various arrangements and regulations (Boltanski 2011: 83–85, 91). The world is the background against which reality is set; with Wittgenstein it is 'everything that is the case' (ibid.: 57). The world is immanence and incessant change, people's immersion in the flow of life, a dynamic lived experience that pays no heed to institutionalized reality (ibid.: 57–61). The world encroaches upon reality when people make experiences that from the point of view of reality were not probable or even possible. The distinction between reality and world involves critical reflexivity and thus constitutes a space from which critiques of the institutionalized reality can be formulated (ibid.: 91). When inconsistencies or even contradictions are registered, they can hollow out reality, making it an utterly brittle construct, vulnerable to denunciation.[11]

Unveiling reality as construction is not my task. My interest lies in discerning those moments when a shift occurs between Rashaida taking something for granted as real and Rashaida questioning their knowledge of reality. For instance, when people focus on a goal that they want to reach together instead of on how to reach it – that is, the divergent ways in which it can be accomplished or whether it is useful to accomplish it at all – uncertainty is limited or even partially bracketed. Reflexivity is low, inconsistencies and contradictions are ignored, and representations of reality are not questioned (Boltanski 2011: 62–67). However, when attention shifts from the ends to be reached to the modalities of action – that is, the *values* and forms associated with it – a code switch occurs.[12] Knowledge is differentiated and uncertainty breaks out.

These moments of reflexive scrutiny demand so-called metapragmatic repertoires of action, which explore the distance between reality and the world (Boltanski 2011: 69). Moments of reflexivity can be differentiated according to two main procedures: confirmation and critique. The former denotes the main institutional function, namely, confirming selected elements from the world to continually reestablish and preserve what was constructed as reality. Critique, in contrast, uses uncertainty to challenge representations of reality. A central point for Boltanski is that critique and confirmation are welded together in a dialectical relationship: critique needs to challenge something and has to be directed against some aspect of reality, while confirmation of something only makes sense against a background where critique is possible and likely (ibid.: 57–62).

Applying Boltanski's distinction of reality and world is a useful tool for conceptualizing qualitative differences between the terms which occupy risk theorists: uncertainty, insecurity/danger and risk. Uncertainty emerges from the difference between reality and world. It entails the more or less radical questioning of what is presented as reality and opens a horizon to imagine other social arrangements. Uncertainty in this sense does not only pertain to what is not known about the future, as many authors emphasize above, but it manifests itself in doubt about the present situation and the ways in which things are arranged. It hence relates to epistemological questions, such as: are things as they appear? How can I know what I know? What is this something that I know? Thus conceived, uncertainty is an experience that, as Dewey eloquently elaborated, results from an always unsatisfiable lack of knowledge and is a main motor of social critique. 'We know that we do not know, but that is almost all that we know: there is no better definition of uncertainty' (Callon et al. 2009: 21).

Uncertainty in its most radical forms is strongly entangled with observations made from being positioned in the world, because 'being in the world', as Boltanski defines it, already denotes having stumbled upon a representation of reality and noticing a difference to lived experience. What was once taken for granted as objective reality has been tarnished by doubt. A reflexive engagement then denotes that reality is perceived as something constructed in a specific way. It allows for thinking otherwise. Or as Boltanski would express it, uncertainty already entails a critical optic, a reflexive answering of questions such as what is and what counts.

Insecurity and risk also entail a lack of knowledge, because if everything was known there would be neither insecurity nor risk. But in contrast to uncertainty, these phenomena denote a certain knowledge concerning what knowledge is lacking. Hence, the notions of insecurity and risk emerge from a perspective that takes the institutionalized reality for granted. 'Insecurity' refers to existential problems, a state that is different from a desirable but unattainable state of security. However, in contrast to uncertainty, insecurity does not lead to a radical questioning of the reality construction but refers to uncontrollable hazards within it. For example, many Rashaida in Kassala engage in cross-border trade with Eritrea, often of alcohol, weapons, electronics and groceries. This activity is branded as smuggling by the government, which has deployed heavily armed police forces to counter the contraband trade. The governmental interventions thus constitute an insecurity for people engaging in these activities that have become integral to their livelihoods. People are concerned with earning an income and making a profit. Thereby they take certain elements of reality for granted while acting. They do not always ask radical questions, such as: is what we are doing actually smuggling? Is it fair that the government forbids this activity without providing alternatives? How can we know that this is an un/acceptable way of doing things? Instead they deal with the insecurity that this type of trade entails and act as if they knew what was going on, taking reality for granted. But in view of the fragility of reality, this way of engaging reality can easily lead to greater reflexivity, when a code switch occurs, what Boltanski (2011: 67, 68) calls metapragmatic registers of action that are marked by uncertainty (cf. Rottenburg 2005a).

'Risk' is here understood as a particular kind of insecurity, namely, calculated insecurity. Risk denotes techniques and the entire calculative apparatus employed in the present to predict and control future insecurities – a goal that can never be fully realized. In contrast to both uncertainty and insecurity, the notion of risk implies that the probability of possible outcomes can be assessed. Boltanski also follows Foucault in seeing risk as a technology of constructing a reality, which can be enacted.[13] It cannot be anything real. It denotes bracketing uncertainties by concentrating on a limited range of unknowns. According to the argument I presented above, in view of the absence of inclusive biopolitical projects in Sudan, which could sift through potentially harmful unknowns and provide some level of security, uncertainty is pronounced for many people in Sudan. Risk is not a primary technology for managing the Sudanese population.

Risks need not be located only at the government level, but can also emerge from more mundane efforts to translate radical uncertainty into something less radical with clearer options for acting. Thereto, I apply a broader understanding of governmentality to encompass all attempts to regulate 'the conduct of conduct', be it that of governments, groups or the self (Dean 1999: 10, 11). O'Malley (2008: 72, 73) points out that all attempts to control and govern the future involve calculation: not only governments but also ordinary people calculate the future and deliberate options in their everyday management of insecurities, even if with much less sophisticated means, applying rules of thumb, ordinary foresight, collecting information, relying on past experiences and so on. In this regard, I further rely on Mary Douglas, for whom human interpretations and responses to various dangerous unknowns are part of a universal but culturally structured phenomenon. Luhmann's juxtaposition of risk and danger is even more important: the attribution of risk to a present decision as opposed to a diffuse danger that cannot be acted upon. This distinction is important in order to gain a nuanced understanding of different qualities of uncertainty and the ways in which people experience and process them.

These positions enable me to extend the notion of risk from numerical and statistical calculation to all situations when people or collective actors consciously calculate, deliberate and evaluate insecurities, frame options, and decide upon them. Risks can be taken or avoided. Risk demands adjusting to insecurities, attempting to master or eschew them. In contrast, insecurity denotes the anticipation of harms coming from the outside, beyond one's control.

To sum up, risk, insecurity and uncertainty are distinct ways of anticipating and controlling futures – probable futures that are subject to statistical regularity, threatening futures related to some known harmful scenarios, and finally open and unique futures (O'Malley 2004: 13, 23). Uncertainty here denotes the lack of assurance, the principal openness and indeterminacy of the future – in a non-normative sense. But it is neither the logical condition of contingency that interests me here nor different groups or societies or how they are being managed by risk technologies at the state level; rather, I focus on how the individual finds herself entangled in various situations and attempts to control her own life and how this motivates or discourages actions that must be coordinated with others in an environment of scarcity.

Engaging with debates about the reality and/or social construction of risks, I assert that the emphasis on uncertainty by definition already includes an understanding of the impossibility of a single reality and a single truth existing out there; it implies that competing realities and interpretations abound. Moreover, relying on Boltanski, and by extension also expanding on much of the orthodox risk literature, I argue that uncertainty also involves an epistemological dimension – not only an observing of the present with regard to the future but an observing of the present with regard to the present or immediate past. Uncertainty in the latter sense, as the observed difference between world and reality, means engaging reflexively with present circumstances; it figures as the main source of doubt and critique. Both the uncertainty regarding the future and its epistemological quality pertaining to the present can produce disconcertment and anxiety. At times uncertainty liberates people from blindly following conventions and leads them to question the propriety of invoked principles, while at other times it inhibits the flow of activity by squarely calling into question all safe references for action. This is at the heart of this study.

Hence, when I talk of the ways of processing uncertainty I refer both to anticipation of the future and reflexive enquiries into present and past arrangements, which the individual takes into consideration while invoking or experimenting with forms in the present. I view uncertainty as the fundamental principle through which other notions, such as insecurity/ danger or risk, can be conceived as special types, defined by their respective relations to reality. In this way, the notions of risk and insecurity are anchored in reality – a single reality – and accept it as the framework out of which to project the future and, if understood as sufficiently predictable or probable, to control it. Risk is conceptualized as calculated insecurity, something that could be averted but that involves engaging insecurities and developing ways of dealing with them. Insecurity is understood as a synonym for danger and unsafety, referring to possible harms beyond the concerned individual's control. Insecurity/danger and risk are also qualitatively different from uncertainty, in that they anticipate negative consequences, future harms or damages, and in the case of risk either losses or gains, which could actually materialize.

By drawing clear analytical distinctions between these notions, I am perhaps pushing beyond what Boltanski intended. He extended the understanding of contingency and agency by placing an uncertainty that I would describe as constitutive at the centre of his discussion of social life in its entirety and he assumes that it is active in all of the different operations, preventing a fixedness of reality. This means that people's means of control and prediction of the future will only achieve partial results, because uncertainty cannot be tamed. I suggest that this move towards qualifying uncertainties is nonetheless justified. The clarity of my argument will profit from differentiating between types of uncertainty, and this will allow me to tease out the different references to reality involved in various ways of processing uncertainty and the different moral understandings that are mobilized to anticipate and organize futures. I thus suspect that the epistemological and deontic dimensions of uncertainty are greatest when discord arises about the modalities of action and when involved parties make their moral judgements explicit. Other moments in which uncertainties can be explored with an ethnographic sensitivity are those when people work hard to dispel doubts and to stabilize certain meanings as matters of fact.

Processing Uncertainty

Establishing Forms

Forms are a key feature of this attempt to introduce a new approach to the study of uncertainty. To process uncertainties, actors engage in the work of transformation or 'form-giving work', which is performed in the interstitial spaces between the specific situation with its temporality, the uncertainty of the individual regarding its correct identification, and the way in which relations, objects and persons are made coherent (cf. Thévenot 1984; Wagner 1993: 466; Bogusz 2010: 35). Dewey's (1896) insights are helpful here again: they posit that any form developed to process uncertainty connects problematic aspects of the situation to an end in view, and its mobilization is a means of enquiring whether an action can clear up the uncertainty or whether any elements in the situation need to be revised. Forms are something decidedly less determined and determining than ideas of structure would suggest: they are props for action, things that hold together and enable a processing of uncertainty. I will first describe Thévenot's idea and its premises, then discuss how it differs from other theoretical takes on forms. I argue with Simmel that following the distinction between form and content is useful for the analysis of uncertainty and its management.

People are immersed daily in a multitude of different situations with different needs of coordination (Thévenot 2001: 57). The question emerges as to where the certainty – or shall we call it confidence – comes that enables people to enter agreements and to cooperate, to even take this state of affairs as normal. With risk the reference is reality – it is taken for granted and offers a range of predictability. Uncertainty, in contrast, if it is not contained, can question all safe reference points and deny all assurances. It poses a great challenge to coordination among people. The problem of how to move from a unique situation that an individual experience to a situation of greater generality shared with other people is facilitated by establishing equivalences, the main forms addressed by many chapters in this book (Blokker and Brighenti 2011: 358).[14]

This highlights another problem that I have yet to address. Processing uncertainty not only concerns the individual and her actions, but it also raises the question of how this can be done jointly with others and whether coordination alters the experience of uncertainty. In view of the problem of how to jointly direct activities towards an uncertain future, I draw upon

Thevenot's 'investments in forms' (1984). It denotes the tedious coding or classifying through which a likeness of things and people is achieved.[15] This process leaves traces in the material world. Forms as things that hold together are institutionalized as parts of reality to which various actors can refer in order to back their claims in situations of doubt. Forms in this sense are predominantly cognitive, such as habits, customs, codes, classifications, rules, standards, qualifications, authentications, legal acts and other institutions, but to gain stability they need to be supported by material, technological, scientific, legal or other elements (Thevenot 2007: 412–13; 1984; Dodier 2011).[16] In spite of their great diversity and the variant efforts that need to be invested in creating and maintaining forms, all forms reduce the effort of coordination and enable people to act in more public situations (Thevenot 2001: 58). Forms are elements of reality. The solidity of the equivalences, and by extension that of reality construction, depends upon their duration in time, their spatial expansion, and their material equipment and therewith their ability to withstand critique (Thévenot 1984: 10–16; 2007: 413).[17]

Niklas Luhmann also adopted a similar point of departure to investigate the conditions of communication, the fundamental operation of social systems. He wondered how communication and order are possible in view of double contingency, the problem of forming expectations about others' expectations (Luhmann 1984: 165). While the success of communication is improbable, every determination – whether purposive, accidental or coincidental – in a social system entails a fixedness of references for following operations and thus implies the emergence of a more comprehensive order (ibid.).

Dealing with the notion of forms in anthropology may suggest Radcliffe-Brown's (1971a: 192) famous earlier distinction between social structure and structural form. Accordingly, social structure is that which can be abstracted from empirical observation, the networks of relationships between people. These relationships are forged by the convergence or adjustment of individual interests in an object; the object is then endowed with a social value for the subjects (Radcliffe-Brown 1971a: 140; 1971b: 199). Importantly, Radcliffe-Brown (1971a: 140) argues that for any society to be constituted, its members have to agree on values. This convergence of interests and the agreement on values create a system of values. The value system's crucial function is to preserve structural form. Structural form is inspired by Durkheimian ideas on the social as a separate sphere of reality, something more than its constituent parts: it is the abstraction of social structures, the general patterns that the analyst deduces from observing the concrete and real networks of relationships. In a structural–functionalist interpretation, structural form thus denotes the general and socially acceptable patterns of behaviour, which are supported and preserved by various social–cultural phenomena and values; this form outlives the involved persons and tends to be inert or return to a state of continuity after upheavals (ibid.: 192–93). In contrast, the pragmatist notion of forms does not assign any relevance or existence outside of social practice; forms are made and unmade in situations. Furthermore, whereas structural functionalist thinking emphasizes the continuity and relative stability of structural form as emerging from an agreement of values, a pragmatist stance underlines the fragility of all agreements and their sociological exceptionality. The most outstanding difference concerns agency: individuals are not accorded any agency by Radcliffe-Brown but are bound by their roles and statuses to maintain and reproduce the structural form, which therein determines behaviours. Following Thévenot (1984), individuals actively and intentionally engage with forms, investing in, establishing or critiquing them through manifold costly investments of time, money, efforts and so on. Forms involve agency and to some degree intention – at least in establishing, justifying or questioning them. For instance, risk as calculated insecurity enables people to act in certain ways and therefore is also viewed as an invested form.

The notion of forms has a much longer history in philosophy than in anthropology. It commonly means a visible figure or gestalt, contours, but also quality, character, kind, species or type. The Greek thinkers who laid the foundation of what Dewey critiqued as the elevation of pure thought and the disparagement of practical activity highlighted forms: for Plato form refers to unchanging, perfect and ideal things, related to the realm of pure thought, uncorrupted by the need for practical involvements in the world (*EPuW* 2005: 521; Dewey 1929: 16).[18] Francis Bacon's treatment of forms, where they emerged as mere patterns to be empirically determined through induction and the generalization of findings, is viewed as the dawn of a gradual move away from ontological and theological problems (*EPuW* 2005: 522). An important contribution to debates on form and matter was made by Isaac Newton, who showed that the physical properties of bodies are determined by their mass, the density and volume of matter as well as inertia, not their form (Bormann et al. 1972: 1013). Kant introduced matter as that which can be practically experienced and forms as those things that provide cognitive certitude;[19] practical experience is not riddled with uncertainty but composed of 'equally complete practical moral assurance' (Dewey 1929: 58). A very different but likewise well-known approach that uses a terminology of forms is Wittgenstein's *Lebensformen* or 'forms of life'. In *Philosophische Untersuchungen* (1977), *Lebensformen* are described as the taken-for-granted, unquestioned, and thus unchallenged things, which enable sense and meaning. Wittgenstein considered different linguistic means and related their use to forms of life, which manifest themselves in language games. Forms of life therein are general principles, which by rules of logic can be attributed to every person.

In view of the rich and varied ideas evoked by the notion of forms, does it make sense to resort to a terminology of forms when in anthropology it may even be mistakenly associated with structural functionalist thinking? What is the advantage when the notion of forms disassociates things that are brought together in the more established notions of norms and rules, namely technical elements and their normative contents? When Georg Simmel is selected as an intellectual ancestor for the notion of forms as technical elements, which imbue certain contents with social life, then certain differences between his conception of form and content and the pragmatic programme come to the fore. In contrast to the ideas formulated in ancient Greek thought, which tend to portray forms as something original, unchanging and pure or an abstraction gained from practical experience, Simmel developed an idea of content as something rather raw and immediate and forms as something emerging, transforming and shaped. The methodological investigation of an analytical distinction between forms and contents was the cornerstone of Simmel's sociology, and in his view the study of forms of sociation is the only legitimation for this science of society (Frisby 1992: 11; Simmel 1992: 20–22).[20] Content is likened to those things, such as drives, interests, inclinations, emotions or psychological states, which emerge from and in reciprocal engagements; it is considered the matter of sociation (*Vergesellschaftung*). Sociation refers to the variant forms that emerge and are realized when individuals – with their interests, intentions and tendencies – interact. It is within these forms that interests can then materialize, that is, the content is endowed with reality in society (Simmel 1992: 18, 19). Form and content for Simmel are entangled; they cannot exist independently of each other.[21] Whereas for Simmel form and content are only analytically separable, in the pragmatic sociology of critique, forms and normative elements can be disassociated and recombined – the very emphasis of the latter approach is upon the situational work of realignment or making forms cohere with various worths or general conventions (cf. Boltanski and Thévenot 2006). Interpretation and evaluation are not more or less fixed as, for instance, the competing ideas of rules or norms would suggest, but rather the idea of form enables interpretative multiplicity and flexibility. Forms, following the pragmatic programme, can be associated with several competing conventions and how exactly people evaluated and (re)combine them depends entirely on the situation.[22]

While acknowledging the ability of reshuffling form and content, to portray forms as merely neutral and technical would disregard the cost or sacrifice which every investment in forms inevitably entails – abandoning the unique for the general (Thévenot 1984: 9). The point is that forms facilitate coordination as regards the epistemological dimensions of uncertainty by providing people with an epistemic foundation for action, and it is precisely the appearance of neutrality of forms that may enable cooperation. A further advantage is that the notion of forms is broad and can encompass various subtypes, such as formats, rules, classifications, codes, habits and so on. Similar to uncertainty, which is here viewed as the overarching category for qualitatively different phenomena (risk and insecurity/danger), forms are viewed as the main category of things that hold together and facilitate coordination. While forms for Thévenot are mainly cognitive, they need to be supported materially to persist, such as through lists, registration forms or other objects.

Equivalences and Cooperation

Since my interest is in how people act and deal with uncertainties and existential insecurities, cooperation is critical. An important point for this pragmatic approach is that forms can be very idiosyncratic, such as the habits conforming to an individual's sense of comfort or aesthetics, but when action needs to be coordinated with others, general forms increasingly need to be found. For example, in a fight no Rashidi will tell his opponent, 'I am fighting with you because I despise your ugly face' or 'because I covet your wife', but he will point to some more general moral failure, such as the other's breaching the norm of hospitality, breaking an agreement, failing to reciprocate and so on. This expansion to generality means that interests, drives and affections need to be expressed in a more general fashion with reference to some common higher principle or value to withstand critique (Thévenot 1984; Boltanski and Thévenot 2006). Cooperation here is envisioned as resting upon an understanding of sameness or equivalence, which first must be produced in view of individuals' unique and particular situations and the uncertainty about what is at stake in every situation. Hence, the analysis is attentive to different 'invested forms' that are referred to and compete to shape or format the situation under analysis, which in my understanding mainly involves cognitive dimensions. In other words, I investigate how people make sense of what is going on and how they engage with what is unknown. Being attentive to how Rashaida in north-eastern Sudan cooperate in a non-reflexive mode to reach a goal, and conversely to how the potentially disparate premises of their engagements are explicitly evaluated, enables one to explore the normative dimension, the general moral understandings that they refer to and apply in a situation to coordinate their activities with others. Guiding questions by way of Boltanski and Thévenot (2006) would be: how do people evaluate and qualify situations and what is at stake in addition to the persons and things involved? How do they – each from their own particular interpretation – reach situations that can be shared with others?

And how do arguments have to be framed to withstand public scrutiny and attain the greatest level of generality?

To theorize how priorities are made in a situation of scarcity, I will draw upon the framework proposed by Boltanski and Thévenot in *On Justification* (2006),[23] which perpetuates Bourdieu's structural heritage but renounces all kinds of determination and rationality (Wagner 1993: 465). In contrast to forms that can be a variety of things with a broadly differing stability, Boltanski and Thévenot suggest that the concept of conventions should refer to broad and commonly accepted interpretative and evaluative frameworks. People may apply these in situations to coordinate their actions and to reduce the uncertainty of how to assign a place to things and persons in a certain hierarchy or so-called 'order of worth' (Boltanski and Thévenot 2006; Salais 2011: 221–22). A convention thus implies a general acceptability; it has to be discursively formulated and thereby its normativity is laid bare. A form, to clearly delineate the difference, appears mostly as a technical element. It does not necessarily expose its normative orientations and thus in principle can be aligned with various conventions. However, a convention could be understood as a very special and general type of form. Conventions, in this sense, are cognitive and normative frameworks; they are always at least virtually plural and competing. But they need to be performed in practice to have any effect on the situation and thereby they are always adjusted, (re) combined and translated in line with the situational exigencies. Conventions are thus important in situations of controversy, when a generally acceptable settlement has to be negotiated or a basis for cooperation has to be reestablished.

To sum up, this book adds to the debates on agency and contingency by tracing how people process uncertainties. I am investigating the ability to cooperate and survive amidst various types of uncertainty – from daily unknowns to life-threatening dangers. Here I differ from Grätz (2010: 73), who argues more modestly and cautiously that his micro-study of gold mining facilitates understandings of risk in relations to factors of social cohesion in an open social field but without macro-sociological abstractions. I tend to be slightly more optimistic. The project to which I have committed myself is to employ my ethnographic data to qualify (sub)types of uncertainty and to reveal how people in Sudan process them in an existential situation. I theorize the particularities of dealing with existential uncertainties and how people engage with different degrees of reflexivity with what cannot be known. My contribution is to show how forms as things that hold together for some time are situationally invoked, used, taken for granted and questioned as props for acting in situations of contingency. Therewith I hope to contribute another perspective to what some have already contoured as an anthropology of uncertainty (cf. Boholm 2003). My study outlines what ordinary people take for granted and how they evaluate and situationally renegotiate their range for manoeuvring. Furthermore, it is attentive to the various everyday practices, methods and non-/probabilistic techniques with which people tame or better seek to tame these uncertainties – individually and collectively. I assume that in order to process uncertainties people invest in forms, that is, they strive to establish some elements as binding, upon which they can draw when interacting with others – this can be applied to institutions on various scales of ordering. Yet all forms, by virtue of their selective and arbitrary nature, are vulnerable to critique. Processing uncertainties can also mean translating them into something more manageable, such as insecurities or risks whereby at least some stable reference points are taken for granted as real.

Notes

1. The most frequent misfortunes that befall Nyole are health failures; failures of prosperity; gender, marital, sexual and reproductive problems; and failures of personal safety, such as traffic accidents, snake bites and so on (Whyte 1997: 16–18).
2. In contrast to authors such as Lévy-Bruhl, Evans-Pritchard (1968: 73) maintained that 'Zande belief in witchcraft in no way contradicts empirical knowledge of cause and effect. ... The attribution of misfortune to witchcraft does not exclude what we call its real causes but is superimposed in them and gives to social events their moral value'.
3. Evans-Pritchard (1968: 351) does contend, however, that there is some freedom within the system of thought: 'Azande cannot go beyond the limits set by their culture and invent notions, but within these limits human behaviour is not rigidly determined by custom and a man has some freedom of action and thought'.
4. A main controversy between these different approaches concerns the objective reality of risks and/or their social construction, the latter being a perspective that dismisses the possibility of the former. The Thomas theorem (Merton 1995) enables the bracketing of this debate: when situations are defined as real, they have real consequences. For example, whereas the real existence of a *ǧinn* (demon) might not be accepted by all observers, especially those adhering to a more orthodox version of Islam, it is still consequential. Fearful of a bad spirit invading them, some Rashaida continue to take certain protective measures, such as writing a Quranic verse on a piece of paper and hiding it in their clothing, although this can also have costly consequences since it is increasingly stigmatized as ignorant and pagan.
5. Shared categories and classification enable people to act without having to question interactions in each and every situation. In this sense Douglas (1986: 48) proposes that institutions do the difficult thinking for people and that by producing collective representations they reduce the uncertainty of future behaviour and thereby preserve social order.
6. The authors ask 'How, then, do people decide which risks to take and which to ignore? On what basis are certain dangers guarded against and others relegated to secondary status?' (Douglas and Wildavsky 1982: 1). They suggest that something is selectable as

a risk based on knowledge of the future and an agreement about what future is desired (ibid.: 5). But this entails cultural bias – some things are perceived as risky, while other, perhaps more threatening dangers are ignored (ibid.: 14). Douglas's tendency to reduce risk to structures and their reproduction was criticized by later proponents of culturalist approaches to risk (Zinn 2008b: 181–82).

7. Boholm (2003: 167) asserts that taboo and risk are counterparts, not equivalents. Taboo is related to fate and certainty of retributions, whereas 'risk stands for calculated uncertainty, a risk can be practically managed, reduced or increased, it could be taken or avoided, depending on one's own and others' actions and motives'.

8. For a critique of this approach, see Rasborg 2012.

9. See O'Malley's (2008: 65) critique of Beck's construction of a totalizing narrative. Further, Tulloch (2008: 149–50) contends that Beck's theory ignores aesthetic, cultural and affective dimensions of risks and that his lack of empirical studies is mirrored in a deficient understanding of how individuals make sense of risks as they go about their daily lives.

10. This is based on another analytical distinction: a first-order observation assumes that risk and dangers are real and that they can be ordered independently of the observer; for example, Beck's early work is interpreted along these lines. A second-order observation refers to the first observation critically and unmasks it as a construction based on the attribution of decisions, which could again be put in relative position by further observations (Luhmann 2005: 131). Luhmann (ibid.: 147) concludes that there is no privileged vantage point from which to observe risks.

11. As Boltanski (2011: 59) summarizes, 'the arrangements which constitute and organize reality are fragile because critique can always draw events from the world that contradict its logic and furnish ingredients for unmasking its "arbitrary" and "hypocritical" character, or for "deconstructing" them'.

12. Boltanski's distinction between reality and world is similar to Rottenburg's (2009a) argument about metacodes as peace treaties. Rottenburg contrasts two different modes of action: moments when goal-oriented action takes centre stage and moments when divergences and contradiction come to the fore. The former demand a metacode to maintain a minimal consensus among involved persons to prevent them from asking fundamental questions and to promote reaching practical ends (Rottenburg 2005a: 270–73).

13. Boltanski (2011: 57) writes: 'in as much as it is probabilizable, risk constitutes one of the instruments for constructing reality invented in the eighteenth century, and is connected (as Michel Foucault has shown) with the liberal mode of governance'.

14. Boltanski and Thévenot have developed their own propositions in dealing with different levels of commonality or generality in action, namely, 'regimes of action' (Boltanski 2011, 2012) and 'regimes of engagement' (Thévenot 2006, 2007) to theorize actions that do not have to meet broad requirements of justice and therefore need not be publicly justifiable.

15. I see resonances between the approach focused on forms and Åsa Boholm's (2003) contribution to anthropological theorizations of uncertainty. He enquired into the possibilities of an anthropology of uncertainty by critically engaging with the cultural theory of risk, which he saw as unduly promoting cultural relativism. Anthropology has to contribute something more than acknowledging the plurality of cultural risk perception. Boholm proposes doing so by unpacking the black-box of culture, which is still too often taken for granted, used as a storage container for miscellanea, which are considered useless for risk calculation. He suggested a conception of culture as a shared

schemata and scripts that define categories and contexts, which allow one to study risk as a meaning-making device, something that establishes and orders relationships among possible harms (risks), objects of harm, and human actions and accountability (Boholm 2003: 175).

16. For example, the notion of 'information' is an invested form, because to be disseminated various cognitive operations need to be transformed into something that is standardized and can be understood widely, presupposing a preparatory process of representation and coding (Thevenot 2007: 412). Here Thévenot's ideas coincide with those of Luhmann on communication.

17. But every generalization comes at a price, also referred to as a loss or sacrifice (Thévenot 2009: 795). Thus, every generalization is inextricably bound up in the question of legitimacy (Diaz-Bone and Thévenot 2010: 4). A doubt about 'the sacrifice' emerges, a doubt that figures as a source of critique in the pragmatic sociology of critique (Blokker and Brighenti 2011: 385–86).

18. Aristotle is attributed with juxtaposing form and matter, which were to become important ontological terms. Form and matter are viewed as basic principles that remain unchanged but are united in composite objects; the latter alone are subject to movement and transformation (Bormann et al. 1972: 983). Much later, in Christian theology, especially the exegesis of Genesis, God emerges as the ultimate and original form-giver, the *Urbild* of all forms and creator of unity through matter and form (*EPuW* 2005: 522; Bormann et al. 1972: 987).

19. For Kant form and matter have no ontological character but rather are terms that guide reflection: matter is that which can be empirically experienced through sensual perception, while form refers to the abilities of the mind, i.e., the orderings and categories the mind can determine by contemplation and thinking (Bormann et al. 1972: 1022).

20. Society in Simmel's view emerges from the interactions of individuals, who in mutually producing effects on each other are united in certain forms of interaction (Simmel 1992: 17, 18).

21. Simmel's (1992: 21) thesis is that different interests can lead to identical forms, whereas identical interests can lead to different forms.

22. This brings to mind another conception of form/matter formulated by Deleuze and Guattari (1987), namely territorialization as the form in which a certain substance materializes, along with the various possibilities of de- and reterritorialization. As Deleuze and Guattari (1987: 41) put it: 'substances are nothing other than formed matters. Forms imply a code, modes of coding and decoding. Substances as formed matters refer to territorialities and degrees of territorialization and deterritorialization. But each articulation has a code and a territoriality; therefore each possesses both form and substance'.

23. A first version of the argument was published in 1987 (*Les Economies de la grandeur*) and the French title *De La Justification* appeared in 1991.

Chapter 2

CONTESTING FORMS

Translating Poverty and Uncertainty

This chapter is about resource distribution, uncertainty and justice in a setting of scarcity. It analyses a series of events that occurred on a day in March 2010 in Um Futeima, a small settlement in the Lower Atbara area of north-eastern Sudan.[1] Representatives of a Kuwaiti charitable foundation arrived to pass out goats and chickens for the poor and to provide the meat of a slaughtered camel for the community. I highlight how uncertainties emerged when reflexivity increased and normative understandings were interrogated.

This situation involved various actors and demanded a certain level of cooperation. Cooperation here is understood as being grounded in formatted information ('invested forms') and is oriented towards a goal – distributing things. But the arrangement of things was questioned and other normative ideas of a fair and good distribution ('conventions') were invoked. A controversy arose that concerned who should be included in the distribution, who really were 'the poor', what was the purpose of the distribution and what should be its purpose instead. Uncertainty ensued. It became unclear how others would act. All made assumptions about other people's actions, watching and evaluating them. People based their claims to reality on various forms, in this case specifically established rules, lists, procedures and social categories, such as 'the poor', 'the sheikhs' and 'the migrants'. I analyse the discursive strategies of the opponents and proponents of the established distributive order (Boltanski and Thévenot 2006). By endorsing or critiquing the way in which resources were distributed, villagers not only shed light upon their understandings of justice but also adapted principles of coordination to their situation, translated them, and invented or imported principles from elsewhere. Of particular interest is how commonality can be produced in a situation of heterogeneity and uncertainty – that is, how equivalences are established/confirmed that move beyond particular interests and hold together as broader compromises among people in a small settlement, and, conversely, what occurs when people begin to doubt the premises of actions.

I begin with a more or less predictable situation, following it to the moment at which people engaged it more critically and reflexively, leading to great uncertainty about the situation, the people involved and the appropriate actions. I use the notion of code switches to theorize the shifts between practical moments and reflexive moments. The former denotes those times when people cooperate through a metacode, which enables the bracketing of indeterminacies and contradictory understandings, and reduces what is relevant about the situation to a minimum (Rottenburg 2005a: 267–71).[2] The latter implies a heightened reflexivity about the prevalence of different understandings and uncertainty about how a situation can be resolved. This ushered in more radical enquiries about the status of knowledges: official representations of reality were no longer taken at face value and the fairness of resource allocations was questioned. In the situation discussed in this chapter, uncertainty became radical. I underscore how it can be a source of liberation.

Approaching the Situation

This chapter is devoted to the analysis of a 'situation' that took place on a single day in rural north-eastern Sudan. What does this notion of 'situation' imply? Instead of making a priori assumptions about social forms, neopragmatist stances start from situations and how meanings emerge and are articulated in actual practices (Wagner 1993; Boltanski 2011). This is in line with recent praxeological approaches in the social sciences, where situations are not restricted to face-to-face interactions but rather figure as complex arrangements of humans, objects, meanings, cognitive formats, institutions and so on (see Schatzki 2001).

Within anthropology there is a long genealogy of tracing processes by analysing the dynamics of situations and extending 'out from the field' in space and time, moving from unique to general, micro to macro, and present to past (Burawoy 1998: 4–5; Evens and Handelman 2005: 1–2). I am thinking of situational analysis/extended case method (ECM), which Max Gluckman developed in the 1940s and which has recently taken the postmodern turn towards becoming and improvisation.[3] A situation figures as a moment (of varied length) of a more general process, whereby the next moment is constantly pending. But authors after Gluckman pointed out that situations were too often taken as mere illustrations of the process.[4] Instead they should be conceived as 'a particular point of entry that opens toward a knowing that is not already apparent' (Kapferer 2005: 92).[5] Hence, it is bound up with uncertainty about outcomes.

A critique of situational analysis is that it does not pay sufficient attention to people's opinions and interpretations, alllowing instead the ethnographic observer to state authoritatively 'what is' (Kapferer 2005: 104). Here the approach of pragmatic sociology of critique comes in handy. Emerging from a critique of Bourdieu's critical sociology that privileged social scientists' ability to uncover hidden domination, it is sensitive to 'what [everyday] actors do, the way they interpret the intentions of others, the way they argue their case, and so on' (Boltanski 2011: 23).

The situation I analyse took place on a day in March 2010 in Um Futeima. The settlement of Um Futeima lies in the hinterlands of the Lower Atbara area, River Nile State, Sudan. At that time it was inhabited by roughly 200 Rashaida (former) pastoralists and a dozen of the landowning Bishariyn. On my first visit in December 2007 only a handful of people had settled there permanently. In 2009 several clay houses had been erected and a small souk with three grocery stores and two cafeterias had opened, and people had begun to sell gasoline to passers-by from large barrels. These commercial activities had become profitable since gold mining commenced in nearby wadis.[6] Um Futeima is not connected to the road system and the electrical power grid. A major innovation was the introduction of a diesel generator in one of the small grocery stores, which was turned on in the evenings to light a lamp, charge multiple mobile phones and run an old small television for a minimal fee. An open shallow well served as the water source. My interlocutors told me they had settled with the hope that state institutions would provide them with health, educational and infrastructural services. To no avail. Some of the much needed services were provided by the Kuwaiti foundation instead. Apart from funding infrastructure projects for the entire village, the foundation also distributed donations for individual poor families. On the day under discussion, a truck was dispatched to pass out two types of transfers: individuals gifts (goats, chicken, building material) for the poor and a camel slaughtered for its meat as a donation to the entire village. My account traces the controversy about the distribution of these resources.

I narrate the events chronologically but interweave some reflections into the narration. I am attentive to 'invested forms' that populated the situation and circulated through it, such as rules, established procedures and social categories. I trace the logics of coordination ('conventions'), both the implicit logics that I identified by observation and those significations that were made explicit through justification and critique. The crucial point is how these forms were interpreted, adapted, translated and enlisted to cooperate with others in the frame of the extant distributive order, and conversely how they were used to challenge the principles upon which the very distributive order hinged. To analyse the situation, I first narrate the events, and then map out the key human, non-human and discursive elements and trace how forms of coordination were stabilized.

Analysing the Distribution

A strange hustle and bustle disrupts the usual early morning calm. I learn that the charitable foundation (Ar. *al-mubarra*, hereinafter 'the charity') is coming today to Um Futeima to distribute livestock. People had told me about the charity before. It is an ethnically oriented charity with headquarters in Kuwait, funded through private endowments. Its explicit purpose is to promote the welfare of Rashaida in Sudan.

Hamda is busy preparing tea and coffee for her guest Rahala, who arrived last night with her four children. Hamda's husband, Hassan, has been working in Kuwait for two years. Hassan's younger brother Tahir stayed behind to take care of Hassan's wife and children as well as their brother Salman, who is referred to as *maǧnūn* (crazy) and *ḥarbān* (deranged). Tahir was my initial contact in Um Futeima. I first met him in late December 2007. Tahir comes from a family of impoverished nomads. He stands out among his siblings and peers in the settlement as having a specific kind of knowledge: Tahir was sent to a boarding school in Atbara, where he acquired not only an education but also the riverine Islamic lifestyle of northern Sudan. As an educated man, he talks about his role in introducing 'our people' (*šaᶜbna*) to a more 'cultivated' (*muṯaqqaf*) and, in his view, settled way of life. In 2006 he led negotiations with Abdelati, the sheikh of the landowning Bishariyn, to acquire land to build a mosque in Um Futeima. Through his brother Hassan, who in those days worked in Saudi Arabia, he had raised funds from a Saudi foundation for its construction. When the mosque was finished in late 2006, Tahir became its imam. This drew other settlers. In 2008 Tahir became president of the rural council after Um Futeima was officially recognized as a village. In early 2010 Tahir had a list of 725 people in his notebook, whom he claimed to represent as sheikh and spokesperson. More than 200 of these lived in Um Futeima, while the rest continued to live as mobile tent-dwellers. Bishariyn in Um Futeima, about ten kindred families, were excluded from Tahir's count, as these were represented by the landowner Abdelati. Due to his position as an educated man, imam and sheikh, Tahir mediated between incoming resources and the people he represented, attempting to channel the flow of goods.

Early in the morning Tahir and his helper Antar transferred his mentally ill brother Salman from his empty one-room clay house to another house. Salman's house was cleaned thoroughly and prepared with simple furnishings and kitchen equipment by Hamda's daughters and the neighbouring women. Then Rahala and her children entered the house, awaiting the arrival of the charity. I learn that the house is not Salman's but belongs to Tahir's sister Rahala. She came yesterday from nearby Goz al-Hila to be included in the distribution. I ask the women whether the charity knows that Salman lives in his house. 'God forbid', Hamda's daughter replies. Puzzled, I turn to Hamda. She whispers that Rahala has some animals, therefore she does not stay in Um Futeima. Rahala and her husband Muslih are not poor, she tells me, but have 'a bit of something'.

A new Toyota pickup truck approaches the mosque in the centre of Um Futeima. One of the men inside introduces himself to me as Masʿoud Salih, candidate of the Rashaida Free Lions for the upcoming election (mid-April 2010) and director of the charity's office in Edamer. Masʿoud Salih is well educated and knows how to use modern information and communication technologies as well as banking services. He was therefore an important mediator between local Rashaida communities and the Kuwaiti charity, but also a person of significance due to his involvement in Sudanese politics as a member of the Rashaida Free Lions party.[7] Working at this interface, he not only assessed villagers' problems and needs but, as a spokesperson for Rashaida in the River Nile State, communicated them to Kuwait. He received the funds in his Sudanese bank account and organized procurement locally. Masʿoud Salih tells me that a truck is approaching to distribute some animals to help 'the poor' (al-masākīn). He drives through Um Futeima campaigning for support in the election and returns to Edamer.

Then the truck arrives and stops next to the mosque. The truck is loaded with six she-goats and their kids, as well as twelve chickens, a camel and the building material for one house. The house is the most valuable gift. The durable building materials were shipped in, but the clay bricks need to be moulded and the house of course still needs to be constructed. The six she-goats and their kids become the main issues of dispute in the situation.[8] The charity's explicit purpose was to alleviate poverty by providing households with productive capital and improving their diets through eggs and milk, but often the animals were sold or eaten and did not have the planned sustainable impact. Nonetheless, regardless of people's use of the livestock, these gifts were sought after by all inhabitants and therefore it is crucial to untangle who managed to lay claim to them. Aside from the animals, there are four men on the truck: a driver and two handymen,[9] as well as a clerk named Barak

Suleih, whom sheikh Tahir greets with an amicable hug. Barak Suleih is a subordinate clerk at the charity's office in Edamer. Whereas Mas'oud Salih's role was in planning and communicating, Barak Suleih was entrusted with overseeing the actual implementation of the projects. Tahir climbs onto the truck and points out the 'right' houses for distribution.

The truck's first stop is the house right next to Tahir's, in which his niece Husna and his paternal cousin Salam (wad 'amm) live. However, neither Husna nor Salam is present; instead, sheikh Tahir, his first wife Matar and their children are standing in front of the house. Tahir later told me that the house was given to him by the charity. He let poor Husna and Salam live in the house intermittently until his second wife was ready to move in. While concealing that others occupy the house, Tahir did not hide that he put himself first in the distribution. Therewith he demonstrated confidence in the validity of his privilege as sheikh. Barak Suleih tells a worker on the truck to give Tahir a goat, its kid and two chickens, approving of Tahir's understanding. Then the clerk attaches to the wall of the house a poster announcing the distribution campaign and takes a photo with a digital camera. The poster declares the charity's mission of doing good deeds and distributing meat.[10] By being photographed, the poster documents the location, the date, the distributed animals, the sponsor and the recipients. After the photo is taken, the poster is detached and moved to the next house. It plays an important role as evidence in justifying the use of resources vis-à-vis the benefactors in Kuwait.

In the meantime a handful of villagers who followed the truck on foot have arrived. They enquire as to who will be included in the distribution. An old lady asks Tahir to give her a goat and a kid. Salima, who claims to be among the first settlers in Um Futeima, sees the building material for the house and demands it. When she is denied the house, she asks: why is she overlooked time and again? Who, if not her, gets the house? She receives no answer. Others come and interrupt. They ask Barak Suleih for animals or money, saying they are poor and have nothing to eat. Barak mentions that everything will be written down and everyone will have his turn – but he does not write anything down. When and how should people know when their turn has come?

Some get upset and leave. Others, like myself, follow the truck on foot to Rahala's house. The case of Rahala and her husband Muslih is peculiar, as this couple did not even live in Um Futeima and their house was used as a space for mentally ill Salman. Much effort was expended to conceal this from Barak Suleih – to my surprise nobody disclosed it. It seems that kin ties were responsible for their inclusion. Rahala is the daughter of Muhammad, who also fathered the three brothers Salman, Hassan and sheikh Tahir. She is married to Muslih, her paternal cousin (wad 'amm); this also makes sheikh

Tahir and Muslih paternal cousins.[11] Yet, Tahir explains the inclusion of Rahala and Muslih because of his respect for Muslih, whom he refers to as noble (*zarīf*) and generous (*karīm*). At Rahala's house, Barak Suleih notices the family's apparently wretched material situation – who else has so few things in their house? '*Masākīn*' (poor ones), he notices and pulls out pen and paper to jot something down for the first time before handing over the animals. An absurdity of this charade was the fact that Barak Suleih, who seemed rather unconcerned with peoples' individual plights, was evidently sufficiently moved by Rahala's miserable housing condition to note her down for further considerations. This act of writing something down is significant in at least two respects: firstly, it shows that the plot succeeded – Barak Suleih believed in Rahala's poverty and the bystanders remained silent; secondly, his attempt to remember her case indicated that he did consult with Mas'oud Salih and thus tried to intervene in the distributive order.

Tahir then directs Barak Suleih a few steps further to his half-sister's and Antar's house. Antar is Tahir's helper. He is completely dependent upon Tahir for his living. During my stay, he ran errands for him, and was loyal in word and deed when Tahir was absent and others criticized him. It seems appropriate to talk of Tahir and Antar in terms of patron and client.[12] This is supported by villagers referring to Antar as *ḍa'īf* and *miskīn* (weak and

Figure 2.1 The clerk documenting the passing out of animals with his camera

miserable) or ridiculing him by saying *yaḫdum* (he serves), which implies a pitiable, servile and above all debased status – not only due to poverty but also the incapacity to earn one's own living (W. Young 1988: 132). The poor were stigmatized. Antar's household likewise receives a goat and its kid, as well as two chickens, the poster is attached to the house, and then the resource transfer is documented photographically.

An old couple, Zeinab and Ahmed Rasoul, meet Tahir and Barak Suleih at Antar's house. 'By God, we have no food', Zeinab exclaims. 'Give me a goat so that I can give my granddaughter milk. She is weak [from a lack of food]'. While Zeinab talks to Tahir, an old woman who still lives in a tent in the woods below the settlement hands Barak Suleih a piece of paper. It reads that she is widowed and poor and deserves a house. Salima intervenes that she should be first, since the other woman is new here. Facing the demands of the dozen assembled villagers, Tahir repeats what he had said before: everyone will receive some of the good (*al-ḫair*) on the next tour. Today is just the beginning. The first six houses on 'the list' (*as-siǧǧil*) will receive something today and the following houses on the list will receive something during the next visit.

Tahir's reference to 'the list' is important. It is a technology of bureaucratic governance in a setting of rampant illiteracy. It reinforces his position as a leader due to his education. Further, it also could be interpreted as an impersonal mode of assigning people a place in the distributive order. However, Zeinab immediately exposes the list's failure. She says that the last time the charity came to distribute carts and donkeys, they also said more would come for everyone. It never did. She is still waiting and she is next on the list. When she is ignored, Zeinab walks over to me. She complains bitterly that she has no money to buy milk for her granddaughter, but always 'the same people' eat everything.

I jump onto the truck as it heads to Abdelati's house at the other end of Um Futeima. Guiding the truck to his house, Tahir plainly states: 'he is the landowner here'. Abdelati is the wealthiest man in Um Futeima, sheikh of the Bishariyn, a member of the rural council and the customary landowner in Wadi Um Futeima. The animals are unloaded and Barak Suleih takes a picture. Next in the distribution was Farah Humeid, sheikh of another clan. Farah is an old man who was injured in a car accident two years ago and has several small children to provide for. In his case neediness and a position of leadership and seniority in his clan coincide. He is given the animals, a picture is taken, and then the truck continues to the schoolteacher's house. Hussein is Masᶜoud Salih's son. His father had helped him to obtain this position as a teacher in Um Futeima. The charity also pays Hussein's modest monthly salary. The same procedure is carried out: the animals are unloaded, the poster is attached and the obligatory picture is taken.

The building materials are taken to the house designated for the doctor. An old man, Salim, lived in it at that time. Salim had come to Um Futeima with his household just two months earlier from Kassala, upon hearing that the charity builds houses in this area. They brought only a few things with them and seemed very poor. Salim's household had no kin ties in Um Futeima and few people visited them. Tahir, however, did not mention his poverty as the reason for giving him the house. Rather, he calls him *baṭal* (hero), referring to his role in fighting with the Rashaida Free Lions from Eritrea against the government in the insurgency in eastern Sudan (1999–2006). As a member of the Free Lions he was well acquainted with Mabrouk Mubarak Salim, the party's founder and also a federal minister in Khartoum.

The workers unload the wood and metal building materials; Barak Suleih talks to two construction workers, who agree to furnish clay bricks and to construct the house for Salim. 'How is it possible?' Salima asks. 'It's not right' (*mā ṣaḥḥ*). Others also wondered why a new resident was so quickly included. Much angry talk ensued about the house, not only because it is much more valuable than the animals but also because it represents permanent residence and inclusion into the community.

As a last stop, Tahir directs the truck to his small shop at the settlement's centre to slaughter the camel. While during the preceding distribution of animals only selected individuals profited, the camel for slaughter, called *karāma* (generosity), is meant as a good deed explicitly for the entire village (*kul al-qarīya*). Its meat is destined to be distributed among all households of Um Futeima (*kul al-buyūt*), announces Barak Suleih. Few Rashidi men are around. Many children and a number of Bishari men, who work in the two restaurants and run small grocery stores, encircle the slaughtered camel with plastic bags in their hands. A large plastic ground cloth is spread out. The men who butcher the camel distribute the meat into about forty piles (see Figure 2.2). Some children snatch pieces of meat and quickly run away. People complain and start getting nervous. How to make sure that every house gets its share? Tahir, who oversees the whole process, wonders loudly, 'Is it not better that we do the slaughtering inside the shop? Then we can give each one his right *(ḥaqq)*'. Barak Suleih disagrees, saying the meat is for the entire village. He insists upon the in-situ public butchering.

When the meat is cut, Tahir begins with the distribution. He calls four old and needy men (*ʿaǧāʾiz*) to step forward and hands each a pile of meat. Next Tahir summons a man with filthy torn clothing with whom I was not acquainted. Tahir stuffs a pile of meat into the man's plastic sack, loudly stating, 'This is a very poor person and he has a big family. Take this also'. He stuffs meat from a second pile into the bag. There is indignation. Too much! Two piles? I want something too! Who is that man anyhow? Why is he getting something? Why is he given meat first? This is not right! Instantly,

Figure 2.2 Piles of camel meat for distribution

everyone grabs whatever he can get hold of. Inside of a few seconds all of the meat is gone. All the while Tahir just stands there and observes meekly and helplessly what is happening. He does not bend down to pick up any meat himself.

I later learned from Antar that the outsider was one of Tahir's paternal cousins, a herder who had come from Goz al-Hila that day to fill his car with gas in Um Futeima. As he owned a car, he was certainly not poor, as Tahir claimed when he put extra meat into this man's plastic bag. Evidently many present suspected that something was afoul – be it because an outsider received a share at all, the share was too large, because they had an inkling that he was related to Tahir, or, most likely, because some had seen him come by car. The order which Tahir strove hard to maintain earlier collapsed right at that moment when doubt was at its height. At this point, I still believed that Tahir was among the losers in this scramble.

After all the meat is gone, I return to the residential quarter, where Hamda and her daughters are waiting together with Rahala and Noura. 'If God wills, Tahir got some meat for us?' they call out to me. I tell them about the chaos, that I stayed until the end, and that Tahir did not hold on to any of the meat. 'We long for meat', the women say, upset. First, they blame Tahir, then Hamda's twelve-year-old son for not grabbing any meat. Then they turn to me, asking why I didn't get any meat. Why, asks my host mother Hamda, when I was there as a *ḫauwāǧīya* (Sudanese Arabic for foreign woman)?

This moment shed light on my role in Um Futeima. I was reproached for having returned empty-handed from the distribution site. For sure, I was anything but an uninvolved observer. Rather, I was there amidst the men, and the women held me responsible for fetching some meat – meat (*laḥm*), the one food that is craved above all, what hungry people dream of and talk about. I figured as an interested party to the distribution, but I had not interpreted my role in the same way. Hamda recognized the potential of my different social status as a *ḫauwāǧa* guest and the certain popularity associated with it. She expected me to employ this instrumentally to appeal to the notion of hospitality and thus to get a share of meat. 'I could not', I say to defend myself. 'I was bashful (*muḥtaššida*)'.[13] But the women, who claimed they could not enter the settlement's centre because it is considered a 'male space', did not agree. They could not make sense of my holding back – why would I be bashful about asking for meat when I was not shy about moving around in the male space in the first place? By not exploiting my status as a foreigner and guest, which would never have occurred to me and which I would have judged unethical in my professional understanding, I did not live up to their expectations.

While the women are still questioning and scolding me, Hamda's son approaches the hut. In his hand is a small transparent plastic bag with meat (meat here refers to all parts of the animal including bones, cartilage, sinews, fat, etc.). Antar had succeeded in getting hold of some meat, which he sent to Hamda. A few minutes later Antar arrives and brings a second larger plastic bag with meat containing the most valued piece – the liver. But how did the liver end up in *dhuwī* Tahir's hands? Tahir had smuggled it into the bundle that he gave the outsider, his paternal cousin, from whom Antar later collected most of the meat. Tahir, however, stood there until people had withdrawn to their respective homes without any meat in his hand, with a disappointed, sullen look on his face.

The women put the liver in a separate bowl. As they cut the liver, Ahmed Rasoul approaches the hut of cloth and wood. Quickly, the women hide the bowl, covering it with a sheet and carrying it inside the attached one-room clay house. Ahmed Rasoul looks around inquisitively and asks whether they have some meat. And then whether they have the liver. No, Hamda replies. Then she repeats my words: 'Tahir got no meat himself, everyone just grabbed it from him'. What is important is that Hamda not only quickly lied but made use of my obviously incomplete and misleading observation that Tahir had not got any meat. All they were sharing were the bits from Antar. Already I am deeply entangled. Ahmed Rasoul leaves. Tahir, his wife and children come over from their house. The liver is cut into small pieces and is eaten raw. At this point, I still did not entirely grasp the full relevance of the liver, although I knew that Sudanese enjoy eating liver. But by eating a piece, I had become complicit with *dhuwī* Tahir.

In the early afternoon, after lunch, while on my way to see Farah Humeid, I meet Salima and Saʿida as I pass the houses of these widows. They call out to me and ask me directly who ate the liver. Put on the spot and startled, I lie that I do not know. Instantly, I have become an accomplice in the cover-up. When I am with Farah Humeid, his daughters ask me whether I ate meat and if 'they' gave me enough. The girls wished they could have had some liver. 'Did Tahir eat it?' the girls ask. 'Did those of Tahir let you try it?' Later that day, some of the Bishariyn inquire about the liver. In the following days, many more people that I met asked me about the liver. Some inquired directly if Tahir 'captured' it, others with more cunning queried if I knew how camel liver tastes, if I had ever eaten it, and on what occasion I had done so. In all of this, I did not give away who ate the liver. I did not want to disclose what I knew only by being a household member and thus circulated an untruth that I felt I had to uphold so as not to compromise my credibility. The liver had taken on a life beyond its materiality. Ahmed Rasoul, the two widows, Farah's daughters and the Bishariyn all suspected that Tahir had taken it and eaten it. The 'who ate the liver?' discourse circulated for days, breeding doubt, suspicion and unease, and leading to accusations levelled against Tahir. The liver had become the metaphor for the unjust distribution of things in Um Futeima and the exclusion of the majority. Mired as I was in the situation, I felt shamed by this discourse of who ate the liver. Yet, I felt I was in a quandary because the alternative would have been to betray the confidence of my hosts.

Incoherences: What Is and What Should Be

The situation was initiated by a Kuwaiti charity coming to a Sudanese village and distributing certain goods. It involved various complex interactions of diverse people, institutions and intentions, such as the trickery in Rahala's case or the underlying rationalities of the charity as a spatio-temporally distant collective actor. Cooperation was needed to distribute items – the main objective in this situation and the reason for the charity's visit. But in view of variant understandings of how this should be achieved, a point of convergence had to be found, a mode of cooperating that was practice- and goal-oriented. This is a crucial point because it indicates that cooperation needs to rest upon a frame of reference or metacode, which overlooks a number of differences for the sake of cooperation (Rottenburg 2005a, 2009a). This enabled people to focus on doing, to accept what otherwise would be radically uncertain, and to pursue a common interest or goal until doubt (re)surfaced. The end of cooperation was indeed prompted by the suspicion of injustice.[14]

The charitable foundation from Kuwait was an entity that tried to achieve a certain outcome (giving to the poor/to all) and therefore had devised some measures to create predictability and to control the situation. But contingency could not be mastered by the charity's planning, and instead a way opened to imagine alternative arrangements. To isolate the gap between the charity's intentions and outcomes, I next differentiate two sets of practices for my analysis, namely, planning and implementation.

Planning and Implementation

By planning I refer to all investments in organizational forms to coordinate and control events, such as projections, plans, budgets, timetables, rules and established ways of doing things that are designed and determined to direct the situation to achieve a certain desired outcome.[15] Because planning is embedded into the contexts of various technical relations, it is here associated primarily with the charity's activities and connotes the official or formal. With regards to planning specific projects, the charitable foundation, albeit not of flesh and blood but a collective actor mediated by its sponsors and employees, certainly emerged as a central calculating and strategically projecting entity.

After designating that the Lower Atbara area should be included in the charity's activities, Mas'oud Salih, Mabrouk Mubarak Salim and two of the charity's Kuwaiti employees visited the area for the first time in their official functions as representatives of the charity in early 2009. The most pressing need was a water source. Hence, the charity's first project was the digging of a deep well. Next, it planned and funded a school and a health centre, which were completed in October 2009. Furthermore, the charity had organized and financed the construction of fifteen clay houses to support needy families, projects for orphans, feedings during Ramadan and other smaller distributions. On a superordinate organizational level, the charity is associated with a political party, the Rashaida Free Lions (RFL).[16] The sites where branch offices are opened and concrete projects are planned by the charity correspond to the RFL realms of activity in Sudan. Thus, the model appears to be similar to one employed by many political parties in the MENA region (e.g., Muslim brotherhood, Hamas, Hisbullah) wherein social services are used to support and generate political constituencies.

The financiers in Kuwait worked closely with the director of its branch office in Edamer, Mas'oud Salih, in designing initiatives for Um Futeima. As an important mediator, he communicated the concerns and problems of local Rashaida communities to representatives of the foundation in Kuwait and informed people in Um Futeima about the rules and prescriptions. Importantly, in order to engage with his Kuwaiti counterparts in suggesting and drafting projects via Skype and Facebook, Masʿoud Salih has been given specific technological skills and the necessary equipment, such as a laptop, video camera, mobile wireless LAN device and head-set.

The poster represented an organizational form, a material–semiotic element that was invested in through planning. Its use was prescribed by the charity as a means of monitoring the transfer of resources. The poster constitutes part of a specific knowledge practice – it witnessed the charity's distributive logic through its inscription. Furthermore, it was associated in a complex technical tangle: as it was photographed by the digital camera, it was integrated into a chain of translations that established proof of the distribution (cf. Latour 2005). The digital photos were transported on the camera to Edamer, where Masʿoud Salih uploaded them onto his laptop and, using his WLAN device, sent them via email to his employers in Kuwait. There the digital photos of the poster figured as evidence in justifying the use of resources vis-à-vis the charity's benefactors. While this instituted procedure of attaching a poster, photographing it and sending it via email as a means of long-distance control enabled an assessment of whether and how resources were distributed, this should not detract from Masʿoud Salih's work of translation in the interstices. After all, he sent the photos along with an email that explained who could be seen in the photographs and therewith had the power to reconfigure the meaning of the poster-photo.

Likewise, Tahir was an important actor already in the planning stage, who cooperated closely with the charity. He pointed out development-related problems of 'Rashaida' in the Lower Atbara area and drew attention to individual grievances in Um Futeima: 'he knows the people', as Masʿoud Salih told me. Therefore, the two discussed, negotiated and predetermined who was to be included in the distributive order witnessed during the day. But this knowledge was not publicized and led to much eager anticipation and finally frustration. 'Invested forms' used in the planning phase was the ethnic category of Rashaida, to prompt ethnic solidarity, as well as the classification of 'the poor' as the recipients of goods, and 'the entire village' as recipients of the meat. The charity defined the poor by formulating a rule to be observed in all resource transfers to Um Futeima: the exclusion of labour migrants to the Gulf from all individual transfers. By founding this institution and providing a normative orientation (charity), the Kuwaiti sponsors framed the qualification of who counts as poor and deserves to be included in the transfers. Therefore the donors' will and rules provided an important reference for the entire distribution and its evaluation. But importantly all knowledge of the charity's will and rules was transmitted via the local representative, namely, Masʿoud Salih.

In contrast to planning, which implies a predetermined goal, implementation refers to the application of official rules but encompasses the pragmatic adaptations of such organizational forms in actual practice on the ground, which is often designated as unofficial or informal. In a classic paper, Meyer and Rowan (1977) assert that organizations, such as the charitable foundation under consideration, do not function according to their rules and procedures; these are conceived as mere myths. Rather, official blueprints are buffered 'from the uncertainties of success by loosely coupling their formal structures and their day-to-day work activities' (Meyer and Rowan 1977: 340–41). This argument was further developed by introducing reflexivity to the equation, maintaining that 'official' and 'unofficial' do not merely refer to calculations and planning versus what actually happens. Instead, 'official' qualifies the assumption that everyone abides by the same frame of reference, whereas 'unofficial' refers to the people's awareness that others cannot adhere to the metacode but must pretend to do so to maintain cooperation (Rottenburg 2009a: 198). The trick is to continually shift between these positions without necessarily clearing up any incoherences.

Implementation is therefore always subject to unpredictability, which different actors must more or less reckon with. Rottenburg (2009a) refers to the gaps between planning and implementation in development cooperation as 'trading zones', a term that draws attention even more to the manifold informal negotiation that occurs in the interstices. For cooperation to succeed, information has to be reduced to a minimum that allows communication but rules out complication. But it is always possible that 'the question arises whether this minimizing strategy has not gone too far … resulting in unpleasant surprises' (Rottenburg 2009a: 194). In this case several actors were in charge of implementing the plans. Tahir's role was crucial, because he seemed to be the only one who had the full picture of what was going on during the distribution. Representing the community, he was involved in both the planning and implementation stages. In the actual distribution, Tahir referred to an allocative technology associated with formal organization, namely, assigning people a number on a list. But the idea of a list is connected to a sequential arrangement and people did not observe a transparent organizational procedure. The list was immediately problematized once it was enunciated.

The charity was represented in the distribution through Barak Suleih. He relied heavily on the information Tahir provided. For instance, when the truck arrived in Um Futeima, Tahir directed it to the houses. Barak Suleih did not know who was to be included in the livestock distribution. He described his own task as merely defending the charity's interests in the distribution, that is, benefitting poor Rashaida and sticking to the plan. This was confirmed when he resisted Tahir's suggestion to butcher the meat inside his shop and instead promoted transparency. Tahir was compelled to trick him by pretending to live in another house, and this was even more obvious in Rahala's case, where poor Salman was taken from his usual living space and the house was arranged to suggest that it was Rahala's home. To avoid allegations of bias or corruption, the clerk underlined that he had no kin ties in Um Futeima. In the Latourian terminology he claimed to be a mere 'intermediary' (Latour 2005: 39) between the charity and the people of Um Futeima, whereas Rahala's case illustrated his mediation: he took note of Rahala's (seeming) poverty in order to remember her when he consulted with Mas'oud Salih about who should be included in future distributions. Barak Suleih also tried to intervene in determining the distributive order, which, however, does not imply that his intention of helping the poor was insincere.

Yet, although the poor were supposed to benefit from the livestock gift, this plan could not be unambiguously implemented, given that the matter of who was to be in/excluded in this category was controversial. Depending on where the uncertain boundaries were drawn, this category could include nearly anyone living in the settlement or only the utterly destitute. Tahir defined poverty in a very broad way, as applying to the impoverished region as a whole. Following the logic that all are poor, the sheikhs could be the prime beneficiaries of the transfers.

The official plan to distribute camel meat for the benefit of the entire village was also subverted in the actual distribution. How to go about the meat distribution? Barak Suleih insisted on a transparent procedure. But still, someone had to be given meat first. Tahir resorted to the principle of seniority coinciding with neediness to determine who received meat first. This logic was then displaced by his hidden selfish interest. Given that the meat distribution resulted in chaos and the plan to include the entire village failed, I wonder why Tahir and not Barak Suleih took charge of distributing in the first place. But even if one assumes that the charity's plan to include all households in the meat distribution would not have been hijacked by the eruption of the chaotic scramble, its implementation still demanded pragmatic adjustments. This has to do with a powerful institution in eastern Sudan, which constrained the access of people to the butchering site: the division of space into men's and women's perimeters. The settlement's centre, where the market and mosque are located, is classified as male space. It is considered shameful ('ayb) for a woman to cross it and a 'betrayal of gender' (W. Young 1988: 38–39); I observed that only very young girls could cross it without being reproached.[17] The instituted difference between male and female in the division of space and the sanctioning of transgression ('ayb) excluded women – except the very old and very young – from a more active participation in the distribution and contradicted the plan to include everyone. Overall, women stayed near their houses, with only some of the old and poor women moving about. In a setting where many men are absent for several days or entire weeks searching for gold or are long-term labour migrants to the Gulf States, this institution hindered women from going to the slaughtering site.

Apart from unequal access opportunities to the site, which impeded implementation of the plan to include the entire village from the beginning, the meat distribution also unfolded to reveal its own incalculable and chaotic dynamics. The meat was taken so quickly that I was unable to determine who exactly got what. But I did see that the young children in particular left the scene weeping and empty-handed, leaving these households without meat. Lastly, it was conspicuous that the reference to all inhabitants of Um Futeima excluded the two small groups of Sudanese construction workers (mainly identified as Nuba, Nuer and Shilluk), who did not even appear for the distribution.

Another factor that probably influenced the implementation of the official rules was my own presence as an external observer who posed questions and took pictures. Barak Suleih was suspicious about my interest in what was happening; perhaps this explained in part why he presented himself as a mere advocate of the charity, whereas Tahir invited me to accompany and watch the distribution. He evidently believed that I would judge the actual distribution, with all its manipulation of the official rules and purposes, as appropriate. Tahir was my entry point to the settlement and I had become a member of his extended household (*dhuwī* Tahir). He undoubtedly read our relationship in terms of generalized reciprocity and believed that my loyalty was an obligation of propriety (*ḥišma*).[18] Furthermore, others addressed their critique of Tahir and of the distribution to me, as if I was there to mediate or to judge. Certainly, the official distributive logic emanating from the charity was not carried out; rather its implementation required adjustments to local circumstances. Whereas people expected a certain amount of tinkering and were aware of tensions between plans and situated actions, this situation transcended the tolerable. In the following I am attentive specifically to the discursive resources that different people deployed as the controversy unfolded.

Arguing for Inclusion

Although the charity provided the blueprints for the distribution, the role of Masʿoud Salih and Tahir roles as intermediaries in channelling the resources was significant to the actual distributive logic. Tahir obviously influenced the distribution of animals in three cases (his own, Rahala, Antar). Facing criticism, he felt compelled to justify the logic of the entire distribution publicly. He did so by applying disparate rationalities.

First, he time and again referred to numbers on a list that guided the distribution. A list (Ar. *as-siğill*) organizes things in a sequence. It is abstract and appears to be neutral but is still a mechanism of exclusion. This technology of bureaucratic governance may have intimidated illiterate people and could have enforced Tahir's position as spokesperson, as he is one of the few educated men who knew how to correctly follow it through. Yet, in view of ongoing criticism, Tahir added other interpretations to the list rankings: accordingly, Antar was included because of his destitution and Farah Humeid because of injuries and impecunity. Tahir, however, did not mention that Farah was also entitled due to his status as a local clan leader. By the same token, the allocation of animals to Abdelati and Tahir himself was not justified but taken as self-evident.

Tahir was silent about Rahala's inclusion. Her case was the most problematic. Here Tahir took a risk and was compelled to trick his closest allies – Mas'oud Salih and Barak Suleih – to believe in the family's neediness. Neither a resident nor needy, Rahala received animals solely based on her husband's personal relationship with Tahir and their ties of generalized reciprocity (Sahlins 1972). This case also indicated that sibship, *'awlād 'amm* and affinal ties in themselves are not decisive for an inclusion in the distribution, nor is neediness – too many others are poor and are related to Tahir via both descent and affinity. As Bourdieu (1990: 16) astutely noted with regard to Kabyle kinship, 'one is more or less "kith and kin", at equivalent genealogical distances, depending on how much interest one has in it and how "interesting" the kinsmen in question are'.

Mas'oud Salih had a say in including his son Hussein in the distribution. Tahir admitted this, but embedded it into a meritocratic argument according to which the schoolteacher had to be compensated for leaving the city to teach the ordinary and simple (*busaṭā*). This meritocratic argument was not contested in Hussein's case, although it overlapped with kin ties. Similarly, giving Salim the house was justified by a meritocratic argument, namely his role as hero (*baṭal*) in the insurgency in eastern Sudan in addition to his poverty. However, this inclusion was probably also motivated by the desire to extend a favour to the powerful politician Salim Mabrouk and to build social capital in their relations with him. Mabrouk visited Um Futeima three days later in the course of his campaign for the elections in April 2010 and specifically enquired of his old friend Salim. In contrast to the schoolteacher's inclusion, Salim's inclusion in the distribution was criticized, partially due to Um Futeima's geographical and social distance from the armed insurgency in eastern Sudan/Eritrea, but also because a rumour had spread a short time later that Salim and his family were not poor but had two clay houses in Kassala, which Tahir was aware of at the time of distribution. Importantly, inclusion was justified with a meritocratic argument, according to which people are recognized for serving the community.

The meat distribution was proclaimed as being for the entire village. According to this democratic logic, all people of Um Futeima, irrespective of kin ties or ethnic affiliation, should principally be included in the distribution of things, as was symbolized by the communal slaughter. This stance was explicitly advanced by Barak Suleih as a representative of the charity and is also one of the official conventions associated with the charity. Such a democratic principle is based on the norm of equality; it contradicts privileging anyone and calls for a neutral distributive principle. Tahir nonetheless prioritized the old and needy as the first recipients of the camel meat. Uncertainty was unleashed at this turning point and cooperation ceased. Although the distributive orders were overhauled at that moment, invoking a democratic logic did not compel anyone to speak for the inclusion of construction workers from other parts of Sudan, who stayed in Um Futeima for extended periods.[19]

Criticizing Exclusion

Given that most people were sidelined in the distribution of livestock, Tahir's justifications were criticized by other villagers. They brought forth different arguments that shed some light on their moral understandings of how resources should be distributed. Both people who were considered well-off and those who were considered poor, irrespective of clan affiliation, refuted Tahir's justification in private conversations by referring to the purpose of the charity to help the poor (masākīn). They argued that those included were not the poorest. In their understandings poverty should relate to material possessions, and as for whom they considered as belonging to 'the poor', they specified mā ʿindahum ḥāǧa (they do not have a thing).

Others pointed out that the charity's official purpose was to further the well-being of Rashaida. They argued that tribal solidarity should have been prioritized, meaning Rashaida ahead of Bishariyn. But the landowner Abdelati was the only Bishari who was included in individual transfers. Some of Tahir's kin felt overlooked and demanded that ethnic belonging be implemented as the axis of in/exclusion, criticizing the fact that the Bishariyn had received some goods. This was an appeal to a more inclusive kin logic. It underscores the fact that whereas kinship exists as a discursive resource and a moral appeal, nonetheless only some kin profit and most are excluded. According to the logic 'if friends make gifts, then gifts make friends' (Sahlins 1972: 186), it appears that the boundaries of kinship are being reworked situationally through various material and symbolic investments in social relationships. Hamda and her daughters advanced another type of critique.

When I returned without meat, they argued that I should have been included in the distribution of meat based on a norm of hospitality.[20] While reflecting further moral understandings of the situation, neither ethnicity nor hospitality as normative claims had much influence on the situation.

Salima opposed the fact that as recent arrivals from Kassala Salim and his family received a house, while they as early settlers were overlooked. She questioned who should be in/excluded in the village. Her criticism referred to a temporal dimension: the entitlement to a share of distributed resources should be connected to the time the claim was made and the claimant's respective position in a queue. Although she did not mention the list, her argument was based on a sequential arrangement and can thus be connected to the idea of the list.

Zeinab's claim to the resources referred to her own poverty, above all her desperation at being unable to provide enough food for her young granddaughter, whom doctors found to be severely malnourished (cf. chapter 6 on Futoum's sickness). Embittered as she was, her criticism was the most direct. She asserted that Tahir unrightfully appropriated and ate the things himself. She backed her claims of injustice by referring to past distribution rounds, declaring that 'the list' was never truly relied upon.

Several other participants in the situation also referred to their *ḥaqq* or Tahir's eating the *ḥaqq* of the people. *Ḥaqq* is perhaps best translated here as entitlement. The term combines notions of property and mutual rights, and therewith also duties (W. Young 1988: 112). Eating someone's *ḥaqq* means that an unjust appropriation or theft has occurred, i.e., it is a form of oppression. Similarly, the liver and the allegation that Tahir ate it alone (with his kin) became a crucial signifier for the injustice of social arrangements in Um Futeima. Eating is an existential issue in many African contexts. Bayart (2010: 233) suggested of the politics of the belly that 'a man who manages "to make good" without ensuring that his network shares in his prosperity brings "shame" upon himself and acquires the reputation of "eating" others in the invisible world: social disapproval and ostracism and, in extreme cases, a death sentence may in time be his reward'. It is significant that this serious accusation was circulating in different, dispersed critiques and was levelled against Tahir. It questioned his leadership role.

Overall, the different critiques underlined the fact that there was a discrepancy between the actual distributive logic that villagers witnessed on that day and their moral expectations of a just distributive order. Before I show how uncertainty about what counts allows one to envision other arrangements, I address Zeinab's claim that the resources are always appropriated by the same people. I examine whether the logic that guided the distribution can be traced back to more stable patterns in the community.

Defining the Poor

The charity began its activities in Um Futeima in 2009. It first concentrated on installing necessary infrastructure in the settlement, digging a deep well, and building a school and a health centre. Next, it donated the materials for fifteen clay houses as well as paid workers to mould clay bricks and build the houses. In order to identify more stable patterns, it is crucial to clarify who profited from the distribution. This discussion will also exemplify how different equivalences were established and translated to fit a specific distributive logic in Um Futeima.

The fifteen houses are easily discernible from the other habitats such as tents, huts or other clay buildings in Um Futeima. They are square, one-room adobe houses with large blue steel doors and a window. Owning a house does not necessarily mean that one lives in it, as Rahala's case indicates. During the livestock distribution Tahir had not only referred several times to the list but also emphasized that the first six houses on the list would receive something. In the following days I asked Tahir about the meaning of the list and the numbers. Who composed the list? Tahir was obviously uncomfortable and did not shed more light upon the list.[21] However, 'every house has a number', he explained. The number was derived from the order in which they were built. He recollected the following sequence, which other people in Um Futeima also confirmed:

1. Muslih and Rahala (inhabited by Salman)
2. Tahir (inhabited by Husna and Salam)
3. Antar and Noura
4. Auwad Barouk (inhabited by his father's sister)
5. Ahmed Rasoul/Zeinab
6. Hussein
7. Noura Ali
8. Farah Humeid
9. Abdelati
10. Salima Mahmoud
11. Saᶜida Muhammad
12. the doctor (inhabited by Salim and his family)
13. doctor's office (inhabited by Birkiya)
14. Ali ᶜId and Salima Salih
15. Guma Salim Salih

Instead of houses 1–6, the houses numbered (1), (2), (3), (6), (8) and (9) were included in the livestock distribution. Therefore, the sequence in which the houses were built does not support the hypothesis that this constitutes 'the list' that Tahir claimed to observe in the livestock distribution. Of the fifteen houses initially built, three are used by Tahir and his close kin, namely, houses (1), (2) and (3). Four houses were given to Mas'oud Salih's kin, that is (6), (7), (14) and (15).[22] In two cases, that of Noura Ali (7) and Antar (3), neediness coincides with kinship. It is their destitution that Tahir named as the explicit reason for their inclusion. The aim to help the poor was used to justify giving houses to Zeinab and Ahmed (5) as well as two widows from Kassala, Sa'ida (10) and Salima (11),[23] who are not closely related to either Mas'oud Salih or Tahir.[24] Farah Humeid was already introduced as a beneficiary in the initial situation (8). He is named among the poor of Um Futeima, but his role as sheikh seems to be more important in the decision to allot him a house. Again, wealthy Abdelati is also included as sheikh and landowner (9). Three houses were reserved for professionals, who provide valuable services for the community: one house for the schoolteacher (6), another for the doctor as a home (12) and one as an office (13). While a doctor is still being sought, the allotting of the house to Hussein was not criticized, although he is the son of Mas'oud Salih, who recommended him as schoolteacher in the first place. This adumbrates the meritocratic principle as one of the more long-standing and uncontested distributive patterns in Um Futeima.

Considering that Mas'oud Salih, Tahir and Barak Suleih endorse the charity's purpose of aiding the poor and stress the rule of excluding Gulf migrants and their families from all individual transfers, as they earn high salaries when compared to the average income in rural Sudan, it is conspicuous that six of the fifteen houses – the charity's most precious resources – were given to some of the wealthiest people of Um Futeima.[25] While none of the people who received a house were in the Gulf States when the houses were built, all of them except Tahir have a record of labour migration to the Gulf States. Tahir, who is in charge of caring for his brother Hassan's family, however, profits greatly from the remittances sent to him every few months.

This last aspect draws attention to the way in which the rule as an invested form was translated to Um Futeima. Firstly, Mas'oud Salih, as mediator between the charity and the people of Um Futeima, had to define the role of things, the charity and the people as well as to identify their wants and needs. To control how resources are used locally and to be able to verify to its financiers as to their equitable distribution, the Kuwaiti donors had defined several forms prior to the distribution: it had qualified the poor by means of a rule. The rule, however, could not be communicated directly, and it was Mas'oud Salih who translated the rule for those in Um Futeima, whereby the villagers, including Tahir, were unable to verify the validity of his representations. Every translation step involves 'inevitable indeterminacy', but the question is whether people notice the mediatory work or not (Rottenburg 2009a: 191). Given that villagers modelled much of their justifications and critique on the normative orientations of the charity, they were confirmed as legitimate. Secondly, Mas'oud Salih and Tahir have translated the rule so that it applies only to current labour migrants in the Gulf. Past episodes are regarded as irrelevant for this distribution. Given the circular character of labour migration, with several months spent abroad and several months spent in Sudan, this interpretation contrasts with the ethic of helping the poor but harmonizes with other principles that oriented the distribution. Thirdly, while Mas'oud Salih still spoke of the exclusion of migrants and their extended families (Ar. *dār*), Tahir reinterpreted the rule by means of a displacement. He instead talked about labour migrants and their house (Ar. *bayt*), referring to family in a very narrow sense as father, mother and their children. Accordingly, the remittances that his brother Hassan sends him as head of an extended family no longer meant his own exclusion, but rather that Hamda and her children were exempted from receiving individual transfers. Fourthly, the rule's translation resulted in the redefinition of the category of the poor. The reinterpretation of what the label designated indicates that the charity's plan of aiding the poor was viewed as the most legitimate rationality in the situation. To summarize, this rule as it was translated to Um Futeima meant that basically all core families (father, mother, children) that did not have a member (unmarried son or father) abroad in labour migration theoretically qualified as poor. This equivalence proved to be a resource for Tahir and his cohorts in the different distribution rounds.

Mas'oud Salih and Tahir strongly influenced what became available for distribution and who benefitted from it by 'translating poverty' to Um Futeima, that is, by identifying actors as members of certain groups with special needs and by developing ideas concerning what must be provided to cover these needs. Thus, by translating between the charity and the people of Um Futeima, by formatting information on equivalences, such as the categories of 'the poor', 'the migrants', 'the sheikhs', 'the orphans' and so forth, and by prioritizing certain categories or people as more deserving of inclusion than others, they have installed themselves in a position where they can exert 'semantic domination' (Boltanski 2011: 9), or they have become what Callon (1986: 205) called 'obligatory passage points'.

To recapitulate, the charity's main reason to include Um Futeima into its transfers was the alleviation of poverty. To that end, it transferred things for the common good (school, health centre, camel meat) and bestowed individual gifts (houses, donkeys and carts, livestock and chicken) on the poor. These were the bones of contention. The challenge to the modalities of distributions, namely the claim that 'the poor' have not benefitted, lingered. In the distribution Tahir responded to criticism by referring to numbers on a list as guiding the distribution – a bureaucratic technology allegedly passed down from the charity – implying that he himself was likewise bound by the same rule. But he did this without clarifying who composed this list, how the numbers came about or why numbers should matter at all.

The distribution of houses shed more light on the list. Zeinab provided an important clue by arguing that she was on the list but that it had not been adhered to. She confirmed the existence of the list but exposed the failure to abide by it as an injustice. There is a link between the allocation of houses and the livestock distribution, namely that all families that received animals had, prior to this, been given a house and therewith a number (1–15). The charity's awareness of different households seems to be intertwined with their being numbered. Whoever has not received a house has not yet been mapped as poor. The charity's awareness of certain households as being out there and being of concern relates to their having a number, that is, their inclusion in the initial distribution of houses, and this was perhaps what Tahir referred to when he mentioned the list. This would also explain why allotting Salim the house was severely criticized. In this sense, the list would figure as a metaphor for the inclusion in individual transfers. This does not preclude that somewhere in the charity's headquarters in Kuwait these people literally might be on some kind of list.

Certainly, the numbers did not correspond to a clear sequence or chronological count. There were slight variations from distribution to distribution. Only a handful of items arrived for each distribution, but it started anew with largely the same set of persons – mainly Tahir's and Mas'oud Salih's kin and the other leadership figures, confirming Zeinab's criticism that the same people always benefitted from the distribution. By not explaining the genesis of the list, Tahir could not dampen the controversy surrounding that issue. Rather, justification was constantly demanded to avoid a charge of arbitrariness, which set off a spiral of justification, critique and justifications in response (Boltanski 2011: 80, 81). Therefore, semantic domination was countered with critique: Tahir was compelled to justify in almost every individual transfer why the recipient was included, leading to a readjustment of the initial justification.

The reinterpreted justifications that Tahir brought forth, however, lacked coherence: they were not based on a common principle but differed from person to person. Apart from the numbers on the list, Tahir highlighted neediness, seniority, leadership and a meritocratic argument. There was confusion concerning what should count, and the plurality of arguments among people mirrored this. In view of these more long-standing patterns of distribution,[26] one must ask why people did not jointly oppose their marginalization in the distribution. The case of 'Id Farid is illuminating.

Challenging Translations

'I asked Tahir many times for a house', ʿId related, about whom it was said, *mā ʿindahu ḥāǧa* (he doesn't have a thing).[27] Given that ʿId was among the first settlers in Um Futeima and is considered poor, he was upset about the distribution of houses in 2009. Why did Ali ʿId get a house, although 'he is not hungry and has a car and a generator?' Or why Guma, who had just recently arrived from New Halfa and has houses there? Wasn't the charity there to help the poor like him, he complained to Tahir? Tensions rose during Ramadan and a fight broke out at ʿId El-Adha in late November 2009. The charity came several times to bring goods for distribution, such as flour, oil, sugar and dates. ʿId claimed to have received nothing. He accused Tahir and Masʿoud Salih of 'eating' the things themselves. Then in January 2010, when donkey carts and donkeys were distributed by the charity, ʿId was again excluded. Moreover, from that time forth a monthly salary of SDG 125 (€ 38) arrived for the muezzin.[28] ʿId had served as muezzin in the local mosque since its construction in 2006, but then Tahir presented him with a discharge from the office of religious affairs in the locality of Edamer.[29] Instead of ʿId, Tahir let his twelve-year-old nephew Abdelrahmen call for prayer, keeping the money for himself. Feeling overlooked and wronged by Tahir and Masʿoud Salih, whom he saw as complicit, ʿId threatened Masʿoud Salih that he would circulate the details of the injustice he had suffered. He would tell everyone that Tahir and Masʿoud Salih were 'eating' people's entitlement (Ar. *ḥaqq*). Masʿoud Salih had ʿId taken to the police station in Seidon, claiming that the latter had stolen money from the charity and accusing him of slander, witnessed by Tahir and another man. A court in Edamer ruled in January 2010 that ʿId was guilty.[30] He was fined 3,000 Sudanese pounds (€ 830), an amount that he could not pay.

On a personal basis other villagers expressed solidarity with ʿId. Several came after his conviction, bringing him small amounts of money to contribute to paying his debt. More importantly, ʿId was supported by Abdelati. The landowner said he had known ʿId and his family a long time – long before he met Tahir. He described ʿId as a good man, whom was being oppressed by Tahir. Abdelati did not provide any details but told me to listen to ʿId: 'everything that ʿId says about Tahir is true'. Significantly, Abdelati lent ʿId most of the money to pay for his penalty. ʿId praised Abdelati's generosity: 'he sees that we are in need and helps us with something'. But ʿId also helped Abdelati on many occasions, describing their relationship as follows, 'Between us it is like an exchange'. Thus, the conflict with Tahir has led ʿId to an intensification of relations with Abdelati, and ʿId even voted for the Bishari candidate in the April 2010 election – a classic example of exchanges between patron and client. ʿId declined from further publicizing his complaint, having experienced its dire consequences (Boltanski 2011: 100). It is likely that his failure to find a following has deterred others from expressing direct criticism.[31]

ʿId's experience is crucial to understanding the specific pattern of justification and critique in Um Futeima: there was much uncertainty regarding the outcomes of criticism. Can it really challenge and overthrow the existing order? While criticism of the distribution was ubiquitous, it was mostly mild and expressed in private conversations, or implicitly by referring to the superordinate principles of the charity that should guide the distribution. When harsher criticism was voiced in my presence, people made sure only family members were within earshot, and this primarily occurred when I was more intimately acquainted with the person. Boltanski, however, argues that the success of critique depends upon its public performance, which can incite others to adopt the challenge it poses to the established order and only then can it rise to a more general level as a 'cause' or 'affaire' (Boltanski 2011: 37). In this situation, people cooperated with the distribution but nonetheless reflexively engaged with 'what is'. In view of the increasing uncertainty, critiques multiplied but they remained fragmented and dispersed. No collective action emerged and no groups formed to engage in an outright protest against the unjust distribution until the meat distribution, when uncertainty became unbearable and cooperation broke down.

De/Stabilizing Forms

In view of the problem of how to jointly direct activities towards a contingent and uncertain future, Thévenot's concept of 'investments in form' (1984) was introduced above, which denotes the coding or classifying that creates equivalences between heterogeneous entities, such as customs, rules, classifications, standards, authentications and so on (Thévenot 2007: 412–13; Blokker and Brighenti 2011: 358). In spite of their great diversity and the continuous work that needs to be performed in the formatting and maintenance of forms, a common feature is that they reduce uncertainty and enable people to quickly pass over their own specificities in order to establish situations that are shared with others (Thévenot 2001: 58). I suggested that Masʿoud Salih and Tahir have managed to create positions for themselves in which they format information, establish equivalences and thus to some extent exert 'semantic domination'. Thévenot (1984; 2009: 795) points to the costliness of this operation of investing in forms that depends upon forfeiting or sacrificing something, e.g., uniqueness for commonality, detail for the general and so on. Suspicion of oppression can be levelled against every form. During the distribution, people who were excluded questioned the legitimacy of diverse 'invested forms', such as the list, the rule or social categories. It is not enough to invest in forms – they also have to be solidified to withstand critiques (Boltanski and Thévenot 2006: 40–42), that is, they need to be institutionalized in line with a certain convention and stabilized with material supports in actual and situational performances (Diaz-Bone and Salais 2011: 13, 18; Diaz-Bone 2011: 47).

How was the form of 'the sheikhs' stabilized? Firstly, certainly through the repeated inclusion of the sheikhs in the various transfers to Um Futeima, which confirmed their status as sheikhs. Secondly, the role of the sheikhs was also supported by their legal/political status, namely that of membership in Um Futeima's popular council; and on a more general level the role of sheikhs in the political sphere was reinforced by the reintroduction of a native administrative system in Sudan from the 1990s (Delmet 2005). Thirdly, in practice the authoritative positions of senior men was hardly contested but rather acknowledged in a normative framework of so-called *ḥišma* relations. *ḥišma* means propriety, humility, modesty and shame. William Young (1988) showed that *ḥišma* – not kinship, descent or affinity – was the defining norm of relations within a nomadic Rashaida camp. It was embedded in reciprocal exchanges between the camp's senior man and its camp members. The latter were expected to be respectful of the senior man and to avoid harming his reputation; he reciprocated this *ḥišma* by providing camp members with security and access to jointly used water, pasture resources and herding collectives (W. Young 1988: 128–36).[32] By privileging the senior men of Um Futeima, an idea of *ḥišma* was adapted to the distribution and therewith translated to the settled context of Um Futeima.[33] Seeing himself as Um Futeima's senior man, Tahir expected other villagers to display *ḥišma* towards him. However, the norm of *ḥišma* was firmly embedded in reciprocal relations and it appears as if the sheikhs – particularly Tahir himself – were falling short of their reciprocal obligations. Many of them rejected their subordination to a hierarchical principle, founded on *ḥišma*, as this would necessitate a much wider redistributive generosity (*karāma*) to be fair. Being *karīm* implies being charitable, gracious and precious, and is a behaviour highly respected by others. People told me about Tahir: 'this is not a sheikh. Haven't you seen, he has nothing to give'. This dissatisfaction with Tahir as sheikh culminated in the refusal to cooperate in the meat distribution.

Related to the rule of excluding international labour migrants from the distribution, the qualification of who counts as poor emerged as a significant and contested form. The rule of excluding migrants was not only interpreted as pertaining to current migrants, but Tahir further applied it to core families (*bayt*), leading to a definition of the poor that opposed ordinary understandings of poverty. Many people repudiated this translation of poverty, backing their claims with the charity's official orientation to help the poor; it should not include the sheikhs. 'They don't have a thing' (*mā ʿindahum ḥāǧa*) was the most common qualification of poverty. It relates to ideas of incapacity, wretchedness and servility. The reference to 'the poor' thus stirred expectations that the recipients would be ranked according to their neediness and not that the village's wealthiest and most honoured persons would be included. The translation of this form was unacceptable.

The alleviation of poverty was the charity's official aim. Giving to the poor relates to ideas of Islamic charity and the norm of *karāma*, which is oriented towards the poor. This is rather different from the notion of *karāma* that Rashaida employed in other situations. Helping the poor was not conceived as a moral obligation, in contrast to helping patrilineal kin (see chapter 6). People who count as poor were generally disdained and viewed as incapable and weak, and thus in a sense responsible for their own condition. Being *miskīn* implies not only poverty, but a pitiable condition, even mental retardation (W. Young 1988: 132). This notion was contrasted with *ʿizza*, a male quality most affiliated with honour, greatness and self-esteem and best expressed through the nomadic ideal of being a self-reliant, independent herd owner. Thus, although formerly embracing other ideals, Rashaida seemed to have accepted the principle of *karāma* for the poor – that is, those who are materially deprived – as an orientation that should be manifested during the distribution. They criticized the discrepancy between the official norm and the actual distribution, challenging the loose and overly inclusive translation of poverty.

Particularly in post-hoc reflections about the distribution, some individuals criticized that it was always 'the same people' who were included, namely *dhuwī* Tahir and *dhuwī* Masʿoud. Literally *dhuwī* means 'those of' and refers to someone's kin group. This is based on a linguistic convention among Rashaida which entails that an extended household is named after its senior male (W. Young 1988: 40–43). While people criticized the lack of a fair alternation of distribution as unjust, they did not explicitly criticize the practice of prioritizing one's kin. This likely relates to a common understanding regarding the importance of brotherly dealings. A person is morally obliged to help his kin, especially the *ʾawlād ʿamm* (paternal cousins) in times of need, participating in the social norm of generalized reciprocity. Failing to help one's kin, when others believe it is in one's power to do so, would severely harm a person's reputation, undermining the support that can be mobilized in times of need. Tahir participated in this norm and therefore was expected to bend the rules to redistribute certain items to his kin. I wondered why people never mentioned Rahala's cheating and believe this may allude to a certain acceptance of this ethics of brotherliness as a distributive principle. Therefore, a reading of the situation as the dealings of one or two corrupt influential men is too reductive and overlooks the networks of personal relations and dependencies by which people are bound in rural Sudan. Poverty is widespread and there are only few goods for distribution. The charity cannot cover all needs.

To deflect criticism Tahir referred to the list as an impersonal allocative principle, which assigned people a position or number. The list could have been a neutral ranking device, delegating all responsibility for in/exclusion to technical aspects. Zeinab's reference to the list indicated that it could have functioned as a boundary object, within which she and Tahir could have acted while pretending to be talking about the same thing (Star and Griesemer 1989). However, there was no transparency about the list's composition and its grounds, no evidence even of its existence. Since Tahir did not explain or justify it, did not transform it into a text, and did not stick to assumptions about how lists work, people criticized it as arbitrary and fictitious, something invoked discursively without being enacted.

The dismissal of ʿId as muezzin could also have been a bureaucratic step – that is, a step that was authenticated and stabilized by an official, stamped letter, issued by the office for religious affairs. But ʿId cannot read and Tahir was unable to produce the letter of dismissal. This leaves much space for doubt and uncertainty about the situation. What if Tahir made up the dismissal and the office in Edamer never issued the letter?

This highlights a dilemma. Qualifications such as the position on a list or the dismissal form from the office of the muezzin could theoretically be confirmed by institutions. Institutions can rank entities according to their internal rules and prescriptions, and often they function remarkably well and remain unchallenged (like the male/female spatial division). But institutions rely on human spokespersons, who like Masʿoud Salih and Tahir pursue their own particular interests (Boltanski 2011: 84, 85). Consequently, misgivings about the integrity of Masʿoud Salih and Tahir and about whether they were truly representing the charity's interest or their own egotistical desires cannot be dissolved. To rehabilitate themselves from criticism, Masʿoud Salih and Tahir appealed to state institutions to intervene in the case of ʿId Farid, which resulted in a verdict against ʿId. They sought to establish the legitimacy of transfers to Um Futeima. While not silencing criticism, this juridical action transformed its character. It reassigned critique that directly challenges the integrity of Masʿoud Salih and Tahir to a more private sphere. The question of how to evaluate Masʿoud Salih's and Tahir's actions hence was 'invested in' and stabilized by the state's legal system. It was an important orientation for how people assess their opportunities 'to act in a specific way without having to pay an exorbitant price for it' (ibid.: 86).

People's moral understandings were not transformed by decree, however, and therefore the controversy did not end there: villagers closely observed the distribution and complained when they believed other conventions should guide it instead. Tahir's constant work at publicly endorsing and confirming the official rules indicated his awareness of potential criticism.

Cooperation and Reflexivity

People modelled their justification and critique on a variety of conventions. Some of the normative dimensions that William Young described in the 1980s among nomadic pastoralists were adapted to the settled context, such as the norm of *ḥišma*. But different actors not only changed and adapted conventions, they also drew upon principles of cooperation that come from elsewhere to express their sense of justice, such as democratic logic, the idea of Islamic charity, or the call to follow bureaucratic procedure. There was certainly heterogeneity in the situation, and uncertainty as to what could safely steer it into less contested terrains. But how did actors deal with this plurality?

Examining the transnational transfers to Um Futeima, it seems that the distribution is largely a compromise negotiated between the charity's official rules and Mas'oud Salih's and Tahir's interpretations thereof in interaction with ordinary peoples' critiques of what is taking place. The charity supplied certain logics for the distribution: ethnic identity as a reference and selection criteria for the site, the alleviation of poverty through the provision of milk and eggs for the animal gifts, and a democratic logic for the slaughtered camel. Furthermore, it stabilized these normative orientations by deploying different material–semiotic tangles: the rule to exclude labour migrants to the Gulf; the numbering of houses to produce knowledge of who is to be considered; and the poster attesting to the foundation's purpose, together with the digital camera and the computer that documented and thereby bore witness to the distribution. Mas'oud Salih's and Tahir's task was to translate these blueprints to Um Futeima. They extracted different elements from different regimes of justification and drew upon disparate, at times contradictory 'orders of worth', reassembling them in a new but contested logic of distribution (Boltanski and Thévenot 2006). Among the principles were prioritizing members of the own kin group, adapting *ḥišma* relations to privilege the sheiks, and reinterpreting the rules regarding the in/exclusion of international labour migrants. This tinkering, readjusting and situational adapting of the official principles is the so-called work of transformation or form-giving work, which must be performed in order to reach any (un)stable agreement (Wagner 1993: 467; Thévenot 1984). Although people voiced criticism, they still to a certain extent cooperated with the distributive order, at least in as much as they did not resort to violence or theft until the turning point during the meat distribution.

Cooperation is hard to conceive of without assuming a certain shared understanding of what is going on and some common reference points. Above, I suggested that cooperation implies a refusal to bother about the details of activities, its grounds and premises, and differences in the ability to define the situation while pursuing a pragmatic agreement, jointly working towards a common end as well as developing selective blind spots (Thévenot 2007). To uphold cooperation and set aside differences during the distribution, different actors had to assume that the metacode, the allegedly neutral frame of reference laid out by the charity, was in fact operative. But reality is fragile.

When people reflexively question forms, they can quickly point out departures from the metacode, i.e., inconsistencies and contradictions. For instance, the contradiction between what people saw as one of the official and therefore legitimate conventions – the bureaucratic principle – and the actual privileging of seniority/leadership in the distribution – or the democratic principle and *ḥišma* for the elders – furnished argumentative material for everyday critiques. There are many more irresolvable tensions. The democratic and bureaucratic conventions invoke similar notions of equality and neutrality, which oppose the superordinate and most legitimate convention to single out deserving individuals in the situation, namely aiding 'the poor'.[34] Most critiques referred to 'the poor' as an invested form and pointed out that it has been disassociated from its official purpose (*karāma*) and aligned with other conventions in the distribution. This association of *karāma* with the category of the poor appears to be a rather recent adaptation, as in the 1980s *karāma* was used among Rashaida in a rather unspecified way for redistributive generosity and often persists to this day. Referring to the poor only temporarily facilitated coordination as long as people held on to the metacode that everything is occurring according to the charity's blueprint. As soon as this understanding was lost, it became a stumbling block. Built upon the sand of irresolvable tensions, metacodes necessarily remain fragile and prone to denunciation, when people are stymied by paradoxes, doubt what is presented to them as reality, and criticize the justice of what they are witnessing (Rottenburg 2005a; Boltanski and Thévenot 2006: 278–83; Boltanski 2011).

During the distribution, cleavages became apparent between reality, the representations of the charity's official norms, and the world, and the way in which these were translated into the actual logic of distribution that people witnessed. People used their experiences of this difference to express their moral expectations of how a just distribution should be organized, exposing the actual distributive practices as unjust.

Conclusion

For most of the situation described in this chapter, I contend that people operated by virtue of a metacode, which enabled them to bracket indeterminacies, overlook contradictory understandings and reduce what was relevant to a minimum; it was about doing something together (Rottenburg 2005a: 267–71). In view of the above critiques of the distributive patterns, however, uncertainty was not entirely contained; rather, people reflected critically on who was included in the distribution and the grounds on which this was justified. The increase of reflexivity meant that reality was no longer treated as something self-evident but was open to interrogation. Incoherences emerged. A code switch occurred between a moment of practice and a moment of reflexive enquiry about the status of different knowledge claims. People no longer took official representations of reality at face value and instead problematized the fairness of resource allocations. Disconcertment emerged concerning what the distribution was about, what it should be about, and how one could ascertain one's claims. Unease and chaos were the results.

During the meat distribution the gap between the prevailing state of affairs and people's ideas of justice grew to its widest point. But can this situation really be aptly classified as one in which radical uncertainty breaks forth, instead of a simple disagreement or people losing patience with the opacity of procedures? Is it not that people were fairly sure of what was going on, namely that 'the same people were eating everything again'? It needs to be pointed out that while Zeinab clearly said that 'always the same people eat everything', it was one qualification of the situation, one test of fixing an interpretation, next to other competing attempts of sense-making.

At the same time other villagers advanced other arguments and critiques, mostly to assert a claim for their own inclusion. If we assume that everyone knew the outcome, why should people bother and take the risks of voicing critique publicly? I would suggest that people mostly cooperated with the sheikhs and the charity's staff in a mode with lesser reflexivity. It was about getting something done and trying to lay hold of something. But then as doubts increased and critiques proliferated, the code switched and attention shifted from the outcomes to the modalities of the distribution.

After the fact it did appear as if Zeinab's critique was the most powerful, but this was not so during the distribution. Nobody but Tahir knew who was to be included. What would happen next was unpredictable from the perspective of the people involved. Even the clerk who was riding in the truck did not know who was to be included. The truck arrived and pulled over at the houses that sheikh Tahir pointed out. Indeed, there were surprises. A poor old man who had recently arrived from Kassala got the building material for a house, the most precious resource. And during the meat distribution, someone who was not known in the village got a large share, officially based on his poverty. It is actually this moment that I referred to as radical uncertainty, not the whole situation: a moment when inconsistencies came to the fore and cooperation collapsed – a stranger got a large share of meat, someone who should not be entitled to get anything, a person about whom it was said that he was poor but whom some had seen fill his car with gas earlier on. There was bewilderment, confusion and anxiety about being overlooked. This situation cannot be reduced to just another opportunity to get something; rather, the course of events was open. Someone had to take meat first, had to grab it and take it away with him. This step was rife with uncertainty too, for what if nobody else had taken anything? What if everyone had stood watching, yelling at the person? Would not the fear of sanctions have inhibited his behaviour, perhaps even motivated him to give it back and wait until his turn came? Quite possibly.

The situation ended in chaos, but things could have been otherwise. The situation cannot be explained merely by a description of the events leading up to it. The meat distribution highlighted the situation's own dynamics and its unforeseeable properties. It resulted in a quite radical uncertainty, which turned it into a moment of 'becoming' or 'agencement' (Deleuze and Guattari 1987). Thus, in concluding this chapter, I reflect on the generative potential of uncertainty. I argue that the challenge to the established institutional order, not only the distributive logic itself, questioned Tahir's and Mas'oud Salih's roles in defining it. Importantly, there was hardly any discernible reciprocity between sheikhs and people. Sheikhdom is associated with certain rights but also duties of generosity (Asad 1970: 233; Sahlins 1972: 189). Tahir faced a dilemma: to be a good and respected sheikh, his redistributive generosity would have to be much broader, but he is only well endowed with cultural capital – his education and urban lifestyle – and the charity brings too few things for him to distribute them widely. While there was evidence of some self-interest – supported by the conventions of leadership and seniority – it needs to be stressed that Tahir also exerted time and spent money to organize things from which the whole community benefitted, such as the mosque, the well, the school and the health centre. Tahir was severely criticized for monopolizing the distribution, but the question of why the charity brings so few things in the first place was never raised. This relates to another much weightier discursive absence: while people criticized how resources were allocated, they did not articulate a larger injustice that the government of Sudan dominates virtually all resources which creates vast margins of excluded people outside of the capital region. They did not address central grievances that have led to a process of mobilization and armed resistance in other parts of Sudan, and also among people ascribing to the same ethnic label Rashaida (Calkins 2014). Some of the cogent questions could be: why does the state fail to provide for and make secure its citizenry? How is it that an organization from another country is seen as the only source of help for the poor? Why does it fund schools, health centres, wells and houses? Critiques radically questioned the order of things locally, not nationally, but they might at some point.

Support for Tahir was eroding. The cooperation between Mas°oud Salih and Tahir was already crumbling. Since I first met Tahir in December 2007 he had been talking about his wish to found a school in Um Futeima, his negotiations with the administrative staff in Seidon, and above all his desire to be the schoolteacher. Mas°oud Salih's son Hussein had taken the place that Tahir had for years prepared to occupy himself. Perhaps emboldened by this, Tahir hid Rahala's background and tricked the charity's representatives. Nonetheless, in spite of such differences, Tahir and Mas°oud Salih cooperated in translating normative orientations into socially valid principles of distribution. Mas°oud Salih furnished the arguments regarding the charity's purpose and Tahir justified the distributive order. Still, Tahir employed deception in Rahala's case and tricked the charity and fellow villagers about the liver, seizing it for himself and his extended household. Comparing the trickery involved in Rahala's case and the case of the liver leads to another point: lying and trickery were not always considered morally wrong – it depended upon who was being deceived. Tahir's neighbours helped him to prepare Rahala's house and he was not reproved or criticized for lying to the charity. Evidently this was acceptable; fooling his fellow villagers in the meat distribution, however, abruptly ended cooperation.

The meat distribution marks the fragility of the order epitomized by Tahir and highlights a common concern around which new forms of coordination and new alliances are emerging. The case of °Id Farid may have temporarily affected the public expression of criticism and led to a situation in which agreement prevailed for a time, but the lingering critiques indicate a cause around which new alliances are forming. Already the relationship between °Id and Abdelati has approached patronage/clientship, another set of reciprocal transfers across economic asymmetries involving both material and symbolic exchanges (Eisenstadt and Roniger 1981). Having Abdelati's backing is an important resource, especially as he is a powerful figure in Um Futeima. Other households that felt sidelined by Tahir also have begun to entertain reciprocal relationships with Abdelati, for instance turning to him to borrow groceries or money. Accusations are being launched against Tahir: 'he oppresses people' and 'he eats people's entitlement'. About Abdelati, in contrast, it is said that he is generous (*karīm*) and good-hearted (*zain al-qalb*), or about °Id that he is *tayyib* (good, kind), *mazlūm* (oppressed) and *miskīn* (pitiable, poor). Hence, in this situation shared understandings of morality and justice define cooperation. The emerging relationships cut across ethnic affiliations between Rashaida and Bishariyn and increasingly contest the role of Tahir as spokesperson and representative of Um Futeima. Uncertainty can indeed be liberating: it can expose the present order of things and challenge its normativities.

Notes

1. To protect my interlocutors from repercussions from the state or the charity, I have changed the name of the settlement, the charity and the persons of whom I write.
2. To cooperate in such complex settings between Kuwait and Sudan, people need to assume that a universal frame of reference exists ('metacode') to 'pragmatically restrict themselves to a limited number of questions, to agree on a procedure, and to represent all that they do to achieve cooperation as founded in objective reality' (Rottenburg 2005a: 273–74).
3. Its rise to fame is attributed to Gluckman's article, 'Analysis of Social Situation in Modern Zululand', which analyses the opening of a bridge in Zululand as a situation that connects colonial officers, Zulu leaders and religious authorities around a common cause and transforms their relationships. From the situation he traces critical constellations in Zululand and arrives at the sociopolitical order in South Africa (Gluckman 1958). The article first appeared in 1940. For nuanced critiques of Gluckman, see Burawoy 1998 and Kapferer 2005.
4. Clyde Mitchell contended that situational analysis largely remained an 'apt illustration'; it could describe the circumstances and historical processes leading up to the situation, but it could not move beyond and illustrate how something new emerged from the situations (Kapferer 2005: 101).
5. Kapferer (2005) extends situational analysis through Deleuze and Guattari's notion of 'agencement', which draws attention to each moment's generative capacities. Situational analysis/ECM thus conceived is in sync with a pragmatist stance in that it discards totalizing and homogenizing concepts such as society and culture, is susceptible to becoming and is better attuned to situational dynamics and unpredictability (see Evens and Handelman 2005: 3–5).
6. Um Futeima was the last settlement south of the then operative gold mines in Wadi al-ʿUshar and Wadi Arab. Treasure hunters arrived here from the west (Atbara and Seidon) but also from the east (Kassala) via the desert road passing near Goz Regeb. Transportation ran from Um Futeima to the gold markets. Furthermore, daily water tankers passed through Um Futeima to fetch water from the river Atbara and sell it at the mines.
7. Masʿoud Salih (the name was changed) was a candidate for the Rashaida Free Lions in the April 2010 election in one of the administrative units in the River Nile State, but he received only a fraction of the votes. The elections resulted from the CPA. In them, the Sudanese elected the president and the state governors, as well as the national and state parliaments.
8. Most Rashaida grew up with some livestock. Chickens, in contrast, are not valued by the formerly mobile pastoralists, who for the most part do not eat eggs or poultry and are unacquainted with raising chickens. Some chickens were eaten, others died or escaped. A few days after the distribution, no chickens remained in Um Futeima.

9. The workers are called Sudanese, basically meaning here non-Rashaida. They abide by Barak Suleih's directions but are not interested in what is going on.

10. The poster reads (my translation): 'bismallah, the state of Kuwait, welfare charity ..., alms [ṣadāqa] and bonding [ṣila, lit. association, bond, but also relatedness]. Good deeds, chicken and distribution of meats. Sent by the benefactor ... – may God safeguard him. Republic of Sudan, River Nile State, Village of ... Year 2010'. The charity's website explicitly points to such distributions as constituting part of their anti-hunger efforts in poor countries. It also displays many photographs attesting to distributions among Rashaida in Kassala. I could not find pictures online of the subject distribution of this chapter.

11. Hamda is the daughter of Ahmed Breik, another son of Muslih and brother to Abdallah and Hamid. Therefore Hamda and Rahala are cognates, patrilineal cousins, but are also related via affinal ties, making them sisters-in-law. The relationship between Hamda and Tahir is also based on descent and affinity: they are 'awlād ʿamm and in-laws. 'Awlād ʿamm (father's brother's children) relations are viewed as the ideal for marriage relations among Rashaida and are conceived of as more binding relations than 'awlād ḫāl (mother's brother's children) relations. People would often tell me: 'nobody helps you but the sons of your father's brothers'. This principle is not only talked about; together with many other principles, it orients actions.

12. See Mühlmann and Llaryora (1968) as well as Eisenstadt and Roninger (1981) for more on patron–client relationships.

13. Muḥtaššida is derived from the root ḥašada and literally means densely packed, crowded. William Young (1988: 117–21) explains how it is used to express a feeling of shyness or bashfulness, an observation that I could also confirm.

14. Of course, there may also be cooperation in spite of disparate understandings of the situation, e.g., due to coercion, intimidation or other violence, or prompted by love and friendship. But given that this situation is about resource transfers to the community, this preliminary definition is apposite.

15. In development cooperation money flows are typically connected to monitoring and controlling mechanisms of the spatially distant financiers and their demands for accountability (Rottenburg 2009a: 192).

16. The Rashaida Free Lions, an ethnically oriented political party, was founded in 1999 by Mabrouk Mubarak Salim. With Mabrouk as leader, the RFL have become the most legitimate representatives and the mouthpiece for Rashaida in Sudan, displacing other, more traditional leadership figures who have not managed to establish their spokespersonship over such a broad form, but rather are restricted to certain tribes (qabāʾil) and clans (Calkins 2014). That people ascribe to and are mobilized by the label 'Rashaida' in the hinterlands of the Lower Atbara area appears to be part of a recent process.

17. I witnessed a situation in which Hamda's unmarried teenage daughter and her friend, both wearing the virgin's veil, were seen near a grocery shop in Um Futeima, wanting to buy some candy for themselves. Their mothers beat them on their return to the house, screaming abuse at them, such as 'are you prostitutes?', and using the word ʿayb (lit. disgrace, shame, blemish). Young children are generally sent on errands to the shops, but as soon as girls wear face covers they are considered too old to go. In the area of permanent residences, the young girls will even walk some extra hundred metres carrying heavy water containers from the well so as not to cross the male space in the centre of the settlement. Women feel more freely able to move around more distant markets, but younger women may only move around in the company of their husbands, brothers, fathers or mothers, and generally a visit to the market for women is connected to taking a child to a health practitioner or seeking treatment herself.

18. Tahir intervened in two cases of sexual harassment, taking this as an offence against his honour, and he continually supported my position and research, also patiently sitting with me for hours recollecting genealogies. In view of the obvious proximity and friendly relations between Tahir and myself, it might seem perplexing that our neighbour Zeinab confided in me by criticizing Tahir and the justice of distributions. She vented her anger that things were always 'eaten' by the same people – mainly referring to Tahir – while I was a member of *dhuwī* Tahir. I read her critique of Tahir as an expression of confidence based on the friendship we had built up in the preceding months during the almost daily mutual visits.

19. Nor did anyone argue that they should be included based on the important Bedouin norm of hospitality, as was asserted on my behalf. Instead, there was a discursive silence that I relate to racist underpinnings against 'the blacks' (*az-zurq*).

20. However, upon my arrival I was told about the Bedouin convention that I would only be a guest during the first three days, after which I would lose such status and become a member of the household. By reinterpreting this convention my hosts adapted the norm of hospitality to the situation.

21. Unlike the situation above, where many people were following and watching the distribution, I here refer to a conversation between Tahir and myself, which took place sometime after the distribution day. Given my persistent interest in the logic of distribution, Tahir switched to rhetorics of justification.

22. Hussein is Masʿoud Salih's son (6), Ali and Masʿoud Salih are cousins (*wad ʿamm*) and Ali's wife Salima is his sister (14). Their daughter, seventeen-year-old Noura Ali, is divorced and lives in another house with her small daughter (7). Masʿoud Salih is Guma's paternal uncle (15).

23. Zeinab is the sister of a respected sheikh of the *dhuwī* Abid clan, who is a member of the rural council in Um Futeima, but he is still mobile with his livestock. The widows Saʿida and Salima came to Um Futeima from Kassala upon hearing of the charity's activities. Both of them lost their husbands in an air strike commonly attributed to the Israeli air force near the Egyptian border in early 2009, which targeted a convoy of cars which were allegedly smuggling weapons destined for the Gaza Strip (See 'Sudan Airstrike Mystery' 2009).

24. The children of the latter two are part of the *kafālat al-yatīm* (supporting the orphans) project of the charity and receive comparatively comfortable monthly payments amounting to roughly €45 per household. Interestingly, Noura's daughter also participates in this programme for orphans, although Noura is only divorced and not widowed. Salih evidently manipulated the charity's instructions to accommodate his niece's needs. All in all five households participate in this programme: four widows of the *dhuwī* Mani clan and Noura, Masʿoud Salih's niece.

25. Namely Muslih (1), Tahir (2), Auwad Barouk (4), Abdelati (9), Ali ʿId (14) and Guma (15). As indicators of wealth I consider here the possession of expensive goods: motorized vehicle, metal detector, diesel generator, mudbrick house and also a herd of livestock. Abdelati, as the single wealthiest person, owns a fairly new pick-up truck (*boksi*), a metal detector, a restaurant with two freezers, a diesel generator and a shop. Ali ʿId owns a pick-up truck, a diesel generator and a television; Guma, a pick-up truck and a metal detector (shared 50/50 with a kinsman), besides houses in New Halfa. Auwad Barouk owns a pick-up truck and two herds, one of camels and another of sheep and goats. Muslih owns a new car and shares in a metal detector, and Tahir owns a motorcycle and a diesel generator with which he operates a mill to grind cereals in his shop.

26. After the houses the charity funded the distribution of seven donkey carts and two donkeys. Here the same set of persons profited on the whole. Tahir and Hussein received

the donkeys, and the carts were given to Tahir, Hussein, Ali ʿId, Farah Humeid, Salim Barouk, Abdelati and Salim from Kassala. The only new person in this is Salim Barouk, the brother of Auwad Barouk, who was away on labour migration in the Gulf. His two wives and their small children were given the cart to make it easier for them to fetch water from the well (normally fetching the water is the task of teenage girls). Significantly, Tahir justified breaking the rule by saying this is 'reasonable' (manṭiqī). But he not only referred to disparate, even contradictory conventions in his justifications, he also broke the rule that he had translated by stating the 'reasonableness' of this step on one occasion (giving the donkey cart to Salim Barouk's wives). This justification sheds light on Tahir's relativist relationship to rules: other people must follow them, but he can bend, change and bypass them. Masʿoud Salih had likewise bent the rule to include his divorced niece's daughter into the project for orphans. Boltanski (2011: 146–47) writes regarding this attitude to rules: 'this kind of wisdom cannot be made public – it would lead to anarchy. To belong to the dominant class is first of all to be convinced that you can break the letter of the rule without betraying its spirit'. People did challenge the fact that Tahir broke the rule but understood it is as part of the overall pattern, yaʾkul ḥaqq an-nās (he eats people's entitlement), as Ahmed Rasoul said.

27. ʿId Farid's wife Salima had appeared during the distribution and had demanded that the house be given to her, claiming to be among the first settlers.

28. I calculated the rate for 15 March 2010 with a currency converter (www.oanda.com). ʿId believed this money came from the charity, while Tahir told me it was from the Edamer office of religious affairs (šuʾūn dīniya).

29. ʿId cannot read and write but this is what Tahir told him. I asked Tahir to let me see the discharge several times, he failed to produce it.

30. ʿId, illiterate and uneducated, did not even understand what he was convicted of – slander or theft. Tahir said he was a convicted thief, while Masʿoud Salih referred to his slander sentence. None of the people I asked about it could confirm one or the other but tended to side with the accused; I was unable to gain access to any documentation related to the hearing.

31. In line with this, Talal Asad (1970: 234) showed in his study on the Kababīsh that agreement or acquiescence in a particular allocation often arises from a relative impotence, the awareness of threats or different short-term goals, such as being included in the very next round of distributions.

32. Violations of ḥišma were understood in terms of ʿudāwa (enmity), that is, relationships marked by distrust and the refusal to cooperate. Violators could no longer be tolerated as camp members (W. Young 1988: 137, 141). In this light, ʿId Farid can be seen as an outright violator of ḥišma towards Tahir and Masʿoud Salih. Amongst mobile Rashaida this would probably have meant ʿId leaving the camp. However, the new immobile habitats pose new challenges to cooperation. Many mentioned that they are not used to living permanently next to people with whom they do not get along. Formerly, dissatisfaction with a sheikh or other camp members meant that the people in question moved their tents and joined a senior whom they respected (ibid.: 117).

33. Seniority does not refer to age alone but to respectable social standing and a position of leadership. Thus it is a purely male property, and the principles of seniority and leadership as mentioned above are strongly intertwined.

34. This is confirmed by Tahir, who put this convention forward when justifying cases where poverty coincided with other conventions, such as leadership or kinship.

Chapter 3

INSISTING ON FORMS

Bracketing Uncertainties in Gold Mining

Rashaida may contest forms when something strikes them as being unfair. In other situations they establish forms to deal with crippling uncertainties. Since 2008 a new source of income for villagers has evolved that is bound up with dreams, dangers and uncertainties. Artisanal gold mining is booming and has led to a far-reaching livelihood transformation in north-eastern Sudan. This activity has become a main source of livelihood for thousands, particularly the rural poor, and including men from Um Futeima. Observing these developments, I was struck by how gold, whose presence in Sudan has long been known and attested to since pharaonic expeditions, was suddenly reconstituted as a crucial resource both in national economic projections and in the imaginations of thousands of small-scale actors (*Africa Research Bulletin* 2011a).[1]

Artisanal gold mining is a highly transient phenomenon, involving mobile people and infrastructures.[2] While it leads to short-term peak incomes, it also exposes people to new uncertainties, when markets which mushroomed around gold mines suddenly turn into ghost towns, leaving behind transformed landscapes. People in Um Futeima did not mention the possible long-term consequences of gold mining but rather concentrated on what they perceived as the more pressing uncertainties – earning one's living through artisanal extraction. The ways in which my interlocutors interpret and process uncertainties connected to the practice of artisanal mining is at the heart of this chapter. While presenting new ethnographic insights into the Sudanese artisanal gold sector, this chapter also deals with a recent technological innovation, namely, the search for gold nuggets with metal detectors. This technology has changed the ways in which people process uncertainties.

Uncertainty presents itself in different guises in the artisanal mining sector: pending governmental prohibition or confiscation of extracted gold or prohibited devices; health concerns related to manual extraction; the threat of crime; and finally the uncertainty of finding gold and thus of knowing whether one's hard labour will earn a livelihood. The latter – economic uncertainty – has the most far-reaching impacts on artisanal gold miners, many of whom, driven by imaginaries of spectacular lucky strikes, have completely abandoned agricultural or pastoral production. The chapter discusses how economic uncertainty is dealt with through technical means – particularly metal detectors and organizational forms. It asks how forms are stabilized and how they mediate actions by allowing miners to momentarily bracket menacing uncertainties or to translate radical uncertainties into something less radical, where at least some reference points are taken to be stable, allowing a broader range within which to make predictions.

Notwithstanding that the artisanal mining sector is shot through with various uncertainties, miners stress that agreement on the modes of coordination prevails as collective and coordinated actions are performed – not only in the actual extractive work but also in the many related sub-sectors. I will trace these rhetorical claims, which create a vision of harmonious cooperation. Thereto, I analyse the everyday discourses on gold mining that were circulating in Um Futeima, a new settlement populated by Rashaida and now a mining community a short car ride south of a large gold field in Wadi al-ᶜUshar. There I also showed people the photos I had taken at the mines, which I had to bring out time and again, i.e., when visitors or more distant neighbours came. This led to animated discussions about the nature of the extractive work and its organization. As well as witnessing the traffic of gold miners and their cyclical comings and goings, many of the daily conversations in the settlement, also among women, revolved around cases of sensational discovery, the quantities produced by neighbours and kin, the hard labour involved, the unpredictability of this work, the goods purchased from gold money, and people's hopes of and wishes for prosperity. In the settlement I also led a dozen semi-structured interviews with miners on their work in the gold sector, specifically their understandings of risks and opportunities. I gained many further insights by paying several single-day visits to the mines at Wadi al-ᶜUshar and Wadi Arab as well as to the respective gold markets, conversing with pit owners, workers in the mines, shopkeepers, and local administrators at the mining site.[3]

The rhetoric of miners endorsed following the rules and presented the social world as an integrated system of rules and regulations, guided by an ethics of brotherliness and friendship. I argue that this rhetoric exaggerates the smoothness of cooperation and thereby downplays the unease as well as the tensions around the distribution of resources in artisanal gold mining. Thus, this chapter suggests that in order to minimize the frictions and existential uncertainties, a type of 'insisting on forms' has emerged. By embracing forms, people create clear orientations for practices, that is, rules and instructions to follow, which enable them not to be debilitated by fear. Doubts about the justice of distributive arrangements and the honesty of miners are thereby stubbornly deferred.

This bracketing of uncertainty that I noticed among Rashaida miners is supported by a social imaginary of instant prosperity, landing a lucky strike, and divine ordination. Everything that is found or not is attributed to the divine will, which can aid in resolving the discrepancy between the dream of gaining wealth and riches without much effort and the dismal reality of meagre, unpredictable incomes from gold mining. Whereas organizational forms in the sector figure as pragmatic responses to economic uncertainty and also support ideas of solidarity and a distribution of profits, certain elements of 'reality' are taken for granted by miners and remain unquestioned, such as the principles underpinning distributive rules and social categories.

I take up the idea of a social imaginary as elaborated by Cornelius Castoriadis (1987). In a critique of the Marxist idea of an economic base as determining the ideological superstructure, the imaginary figures as a fountain of creativity and as a world-making force, 'the unceasing and essentially *undetermined* creation of figures/forms/images' (Castoriadis 1987: 145). This conception enables the linking of forms, significations, values and ideas – which in turn enable highly coordinated collective actions in gold mining – to the slippery underground of the social imaginary of getting rich quickly and doing so by virtue of divine assistance – importantly, in an non-deterministic manner.

Extracting Gold Artisanally

But first, how to get the gold out of the ground? In north-eastern Sudan, there are two main technologies of extraction: hard-rock mining and detector prospecting. Artisanal gold extraction from hard-rock veins is laborious: mines are dug; gold-bearing quartz ores are cut out from the underground rock with pickaxes, chisels and sledgehammers; the ores are then broken down to pebble-size with hammers and ground to a fine powder in mechanical mills. Then the gold-bearing powdered ore is washed in water. The resulting slurry is brought into contact with mercury, which forms an amalgam with the gold particles. The gold amalgam is heated to separate the gold and mercury, whereby the latter evaporates. Searching for gold with a metal detector is viewed as a potentially lucrative and less hazardous alternative. Metal detectors are designed to indicate metal deposits – nuggets, grains or flakes of gold – in the top layers of the soil through electromagnetic prospecting. Unlike the gold in quartz deposits, extracted nuggets or flakes are called clean gold (*dahab ṣāfī*), meaning that they do not have to undergo labour-intensive processing but can be sold immediately at the gold markets. The use of metal detectors is a more recent innovation in Sudan, and has not been studied extensively elsewhere.[4] Apart from discussing a new extractive technology, my study offers a thematic contribution to the vast literature on gold mining in Africa. It is the first ethnographic account of recent developments in the burgeoning gold mining sector in north-eastern Sudan.[5]

Studies on gold mining in Africa still tend to be divided according to disciplinary interests, whereby 'hard sciences' such as geology focus on the technological–ergological aspects of mining industries, while social sciences – anthropology in particular – study the social organization of informal activities, cosmologies, and changing lifestyles.[6] In a seminal article on the anthropology of mining, Ricardo Godoy (1985) criticized this self-restriction to issues of social organization and migration in anthropological studies of gold mining because it does not engage with the complex geological and economic infrastructures of the mining sector. I add to recent scholarship that has sought to transcend such self-confining disciplinary boundaries and the limits these impose on the object of enquiry and the type of questions posed (Luning 2008, 2012; Grätz 2010). Taking up Godoy's concern, almost twenty years later Ballard and Banks (2003) also wonder why ethnographic studies on mining have remained parochial and undertheorized.[7]

The experience of Katja Werthmann (2009: 23) indicates why anthropological studies of mining often do not desire to fill this gap. Mining was not Werthmann's initial object of enquiry, but as miners suddenly appeared and became the concern of people in the field, the theme demanded attention.[8] My experience was similar. My main focus was on ways of coping in an existential setting, but suddenly gold had emerged as a crucial source of revenue, imagination and angst. I thus am also responding to a concern of my interlocutors in Sudan and would likewise situate my study in the anthropological body of literature on gold mining, but I seek to more directly engage its critiques. While detailing the significations with which gold is associated in Sudan, I am also attentive to the interplay between materiality and organization – specifically the links between uncertainty, its management and the interactions between metal detectors as inscribed technologies, their users, and local assumptions regarding the properties of the devices and their proper handling.

An ethnography that extends its analysis across different sectors and countries is Tilo Grätz's *Goldgräber in Westafrika* (2010). It provides a detailed examination of the organization of artisanal extraction in Benin, describing the direct bodily performance of work, its regulation through expectations and sanctions, as well as the situational improvisation of norms. This chapter shares Grätz's focus on risks, coping strategies and the in-situ negotiation of norms. But whereas he creates an overall harmonious picture of cooperation among gold miners, highlighting reciprocities and friendships, I am more interested in the state of mind that allows miners to downplay the tensions that surface time and again. This chapter therefore adopts a pragmatist stance. Inspired by Boltanski (2011), it begins from an assumption of rampant uncertainty and then looks at the ways in which people situationally understand and process it through forms.

Gold as a New Dynamic in Rural Sudan

At dusk as Hamda is preparing the evening coffee, a car approaches from afar. Some of the neighbours are sitting together on a mat in front of Hamda's house wondering who it is. The car passes by and stops at a tent on the fringes of the settlement. Car doors are opened and closed, voices fill the air. 'Nafi^c is back', Salam says and gets on his feet to greet him at his tent. 'God willing he found houses and cars', some of the women mumble. After a short while, Salam returns with news and a handful of dates and candy, which he distributes among the women and children present. Nafi^c had been gone for nearly twenty days searching for gold with a metal detector and there had been no information on his whereabouts. Salam reports that his mining team found gold worth six million (SDG 6,000 = € 1,824)[9] in Wadi al-Miskin. Nafi^c received 1.5 million (SDG 1,500 = € 456) and Qismallah 750,000 (SDG 750 = € 228). Nafi^c and Qismallah brought camel meat, fresh fruit and dates from the gold market in Wadi al-^{c}Ushar, and Qismallah presented his wife with a box of sweets. '*Mā sha' allāh*' (what God wants), the women retort. They ask about the amount of camel meat and whether the women would also receive new dresses from the market. Salam is then ridiculed for having fetched only SDG 45 (€ 14) two days earlier.

Nafi^c is a middle-aged man, perhaps in his early fifties, a father of seven small children. Before settling in Um Futeima in 2008, the family lived near the city of Kassala. Nafi^c owned a water tanker and Qismallah drove it. The water tanker was what he bought from his salary in Abu Dhabi, where he was herding racing camels for several years. He earned a steady income from it, but then he heard of gold, and stories of people who worked only three days and earned enough to never have to worry about work again. Some are said to have found several trillion; they just went and dug in the ground and became immensely rich overnight, buying cars and houses. These people now enjoy themselves, leading lives of privilege. Such stories caused Nafiᶜ to think and dream. Why should he not try and see whether God had not written down such a course for him? He sold the water tanker and purchased a manoeuvrable pick-up truck to follow the gold. He took his wife and children and pitched his tent in Um Futeima in late 2008, together with his relative Qismallah, to leave them behind in a safe environment and to be close to the mines of Wadi al-ᶜUshar.

Nafiᶜ remembers going to the gold mines for the first time, feeling nervous and excited, with no idea of what to expect, how to extract gold or what to do. He did not even know the exact location of the mines. Departing from Um Futeima, Nafiᶜ sought the company of some young Rashaida men from the area, who showed him the way. At the gold market in Wadi al-ᶜUshar, he found Abdelrahman, a mine owner from his tribe. They began digging a pit and were working at the surface, extracting stones with gold ore. He was told to crush extracted stones with a hammer, filling sacks with stones that someone with more experience had inspected. The first shift Nafiᶜ joined lasted fifteen days. He earned a share of SDG 200 (€ 61) and returned to his family to rest for several days. Later he worked twice again on shifts in Abdelrahman's mine, but then it got too risky for him. Abdelrahman's mine is legendary and turned him into a rich tribesman. After one and a half years, it was still producing. Nafiᶜ estimated in 2010 that the mine might descend one or two hundred metres into the ground. But Nafiᶜ will no longer work there. He is afraid. It is too deep for him, he says. He is not young anymore and he has children to feed. Too many people have died there, suffocating from bad air (gases) and collapsing gangways.

Since 2008 Nafiᶜ has been coming and going to the gold mines. He tried digging his own mine, ten times paying for a backhoe, but he only lost money. He gave up. Then in 2009 metal detectors began to proliferate. Nafiᶜ contributed a small share towards buying a detector that was smuggled into Sudan. He paid SDG 1,500 and now receives part of the profits. He joined a detector team four times as a worker, but remarks that it is very exhausting for him – the work at night, physical deprivations and the constant anxiety about not finding anything, returning home without money to buy food. Meanwhile he works mainly with his car. Either he offers transportation services between Um Futeima and the gold mines for a fixed fee, or he drops people off at certain locations for special hire or participates in detector teams with his car on a profit-sharing basis. Sometimes he earns little, sometimes a lot, which in his view accords with what God has ordained for him.

Gold mining has become a major source of income for rural people in north-eastern Sudan. The burgeoning of artisanal mining has transformed the ways in which people regard areas formerly reserved for rain-fed farming and herding, namely, as a resource-base waiting for private exploration. In late 2008 gold was found in Wadi al-ᶜUshar, north of Um Futeima. A new mining front opened, pits and mounds of dirt proliferated and thousands of people were drawn into the area. A marketplace developed in Wadi al-ᶜUshar with grinders, washing pools, restaurants, grocery shops, gas stations, electricians, gold vendors from Khartoum and so forth, offering abundant sources of income.[10] Nafiᶜ is an example of the thousands of men and young boys who streamed to the vicinity of the gold mines in north-eastern Sudan, hoping to land a lucky strike. Although gold mining provides highly unstable and uncertain incomes, the lack of economic alternatives makes it seductive to the rural poor. This corresponds with literature on small-scale mining in Africa, which argues that the sector is poverty-driven (Pardie and Hilson 2006; Hilson and Banchirigah 2009; Hilson 2010; Cartier and Bürge 2011).[11] Women play an important role in the gold processing chain in many African countries, especially working in the manual pulverization of gold ore, tending to bars or offering sex services (cf. Werthmann 2009; Grätz 2010). This also applies to Sudan's Ingessana Hills in Blue Nile State (Medani 2003). However, gold mining in north-eastern Sudan is classified as a male activity. Only men and boys are permitted in these sites of activity.

Due to the unabated spread of artisanal gold mining in recent years, there is strong competition for the ores between mining consortia and small miners (Calkins and Ille 2014). Governmental prohibitions thus far have done little to halt artisanal mining activities.[12] Nonetheless, the government closely monitors artisanal mining activities.[13] It estimates that while in 2007 a few hundred people were busy mining for gold, in early 2010 that number had already risen to 40,000–50,000 (Ibrahim and Abdel Baqi 2010). More recent estimations range from 250,000–500,000 people occupied in artisanal mining.[14] The difficulty in producing accurate estimates relates to the high mobility of small miners, who continually venture forth to explore new sites in the desert, extracting from mines but also searching with metal detectors. Furthermore, many miners are busy throughout the year, but some only seasonally engage in mining to supplement agricultural and pastoral activities, while others pursue different trades and only occasionally try their luck at mining. Producing reliable figures is further complicated by the transience and high mobility not only of people and their vehicles, but also of entire mining infrastructures that relocate according to the productivity of mines.[15]

But where in Sudan can gold be found? Metal detectors and hard-rock mining, as extractive technologies with their respective infrastructures, develop in view of theories of natural resource deposits. These may be official

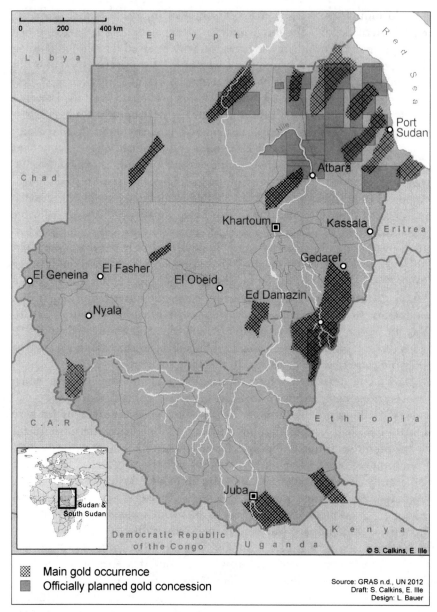

Figure 3.1 Official estimates of gold occurrences and concession areas

geological studies or lay theories, which result in assumptions about proper methods of gold extraction. According to geological studies, gold occurs in alluvial deposits of sand, clay and silt, typically along riverbeds, or in variant associations with rocks, for instance, as inclusion deposits in granite rocks (Launay 2010: 8–55). In order to exploit alluvial deposits in small-scale mining, gold needs to be separated from the detritus by weight. The panning for gold employed in Blue Nile State is one of the technologies used to extract such deposits (Ibrahim 2003; Medani 2003).[16] Surveys of the Geological Research Authority of Sudan (GRAS) focus on profitable hard-rock deposits in north-eastern Sudan: quartz veins, shear zones, and associations with sulphides and barites (see Figure 3.1).[17] In north-eastern Sudan gold is thought to exist mainly in quartz veins. When associated with sulphidic ores, these veins are estimated to measure up to three metres in width and two kilometres in length. However, because of tectonic events, they may be discontinuous, fragmented or dendritic and vary significantly as to their gold content.[18] 'Clean gold' explored by detectors is not the object of governmental geological studies.

As Nafiᶜ's example indicates, gold extraction in the beginning was confined to digging mines and extracting gold ore from hard-rock veins, a technology that still accounts for the bulk of the artisanal gold sector. The other extractive technology emerged later and in 2010 still involved comparatively few people. Since around mid-2009, metal detectors have been used to explore surface deposits. I was able to follow these developments through various visits to the region: on my first visit to the area in December 2007, Um Futeima was only a tiny hamlet with three or four permanent buildings. Back then, gold mining was not yet an economic option. On a return visit to Um Futeima in late 2008, only a few men were engaged in gold mining. Upon my return for further empirical research in 2009, there was much excitement about gold in the area and a gold market had emerged in Wadi al-ᶜUshar. Also detectors had begun to proliferate and continued to do so until I left the area in May 2010. The settlement had expanded through new building activity. The absence of men from the village was striking. Most had become gold miners, returning only intermittently to rest at the settlement.

My analyses in the following sections are based upon my stay in Um Futeima and upon several visits to the gold mines in Wadi al-ᶜUshar. Um Futeima lies dozens of kilometres south of the mines, putting the settlement on the map of mining traffic. I observed the cyclical comings and goings of gold miners and was able to record the intervals of their trips, the composition and constitution of mining teams, their mobility patterns, and the amounts of money made, as well as opinions on this kind of work. In March 2010 Wadi al-ᶜUshar experienced its first decline as miners moved north in search of new excavation sites.[19]

As a result my analysis is situated in a specific way. It traces mainly the discourses and perspectives of Rashaida from Um Futeima in a large and heterogeneous social world of artisanal gold mining. However, the ethnic group is not an intuitive analytical unit in artisanal mining. The social world of gold mining is rather characterized by its fleet of workers from diverse regional, occupational and ethnic backgrounds (Grätz 2002). But whereas the mines and gold markets are ethnically heterogeneous sites where people from diverse walks of life work together, kinship and personal ties play a more important role in the search for gold via metal detector. Of particular interest is why the latter activity is organized differently. In other words, why do kin ties and ethnic belonging figure as principles of coordination in detector prospecting? This chapter suggests that the uncertainties peculiar to the two extractive technologies are entangled with different kinds of organizational forms, promoting different kinds of solidarity.

In the settlement of Um Futeima people's daily conversations dwell on the blessings and hazards involved in gold mining. In the subsequent section, I will highlight four paramount sources of uncertainty in gold mining, which occupy people in the settlement. Often when we were sitting together in the evenings at the hearth or chatting in the afternoon over coffee, talk revolved around sensational stories, of large discoveries or extreme misfortunes, serious accidents, violent crimes and murders. In the interviews that I led with a dozen miners, many also talked about their personal fears and physical discomforts. However, there are also some vulnerabilities pertaining to miners' health that they are largely unaware of but that I mention here briefly as they may have future repercussions. To that end, I quote from governmental and NGO reports dealing with small-scale mining in Africa.

State Intervention

The interests and plans of the state are opaque and uncertain. From the perspective of artisanal miners the question of state intervention and regulation of the sector above all gives rise to insecurity. In the earlier discussion I defined insecurity as akin to a danger, something potentially harmful, which cannot be attributed to individual decisions and actions but lies beyond them. All unlicenced mining activities in Sudan are prohibited, but these prohibitions are not enforced, leading to questions about the government's will and ability to implement policies.[20] In early 2010 it seemed that the authorities in Khartoum would try to intervene and suppress the informal mining sector to protect the government's own shares in industrial enterprises, because miners were spreading into areas allocated to private investors as concessions. Meanwhile, due to a severe economic crisis and connected political unrest in the capital, the Sudanese government's interests appear to be geared to short-term goals, namely making as much money from gold as possible to buffer the loss of oil revenues.[21] Therefore the political will to implement these measures seems to be lacking; the government of Sudan encourages the emergence of manifold informal practices and is a source of perennial insecurity.[22] In the northern Sudanese hinterlands 'the state' appears as something so distant that some gold miners are not even aware of the sector's overall illegality. Others interpret the government's turning a blind eye to such activities as indication of its goodwill. As Hamda's son-in-law Salam said, 'It's a good government. It wants the people to benefit'.

Detector users, however, frequently referred to the prohibition of metal detectors and the dangers of confiscation. The government meanwhile has passed a bill that enables the import of detectors, so as to siphon off some custom duties and extract some money for licencing. But none of the people I met in the Lower Atbara area had been through the expensive and time-consuming process of licencing. Owning unlicenced detectors, these people took precautions. Farah stated:

> when they find the detector, that's it. They take it from you. They take your money, they search through your pockets, your car, everything, for gold. If you have money, they will take it and say you have it from stealing gold from the government. Maybe they take you to prison. They say you have to pay so and so much money. So you have to hide it. You don't take it into the marketplace. You only take it to your house at night.

Insecurity here means a nebulous danger or potential harm (confiscation, arrest) emanating from the government of Sudan, related to the status of these activities. It is particularly pronounced in detector prospecting. People cannot calculate this insecurity or master it, but they still take some precautionary measures: they increasingly place attention on navigational skills (avoiding main roads and checkpoints) and invent creative ways of hiding the detector, such as wearing its coil under one's clothing, or attaching a hidden carrying system to the car.

Crime

Another insecurity concerns crime. Many stories circulate about violent incidents, but importantly these all pertain to detector work or to travel in isolated areas. In contrast to the calm situation in the Lower Atbara area in 2010, violent fighting for the control of gold mines erupted in Darfur, causing many deaths and massive displacements from January 2013.[23] While sitting around the hearth in the evening, Salam recounted one story to the women, who were trembling with excitement and fear:

A lucky man had found a kilo of gold and was returning home from the mines at Um Ruweishid. A strange and poor man approached him and asked for a free ride. The other man told him '*irkab*', ride with me. When they were taking a rest in the desert and had just washed themselves (to pray), the lucky miner bent down on his mat to pray. The other man came from behind, put a shawl around his neck and strangled him. He took all of his money and disappeared. All they found later was the dead robbed man on his prayer mat and his deserted car.

Crime is an insecurity. It is a potential harm, a danger that looms. Its probability cannot be calculated and attributed to individual decision. Its occurrence is beyond the individual's control and means of prediction. Fear of being the target of violent crimes, particularly armed robbery of extracted material, theft and murder are widespread, especially in the more isolated extraction sites. 'In the desert, people are afraid of each other', explained Salam. The mines and gold markets as clearly regulated spaces were considered comparatively safe from the threat of armed robbery or murder. Regarding detector prospecting, Salam noted:

often it is not safe. … If they see that someone found something, perhaps they will slaughter him. Or they start to fight, there is a lot of fighting. He will say, 'This is mine. I was here first'. You won't go with anyone, unless you really know him, like a close friend or your kin. … At the mines, there are many Rashaida of course, but even with them you won't go. Each one sticks to his own people out of fear.

This insecurity has a strong effect on the organization of artisanal extraction, above all the search for gold with metal detectors in isolated areas. Miners confirmed that for this reason, they would only take people along in their cars whom they knew and could trust. Out of fear, many also acquired a rifle.

Health Hazards

Another source of uncertainty relates to the various possible physical repercussions of artisanal gold mining. Many miners told me that they had suffered from severe diarrhoea and colic, which had forced some to return home prematurely.[24] Another source of concern is mercury, a highly poisonous metal that due to its qualities is employed in the artisanal sector to amalgamate gold particles. Mercury is added when ground gold ore is washed in large troughs; it amalgamates with the gold dust and, being heavier than the dirt, settles down in the troughs and can be sifted out from the dirt. In line with Foucault's (2007) conception of risk as technology, I conceive of the harms associated with mercury as a vulnerability, a technique employed to assemble people and things around an assumption – the need to normalize vulnerable things by rendering them safe. It calls for planned strategic action and the deployment of various methods to anticipate and control harms. For instance, artisanal mining activities in Blue Nile State were monitored as part of the Global Mercury Project, which attempts to introduce 'cleaner methods of production' (Ibrahim 2003; Medani 2003). International non-governmental organizations are active across Africa, drawing attention to the dangers and damages associated with mercury pollution.[25] Residues of mercury leak into the environment while washing and when it is burned to separate it from the gold. Mercury is heated directly without precautionary measures or technologies of distilling it, thereby exposing workers to the poisonous vapours. These men may inhale large quantities of mercury vapour and are especially at risk of being poisoned, possibly resulting in nervous conditions, loss of hearing and infertility (Veiga and Baker 2004). Vulnerability here is thus conceptualized as a technique of government akin to risk to attribute potential harms (related to mercury exposure) to people unaware of danger and regulating them. For instance, Qismallah, who began his gold-related work in the washing process, referred to the work as 'nice' and worth what he was paid for it (*ḥaqquhu*) and contrasted it to the more direct hazards of labouring in badly reinforced shafts in the mines.

Consider the case of Hamid, who is only seventeen. In October 2008 then fifteen-year-old Hamid worked a shift in a mine in Wadi al-ᶜUshar. He had been there only a few days as a porter carrying out chiselled stones when a gangway collapsed on him, a friend and others. Hamid was knocked unconscious, but his working team was able to dig him out in time. He survived, but his friend Suleim and two other workers, trapped beneath him, died of suffocation. Hamid's foot was badly crushed in the collapse, and after several costly operations, which exceeded many times his earnings from gold mining, he now limps and his ability to perform hard work is impaired.

Such tragic experiences are considered the greatest health hazard by many men. This hazard can be assessed by deliberating the advantages/disadvantages of this type of work. In this case, men weigh the high probability of making money against these health hazards. For instance Nafiᶜ, who was introduced above, refrained from working in the productive mine of Abdelrahman because he feared for his life and health. It is a calculative engagement where actions can be attributed to decisions and it makes sense to speak of this as a risk.

Overall, work in the gold mining sector involves a number of health uncertainties, such as a vulnerability related to mercury, the spread of infectious diseases and severe health risks related to underground ore extraction. The rough, difficult work underground in the mines can result in various injuries, from abrasions and bruises to the risk of unfortified shafts or gangways collapsing and injuring or killing the miners trapped inside. These health risks pertain to hard-rock extraction; detector work in contrast is viewed as comparatively safe.

Finding Gold

The most fundamental uncertainty concerns miners' livelihoods. It is the fear of futility, of expending time and energy and risking one's health and security, and then not finding anything. Finding gold is never a certainty. Imaginations are stirred by countless stories that circulate about spectacular finds, such as discovering several kilos of gold in just a few days. For example, Farah told of a team of prospectors among Rashaida who bought a detector and just got it out next to the road where everyone drives to the gold mines. Nobody searched there. 'What did they find?' asked Farah. 'God allotted 3 kg to them! Three kilos! Can you believe? Those boys became rich overnight'. This desire for quick success motivated miners, who expressed time and again that God willing they would 'find cars and houses of stone'.[26] In contrast to the dream of quick money, artisanal gold extraction itself is viewed as hard and burdensome. Detector prospecting is carried out in isolated areas, leading to further physical discomforts: not being able to wash, forgoing sleep and eating inferior, often dirty food.

The most critical point about this exertion is that miners can never be sure anything will result from their hard labour. Salam stated: 'it's true some go and find nothing. That is their destiny (*qadar*). There is earth which contains no gold and earth with gold inside. … One finds, one doesn't. It's from God'. Nafi[c] explained: 'sometimes our labour just rises into the air'. The same uncertainty was also confirmed by Farah, who worked on detector teams: 'it's not known whether one finds something. … One time we find two million [SDG 2,000 = € 608], one time we don't find anything. … It's all luck (*ḥaẓẓ*) and, if God wills, a means of living (*rizq*)'.[27]

Processing Economic Uncertainty

Gold miners experience different types of uncertainty: insecurity pertaining to the role of the state and the threat of crimes, health risks and hazards, as well as an overall unpredictability of income. To engage in artisanal gold mining, these uncertainties have to be lived through and processed. How is this done? I will identify a range of ways. These may be very direct technical responses to a specific uncertainty, such as using metal detectors to increase the likelihood of localizing gold deposits, or may be complex organizational forms, which embody much social work, i.e., the rules of revenue distribution or fixed work shifts. In contrast to dreams of great and instant wealth, these ways of dealing with uncertainties represent technical solutions and mostly establish a reference to a pragmatic objective – the idea that all should be able to earn a living. This solidarity diminishes the risk of ending up without an income, and enables people to set aside differences and pass over uncertainties in the artisanal gold mining sector.

Finding Hard-Rock Deposits

Diverse forms emerged to process economic uncertainty. Here I am investigating the question of how to localize the best prospects for gold in such a vast terrain. This subsection concentrates on two issues: first it briefly explores how miners managed to moderate the uncertainty of finding gold deposits in hard-rock mining; it then deals with how technical devices are employed to track down 'clean gold'.

How do miners make sense of expending time, effort and money in this highly speculative and uncertain activity? Regarding hard-rock mining, Nafic related: 'you want to dig, then you dig. ... I choose any place where I see mines and see people digging and see that they have found something. Then I go and dig next to them'.[28] Backhoes excavate shallow pits, but locating a mine through digging is uncertain. Only a fraction of excavated pits are productive. These mines are then gradually expanded with the extractive work, either as pit mines or various deep underground shafts. 'It's possible that you get more than you can imagine, it is possible that you find nothing at all. ... It is fate (*qisma*)', Nafic confirmed. This imaginary of a divine being passing out lots explains why the discovery of gold was seen as entitling a person to exploit it. Whereas miners from Um Futeima emphasized ideas of luck and fate in striking a gold vein, they did not provide any information on the exact strategies in locating deposits – apart from digging next to others, I continue to wonder how they knew the shape of the deposit and how to plan the shafts needed for extracting. Godoy (1985: 200) endorsed the need for anthropological studies of mining economies, whereby 'the questions that need to be explored include the methods and rules of thumb utilized by miners in localizing mineralized deposits. Having found the deposit, how do they categorize/conceptualize geological/mineral formations and different ore grades; and, based on native distinctions, how do miners decide where the cut-off grade is' (ibid.: 211). Miners from Um Futeima did not give me any clues on such issues but rather mystified their practices by reference to divine ordination.

Even though Rashaida I met interpreted the economic uncertainty as being subject to predetermination, this does not exclude their simultaneous pursuit of pragmatic and cooperative relations. For example, many men did not have enough money to pay for the backhoe. Hence, a number of men often pooled their resources, sharing the costs for it. If gold was found they shared the returns and, if not, they shared the losses. Pooling thus constitutes a way of reducing economic uncertainty. At the same time this type of cooperation runs counter to the idea of individual fate, because retrieved gold is distributed in line with technical criteria, that is according to shares, irrespective of who found the piece of stone or decided upon digging at a specific location. This paradox will resurface in the discussion below.

Anyone can seek his luck and try to find a mine, but when it produces he must comply with organizational procedures. Registering a mine is a way of protecting what is conceived as the discoverer's right (ḥaqq) from usurpers. To register a mine in his name in Wadi al-ʿUshar, the claimant needs to approach a hut housing a small police station and three armed officers, belonging to the local administrators in the west of the gold market.[29] There, the local administrator, a sheikh of the Garab, a subgroup of the customary landowning Bishariyn, issues authentication papers. It reads taḥṣīl as-sūq, or trade license. The paper bears the name of the administrative unit, the locality, blank lines for the claimant's name, a large field for explanations, and lines for the date as well as the administrator's and owner's signatures. This document was developed to register regular market activities in the resident communities but is now being used in the mines to authenticate the right of exploitation. Registration also involves the signing and stamping of the paper and the payment of SDG 10. The SDG 10 fee is nominal, but remains symbolically significant as it is part of an evidentiary practice that firms up this form of cooperation. It recognizes the landowning group's customary rights and acknowledges the discoverer's right of exploitation and it can be referred to in cases of dispute. This form, in the sense of Thévenot (1984), backed by the paper proof, is quite stable and supports claims to the ownership of mines. It thus facilitates coordination and thereby reduces uncertainty about how to act. However, it is also vulnerable because people can challenge it, highlighting that this is a mine and not a souk and that this type of mining is in any event prohibited by the government. This only confirms the point that all forms are fragile and their stability hinges on how they are invoked, taken for granted, doubted or challenged when people interact.

Localizing Gold Nuggets

Returning to the overall gamble of finding gold, the metal detector itself is a technical reply to the very same uncertainty. While these devices are intended to reduce the level of economic uncertainty, at the same time in Sudan they remain within the dominant imaginary of a preordaining Islamic God. No matter how powerful a device, it is viewed as futile if God has not ordained a find for a miner. Nonetheless, this does not in itself solve the question of where to use the detector in a vast terrain.

Most detector teams do not move around without a plan of some sort. They are resourceful in allaying the uncertainty of finding gold in a specific locale: they attentively listen to other miners and stories of sensational finds. Many tap into their knowledge of the landscape and employ greater foresight. Some Rashaida described approaching landmarks that they remembered from herding camels, such as certain stone formations or seasonal watercourses, to search in one or the other location, where due to the colours of the stones they suspected gold might be found. This landscape cognition bears an advantage that goes beyond merely reducing the uncertainty of where to search in the vast deserts: in navigating the car through the desert, these miners can avoid both governmental control posts on the main roads and the risk of losing one's way in the steppe.

To compensate for these navigational skills, which others acquired by herding, some, like Guma, have adopted other technical means. Guma was raised in New Halfa in a more settled and urban environment. He has no experience of herding and orienting himself in the desert. He invested his first returns from gold mining in a GPS. Guma paid SDG 1,200 (€ 365), an amount he viewed as very expensive. But the GPS is invaluable as he can therewith navigate the desert without getting lost. The ability to mark a specific location with the GPS for further exploration enables him to leave the site, sell extracted material, and then to return to exactly the same spot later, even at night, and in this way the GPS surpasses embodied navigational skills. Nonetheless, the GPS did not guarantee that Guma would find what he imagined. He too emphasized the unpredictability of returns, 'We just go according to God's blessing', and told of both gains and losses.

The GPX 4500 – Inscriptions and De-scriptions

In the following I analyse how metal detectors – devices that are designed to electronically indicate the location of near-surface metal deposits – are used to process economic uncertainty. I will present the most widespread and preferred model among my interlocutors, the GPX 4500, and discuss its inscription with functions and programmes and their de-scription in the sense of Akrich (1992) in relation to the environment of northern Sudan. I show that in this new branch of gold mining, the task of reducing economic uncertainty is delegated to the metal detector, and as metal detectors perform their work, the extractive work and its bodily performance are organized around it.

Social studies of science and technology have shown that designers, when developing a new piece of technology, project certain qualities, competences and types of usage onto potential users, '"inscribing" this vision (or prediction) about the world in the technical content of the new object' (Akrich 1992: 208). This inscribed vision of the world, 'the technical realization of the innovator's belief about the relationships between an object and its surrounding actors', seeks to define users' perceptions and practices through notions of proper and correct usage, called a 'script' (ibid.: 208). However, there is always a gap between a theory of usage and the actual usage of a technology. It can be more or less wide, according to the obduracy of the technology, that is the prescriptions inscribed into the technology (ibid.: 206). In their article on the Zimbabwean bush pump, De Laet and Mol (2000) have argued in this context that a more fluid and less prescriptive technology is often more successfully adapted by users.

As artefacts to lessen the uncertainty of where it is useful to dig for gold, metal detectors were developed to detect underground metal objects. The GPX 4500, according to the advertisement of its manufacturer Minelab, was developed for recreational treasure hunters, specifically gold prospectors. Thus, it was designed particularly with regard to scientific theories of gold resources. According to one widely known scientific hypothesis about seismic activity in the earth's history (cf. Launay 2010), fluid metal was formed at great heat underground and then was dispersed through tectonic events, in part ending as gold flakes, grains or nuggets in the topsoil layers. The detector is designed to find these scattered gold lumps in the near-surface layer of the soil. My Sudanese interlocutors called these deposits 'clean gold' (*dahab ṣāfī*). The idea of clean gold accentuates purity and denotes a difference between this type of deposit and gold ore whose processing is labour-intensive. In the following, I will investigate some of the GPX 4500's inscriptions, that is, some of the assumptions and properties that designers at Minelab implement to affect how the extractive work is organized and performed. I will relate this to actual practices and the organization of extraction in Sudan where the technology is transferred.

The GPX 4500 comes in a long cardboard package with a rechargeable battery and an adapter for the car. The detector is made up of a round flat disk, called the coil, which does the prospecting, and is connected to a long shaft with an armrest for carrying. It also comes with a set of headphones; a heavy battery, which is strapped high to the miner's back in a harness to avoid interfering with the detector; an adapter for the car; an LCD display; and a number of other appliances. But how does it operate? The coil is connected to a battery, which electrically induces a magnetic field. The coil then is moved over the earth. When the coil detects a gold nugget or other metal, it reacts and produces another electromagnetic field, changing the detector's magnetic field (Rickford 2006). This change of electromagnetic field is signalled acoustically. The pitch and volume of sounds that the detector emits then varies. More abstractly, the detector translates complex underground composites according to a metal/non-metal code into sounds. The emitted sounds then allow the user to identify metal objects and qualify the type of deposit. As it is said in Sudan, experienced prospectors begin to 'hear' the gold.

To a certain extent, metal detectors have become black-boxed technologies, their use somewhat standardized and stabilized. All users of this technology in Sudan know how the detector has to be worn and held, without paying any particular attention to the work of the designers. The inscriptions that define how it is proper to hold and move the device are taken for granted (Akrich 1992: 211). Even small children who imitate detector people in their play know the 'correct' posture (see Figures 3.2 and 3.3).

Whereas the 'correct' posture remains unquestioned and is taken for granted by prospectors, the device's designers envision a much greater variety of movements with the detector than those performed in Sudan. The GPX 4500 is endowed with three different modes of search for different soil types, which can be selected through the menu on the LCD display: general, deep and custom. The custom search mode in turn has four sub-modes for prospecting: patch, for a quick overview of unknown terrain; hi-mineral, which stabilizes interference for highly mineralized soils; hi-trash, which raises

Figure 3.2 Hamda's grandson ʿUbeid playing with a toy detector

Figure 3.3 A young man demonstrating the proper posture for detector prospecting

the threshold for signals in areas with a lot of iron trash; and test, the default mode for experimentation (Minelab n.d. 28–31). According to the manual, these modes of search are connected to diverse body movements. Searching deeply, for example, demands rhythmic and slow movements, whereas in the more shallow and less sensitive mode, the detector can be moved briskly. Overall, the assumed user is a literate user, who can read the manual, identify soil types and monitor the detector's reaction to ground interferences and its balancing. In short, the user is seen as someone who is capable of selecting the appropriate search mode. Yet, most Rashaida working with detectors that I met could neither read nor write at a minimum level of proficiency, let alone well enough to understand the somewhat technical language of the manual. Even the more educated, like Guma who in principle could access Minelab's Arabic manual, ran the detector only in its standard setting ('general'), achieving a sensitivity of median depths.[30] Differences between these three settings or other functions of the detectors were not noticed by users I encountered; rather, the detector was conceived of as being endowed with a uniform property to detect metals at a certain approximate depth while moving it rhythmically. Users of detectors in Sudan stated that the depth of prospecting is approximately up to one metre.

The use of the detector in the standard setting affects how the work is performed: Guma states that the stability of sounds emitted is important. Therefore, the detector's coil is moved parallel to the ground in sweeping movements from left to right, which take about five or six seconds. These movements have to be carried out for between half an hour and two hours according to the number of people and the organization of shifts. Guma stresses the importance of moving the detector symmetrically during a shift, which constitutes its 'correct usage': he determines an area in which to search and then workers walk in straight lines, covering an entire strip of land, one next to the other, so as to thoroughly prospect a certain patch of land and not to miss any gold. When the detector is turned on, it emanates a sound in a standard pitch. On moving it, this pitch is altered, leading to a wide range of sounds that can result from various sources such as ground noises or electromagnetic interferences. When metal objects are in the ground, the detector emanates a short and sharp screech. 'A good miner is patient and keeps his concentration', Guma stressed. Therefore, the person operating the detector wears headphones to hear even the slightest alterations in the detector's pitch, which could indicate a gold deposit.

The GPX 4500 assumes not only a literate, competent user but also a recreational gold prospector operating in moderate climatic zones. The GPX 4500's manual warns of exposing the device to high temperatures. The anticipated range for operating the battery lies between 5 and 25°C, whereas 45°C is declared as the utter limit (Minelab n.d.: 98, 99). In the dry season in north-eastern Sudan, temperatures not only reach but frequently exceed 45°C. Electronic damage of the battery due to overheating occurs frequently, at times leading to irreparable damage. In October 2009 Farah was responsible for a total failure of a detector. He left it in the closed cabin of a pickup truck while it was charging. The electricians at the gold market were unable to fix it. 'But that was when detectors were new', Farah reminded me. 'Now they can repair almost anything'.

Still, overheating is a costly technical risk, which miners seek to avoid. Guma, for instance, has organized the working shifts to lessen the risk of breakdown due to overheating. He schedules the work in the cooler phases mainly between four or five in the afternoon and four or five in the morning. Two people are on each shift. One person walks with the detector, while the other holds the flashlight and the shovel to dig. Then work is halted until six or seven in the morning, when another two or three hours of work are performed.[31] This schedule of work results from the interplay of the technical activity, that is the work with the detector, the perception of the detector's properties, environmental conditions, and the workers' need to rest. Workers experience this response to the risk of overheating as burdensome due to the lack of sleep at night.

Mobility is a core feature of this type of gold extraction and this is enabled by battery power. The time for uninterrupted prospecting is limited by the strength of the battery and the need to recharge it. According to the Minelab's user manual, the GPX 4500's battery can last up to twelve hours. In Sudan detector people ('ahl al-ǧihāz) operate the detector only seven to nine hours or at times significantly less until it has to be recharged. The work cycle Guma described above thus not only relates to what he perceives as the risk of overheating but also the battery's limited capacity. The battery is recharged by car via an adapter. Guma explained that he never charges the battery when the car's motor is turned off, because this increases the danger of depleting the car's battery and finding oneself stranded in an isolated area. The car's motor needs to be kept running. Guma often used the recharging time to relocate to other sites or to drive to the market and eat at a cafeteria. The need to recharge the detector's battery on a daily basis thus contributes to the high mobility of detector teams.

What is more, the detector is interpreted as working according to divine ordination. Ideas of luck (ḥazz, baḫt) and divine predetestination (qadar, qisma, ḫaṭṭ) are invoked; they are not seen as mutually exclusive concepts. Rather, Rashaida I encountered interpret luck as being of divine providence to make sense of why some people find gold with detectors while others fail to do so. This forms part of an imaginary according to which God's foreordaining of events infallibly guides people (ḫuṭṭa min allāh). This interpretative pattern is applied to the entire mining sector. While Rashaida invoked an Islamic God to interpret why some are successful and others are not, every miner nonetheless experienced the uncertainty of finding gold. Many mention the lack of predictability of returns and the problems they confront in achieving a sustainable livelihood (rizq). Miners expressed the feeling that *rizq* is something everyone should be entitled to as a God-given blessing. As such it affects the organizational forms in the sector.

Metal detectors, like all technologies, are designed and promoted with ideas of 'correct' and 'appropriate' usage in the manual and user guide. Correct usage includes knowing how to adjust the detector to the type of soil or how to fine-tune the depth. To a certain extent, users in Sudan were disassociated from some of the ideas in the manual, which are also advanced through branding and marketing and are connected to guarantees given by Minelab salesmen. Most of the detectors that were used in Sudan in 2009 and 2010 were contraband goods. Many purchased their detectors in Kassala. They were smuggled into the country through its porous eastern borders, most likely across the Red Sea; the trade in detectors was therefore based on immediate exchange. At the moment of purchase the tie between the seller and buyer of the detector was dissolved. Therefore, users were unable to take advantage of the provisions of the warranty, if necessary, either from the trader or the producing firm. For repairs, they relied on local electricians, their own abilities, and more or less successful in-situ adaptations. The importance of handling them cautiously to avoid damage was therefore stressed by several people who oversaw the work with detectors.

To sum up, detectors are a technology that was transferred to Sudan and enabled people to exploit another type of gold deposit, so-called 'clean gold' near the surface. The uncertainty of where to dig for gold is delegated to these devices. As the most significant devices in this type of artisanal extraction, they are designed and inscribed in view of certain assumptions that arise from some of their technical properties, such as the battery life, having to recharge by car, and having to adopt certain body postures and movements during prospecting. As was shown, when detectors travel to Sudan, they are employed in different climatic zones, isolated areas, legal contexts that disassociate them from warranties, and also variant sociocultural and economic settings that strongly affect how their inscriptions are perceived and translated. Or as Akrich (1992) would have it, they are de-scripted by the user, who realizes the technology and puts it to work in his specific context, which is also being shaped by its introduction. De-scription denotes 'the inventory and analysis of the mechanisms that allow the relation between a form and a meaning constituted by and constitutive of the technical object to come into being' (ibid.: 216). In north-eastern Sudan detector prospecting is not recognized as merely a technically mediated activity, wherein a technical device operates in line with its official purpose and an established scientific theory. Rather, the technology is interpreted as a tool to pursue 'what God has written down' for a person. Success in mining and wealth then become indicators of divine favour, thus creating an association between the technology itself and other moral understandings, as will be further expounded below. The next section focuses on the role of metal detectors in defining relationships between diverse people and things.

Reshuffling Relationships

A detector is a piece of technology. It can be bought in a cardboard package for a specified price. As such, its materiality appears to be neatly circumscribed. But is it? Difficulties in drawing the boundaries begin when one thinks of the capital needed to acquire the device or the costs – in terms of the gasoline needed to fuel the car that is used to charge the battery – of operating it. Or the above-mentioned dangers of violent crimes in isolated areas, which means working in groups to ensure that the activity is conducted in safety. The performance of detector extraction in the northern Sudanese setting creates various relationships, whereby social roles and categories are defined, and rules and other organizational forms are established.

I begin with the investment costs and the links created. Given that detectors are expensive contraband goods, ranging from SDG 35,000–50,000 (€ 10,641–15,201) in mid-2009[32] and SDG 16,000–35,000 (€ 4,864–10,641) in early 2010 according to brand and market availability, investing in such a device is viewed as risky. After all, even with the most expensive device, returns remain unpredictable. Secondly, as an unlicenced, illegal good, it may fall prey to a governmental raid or confiscation, resolving not only in the loss of the detector but perhaps even leading to the imposition of fines or imprisonment. To buffer themselves against the risk of high losses, a group of people commonly pooled resources to buy a detector. Thereby individuals contributed various amounts of money – from paying a half to paying only a fraction like Nafiᶜ, who was mentioned above. His share amounted to only SDG 1,500 (€ 456) for a GPX 4500 that cost SDG 46,000 (€ 13,985). Money that is made with the detector is distributed 'according to calculation. … Whose share was large gets more, whose share was small gets less', Qismallah recounted. Importantly, providing the capital to purchase the detector is crucial to constituting a social category – the owners.

This shared ownership of a technical device introduces complexities and a substantive uncertainty into the organization of gold extraction. Many of those investing in detectors labour abroad in the Gulf States. How does the individual who contributed to buying a detector ensure that his investment is respected and that he receives a fair share of what is gained far away in Sudan? In view of such unsettling issues – a latent suspicion of cheating and the larger existential uncertainty of whether anything will be found at all – people need something to orient their actions, something to reassure them. Migrant co-owners usually manage the uncertainty of returns on their investment and their inability to control it from afar by appointing one of their kinsmen as their trustee (*wakīl*).

Assigning someone as a trustee, who enquires as to one's share, only makes sense if there is someone in charge who can authoritatively be approached. Qismallah confirmed:

> [The regular *wakīl*] walks with the detector and works with it. He carries it and works with it in the place of the other person. ... but [Abdelrahman] is the great trustee of the detector. He follows the detector and takes all the money for the detector. Then he calls the people by telephone and tells them 'your share (*ḥaqq*) is this that I have written down'. ... Abdelrahman bought the detector, a GPX, in Kassala for 46 million. ... He organized it and told the others that he holds on to their shares. When they return from abroad he gives them their money ... He knows mathematics. He hits the calculator and he had a pen and a notebook. ... Abdelrahman knows everything. He also writes down the schedules in his notebook. Everything is organized. There is no room for mistakes. And the calculation and the money that is brought, he writes it all down.

A person endowed with special administrative or other competences is called the great trustee of the detector or its director (*mudīr al-ğihāz*). The trustee is in charge of the purchase, the organization of the technical activity, and the just distribution of revenues. He selects the workers for a mining team as well as the car taken for a prospecting trip. By indicating that Abdelrahman 'knows everything', Qismallah drew attention to the crucial competences of trustees. Abdelrahman knows how to read and write, use the calculator, and employ a notebook to keep track of the money made, the schedule of rounds and people in it as well as the shares of different people. 'He is a big man and we help him and respect him and his hand is not too short with us', Qismallah explained about Abdelrahman. 'All of us are brothers and all trust him'. By emphasizing the respectability of the 'big man', his trustworthiness, and the fact that his dealings are made according to the system and correct calculations, ordinary workers on mining teams do not leave any room for doubts and thus enable the smooth cooperation between workers and owners of the means of extraction, thereby also confirming these social categories.

Operating the detector is also costly. As was stated above, a group is needed to perform the work. Workers, along with their tools and supplies, need to be transported and fed. A car is thus indispensable to detector prospecting. Furthermore, a car is not only needed to move across isolated wadis and mountain foothills, in order to relocate frequently, but also to charge the battery daily. Rashaida who had access to migrant remittances from the Gulf States were able to furnish the capital to buy cars and contribute to detectors (Calkins 2009, 2014). This makes Rashaida especially receptive to this technology and prominent in the detector subworld.

The reliance on cars to engage in detector prospecting also affects the organization of work. Space in the car is limited, but the men's desire to join detector teams appears to be unlimited. In view of the high demand and the comparatively few detector teams, the issue of how the latter are organized and composed is crucial. Although the owner of the detector and the car are rarely the same person, the detector is placed at the centre of this activity and therefore its owner or director is in charge of composing and scheduling teams for prospecting. Firstly, the number of people who can go on one round is limited to a handful. Aside from the limited space in the car, Farah mentions another reason for this: '(the detector's owner) says it is better I take five people in case one finds something, he profits. ... If he took twenty or thirty people along, he couldn't cover them. He wouldn't profit very much'. Besides, workers expect to be fed and they only reimburse costs for food and drink when gold is found. Taking too many people along would thus impose an unnecessary and avoidable financial burden, especially in view of the sequential performance of the technical activity with only one detector. Secondly, the group of people taken along on detector tours alternates. Miners mentioned that trustees of detectors test the luck and stamina of different people through alternation. 'This one perhaps is lucky, this one is unlucky. ... This one is good, this one is not good', expounded Farah. Salam mentioned another important principle that motivates the organization of detector teams, namely one's reputation among the extended family:

> If [the detector's owner] always took the same persons along, his people (*'ahl*) would feel sad and angry at him, 'Why did you leave me and take this one and that one?' Of course there will always be some sadness, but he wants to please them also. You know how people are here. They get mad about this. They will say, 'You took your mother's brother's son, am I not your mother's brother's son also? Why don't you take me? Am I not your father's brother's son?' ... You know how large the families are. They will accuse you and say you did this purposely: 'bad, bad, bad, why this one, this one and not me?'

Hence, the detector's trustee selects a handful of workers to search with the detector for one round, then another group is dispatched. This rotating of people is intended to allow a great number of kin to derive a benefit and prevents damage to the owner's reputation. By testing the luck and ability to work of different individuals and forging broad ties, this alternation is also a form that, from the detector owner's perspective, reduces economic uncertainty and increases the probability of finding something. From the workers' perspective, the issue of being taken care of is particularly crucial: by joining a detector team, even if nothing is found, at least their costs for food will have been covered and debts will not have to been incurred.

Qismallah mentioned another organizational form that increases predictability and calculability in a sector marked by rampant uncertainties – the appointment (*mauᶜid*). A round in a detector team is scheduled to last from seven to ten days. Farah and Qismallah, who participated in different detector teams, confirmed that after a round has been completed an approximate date is agreed upon with the detector's owner for the next tour. Two or three days before the date they call the detector's owner via mobile phone for more information. Is the car back? When is it going and from where? Where are they meeting? When the detector's director cannot be reached, the miners for the next round will call someone from his kin to see whether he has returned from the past round. When much gold is found, the owner or director may decide to extend the tour, staying away two or three weeks. As the person in charge, he can alter the schedule as needed.[33]

Disagreement on who is entitled or who should be selected to go is prone to occur, as Salam's comments above illustrate. They are negotiated and settled by the detector's trustee, who dispatches one team and tells the other aspirants to be patient (*'uṣbur*). Miners frequently highlight the qualities of big men, mentioning that they need to be good arbiters, listening to all sides. This is peculiar given that miners largely deny the existence of disagreements, glossing over them with the rhetoric of brotherliness and impeccable calculations.

Who is in/excluded from a detector prospecting team is a crucial concern. Ethnic homogeneity is rhetorically confirmed. Detector people (*'ahl al-ǧihāz*) emphasize that no one will be rejected and that in principle anyone can join a detector team, that is, any of the great trustee's paternal kin (and often enough maternal kin). People from the outside are excluded. There are three explicit reasons for this form. Firstly, according to the prospectors, there is the issue of insecurity: the fear of foreigners who 'kill men', as Salam indicated, and the fear of being robbed in the desert, as well as generally not knowing whether other people are hostile or not. Therefore, they talked of the need to rely on 'your people' and 'your group'. Secondly, the preference of kin over other people pertains to cheating. Miners' rhetoric stressed the need for trust among members on detector teams. Absentee owners of the detector are vulnerable to being cheated and therefore need to have confidence that the trustee and the few people on the prospecting team will protect their interests and not try to cheat them out of their share. Nafiᶜ stated, 'Nobody will betray the others. There is one sense of responsibility and we are one as brothers'. This was also confirmed by Qismallah, who mentioned that among detector people there was no room for mistakes. This ethos of not cheating or otherwise deceiving in the face of kin ties was discursively confirmed over and over by different prospectors I encountered. As a way of surmounting the uncertainty of incomes, it stands in stark contrast to the toleration of moderate cheating that Werthmann (2009: 113) observed in Burkina Faso. Thirdly, preferring one's kin and excluding others is explained as logical, because those related to the detector owners should benefit and not outsiders. By enabling a large number of different members from the kin group to earn money and thus by extending them this favour, personal relations are strengthened between the big man and the workers. To a certain extent those on the receiving end become indebted in that they are obliged to reciprocate at some time in the future – if possible (Sahlins 1972).

To define more clearly the peculiar character of the organization of detector prospecting, it is useful to contrast the kin logic that orients relationships between the detector's director and the workers on the team to the composition of working teams in hard-rock mining. Nafiᶜ remembered working at mines:

> People just come and say: we want work. Anyone. They come and congregate, the people want to make a profit. One time five, one time ten, one time eight, one time six, one time twenty, one time thirty. … Among them are Rashaida, Sudanese, people from other areas in Sudan, from eastern and western Sudan, from the north and the south.

The mine owner then selects a certain number of workers from the assembled men to form a team. As in other African gold mining camps, these teams are ethnically heterogeneous, composed of people from diverse backgrounds and locations (Grätz 2010: 57–61). The different extractive technologies – hard-rock mining and detector prospecting – and their different organizational structures thus lead to different solidarities.

Calculating Shares: Ignoring Inconsistencies

In view of the multiple uncertainties in artisanal gold mining, particularly the uncertain incomes, the way in which revenues are distributed is relevant. In the sector there are fixed rules of revenue distribution, forms which help to avoid disagreements and fights over who is entitled to how much of a share. A person's return or share, according to the rules of revenue sharing, occupied significant space in people's everyday conversations, not only in detector prospecting but in all avenues of artisanal mining. Rashaida in Um Futeima cited these principles as fixed rules, referring to them as a system (niẓām) and to their shares as their entitlement (ḥaqq).

Detectors were first employed in the mines to search for gold nuggets in the excavated pits and mounds of dirt. The introduction of detectors led to a reconfiguration of the patterns of sharing in the mine: a new role for the detector was introduced. Returns in the mine were principally halved between the mine owner and the workers in the mine.[34] Instead of halving the extracted gold between patron and workers, when detectors were used during a working shift in the mine, revenues from gold extraction were distributed equally among three groups: the mine owner, the workers in the mine and the detector group ('ahl al-ǧihāz). The detector group's internal system for sharing returns is divided by three – both in the mines and in the desert. The three parties that each receive a third are the car owner, the detector owners and the group of workers. This distributive rule was confirmed by nearly all detector groups. However, the use of detectors in mines was not continually desired by the patron or mine owner and the workers, given the high demand placed upon the extracted gold, most of which in a productive mine is derived from the underground rock and not by the detector. Therefore participation in the search with detectors was frequently limited to a few days, whenever new mounds of excavated material had accumulated or the question arose in a pit mine as to where to dig deeper. From the point of view of the detector team, searching near a gold mine might be a risk-minimizing strategy, because scattered gold nuggets are likely to be found in the mounds of extracted material near a gold vein. On the other hand, given the comparatively small share of individual workers, most preferred to try their luck in the desert, where they could receive a third and not a ninth of revenues, when compared to the mines.

In detector prospecting, profits were divided into three equal parts among owners of cars, owners of detectors, and the workers operating the devices, whereby the workers' share is equally divided among the number of participants in a mining team. This was understood as solidarity. All workers on the shift believed that they were working towards the same goal – their *rizq* (livelihood) – and deserved the same share. 'There is nothing like one takes much and the other little', Farah said, confirming this principle of distribution. The equal sharing of what was extracted jointly, albeit with various engagements, was viewed as a type of insurance and many expressed the feeling that this also constitutes a kind of assistance for the older and the poor. Referring to this solidarity, Farah's friend Salam mentioned that it means there is no anger among the mining team. This principle thus is a significant way of redistributing risks and returns among a group, whereby income discrepancies within the group of workers are ruled out. However, in several instances the trustee, although he did not join the workers in performing the activity, still received a share with the workers merely by virtue of his participation in the mining trips. Qismallah stated regarding Abdelrahman, 'When he demands some kind of help, he is like a brother amongst us, we help him. Sometimes … he goes and relaxes, we take his place when looking for gold. ... His hand is never short with us'. Workers were more interested in the overall reciprocity between them and the trustee, ignoring the fact that the trustees thus received multiple shares, those allotted from the detector's share, the car's share and the workers' share. Potential stumbling blocks to cooperation were brushed aside.

The detector's share of a third of the revenues was explained by relating it to the very high investment costs involved in purchasing this smuggled good, the threat of confiscation and the risk of breaking the electronic device. Costs for repairing the detector were assumed by the owners. Therefore, allotting the detector, that is, its owners, a third of all the procured gold was not criticized or questioned by any of the involved miners I met. The car's allotment was somewhat different. People mentioned that in contrast to detectors – that in the beginning cost up to SDG 50,000 (€ 15,201) – decent cars could be purchased for less than a third of that. Then how is the share of a third for the car explained?

Giving the car's owner a third of the gold revenues was justified by reference to the solidarity between the owner of a car and the workers with a detector: the former is entitled to the car's third (ḥaqq as-saiyāra) when something is found, and in turn provides the workers on shift with food (i.e., wheat, oil, sugar, coffee, tea, rice, onions), pays for the gasoline and undertakes eventual repairs on the car at his own expense. As mentioned above, when nothing is found, the car owner pays all expenses and does not ask for recompense. The uncertainty of winning or losing thus is placed on the car owner's shoulders. Many prospectors thought this justifies the car's high share.

Farah expressed this overall approach as a solidarity or a kind of security for the individual worker. A worker on a detector team may return without money and benefit, but also without financial debts. This was a stark contrast to the situation at the gold markets near the mines. In these artificial towns, where all goods need to be imported, costs of living are high and unlucky miners regularly returned with debts at grocery stores and restaurants, with severe consequences for the families of miners (see the case of Birkiya in chapter 4). These patterns of reciprocal exchanges between owners and workers on a detector team led to more long-standing structures of obligation and exchange between workers and owners, best understood in terms of generalized reciprocity.

Yet, although people confirmed and defended the car's share as legitimate, another model of cooperation was also practised. Nafiᶜ, a car owner, did not receive a third. Rather, he recounted that on one trip revenues were split 50/50 between the workers and the detector's owner. The car received a workman's share, that is Nafiᶜ received his own share as a worker and then a second share for the car, considerably lessening the car owner's share and augmenting that of the individual worker. This distributive pattern is less widely used, but Nafiᶜ was not the only one applying it. This system of distribution is justified by reference to the same principles, namely, the need to reimburse the car owner for his expenses of gasoline and at the same time as help for the poor. I wondered why Nafiᶜ agreed to this unfavourable distributive arrangement, when everyone claimed that the car's third is fixed and this strongly disadvantaged him by reducing his share. Nafiᶜ either did not understand my question or did not want to respond to it. He continued to talk about the distribution in his round and recounted the above reasons to explicate his small share, passing over the discrepancy between the two modalities of revenue sharing.

Even Qismallah, who had accompanied Nafiᶜ, did not discriminate between the modalities of distribution. Given that all members of a mining team claim to know the shares of other team members, Qismallah must have noticed that his next-door neighbour in Um Futeima and close friend Nafiᶜ did not receive what he should have by applying the rule. This went unmentioned. Rather Qismallah, like other detector people I talked to and interviewed, justified the third of the car by referring to the expenses in acquiring a car, the expenses for gasoline and repairs as well as the shouldering of all costs if no gold is found, although the third was not a third but a worker's share. When I explicitly asked him why Nafiᶜ's car was only allotted a worker's share, he confirmed the amount that Nafiᶜ received, SDG 160 (€ 49) as opposed to his SDG 80 (€ 24), but did not dwell on the logic of revenue sharing. Rather, he reiterated the very same justification, not noticing the two different modalities. The discrepancy between what Nafiᶜ received and should have received, the car's entitlement to a worker's share versus a third of revenues, could have led to doubt, the critique of the entire distributive arrangement, and even an end of cooperation.

Why Nafiᶜ agreed to this unfavourable distributive arrangement is puzzling, but can be explained by the power asymmetries inherent in detector work. The detector's trustee did not join the group with Nafiᶜ and Qismallah but rather stayed at home. Nonetheless, he was interested in obtaining a large share. Reducing the car's share to a mere worker's share therewith also increased the detector's share to half. That Nafiᶜ did not criticize this peculiar arrangement as exploitive or that Qismallah did not use the situation to argue for a reconfiguration of the distributive arrangement to the workers' benefit connects to the director's ability to simply exclude troublemakers. Willing substitutes can be found with ease among his extended kin networks. Voicing critique would thus bear the risk of exclusion from the system of rounds and associated income opportunities.

Instead of using this distributive principle, which from a worker's perspective is more advantageous, to principally criticize the system of thirds or to voice some doubt about the justice of the latter distributive arrangement, workers on detector teams confirmed the distribution by thirds as 'this is how it's done' and 'there are three parts'. Overall, this supports the thesis that in view of existential uncertainties, people for the sake of action in common may turn a blind eye to incoherences and tensions, refusing to notice and utter things which might endanger cooperation. The stubborn instance on 'the rules' and the alignment of two different modalities of distribution with the same justification are therefore ways of dealing with uncertainty. The rules of distribution herein figure as invested forms that meanwhile have stabilized and therefore hold together – or are held together – by engaging them with little reflexivity as neutral, purely technical solutions to a problem of coordination.

A further critical issue that is highlighted by the rules of revenue distribution and the example of Nafic is calculation. Numbers were a main area of discussion and had the potential to lead to unease: what to make of discrepancies among the shares that different members of the same mining team report? Such differences were either ignored or immediately settled by collective calculations, explaining the error by a failure to remember correctly and jointly establishing what must have been the correct shares. My presence was another source of unease. To follow miners' narrations, I calculated the various amounts and quite often identified gaps of several hundred Sudanese pounds, which suggested that the group of owners were cheating. When I enquired about such issues, my question was rebutted. 'Impossible' or 'you got it wrong, there is no cheating among brothers'. There could be no mistakes in calculation.

Confirming the 'rightness' of the rules of distribution, the men sought the error elsewhere, not in the *wakīl* or the owner but mostly due to their own memories,[35] closing their eyes again to things that would complicate cooperation between these two categories. The ability to calculate thus is of utter importance. Calculations are here used as a means to reestablish agreement, but they also could serve as a source of critique between what should be and what is and therewith could pose a challenge to the distributive arrangement. It is perhaps unsurprising that the ability to calculate, and also to read and write, is especially pronounced among trustees of detectors. These faculties are essential for people who wish to establish themselves as new entrepreneurs and patrons ordering and organizing the extractive work. Thereby, they continually enforce and confirm their crucial positions.

Regulating Predictability through Shifts

Some of the most cited and taken-for-granted forms are the various working shifts. These forms are central to the extractive activity and therefore their relative stability is a pillar in a social world marked by widespread uncertainties.

There are three types of 'shift' (*wardīya*): a reciprocal agreement between a local landowning sheikh as representative of the resident community and immigrant miners that allows the latter to dig on the former's land; an agreement between mine owner and workers to collaborate and exchange various items and services during an extractive shift of variant length in a mine; and a detector team's clearly regulated round of several days, forming part of an overall timetable according to which the detector's trustee organizes workers. I focus below on the third type and discuss how participating in combination with the rules of revenue distribution entitles each member of the team to a share of what was earned with the detector.

An important difference between a shift in a mine and a shift with a detector is the length of time. The former is flexibly adjusted to the volume of production and can last up to several weeks and months, whereby reaching an amount that is neither too large nor too small to be easily and cheaply processed is desired. Shifts in detector teams are temporally predefined, usually limited to extractive rounds of several days. Shifts among detector teams are embedded in more rigid overall schedules, which project the extractive work several weeks into the future and attempt to balance many interests to maintain or strengthen kin ties. The schedule of rounds in the search for gold via detectors is mostly written down in lists and tables in a notebook and is supported by appointments which the trustee makes with different miners as far as six weeks ahead of time. Importantly, in contrast to the mines where a patron and workers may collaborate only during a single shift, the schedule implies repetitive episodes of collaboration and therefore long-standing ties. Keeping records of the different schedules helps the trustee to determine who is entitled/deserves to go and who has waited a long time, and also aids in justifying his decisions when people complain. As emphasized above, the trustee's role is central in composing the detector teams and therefore in prioritizing people. This inevitably leads to some 'disappointment' and even accusations of malicious intent, as Salam indicated. The trustee must therefore be a respectable 'big man', one who is well known as an arbiter and adept at keeping the peace. This alludes to considerable tensions about the question of inclusion in the different prospecting rounds – a tension which, however, people do not dwell on in their conversations.

Bracketing Uncertainty

Miners live through multiple uncertainties in searching for and extracting the valuable metal. They process uncertainties in different ways, i.e., delegating an economic uncertainty to technical devices and at the same time holding on to diverse pragmatic patterns of cooperation: pooling money to spread the risk of losses (financing an excavator, purchasing a detector, etc.) and abiding by clear distributive rules between different social categories. But there is always uncertainty about where the gold is. The forms (social categories, shifts, rules of distribution, etc.) established in the course of this technical activity express different orientations: the rules of revenue distribution and the idea of profit-sharing are technical solutions to the problem of coordination in that they allow some space for luck and spread both risks and benefits vertically – unequally between different categories (workers/owners) – and horizontally – equally within the category of the workers. In hard-rock mining commonality was produced for an agreed duration through group membership, irrespective of belonging and the ability to work, whereas in detector prospecting membership in the group and kinship were fused, producing long-standing commitments.

Given the exceptional, fragile and problematic character of agreement (Boltanski 2011) in a setting of wide-ranging existential needs, it appears significant that ordinary gold miners present the modes of coordination in the self-organized and officially banned world of artisanal gold extraction as cohesive and that they adhere to a narrative of fixed rules and systems as well as flawless calculations. The discourses of gold exploration and the employed technologies, the processing of gold and the organization of the entire gold market indicate a high level of coordinated collective actions in artisanal gold mining and an ethos of abiding by the rules, which might seem surprising in view of the sector's transience, mobility and illegality. With Thévenot (1984) coordination is theorized as being based upon 'invested forms', that is various classificatory practices that assemble disparate entities and produce a sameness of things and people, facilitating cooperation by reducing the individual's uncertainty regarding how to interpret and act in a situation. Gold prospectors understood these forms as fixed sets of rules and regulations that guide their actions, recounting 'this is how it's done', 'gold mining is like this', 'there is nothing more to it' and so on. They did not engage them reflexively. I therefore read these forms and their rhetorical confirmation as 'insisting on forms', that is as ways of bracketing the sector's rampant uncertainties – a process, however, that can never be complete, as the contributions of Dewey, Luhmann and Boltanski make clear.

At the outset of the chapter I drew attention to the multiple uncertainties in artisanal gold mining and then identified the ways in which people process uncertainties. Here I show how forms, as ways of intercepting uncertainties and a specific social imaginary, are articulated. I will argue that the introduction of detectors as a new technology is coupled with strengthening clientelistic relationships among kin, and therefore the introduction of detectors and the organization of gold extraction results in a peculiar distribution of resources in society. I will show that a social imaginary, which connects a lucky strike to the divine allocation of lots, reinforces this process. The burden of my argument is to show how the imaginary creates various organizational forms and why what I identify as a tendency of 'insisting on forms' has emerged in artisanal gold mining.

Detectors and New Patrons

One of the most recent innovations in the social world of artisanal mining has been the introduction of metal detectors. Above I discussed the GPX 4500's inscription with specific properties and programmes, which interact with other elements in the coordination of labour, such as its battery life, the need to recharge it by car and its sensitivity to heat, and in turn moulds its perception and the bodily performance of work. There is a long debate on whether things have agency or whether it is only the human who projects his agency on things (see, for example Latour 1993, 1999; Bloor 1999). Pondering the slogan of the US National Rifle Association, 'Guns don't kill people. People kill people', and critics who would argue that guns do kill people, Bruno Latour (1999: 246) argued that neither holds true. People and things are seen as forming a collective, whereby humans and nonhumans are endowed with a potential for action, called a subprogramme. These are neither arbitrary nor determine the situation. But together they create a hybrid: a new corporate body emerges through the mutual translation of subprogrammes, which leads to unintended consequences (ibid.). This has inspired and sensitized my approach, given that the organization of the extractive work cannot be reduced to the convenience and preferences of the workers or to the properties of the detector.

My account showed that the organization of extraction with detectors results from a mesh of individual human needs and wants, social coordination, the material environment, and inscriptions and de-scriptions that occur when the technological forms are related to new moral contents. I have demonstrated how the introduction of gold detectors has played a crucial role in reconfiguring relationships among various people and things, defining their roles in the extractive enterprise and their entitlement to shares. Drawing rigid boundaries between technological and social aspects of detector prospecting would fail to account for the reciprocal or mutual shaping of practices and knowledge through diverse social, individual and material elements (Akrich 1992; Pfaffenberger 1992a: 508; cf. Latour 1993).

Therefore, a gold detector can not figure only as something functional, but is also always ideologically charged (Pfaffenberger 1992b: 283), in this case reinforcing differentials of power and wealth in society, particularly differences between owners and workers. The ownership of a detector is the reference for the classification of people as 'owners/trustees' as distinct from 'workers', which facilitates the coordination of labour. The owner of a detector – or rather in most cases the trustee, representing a group of owners – is crucial in instigating this work: the money needs to be mobilized and collected, the detector needs to be purchased, specific know-how to operate the device has to be acquired, and its properties and 'proper' handling need to be understood, transmitted and monitored. Extraction, the duration of shifts, the mobility of teams and the length of work intervals have to be orchestrated. Workers and a car need to be arranged, diverging interests of various (potential) workers have to be arbitrated, and the shares of absentee owners have to be calculated, fairly and transparently. Through this process of 'investments in forms' in the frame of the performance of this technical activity, the roles of things and people, the detector, the car, the human participants as owners and workers as well as mutual rights and obligations are defined and fixed (Callon 1986).

The coordination among detector teams was supported by a discourse of an ethics of brotherliness. The explicit logic of guiding the composition of detector teams is to benefit one's kin ahead of other people and at the same time to employ people who can be trusted, due to kin ties. The trustworthiness of all was affirmed time and again in the conversation of miners. Many outrightly denied the possibility of fraud by virtue of 'brotherhood' (*kulna iḫwān*). Moreover, when discrepancies appeared, they were ignored or even denied: 'impossible' or 'you got it wrong, there is no cheating among brothers'. There could be no mistakes in calculation. Thereby, miners confirmed the crucial positions of trustees or owners of metal detectors through which they can define and evaluate other entities. Furthermore, by taking different people along in successive rounds, these new entrepreneurs were able to create networks of people who are indebted to them.

The organization of this segment of the social world of artisanal mining indicates the growing importance of patron–client relations within kinship networks. This is not an altogether new development related only to detector prospecting; it already existed through the participation of many Rashaida men in labour migration, where individuals supported and often still support a broad array of relations with their transnational transfers of money (cf. Calkins 2009). A significant point is that all the people I met who possessed either cars or detectors had a history of cyclical labour migration to the Gulf States. This indicates that labour migration, by providing the investment capital for these expensive technologies, is still the most important stepping stone to becoming an owner in extraction via detector. Even mine ownership among Rashaida is facilitated by incomes from labour migration. Of five Rashidi mine owners that I met, all but one had migrated to the Gulf and thus accumulated enough capital to pay for the backhoe, purchasing tools and sometimes lending to their workers, and paying the costs for food and drink for days or weeks until the gold vein was laid bare. Grätz (2010: 59–61) refers to this arrangement as proto-patronage because cooperation between a mine owner and the workers from diverse ethnic and regional backgrounds, in most cases, only lasts or is agreed upon for one shift. In contrast, the owners, or specifically the detector's trustee, have entered into more long-term relationships, supporting networks of 'indebted' people, and, through their power to decide on the composition of detector teams and the schedules of extraction, have installed themselves as obligatory passage points (Callon 1986; Rottenburg 1995) – that is, nodal points in their social networks that the individual must pass in order to engage in this kind of work. However, whereas these ties tend to focus on the workers' personal relationship with a patron, they are becoming increasingly complex as several owners hold shares to various detectors and may try to influence the trustee's decisions, and also as detectors proliferate and miners may be entitled to join several detector teams with variant schedules.

These emerging structures around the detector work are clientelistic as they entail both specific and generalized exchanges that are asymmetrical but are viewed as mutually beneficial (see, for instance, Eisenstadt and Roninger 1981).[36] Specific exchange arrangements in detector teams are, for instance, workers' provision of services and labour in return for food and transportation and an opportunity to share in the profit provided by the owners. This specific exchange is embedded in kin ties and more long-term generalized exchange, involving workers' loyalty in return for solidarity, such as paying for their food although no gold has been found or ignoring inconsistencies when they arise. These package–exchanges are based on a dialectic between inequality and solidarity: patrons have access to the technological means of production (detectors, cars) but also generally have other qualifications, such as reading and writing skills as well as the ability to calculate and maintain the account books, which enable them to further their interests. This economically and politically powerful position allows them to display solidarity with the workers, i.e., shouldering the costs for food and gasoline. These two kinds of exchange are overlapping and may provide an answer to the issue of cheating.

Such exchange patterns do not necessarily clarify whether or not people cheat; rather, they indicate that these exchanges are connected to personal relationships and are oriented to ideas of honour and obligation (Eisenstadt and Roninger 1981: 285). Honour defines a person's trustworthiness, whereas stealing would make a person unfit as a patron or client – something that might lead to a breakdown of cooperative relationships.[37] People rather insisted on forms, on abiding by the rules, and on their correctness as a way to crowd out doubts, thereby taking the fairness of organizational forms for granted. Organizational forms connected to detector prospecting appear as extensions of the technology itself, something that self-evidently and naturally belongs to this type of activity and thus is neutral. However, the introduction of detectors as a new technology has strengthened clientelistic structures in kin networks. The interplay of new technologies and organizational forms supports an asymmetrical distribution of resources in society.

Social Imaginaries and the Insistence on Forms

The use of metal detectors has reshuffled relationships but it has not led to critical engagement on the justice of changes. Technologies are often buttressed by symbolic discourses, which disguise coercive properties and protect them from critique (Pfaffenberger 1992a: 501; 1992b). In the following I address the insistence on forms and ask why the level of reflexivity with which uncertainties are processed is low and why doubts of arrangements are rarely raised. The significations with which gold mining is associated provide some tentative answers.

An interesting literature has burgeoned in the past decade that seeks to capture the transformation of social imaginaries in contemporary African societies.[38] Mbembe (2002: 270) identifies a particular ambiguity:

> This is the phenomenon ... of an economy of desired goods that are known, that may sometimes be seen, that one wants to enjoy, but to which one will never have material access. ... The powers of imagination are stimulated, intensified by the very unavailability of the objects of desire. ... Here, the course of life is assimilated to a game of chance, a lottery, in which the existential temporal horizon is colonized by the immediate present and by prosaic short-term calculations.

This echoes what James Ferguson (2006: 147) has described for Zambia, namely that the faith in societal development and progress has gradually been replaced by hopes of an individual breakthrough related to one's ingenuity and luck. A similar chord was struck by Jean and John Comaroff (2001: 5, 6), who described the effects of present-day millennial capitalism: as the security of investment returns is increasingly mystified and therewith the overall livelihood security, people are seen as increasingly turning to uncanny means to regain some control over their subsistence. But the Comaroffs suggest that this is nothing peculiar to Sudan or Third World countries – in Western capitalist societies as well, wealth-gaining strategies are on the rise, which cannot be accounted for without reference to metaphysical explanations. Drawing attention to the entanglements between socio-economic and religious/cosmological transformations, they speak of the 'odd coupling' of hyperrationality and the spread of novel magical practices (ibid.: 2). The emergence of dreams to generate high profits through alchemy, disenfranchized from productive enterprises, is connected to the insecurity of returns in millennial capitalism (ibid.: 19–23). Similarly, one could suggest that the imaginary of novel, instant prosperity among the disenfranchised, which is strongly entangled with ideas of divine ordination, is connected to the experience of existential uncertainty and an exclusion that cannot be overcome by ordinary means.

The fullest conceptualization of a social imaginary is perhaps found in Cornelius Castoriadis's *The Imaginary Institution of Society* (1987). This is an attempt to rethink 'the social' on the basis of the social imaginary as a fountain of creativity and as a world-making force. The imaginary is depicted as magma, a fleeting, viscous underground of all meaning-making. Nonetheless, it is open to empirical investigation by focusing on the determined forms, that is, more or less fixed meanings that issue from the imaginary: 'the tools and instruments of a society are its significations; they are the "materialization" of the imaginary' (ibid.: 361).[39] Significations then enable the perception of something as real and the creation of distinctions between thing/image, real/fake and so on (ibid.: 182; Joas 1989: 594).[40]

The imaginary is not a distorted derivative of real things. Society or any social forms cannot be explained by or reduced to events leading to a certain constellation but is something that creates itself and institutes itself into new ontological forms: 'what is given in and through history is not the determined sequence of the determined but the emergence of radical otherness, immanent creation, non-trivial novelty' (Castoriadis 1987: 184).[41] Nonetheless, Castoriadis realizes that everyday doing and saying needs some level of determinacy, but to be determined for him does not mean being constrained by outside forces, it rather means being located in a certain horizon of imagination (Joas 1989: 593–94). The imaginary thus provides some references for acting, that is, orientations about values in a certain situation. It enables some containment of uncertainty.

Returning to Pfaffenberger's (1992b: 284) assertion that the coercive properties of technologies need to be legitimated by symbolic discourses or rituals to gain stability, care needs to be exercised to avoid reducing social imaginaries merely to their functions in supporting socio-technical arrangements. Applying Castoriadis's ideas is helpful in eschewing overly functionalist interpretations, social constructivist arguments, which place responsibility squarely on human actors, and technological determinism, which highlights the coercion exerted by technologies (see Akrich 1992 and Pinch 2008 for critiques of such arguments). The social imaginary as a fluid underground of hopes and dreams is a social communication from which organizational forms and principles of coordination in artisanal gold mining emanate. It can be qualified by looking at its materializations in the significations, values and ideas to which individuals relate.

The imaginary contains two main ideas: the promise of spectacular riches through a lucky strike and the divine predetermination of an individual's fate with regard to what he does or does not find. The former, the imaginary of instant wealth, draws thousands to gold mining and has led to a new narrative in the Lower Atbara area: people were poor at first, but then in view of God's mercy for the land found cars and houses in gold mining. But this narrative cannot be confirmed for any of the gold miners from Um Futeima. The above-mentioned organization of detector prospecting and extraction, with its elaborate rules of revenues distribution and their pragmatic orientation toward a horizontally equal and vertically unequal redistribution, exemplified that the various cooperative forms significantly narrow what an individual, primarily the individual worker, can gain from mining. It is this discrepancy between the imaginary of instant prosperity and the reality of meagre, insecure incomes from gold mining that favours the enlisting of an Islamic God. To recapitulate the second important idea of the imaginary, people interpret their uncertainty of finding gold as divine providence, something known to God but not human beings. The semantic field available to express these ideas is broad. Most often people referred to lot (*ḥaṭṭ*), fate and predestination (*tauqīd, qadar, qisma*), applying this to instances when much or little was found, whereas ideas of luck and good fortune (*baḥt* and *ḥazz*) were used to denote mainly a success in mining. People also talked more abstractly of 'the gold' as a divine blessing (*barakatu 'llāh*), God's mercy (*raḥmatu 'llāh*) or God-given rest from anxiety (*rāḥatu 'llāh*).

Promises of quick wealth and an apportioning God are part of the social imaginary from which forms and images are created in artisanal gold mining. The ways in which these two central significations of the social imaginary are linked bears some analogy to what the Comaroffs (2001) describe as an increasing mystification of subsistence. The imaginary gives rise to significations that are hard to untangle, that hold together and repel critique, even if the concrete forms of cooperation and their principles are creatively and unceasingly adapted to new circumstances, as was the case when metal detectors were introduced as a new extractive technology. The imaginary thus places the miner in a certain horizon and affects how people perceive, think and act upon their engagements: as was argued above concerning detector prospecting, miners insist on forms. Radical uncertainty, which entails semantic, deontic and epistemological challenges to a state of affairs, is avoided, possibly in view of the overriding and acutely existential uncertainty of incomes. In the following I want to draw out some of the ambiguities regarding how elements of the imaginary relate to forms of cooperation and then will relate this to the reflexivity with which the overriding uncertainty of incomes is engaged.

Several tensions between the social imaginary and invested forms were outlined in view of great economic uncertainty. Often when comparing different miners' accounts or when they were sitting at the fire in the evening discussing what each member of a detector team had earned, differences emerged. These differences did not lead to doubts about what happened but rather to doubts about the ability to remember correctly. Cheating was not even introduced as an option. Instead of inconsistencies or paradoxes, discourses focused on solidarity and help, the following of rules and their correctness. I have called this an 'insistence on forms', which dispels tension in situations that people experience as radically uncertain and is leveraged for cooperation.

Consider the institutionalization of profit-sharing between owners and workers. Some recent publications criticized such relations as exploitive, as workers often ended up without an income if the mine was not productive (see Jønesson and Fold 2009: 217–21). All prospectors with detectors and hard-rock miners with whom I talked confirmed that at times they would receive nothing or so little that it did not justify their efforts. Still, none of the men talked of exploitation or would exchange their share for a regular and stable salary. The uncertainty of income also entails benefits, in that it does not rule out the possibility of a lucky strike – an element of the social imaginary that lures thousands to the gold sector in the first place. The idea of striking a rich vein thus moulds the organizational form of profit-sharing, making the gamble more attractive than a stable and secure salary. As Godoy put it (1985: 201): 'the greater the share of exploration risks borne, the greater the expected return'.

In contrast to a system of salaries, profit-sharing is wholly shot through with the uncertainty of finding gold. Yet, in combination with rules of revenue distribution that stipulate the shareholders and the size of shares, profit-sharing nonetheless expresses solidarity with the individual. The equal distribution of workers' shares was evaluated positively as a main source of support in the artisanal gold mining sector: the lucky or strong worker supports the unlucky and weaker team members.[42]

But how does this practice interact with ideas of divine ordination, that is, the divine dictation governing finds for individuals? In Sudan the divine blessing of finding gold, which was bestowed upon individual miners, is technically refracted by means of the rules of distribution, conferring the blessing allocated to one upon the entire mining team. This, however, entails a narrowing of individual gains (for the lucky one). This peculiar solidarity in Sudan is a pragmatic and above all technical solution to uncertain incomes. As a form it was created by and through the same social imaginary, particularly the tension between the dream of rich yields and the experiences in gold mining. It mitigates uncertainty. Sticking to the examples from detector prospecting, uncertainty for the participant on a detector team is no longer extreme, particularly given that rules of revenue distribution are connected to broader reciprocities between workers and owners. A worker can join a mining team assured that he will not end up with more debts after an unsuccessful tour. Furthermore, his income is not dependent on what he personally finds, but rather on what is found by the team. 'Maybe I don't find, but my brother will find something or God has written something down for the other comrade', confirms Salam. 'It is more likely somebody will find something if you are on a team, even if only a grain of gold'. Uncertainty is engaged in a more probabilistic fashion. It is not extreme, because forms of cooperation, rules of distribution and social categories intervene and render many elements in the equation calculable and predictable, without taming the fundamental uncertainty of incomes. In view of this conscious calculation of possible gains/losses, uncertainty is transformed through various 'investments of forms' into a risk as defined above with recourse to Luhmann's (1991) distinction between risk and danger: in this situation future outcomes are attributed to the decision to join a detector prospecting team.

Miners not only combine paradoxical ideas, to wit, hoping for instant, individual enrichment and expecting a redistribution of finds among the team of workers, but with regard to the latter principle also pass over other differences for the sake of cooperation. Miners insisted on the equality of all in the category of the workers, be it in the mines and/or among a detector team. But when the detector is employed in the mine, the workers are not all one. Rather, the rules of distribution privilege the workers in the mine over the workers with the detector, allotting them a much higher share (1/3 vs. 1/9). Although both groups are called 'workers', this difference is not criticized. This again points to the successful form-giving work (Thévenot 1984) that established these two categories of workers as separate. For people there is no contradiction between confirming the principle of equality among workers and differentiating between different types of workers. Another example mentioned above was the small share for Nafiᶜ's car. Miners did not dwell on such inconsistencies. They rather interpreted the overall sharing mode as help and solidarity.

The miners' insistence on sharing the part of the workers equally is noteworthy as well, given the overall asymmetrical arrangement, which does not ensure any equality between owners and workers. These professional categories as 'invested forms' are accepted uncritically and are the reference for the rules of distribution. This reference is fixed and confirmed by the institution of private property – owning something enables one to decide on its use. Thereby the rules of distribution are at once useful and abusive: they figure as technical means to process the uncertainty of incomes among participating workers and concomitantly enforce class differences between owners of means of gold extraction and mere workers.

While finding gold is associated with a divine will, there seems to be a degree of stratification in the social organization of detector prospecting that appears more worldly than sacred: the seemingly classical division between labourers, who are disenfranchised from the means of production, and something like a bourgeoisie that siphons off greater shares – though not surplus value in a classical Marxist sense – through the labour inputs of the former. Highlighting the large investments, the higher risks and responsibilities for the group, owners justify receiving a larger share of the profits. These arguments were not contested but rather affirmed by the workers. There was no critique of nor resistance to the higher shares of owners, be they owners of detectors, cars or mines (in hard-rock mining), whereas the labourers bore the work's hardships and health risks. Although new incomes can be generated from the burgeoning of artisanal gold mining, my analysis suggests that the profitability of this engagement – far from the oft-invoked ideas of spontaneous, unknowable and divine providence – depends upon the ownership of the means of production and the emergence of organizational forms that support a distinction between owners and workers. Nonetheless, the juxtaposition of hard-rock mining and detector prospecting suggests that, particularly in the latter branch, more long-standing ties based on generalized reciprocity are emerging around trustees, who figure as new types of patrons and entrepreneurs.

To sum up, it appears significant that forms of cooperation in this self-organized and illegal sector are institutionalized and continually reinstitutionalized by the affirmative discourses of the miners. Differences in wealth and in the ownership of the means of production are not used to explain why some profit and others do not. 'We take the good and the bad and see what God has written for us', confirms Salam. Therefore, the attribution of luck to a preordaining God enables them to push away things that challenge the institutionalized social imaginary and endanger cooperation, but only to a certain extent because fatalism is counteracted by the technical and pragmatic ways of dealing with uncertainty. They support the various arrangements and regulations in the artisanal mining sector by connecting them to more broadly held values, but reality is ambivalent and fragile because miners do not accept the God-givenness of everything but pursue pragmatic solutions.

Boltanski distinguishes reality from the world. The world is immanence and incessant change, people's immersion in the flow of life, a lived experience that often contradicts the institutionalized reality, hollowing it out (Boltanski 2011: 57–61, 91). As was shown above, people do not fatalistically accept their divine lots but simultaneously engage pragmatically with their environment, recognizing the use of specific forms of knowledge in navigating the terrain or identifying gold-bearing stones. They furthermore process uncertainties by technical means, using GPS to navigate more successfully, delegating uncertainty to metal detectors, and coming up with intricate systems of revenue distribution that ostensibly offer solutions to uncertain livelihoods. Furthermore, the organizational forms on which prospectors insist indicate a sort of ordinary everyday moral understanding that hard work should pay off and lead to some entitlement. 'Reality' is therefore fragile due to the hiatus between reality and the world experienced by the miner, particularly its assembling and confirming of heterogeneous and at times paradoxical elements, such as the imaginary of ordination and pragmatic rules of revenue distribution.[43] Whereas this inconsistency of reality and its distance from the world imports the possibility of doubt and critique (ibid.: 57–61), a possibility of negotiating new agreements and forging other social bonds, this option was not used. Rather, the difference between reality and the world was overcome by an oscillation between the institutionalized imaginary of luck and ordination by a divine being, and the pragmatic solutions to economic uncertainty in an everyday order, concerned with securing a living. I relate this moving back and forth to the uncertainty of incomes deriving from artisanal gold extraction and the need for cooperation in the labour-intensive work, which enables people to selectively ignore elements that would disrupt cooperation.

Conclusion

The tension between hopes of high potential incomes and the utter unpredictability of realizing them marks the artisanal gold mining sector in Sudan. The social imaginary of divine ordination and phenomenal, instant wealth is a source of orientation for miners, moulding organizational forms for artisanal gold extraction.

Miners need to process this uncertainty that pertains to their livelihoods. They engage in various practices to reduce it and bracket it, invoking established organizational forms which redistribute potential gains and losses. This chapter highlighted that forms are related to a social imaginary of new prosperity and of a God who hands out lots, upon which they can reflect and act. This imaginary tends to mystify economic uncertainty by suggesting a causal link between wealth and divine ordination. Thereby it directly impacts several forms: I have shown how organizational forms develop through an interplay of various human and non-human elements, such as the environment, technical devices and human properties. I further suggested that the social imaginary also brought forth forms which are pragmatic and above all technical solutions to handle economic uncertainty. Relating to multiple uncertainties and the need for cooperation in the labour-intensive work, I suggest that this ongoing alternation between reality and world in the sense of Boltanski – to wit, an imaginary of luck and wealth, where the order of things can be justified by reference to a preordaining divine being, and pragmatic solutions to uncertainties in an everyday order, concerned with securing a living – enables people to pass over elements that would raise more radical questions and might disrupt the activity. My analysis of miners' rhetoric suggests an insistence on forms as a way of dealing with economic uncertainty and the mystification of links between material endowments and incomes. The insistence on redistributive forms in detector prospecting can also be read as a response to significations of the social imaginary, particularly the suggestive association of wealth and divine favour. Because an order of things in which one takes all would be intolerable.

Reflexivity about the unknown is therefore low. Miners tend to bracket uncertainties or to translate them into something more calculable such as risks. They create an image of a harmonious whole, confirming and institutionalizing a 'reality' by denying or pushing away tensions or conflicts, refusing to even dwell on elements that could endanger cooperation. The next chapter explores the exhausting uncertainty of daily village life that results from the frequent absence of men and the unpredictability of their incomes. This creates new pressures on women in Um Futeima to find ways to stretch food supplies and to build cooperative relations with others.[44]

Notes

1. Calkins and Ille (2014) discuss competition between industrial and artisanal mining sectors. In the past few years the number of international mining deals signed in Sudan has soared. Compare the following: *Africa Research Bulletin* (2011b); 'Sudan Signs 10 Gold, Iron Mining Exploration Agreements, Minister Says' (2010); 'Sudan Pins Economic Hopes on Gold Prospects' (2012); 'North Sudan Expands Its Gold Mining Sector' (2012).
2. Scholarship on mining often differentiates between illegal and legal activities, calling the former artisanal mining, and referring to licenced mining activities as small-scale mining (UNEP 2011a). I find this distinction based on legality somewhat difficult in a state such as Sudan, where the rule of law is to a large degree absent, and therefore use the term artisanal mining to denote a difference in both scale and mode of extraction from industrial mining plants and infrastructures.
3. In Khartoum I interviewed officials at the Ministry of Energy and Mining (now the Ministry of Minerals), analysed official reports and legal acts, and followed newspaper reports and other media for more recent developments.
4. I found two articles on gold mining that mention metal detectors: Rickford (2006: 449) devotes a small section on one page to describing the principles by which detectors work as a clean alternative to mercury use in Guiana; Jønesson and Fold (2009) merely mention that detectors were introduced to small-scale mining in Tanzania after 2000.

5. Apart from Ille's (2011) book about historical narratives on Shaybun gold and two recent papers (Calkins and Ille 2014; Ille and Calkins 2013) on the competition between artisanal and industrial gold mining, this phenomenon has not been addressed by academic studies. However, a handful of papers and reports were produced during the project phase of the Global Mercury Project (2002–2007) in the Blue Nile State (Ibrahim 2003). Recently, a new mining law was passed in South Sudan, which confirms a right for communal landowners; for more on this, see Deng, Mertenskoetter and Vondervoort 2013.

6. More nuanced distinctions and disciplinary interest could of course be drawn. Political sciences and economics tend to deal mainly with the legal frameworks, national development plans and projected and real profits/costs of industrial and possibly artisanal gold mining. Development and area studies focus more or less on the artisanal mining sector, i.e., the ecological/environmental and social impacts of artisanal mining and the use of child labour (Hilson 2002, 2007; Rickford 2006; Hilson and Banchirigah 2009; Tschakert 2009; Grätz 2010). Anthropological studies in particular have displayed a proclivity towards investigating the sociocultural contexts of artisanal gold mining activities, dealing with issues such as risk management, social organization, cosmologies and transforming lifestyles (Nash 1979; Taussig 1980; Luning 2008; Werthmann 2009; Grätz 2010).

7. They identify the lack of studies on multinational mining corporations as an enduring lacuna that relates to mining corporation's strategic opacity and means of corporate security (Ballard and Banks 2003: 290), a lacuna this study does not close.

8. Werthmann's anthropological study investigates the sociocultural contexts of gold mining. She shows how gold in Burkina Faso is associated with ideas of 'heat', 'bitterness' and 'the diabolic' and needs to be purified before it can be extracted and used in other economic spheres (Werthmann 2009: 159–76).

9. There is a confusing linguistic convention referring to the old Sudanese pound, which was replaced by the dinar (and by the new pound in July 2011), whereby the three last zeros were deleted. However, as indicated in the example above, everyday language never adapted to this change. I use the exchange rates to give the reader a rough idea of the monetary equivalent. The rates were determined using the online calculator at oanda. com. I do not know the dates when items were purchased, but the exchange rate for the Sudanese pound was more or less stable between mid-2009 and mid-2010. I therefore have chosen an arbitrary date, namely, 1 February 2010 (SDG 1 = € 0.3). With regard to the pound, 0.1–0.5 are rounded down, 0.6–0.9 are rounded up.

10. The government estimated that 3,000–7,000 people work in Wadi al-ᶜUshar market alone (Ibrahim and Abdel Baqi 2010: 3).

11. The emergence of small-scale mining activities is often linked to a broader process of livelihood diversification in Africa, interrelated with dwindling farming incomes and the sector's overall unprofitability since the prescription of structural adjustment programmes in the past decades (Hilson and Banchirigah 2009; see also Bryceson and Jønsson 2010). So-called alternative livelihood projects were therefore introduced in various states in sub-Saharan Africa, promoting activities such as snail cultivation, mushroom farming, rearing stock, or grass cutting (Tschakert 2009). But due to their overall unprofitability they hardly figured as alternatives to gold mining (Hilson and Banchirigah 2009).

12. Artisanal gold extraction is only officially permitted after an expensive and lengthy process of registration and authorization in Khartoum. See Calkins and Ille (2014) for more details on the formal procedures and costs involved in acquiring permits for explorations (concessions), mining and detectors, and Fisher (2007, 2008) for more on the position of artisanal miners within the Tanzanian state.

13. Mining companies exert increasing pressure on the government to enforce their contracts and to prosecute artisanal miners for encroaching on their concessions. Since the government is entitled to a 25 per cent share of net profits, this may motivate it to introduce further measures to inhibit these illegal artisanal mining activities. But the government of Sudan's economic despair seems to direct its policies more towards quick short-term revenues. Therefore it integrates small miners into the Sudanese economy by centrally purchasing their gold for export, making them part of a global supply chain.

14. 'Sudan Pins Economic Hopes on Gold Prospects' (2012) estimated that there were 250,000 miners in July 2012, and 'Heavy Fighting over Gold Mine in Sudan' (2013) estimated 500,000.

15. Official calculations put the informally extracted gold that is daily sent to Khartoum at 10 kg in 2010, but given the illegal nature of informal gold mining and black market sales, officials are unable to even approximately measure it. Other officials presume that the extracted amount may be much higher, fluctuating between 50 and 100 kg per week (Ibrahim and Abdel Baqi 2010: 3). Meanwhile, the government acknowledges that most of its gold is produced in the artisanal sector; the Ministry of Mining figures estimate this as being as much as 90 per cent ('Sudan Predicted to be Africa's Largest Gold Producer by 2018' 2014).

16. GRAS indicates that alluvial deposits can be found in the Blue Nile State and in southern Sudan, but not in north-eastern Sudan, the area under consideration here. Panning for gold in the rivers was not mentioned by any of the interlocutors nor was it observed. Ille (2011) indicates that alluvial deposits were exploited from South Kordofan. The long history of gold exploitation in northern Sudan perhaps implies that the easily exploitable alluvial deposits have been depleted and therefore panning is not applied, although it still may be used in some parts of Sudan (cf. Launay 2010: 17). For ethnographic descriptions of panning, see Werthmann (2009) and Grätz (2010: 49–52) for West Africa.

17. In northern and north-eastern Sudan a GRAS report identifies four main gold belts: Ariab-Arbaat, Gebeit-Serakoit, Aberkateib-Hamissana and Derudeb-Sinkat.

18. For instance, a ton of quartz may contain just a few grams of gold or up to 200 g of gold, as in the Ariab mine (GRAS), which is being exploited industrially. Regarding the structure of mines, Werthmann quotes Dumett: 'shafts came in a variety of shapes and sizes, ranging from the chimney type, large enough for one man (the most common form), to a rectangular type, to sloping types with steps cut in, and long snakelike tubes that follow the line of the reef'. But she also points out that the form of shafts depends upon the type of gold deposit: 'if the gold deposit forms an underground "mat", the surface above the deposit is pierced by narrow tubular shafts that may branch out into underground galleries. If the gold deposit takes the form of a linear vein, tubular or rectangular shafts along the vein will eventually merge to form one large open mine. In some gold mines in Burkina Faso, vertical shafts reach a depth of more than 100 m' (Werthmann 2006: 124). Seven industrial mines are presently being operated in Sudan, partially owned by foreign investors, which prospect and exploit the richest ores (*African Research Bulletin* 2011b).

19. The market saw an intermittent decline, when hundreds of people – gold miners and workers / entrepreneurs in the market – left for Um Ruweishid, a new mining site in the Butana. Yet, when returns there were lower than expected, many shopkeepers and miners returned. Others, however, moved on to some of the newer sites in the Red Sea Hills.

20. An important internal report by GRAS from early 2010 recommended several policies to regulate the sector: implementing a clear policy for the prosecution of illegal mining activities; placing greater responsibility for prosecution upon administrative districts;

establishing mining cooperatives and unions as well as local branch offices of GRAS, to unite small miners in delimited sites for gold mining under the joint supervision of local mining authorities and GRAS; granting small miners access to sites, where industrial extraction is no longer profitable; issuing more small concessions; and intensifying efforts to confiscate and prosecute the possession of detectors without official licences (Ibrahim and Abdel Baqi 2010: 14).

21. See Calkins and Ille (2014). For news reports covering these developments, see 'Gold Last Hope for Sudan to Avert Economic Collapse' (2012) and 'North Sudan Expands Its Gold Mining Sector' (2012).

22. In contrast to the lax governmental interventions in Sudan, artisanal gold mining is policed more strictly in other African countries. In Benin, for instance, following a phase of toleration the government attempted to control the artisanal gold sector through crackdowns, confiscations and displacements, blowing up mines and shafts or regulating the access to mining sites. This led to the emergence of more transient patterns of organization, such as the foundation of smaller, more temporary camps, the immediate splitting of revenues, and faster but more insecure methods of extraction (Grätz 2010: 117–23, 132). Similar government operations have been reported for Ghana (Tschakert 2009: 717), but often mining corporations also hire their own security personnel (Hilson and Banchirigah 2009: 166).

23. See 'Heavy Fighting over Gold Mine in Sudan' (2013), and 'Tribal Clashes Kill Dozens near Gold Mine in Sudan's Darfur' (2013).

24. My neighbour Salam's brother Ahmed, for example, was brought to my host Hamda's house with severe abdominal pains and diarrhoea from which he suffered for weeks. The nurse in Seidon diagnosed amoebic dysentery, indicating that he had likely eaten foods polluted with faeces in Wadi al-ʿUshar. But this is not self-evident, because amoebic dysentery is very widespread in the Lower Atbara area. A health concern raised by the GRAS report is the spread of infectious diseases, such as cholera or typhoid, due to the lack of hygiene at the mining camps (Ibrahim and Abdel Baqi 2010: 13).

25. See, for instance, Spiegel and Veiga 2005, 2010; UNIDO 2007; UNEP 2011b; cf. Pardie and Hilson 2006; Tschakert and Singha 2007; Hilson and Clifford 2010.

26. For instance, Guma sits in his one-room clay house and dreams: 'in sha' allāh, when you come back to us here from Germany, we will have built long buildings from the gold. Long buildings with air conditioning. Then you will sit with us and get acclimatized, and you will be comfortable in a room with air conditioning. We will serve you cold drinks. And Hantuta [his wife] will have gold everywhere'.

27. Rizq literally means livelihood, sustenance and shelter, but it also signifies divine benefaction. Not finding gold may translate into a crisis for the family – for instance, a lack of food supplies or inadequate money for medical treatments.

28. The backhoes are paid for by the people who seek to dig in a specified location. The price of the backhoe is SDG 500 (€ 152) per hour. Most miners let the excavator dig for fifteen minutes for the fixed rate of SDG 125 (€ 38) and then inspect the site to see if any valuable stones came up. When a miner abandons a mine, he cannot reclaim it if somebody else later digs deeper and reaches a gold vein.

29. Wadi Arab is administered by a sheikh of a different Bishariyn subgroup and belongs administratively to the municipality of Haiya.

30. It is perhaps peculiar that the GPX 4500 – hundreds, if not thousands, of which are now being used in Sudan – is the only detector on the US company Minelab's website that was provided with an Arabic manual. See www.minelab.com/__files/f/73282/4901-0116-1%20 Instruction%20Manual%20GPX-4500%20ARABIC.pdf, retrieved 7 November 2012.

31. Guma was the only one of my interlocutors who consistently planned a short morning shift in his work cycle. The shortness of this shift is dictated by the overall pattern of this socio-technical activity and the fact that the detector needs several hours to recharge completely, although it can be operated intermittently without being fully charged.

32. I used the exchange rate of 30 June 2009 and calculated the rate with oanda.com. In comparison to the very high price in Sudan, which is due to the added costs associated with smuggling, the GPX 4500 can be purchased in Germany or on the internet for € 4,500.

33. Often the detector team will be in an isolated location, which is not covered by the telecommunication network. But given the mobility of such mining teams, at some point in time the team will again be within the reach of mobile services. Therefore, the mobile phone has become a highly important source of information and communication and also a means of claiming one's entitlement to join a round. The latter aspect is important because people who are included in a scheduled round view this as their entitlement and will criticize any break in the schedule.

34. Returns are divided between the mine owner and the workers in the mine according to two systems – one in kind and one in cash. Both, however, specify 50/50 shares. First, in the cash system, the mine owner and the workers form a team until the gold is sold; the mine owner subtracts the costs for processing the gold, which he advanced (grinding, washing, transportation, etc.), and then hands half of the remaining amount in cash to the group of workers, who divide it into equal shares among themselves. In Sudan this system is only applied when a few sacks have been filled with stones. In the second system of distribution, when a large amount of stones has been amassed, these are split between the mine owner and the workers (50/50), whereby both parties are in charge of grinding and washing their own shares. The latter procedure is more common. Peculiarly, the distributive rule of sharing profits 50/50 between the mine owner(s) and the workers in the mine is also applied in West African artisanal mines, where, however, the owner seems to assume more comprehensive responsibilities for the miners, their health and nutrition (Grätz 2010: 58, 66–70). Why can the same rules be found in such heterogeneous circumstances, spanning thousands of kilometres, and what does this indicate about understandings of justice? Thus far the travel or diffusion of such distributive models has not been addressed in literature on gold mining, apart from the seemingly obvious cases of cross-border migrations in West Africa, and remains puzzling. Not to miners, however, who state, 'This is how it's done'

35. I could not accompany the men into the desert and therefore I have no idea of the space allowed for tinkering with the rules and shares. Werthmann (2009: 112, 113) cites it as widespread in each step of the operational chain in West Africa. In Um Futeima little was mentioned about cheating and stealing, possibly as this was believed to tarnish the honour ('izza) of a person.

36. See Marcel Mauss (1954) for a comparative treatment of various exchange systems. He showed that gift giving, while purporting to be disinterested and altruistic, is part of a highly structured exchange system, based on the social norm of reciprocity. See Sahlins 1972 for an analytical treatment of different forms of reciprocity.

37. Some literature has suggested that the asymmetrical relationship between patron and client is based on the patron's fame and reputation, connecting the morality of honour and shame to patron–client systems (Eisenstadt and Roninger 1981: 285; cf. Abu Lughod 1986: 78–117). A further important link between patronage and political systems was indicated by Ernest Gellner (1977: 4), namely that 'where power is effectively centralized, or on the other hand, well-diffused, patronage is correspondingly less common'.

38. Anthropological studies of mining have elaborated extensively on cosmological transformations associated with extractive economies, such as spirits, the devil or the lord of the hill (see Nash 1979; Taussig 1980; Jorgensen 1998). Nash interpreted occult rituals functionally as promoting group cohesion, while Taussig resorted to a 'symbolic neofunctionalism, in which belief systems serve the role of mediating between tensions'; both were criticized for overstating the devil in the spread of capitalist production systems and for their functional interpretations of occult practices (Godoy 1985: 210; Parry and Bloch 1989). Notwithstanding Taussig's interpretation this inspired a recent study of Albino murders in Tanzanian mining areas. Bryceson et al. (2010) describe how the bodies of murdered Albinos are commodified to furnish various lucky charms, which are held to enhance the luck and success of miners. This novel (and grisly) practice is associated with tensions between beliefs from an agricultural past, mediated by traditional healers, and external pressures connected to miners' integration into global capitalist market processes. Werthmann (2009: 225, 226) cautions that similar functionalist approaches simplify the complexities and ambiguities of belief systems, conflating their rich sociocultural and historical roots to recent socio-economic changes. Grätz (2010) describes various occult practices such as wearing amulets, refraining from exploiting certain reefs or resorting to supernatural interpretations of accidents in Benin, but he does not attempt to integrate this into a single cosmology. He recalls the importance of considering the situatedness of all knowledge and practices in different communities and places. My analysis is situated in as much as I concentrated on different ideas circulating among Rashaida from the hinterlands of the Lower Abara area, people ascribing to an Arab-Muslim identity. I assume that a plethora of rituals and occult practices of people from various religious and ethnic communities coexist at the mining site and there are several competing interpretative frameworks to make sense of luck and misfortune.

39. He wrote: 'The imaginary of which I am speaking is not an image *of*. It is the unceasing and essentially *undetermined* (social-historical and psychical) creation of figures/forms/images, on the basis of which along there can ever be the question *of "something"*. What we call "reality" and "rationality" are its works' (Castoriadis 1987: 3, his emphasis).

40. Similar to Castoriadis, Boltanski (2011), whose theoretical proposition was referred to in the introduction, conceives of reality as a state of affairs that is supported by various qualifying significations.

41. Castoriadis does not neglect prior institutionalizations and their materialities; rather, in his social theory they account for socio-historical differences between societies. The imaginary, the world-making and meaning-bestowing force, is seen as the source of such processes of institutionalization, which nonetheless are depicted as irreducibly creative and indeterminate.

42. In contrast to this levelling of the workers, Grätz (2010: 65) indicates a meritocratic principle for distribution in Benin, where workers who do the heaviest work chiselling off the stones in the shafts get larger shares than workers who perform lighter jobs.

43. The idea of divine predetermination in finding gold and the moral understanding that the land on which gold is found is not free but belongs to certain autochthons, who should be included in what good their land bears, led to a compromise – the shift arrangement between local sheikhs and immigrant mine owners.

44. Polier (1996) referred to this consequence of male mining activities as the 'feminization of subsistence'.

Chapter 4

STANDARDIZING FORMS

Uncertain Food Supplies

This chapter is devoted to the mundane, specifically with regard to the experience of women. Instead of focusing on the great uncertainties and risks of gold mining, it delves into the subtler, more gruelling everyday uncertainties that result from the absence of men and the unpredictable incomes they provide. Women, who remain in the settlement without men for extended periods, frequently experience an existential situation: running out of food. What should a woman do – who knows neither when her husband will return from gold mining nor whether he will return with money or debts – when her flour stock runs out? In view of this uncertainty and the probability of hunger, how does a woman coordinate her actions with other women in the settlement, who face the same uncertainty of absent husbands and the added uncertainty of not knowing if and when this woman will be able to repay the flour? Should they risk causing a gap in their own flour supplies?

These everyday uncertainties that women have to digest are the starting point for this chapter. It traces how women in the settlement of Um Futeima cooperate to bridge gaps in the food supply. On a theoretical level, it connects to broader debates on contingency and agency, by detailing how forms of cooperation are established and employed as buttresses to manage uncertainties that permeate daily life. Thereby it also adds to discussions of reciprocity (Sahlins 1972) as a principle of coordination. Two types of exchange are identified: staples and cooked food. The latter is oriented by generalized reciprocity, whereby rhetoric highlights generosity, denying the character of exchange. Conversely, the exchange of staples is based on balanced reciprocity, the principle of tit-for-tat. Yet, instead of taking the equivalence of exchanged entities for granted and assuming them as a given, this chapter is attentive to womens' struggles in establishing equivalency and maintaining a standard or guarantee of equal exchanges. By addressing the relationship between equivalences, ideas of fairness and social relationships, this chapter further connects with debates in anthropology which suggest that food is not commonly the subject of direct exchange. Towards the end of the chapter, I reflect upon the peculiar quality of female agency in existential situations, in order to interpret attempts by women to establish equivalents.

Existential Uncertainties: Gaps in Food Supply

When I approach Birkiya's houses on the outskirts of Um Futeima, her busy clattering indicates that tea is being prepared. She must have seen me. When Birkiya serves me the tea, she apologizes for how little sugar is in it. While we are chatting, we hear the noises of a car engine. Birkiya jumps to her feet, walks to the window and pushes the plastic drape aside to peer out. The car drives by. She returns to sit next to me on the mat. Birkiya is desperate for news from her husband. He left more than two weeks ago for the gold mines and she has not heard from him since. Birkiya is anxious. When he departed, he left her and her four children a small supply of flour, oil, tea, coffee and sugar. Birkiya's stock is nearly exhausted, causing her sleepless nights. We sit and talk, while she clasps my hand tightly. She wonders what she will do. Her husband leaves to search for gold and they have to cope. When their supplies run out, all she and her children can do is 'avoid eating' (*tağannub al-'akl*). For the last four days they have eaten less. Every day Birkiya prepares one *ᶜabūda*, a bread of fermented sorghum dough baked between two large metal discs. They eat it for breakfast and lunch with some water and oil. She has sugar only for the next morning. Her flour stock will last her only a few more days. She prays her husband will return.

Birkiya lets go of my hand and peers through the window again. A car is approaching the settlement. Her husband is not in it. We then talk about gold mining. She bitterly wonders what makes her husband go and why he never returns with anything. He has left six times and has yet to find even a grain of gold. To supply her with a few consumables, he buys them on credit from the stores in Wadi al-ᶜUshar and borrows money from his fathers' brothers, from his mothers' brothers – so far the gold mines have brought him nothing but debts. Last time he left her with very little flour and sugar.

Will he return in time and will he bring food? When I leave, I promise to visit again soon to see how she is doing.

Birkiya's flour lasts exactly three days. She makes up her mind and decides that she will wait the evening for her husband to return, then she has to act. On day four, right after the morning prayers, she wakes her children, collects a few items, takes a full water canister, and they start walking. With empty stomachs, she and her children walk several hours in search of her mother's camping cluster. She and her eleven-year-old daughter take turns in carrying the two-year-old. In this dry season her mother's tent is somewhere down by the river Atbara, so that her father's small stock can be watered. Birkiya and her children arrive before noon. They rest and are fed. She later described a calm that washed over her, staying with her mother, a rest for her worried heart.

Meanwhile back in Um Futeima, I return to Birkiya's house. I ask the closest neighbours where she has gone. She left, I am told. For good or will she return? Nobody knows or wants to tell me. I only learned about how she fared, when after a couple of days, a car stops in front of Birkiya's house. Birkiya and her children get out. Her father had arranged her transport. Birkiya returns with some goods, flour, sugar and oil, and SDG 40 (€ 12), which her mother gave her. She sits and waits again. She makes bread twice a day and they eat breakfast, lunch and dinner from it. There is still no sign of her husband.

Birkiya's dramatic exit bespeaks the existential situation women live through, related to the breadwinners' absence and their uncertain incomes from gold mining. Birkiya has only recently settled in Um Futeima. Her husband hoped that as poor people, they would be allotted a house by the charitable foundation from Kuwait, which had been active in Um Futeima since 2009. Neither her husband nor Birkiya has any kinship or affinal ties in Um Futeima. They were given a house to live in intermittently, a house the charity built for the doctor, who is still sought to operate the health centre. This house is on the fringes of the settlement and other women do not like to visit Birkiya there, given its exposure to the open 'male' desert space behind. Birkiya has few contacts in the settlement. She visits three neighbouring women, but she cannot ask them for help. She recently borrowed some oil and flour, which she could not return to the women. Birkiya explains that she felt bashfulness (taḥaššud), which held her back from demanding more. Anyhow, Birkiya is convinced that they would not give her anything and will berate her if she comes back before several months have passed. Birkiya's example indicates the stress women face when their food stocks run low, especially when they cannot rely on a network of cooperative relations in the settlement.

The experience of this physically and emotionally draining uncertainty is gendered: women and children stay behind in the villages, whereas men predominantly work in gold mining with irregular incomes and absences, causing the former to suffer gaps in their food supplies. Men, in view of their greater mobility, their relations with different shopkeepers and their ability to travel to kin, have other means by which to acquire money or staples. Family fathers or their appointed trustees are responsible for provisioning their households with food but often are unable to live up to this normative expectation. Since they have joined the settlement, most women no longer engage in productive activities, such as small stock breeding and herding. It appears that settlement and close cohabitation have confined the radius and diversity of activities in which women can engage without causing them disgrace (*ᶜayb*).[1] Women in the settlement are unable to go to the grocery stores or to the market, as these are considered purely male spaces. Establishing credit relations with shopkeepers is likewise not an option for women who stay behind on their own, and thus children must play the mediating role.[2] Birkiya said that to 'avoid eating' is the only thing she could do in this situation.[3]

To avoid eating, however, is not a new strategy for rationing food supplies. Many adults remember episodes in their lives as mobile pastoralists when they had to reduce their daily food intake. It was one of the first responses to drought to preserve the herd, the productive resource.[4] Whereas this way of coping with adversity is long-established, people interpreted the occurrence of this pattern in the settlement as indicative of their poverty. One reading could be that the pastoral economy demanded the possession of but a few items, resulting in a relative limitation of what was considered as a need in the first place.[5] Now that they are no longer mobile, people appear to have become oriented towards accumulation. This is reinforced by the social imaginary of a lucky strike in artisanal gold mining, which instantly lifts people from their dismal living situations. I have argued that this imaginary produces specific collective forms of risk taking/sharing. But a more pertinent explanation as to why reducing food intake in settled circumstances no longer figures as an acceptable way of coping with insecurities is not the orientation towards accumulation and the imaginary itself, but rather the move away from subsistence production. Many people, due to the gold boom, have forfeited the meagre but steady incomes related to pastoralism or agriculture. A subsistence-oriented economy turned into a mining economy, introducing new uncertainties and increasing people's dependence upon money for nearly all their food staples. The burgeoning of artisanal gold mining has led to a new kind of livelihood uncertainty – an uncertainty that women and children quite literally digest. This highlights the fact that women's options in situations that threaten their reproduction are limited by diverse factors. The consequences are anxiety, hunger and a vulnerability to disease.

Birkiya and her husband moved away a few days after her husband's return from the gold fields, settling next to the tent of her husband's uncle (ʿamm) at another location. Birkiya's case stirs up questions about solidarity between community members in settings of scarcity.[6] Are there any support mechanisms in place? If so, why was Birkiya not included in them? I show that food exchange is not a way of transmitting wealth to the poor, but rather a type of exchange that prioritizes solidarity among a group of women, who face the same uncertainties in managing their food supplies. In the following sections, I will analyse how women share and/or exchange food as well as the principles upon which cooperation hinges. Staple foods are more important in buffering gaps in food supply and will be discussed in greater detail than cooked foods.

Morality and Exchange

Discarding dichotomies such as interest/affect, profit/solidarity or money/love, I pay attention to everyday negotiations of interest and affect and focus the discussion on the establishment of equivalence.[7] This point of departure draws attention to how exchange is patterned, the explicit discourses on exchange and generosity as well as how practical deviations – that is, tinkerings and trade-offs that occur in situ – relate to moral understandings concerning what is appropriate or fair in a particular setting.

Cooked foods, for instance, are announced by women in Um Futeima as 'generosity' and 'gifts'. Nonetheless, they create obligations to reciprocate, a point made famous by Marcel Mauss (1954: 3). In his terminology a gift is a 'total social phenomenon' involving not only social relations but also economics, law, aesthetics, mythology and religion. This notion of prestation is significant as it undermines conceptions of pure market and non-market exchanges. To capture the continuum between these two ideal types – market and non-market exchange – the concept of reciprocity emerged in anthropological literature, denoting above all the quality of social relations between people (Gregory 1994: 923). Sahlins (1972) defined generalized and negative reciprocity as extremes of solidarity and unsociability. Negative reciprocity is 'the attempt to get something for nothing with impunity' (Sahlins 1972: 195). It refers to haggling, barter, theft and other types of seizure, while generalized reciprocity is putatively altruistic, expressing ideas of generosity, help and food-sharing, which engender social obligations and exclude the calculation of equivalents. Balanced reciprocity refers to direct exchanges of equivalent values within a limited period of time, e.g., market exchanges (ibid.: 193–95). In contrast to reciprocity, the notion of exchange emphasizes the material transmission of a thing from one party to the next (Gregory 1994: 911).[8] The concepts of reciprocity and exchange both encompass moral and material aspects, but each highlights inverse nuances of the other.

Monetary exchange is special; it offers some possibilities that commodity exchange forecloses, such as the easy transfer of profits or the dissolution of relationships between exchange parties (Parry and Bloch 1989: 5). Furthermore, it enables equality by putting things into an exact, coherent equation (Gregory 1994), such as one cup of coffee equals € 2.60 and two cups of coffee equal € 5.20. Focusing on equivalences invites messiness. Malinowski (1922: 355) used the notion of equivalence to denote the relation between objects exchanged as gifts. It thus expresses a qualitative relationship. A striking example is bride wealth, which figures as the equivalent of a woman (Lévi-Strauss 1969a: 470). This chapter shows how equivalences are established in the exchange of staples. The encountered equivalences are special in that they mix some of the above elements. Firstly, equivalences pertain only to one kind of staple and do not establish qualitative relations between different kinds of staples. Secondly, there is a short and indeterminate time lag between borrowing and returning, as opposed to the indeterminate delays with regard to cooked foods. Thirdly, equivalences in the situation express commonality among a group of women and emotional distance, indicating that balanced reciprocity is the principle of coordination in spite of the delay. Lastly, oriented towards equality, women attempt to standardize exchange through equivalences (staples) and stabilize relationships through gifts (cooked food).

In analysing two kinds of exchange, this chapter is inspired by Frederik Barth's (1967) article on economic spheres in Darfur. Yet, it uses a somewhat different terminology, namely that of 'invested forms' (Thévenot 1984). Barth (1967) argued that circulation in an economic system is ordered into spheres of exchange. To wit, independent classes of objects are connected to specific transmissions and separated from each other through instituted barriers.[9] Exchanges within a sphere were considered unproblematic, but moving between the spheres to which people acquiesce due to a pressing need or particular ingenuity was morally evaluated. Such approaches tend to overestimate the role of money in driving social change (Parry and Bloch 1989: 12–16);[10] they also presuppose agreement on systems of classification and take the equivalence of exchanged items 'within' a sphere for granted. Further, by concentrating on hierarchies between the spheres (Bohannon and Bohannon 1968) or barriers that sanction transmission between the spheres (Barth 1967), such an approach is attentive neither to the efforts of comparison and the agreement on common terms nor to the work that needs to be expended to render things into an equivalent 'form'. I am inspired by Kopytoff (1986: 71–73) and others who highlight the difficult classificatory work of categorizing what things go together as a group and of putting them in value relations (see also Appadurai 1986: 14). Kopytoff (1986) asserted that spheres of exchange are universal. They also exist in Western societies and draw attention to boundaries between classes of value. Applying this sensitivity to the problematics of value equivalence to Sudan, I not only show how equivalences are established but also describe the 'form investment' needed to stabilize them – in some cases until they are taken for granted as standards.

Further, Barth (1967: 157–62) assumes that the village economy is an aggregate of individual decisions, whereby each individual is driven by one rationality – to maximize utility.[11] The approach that takes the 'form-giving' work seriously, in contrast, asserts that both humans and non-humans have potentials to act and that their operations are subjected to situational evaluations, whereby diverse rationalities compete (Boltanski and Thévenot 2006: 1).[12] Thus, in my analysis of the principles of coordination for the exchange of food, the relations between equivalency, understandings of justice, and social relationships are key issues.

Food and Eating

Food is vital for human survival. It is a daily need and is often connected to routinized eating situations. As a cultural artefact, food is also a reservoir of social meanings and distinctions, which manifest themselves as tastes, expressing personal and cultural identities (Sutton 2010: 209–11; cf. Bourdieu 1984).[13] That a simple ingredient such as a potato can be turned into vastly different dishes in different cuisines, such as American hash browns, German dumplings or Indian curries, supports this. Food is incorporated biologically by providing energy to sustain the body and in terms of representations and beliefs concerning how certain foods affect the body (Fischler 1988: 278–80). The well-known German pun *man ist, was man isst* (one is what one eats) alludes to this connection between how the individual is constituted by swallowing and digesting both the materialities of food and the associated significations (Fischler 1988: 275).[14] 'No other cultural artefact penetrates our body in such an immediate, direct and intense manner' (Avieli 2009: 223).[15]

Recent studies have also emphasized that food engenders affection and solidarity. Food dealings 'are a delicate barometer ... of social relations and food is thus employed instrumentally as a starting, a sustaining, or a destroying mechanism of sociability' (Sahlins 1972: 215).[16] For instance, Notermans (2008: 369), in her study of children's perspectives on fosterage in East Cameroon, quotes eight-year-old Nadia who concluded that a foster parent loved her very much because in contrast to other caretakers he gave her food. Notermans follows Carsten (2004: 35) in seeing how intimacy and kinship are created and maintained by sharing food in the homes.[17]

A similar point is made by Alexeyeff (2004) in an article on how food is used to express love and affection. She describes the travel of Mama Mata, a cook from a Polynesian island, to New Zealand, where she presented her emigrated kin with 239 kg of island delicacies. Mama Mata returned home with gifts of more economic value: money for a motorcycle, a new iron, bedsheets and loads of food from New Zealand. Alexeyeff (2004: 77, 78) cautions against reading this as an unequal economic exchange. The exchange is reciprocated, but Mama Mata's foods had a much higher affective value; it was about finding an equivalent for the love Mama Mata had expressed through cooking. This idea challenges the observations that food generally has to be exchanged without seeking to establish equivalences within the community (Sahlins 1972: 215–19).

This chapter contributes to this strand of scholarship by being attentive to two different categories of exchanged food, namely, 'raw' staples and cooked foods[18] in relation to equivalences: in the settlement of Um Futeima, even among kin and close neighbours, the accuracy of exchanges when staples are borrowed and lent is important. Simultaneously, women place significant emphasis on the exchange of cooked foods as a non-calculative expression of emotion, namely generosity (karāma).

In Um Futeima food is scarce and eating involves some urgency. When people talked about weddings, the name-giving feast for a child or a trip to the gold mines, their conversations invariably turned to the kinds of food consumed, their preparation and the amounts of meat presented. Eating takes a prominent place in social organization. Rashaida households revolve around the social and symbolic organization of the hearth. Every marriage, as I was told and was able to observe at weddings I attended, has to begin with the institution of a new place of dwelling – a tent, a hut or a house for the new wife. At the centre of the new habitat is the hearth, which also plays an important part in marriage rituals. The bride uses the hearth to prepare coffee for her spouse immediately after entering the new place of dwelling and during her first private moments with her groom (W. Young 1988: 411). Every married woman is thus mistress of a hearth and in principle is expected to cook for her husband and children. Yet, due to the scarcity of resources, young married couples often do not cook their own foods and are connected to the hearth of the senior woman, usually the bride's mother. In my host Hamda's case, three of her married daughters and their husbands ate all their meals together.[19] Her married daughters took turns or aided their mother in preparing the daily bread. It is this preeminent role of women over food and its preparation that explains why the exchange of food is an exclusively female sphere.

Food is eaten from communal plates with the right hand, thereby a gender and age division is observed related to ideas of cleanliness: men are served first, then children, while women eat last.[20] Women thus are in a subordinate position to males and children, but still are able to influence intrahousehold food distribution. They prepare meals and can sometimes scrounge titbits for themselves and for some of their children. Furthermore, they arrange the food on the plates, allotting the shares. In Hamda's household, the women's plate is the largest, as women by far outnumber men, who are not only living in the settlement.[21] Only on the rare occasions during which meat was consumed did men preside over its cooking and distribution, reserving good pieces for themselves. The next section elaborates on food exchange among women, especially the modalities of cooperation to buffer gaps in the food supply.

Exchanging Food: Calculation and Generosity

Staple Food: Standards for Direct Exchanges

Woe to those that deal in fraud, who, when they take a measure from people, exact full measure, but when they give by measure or weight to men, they give less than what is due.
– The Holy Qur'an, Sura Mutaffifin 83:1–3,
Yusuf Ali Translation (1934)

The LORD demands accurate scales and balances; he sets the standards for fairness.
– The Holy Bible, Proverbs 16:11,
New Living Translation (2007)

There are three main staple foods in Um Futeima: sorghum flour, oil and sugar. Sorghum flour figures as the most essential staple from which the daily bread is derived. Not having sufficient flour is called 'being hungry' – those who are chronically (rather than occasionally) short of this staple are called 'hungry ones'. Mainly meals consist of sorghum as a bread or porridge along with oil and onion. Few other things are consumed at all during the two or three daily meals. Occasionally different vegetables, such as tomatoes or dried pulverized okra, are added. Apart from bread and oil, sugar is considered as another necessary daily staple. It is consumed in large quantities in tea or coffee throughout the day. The morning tea frequently also contains milk, either fresh goat milk or milk powder. Overall, food is monotonous and is consumed rather routinely without much variation of ingredients.

'We have no flour. Go and fetch some from Umikhras', Hamda tells her young daughter, handing her a metal bowl. The girl returns with flour and hands the bowl over to her mother. A week later, after Tahir has been shopping at the market in Seidon, Hamda sends her granddaughter with a bowl of flour on her head to Umikhras. The traffic of children with bowls between different houses is a common part of daily life in Um Futeima (see Figure 4.1). I will describe and analyse these exchanges and the 'form-giving' work they premise (Thévenot 1984), based on observations and insights I gained by living in Hamda's household. Hamda cooperates with six women from her neighbourhood.[22] As the household's senior woman, she presides over cooking and the food stocks. In moments of need, she specifies houses and sends her children there.

Although Hamda's husband does not participate in gold mining but works in Kuwait for a stable and comparatively comfortable salary, she still experiences the same gaps in food supplies with which other women in the settlement struggle. This relates to institutionalized structures of provisioning in the settlement and the dependence of women upon males: Hamda and

Figure 4.1 A girl fetching flour in a small bowl (with another girl offering her a cup of water).

her children have to rely upon her brother-in-law, sheikh Tahir, who receives the money from Kuwait in his bank account and is in charge of supplying them with necessities. She has no money to spend from her own purse; Tahir makes all decisions on consumption by shopping for her. Since Tahir started gold mining and has a new wife, who lives some kilometres away in the nomadic hinterlands, he is more often absent than present and Hamda's supplies also tend to become exhausted.

That Hamda returned the approximate amount of flour in a narrow period of time to Umikhras indicates that the exchange of staple foods is based on a logic of balanced reciprocity (see Sahlins 1972: 194–95). Hamda confirmed, 'We take something and when we get something, we send it back'. One of her grown daughters added, 'And when they need something from us, they take it. When their man brings money and buys things, they send it back to us'. The women also referred to these practices as borrowing or lending food. This frankness about engaging in direct exchange may be surprising. Classical studies have stressed the tendency towards generosity and generalized exchanges concerning food, especially staples, within small communities.[23]

Hamda's engagements with other married women occur against a backdrop of almost daily fights about food among members of her extended household. Mostly these are petty fights concerning who ate how much, but at times these disagreements escalate into insults and abusive speech or even fisticuffs – situations that are harder to mend. Petty struggles occurred, for instance, between Hamda's son and her teenage daughter regarding the former's eating of tomatoes before food was served. During my presence more serious fights broke out between one of Hamda's daughters and her brother-in-law concerning watermelons that I had brought, whereby the latter and his wife were insulted and withdrew from joint meals for four days. Fights among Hamda's children, sons-in-law and sheikh Tahir's wife were ongoing, whereby the latter was accused of sending her children to Hamda to eat, but not adequately reciprocating. These conflicts around the intrafamilial distribution of food highlight that when people have to put up with existential uncertainties, the home is not necessarily a locus where people experience help and solidarity but rather is frequently also marked by neglect, strife and competition (Cooper 2012).[24] Sahlins (1972: 128–37) has suggested that generosity is greater in communities with differences in wealth, a situation which often results in patron–client relations, but decreases in times of widespread hardship and crisis, leading to an 'atomization' of kin groups and the integration of the nuclear family. Whereas this argument could explain the lack of generosity in view of the overall plateau of wealth on a subsistence level in Um Futeima, the family is conversely not more cohesive.

For the described exchanges of staple foods, kin ties are not important. The seven senior women who cooperate with each other in the exchange of staples are partly from the same lineage, partly from disparate lineages. They all live in the same neighbourhood of Um Futeima. Apart from these seven women, there are six other married women in the same quarter of the settlement, who do not participate in the exchange of staples. Three of these are Hamda's daughters, who receive food from their mother's hearth, and three other women. All six are considered poor.[25] The condition for participating in the circle of women, who lend and borrow from each other, is given by the principle of balanced reciprocity itself: having, taking and being able to return within a short period of time. Poor people are excluded from this continual borrowing and lending activity. This clarifies why Birkiya's options were limited in the situation. She had borrowed some staples from her neighbours but could not reciprocate, disassociating her from further engagements with neighbouring women. Birkiya explained this in terms of her bashfulness (*taḥaššud*), a feeling caused by indebtedness and the failure to live up to the moral obligation to reciprocate. Poor people who too infrequently manage to replenish their staples to participate must rely on other networks of solidarity and care – the family and kin.

Thinking about exchange (of different sorts of capitals), Bourdieu (1983: 191) stressed that the mutual recognition which is institutionalized in exchange relations presupposes that involved actors recognize themselves objectively as minimally homogeneous. As a basis for this exchange of staples, the seven women, who regularly deplete their own food reservoir to help one another to meet basic food requirements, must understand themselves in some ways as 'the same', being of one economic kind, enabling both cooperation and efforts in establishing an equal balance after completing a bilateral exchange (A=gives and B=takes, B=gives and A=takes). Whereas social ties are also important for these exchanges of staples, balanced reciprocity hinges more upon the material than social dimensions – the equivalence of exchanged items. Instead of ideas of generosity and generalized exchange – trusting that sometime in the future something will return – women seek to establish standards which ensure the fairness and equality of exchanged items. But first I will discuss the crucial mediation of children.

Children as Porters

Porterage of heavy things, above all water and firewood, in this rural settlement is predominantly the chore of young unmarried girls (cf. Porter et al. 2012).[26] Hamda's young daughters get water in the morning after breakfast. They also get firewood two to three times a week in the afternoon.[27] Infants and toddlers are exempted from work, but as soon as young boys and girls reach a stage of maturity[28] – perhaps three or four years – they are entrusted with first tasks, such as carrying items between different houses, fetching things from shops, borrowing tools, tethering the goats and so on. As mothers constantly send their children on errands, making their porterage so ubiquitous, trivial and normal, it does not draw any attention.

This unaffected ease and seeming naturalness with which small children move from house to house transporting the bowls, bottles and other items influences the transactions and enables the adults to engage in exchange with greater ease. By using children as porters and messengers, women can avoid proper decorum and politeness, which they would need to display if they went themselves. The women can focus on the envisioned exchange without being distracted by ritual hospitality. For example, often neighbour children peered into Hamda's hut and interrupted the conversation, asking for flour for their mother with the bowl in their hands. Because they were children, Hamda could either give them something or could chase them away, denying them flour by saying she has none. By means of the children's mediation, women avoid potentially embarrassing situations when attempting to borrow staples, which could impinge upon their relationships. Girls are the more frequent porters; by being immersed in these different, at times delicate exchange situations, they learn much about the fabric of social relations and already before adolescence have acquired a deep understanding of the exchange principles in relation to different social ties. Next, I will show which materialities women deploy in their food dealings and how they use a technique of measurement to test the equivalence of exchanged amounts.

Standardizing Vessels for Exchange

I here focus on how the staples of flour, oil and sugar are moved from house to house. I discussed the role of the children in carrying them, but have not yet enlarged on the vessels themselves. Of the three staples, sugar is the least important. It is moved from house to house in small quantities either in cups, glasses or plastic and paper bags, in which it is also sold at the local grocery stores. A bargaining spirit prevails. Women are careful not to be taken advantage of, and complain when they perceive that the returned amount is less than what they have lent. It is about matching an expectation of approximate amounts; less attention is paid to enforcing equivalency. This can be explained by the consideration that sugar is neither as expensive nor as essential in satisfying hunger as flour and oil, where industrially produced standardized vessels are employed.

The women place greater emphasis on the equivalence of exchanged oil. Some of the wealthier people purchase oil in five-litre containers. Others buy smaller amounts by weight in the grocery store,[29] which are poured into an empty half-litre plastic bottle. The same empty plastic bottles circulate in borrowing and lending oil. The bottles are fairly widespread in the settlement.

Figure 4.2 Typical kitchen equipment

People, for instance, buy a bottle of clean water from a shop in town, following the doctor's prescriptions, when one of their children is sick with typhoid or dysentery. These bottles then are washed and used as containers for oil or fresh milk. Most women do not own large stocks of oil. They only exchange a small sip of it in a bottle. The women have no scales and employ no other means of measuring the exchanged quantities of oil. Yet, Hamda affirmed, she did so with her eyes. She claimed to remember how much she received and to reciprocate the same quantity of oil. In spite of the ambiguities involved and the reliance on different perceptions, I only once witnessed an ugly dispute about the quantities of oil exchanged. Hamda was accusing her sister-in-law, sheikh Tahir's wife, of returning an absurdly small amount of oil in return for what she had borrowed ten days earlier. Hamda's sister-in-law disagreed, arguing that even if it had been less, in view of other exchanges between her husband and Hamda, the latter should accept it. Hamda strongly disagreed. Her daughters intervened on her side and it all ended with several days of total avoidance between the women of the extended household.

Flour is the most frequently exchanged and essential staple. Its exchange is serious. It is transported in metal bowls. At marriage, the groom is expected to supply his bride with various presents, including kitchen equipment and at least two sets of metal bowls. The bowls can be purchased at market towns across north-eastern Sudan. Every married Rashaida women I met owned a minimum of two sets of bowls and used them for the daily eating, drinking and cooking activities: these were large bowls with a flattened bottom and a broad rim, used as trays for eating or troughs for feeding small stock, and a variety of round bowls with only a small flat bottom and a small slim rim, which have a much greater volume and are used for drinking water, milking stock, pouring water into the cooking pot and so on. The bowls can be nested into one another, but each individual bowl in a set is of a standard shape and size.

The round bowls (*zabdīya*) reserved for dealing with liquids are also used as vessels to exchange flour. I observed that only three different-sized bowls are employed, called the big, the medium and the small bowl. The women remember for each act of borrowing or lending which size was used, and have to reciprocate or demand accordingly. Hamda sent her daughter with an empty medium bowl to Umikhras, and she returned a medium bowl of flour. At other times, however, I noticed that women sent their children to ask for flour without a bowl. Then the lending woman – if she agrees to give – can decide on how much she can spare from her supplies. The women did not mention explicitly why everyone uses the same three kinds of bowls or why they use bowls at all, instead of other vessels, pots or plastic bags. Yet, it was clear that from a woman's set of bowls only the three kinds of bowl (large, medium and small) could be used. That only these three kinds of bowls were transported between the houses indicates that a standard of exchange had been established, even if it was too subtle and mundane to merit mention.

This resonates with how Lawrence Busch (2011) describes standards, to wit, as the taken-for-granted aspects of daily life, or, as Lampland and Star (2009: 13) put it, the boring backstage components of our lives. Standards are understood as 'measured comparisons': by encompassing a sort of simile or metaphor, standards enable one to test and evaluate people and things (Busch 2011: 10–12).[30] Citing examples from the Quran and the Bible, Busch (2011: 18) recalls the ancient historical use of exemplary measures, weights or volumes as standards in exchanges – an important contribution in view of the more recent tendency to associate standardization with hyper-modernity and totalizing processes such as globalization (see, for example, Lampland and Star 2009; Timmermans and Epstein 2010). Similarly, by employing standardized metal bowls, the bowls and their respective sizes themselves become measures to compare amounts of flour and therewith establish standards to which the women's interactions refer.

Scholarship on standards stresses that they embody information about the ways in which we organize living together and at the same time are black-boxed, muted, taken for granted, ubiquitous, unquestioned, accepted as necessary and not given thought until they fail and result in conflicts.

The goal of standards and standardization is 'to render the world equivalent across cultures, times, and geography' (Timmermans and Epstein 2010: 69); 'to streamline procedures or regulate behaviors, to demand specific results, or to prevent harm' (Lampland and Star 2009: 8, 10); to prescribe the rules that others have to follow and frame a number of options, and to facilitate coordination (Busch 2011: 28, 29; Thévenot 1984). When they have been successfully established, they work as 'recipes that we use to hold the world of people and things together' (Busch 2011: 5). The point that standards are the raw material through which reality is represented is important. Above, the same idea was formulated in more general terms, namely that the process of investing in forms is an inevitable selective process, whereby some elements are sifted out and stabilized to hold together, while others are sacrificed (Thévenot 1984, 2009).[31] According to Busch, standards make things *zuhanden*. He draws upon Heidegger's ideas of *Zuhandenheit*, which denotes the handiness or readiness-to-hand of tools in relation to human practice and not their mere being there (*Vorhandensein*) (Busch 2011: 30). A saw when used can reveal other things about a tree than just its value as an object of contemplation. When standards make things *zuhanden*, this means that the very application/implementation of standards enables the users to perceive properties of the world that otherwise would not be revealed. Further, it enables them to have certain aspects of the world enframed, ready-to-hand, as a 'standing reserve' that can be converted into a resource for action (ibid.: 30–32). The bowls and bottles are crucial and function as standards in a setting where the fairness of exchanges is an issue; they provide women with some security in acting.

Measurements – Evidence of Equivalence

There is a standard concerning which bottle to use for oil and which bowls to use to exchange flour. Yet, even when the same bowl size is employed, because only the volume is measured, its content can vary significantly. Next, I analyse the way in which women seek to determine the equivalency of exchanges – that is, precisely how full the bowl should be.

It is already an unbearably hot morning. I am sick with a fever and digestive problems, feeling too ill to get up. I am lying on an old bed in Hamda's hut, facing towards the wall to signal that I want peace and quiet and to be left alone. Only Hamda is inside the house, working on some embroidery. I hear her seven-year-old daughter enter. Hamda gasps, then reviles someone as *šarmūṭa* (slut, prostitute). Startled, I turn around and see Hamda squatting near her hearth with a small metal bowl in her hand. She and her daughter look at the flour inside the bowl. Then she places the bowl on the floor and gently taps it on the side with her fingers until it levels out.

Hamda forms a fist with her right hand and stretches her little finger out straight, extending it into the bowl. The hand rests on the rim. Her fingertip sits on the flour's surface and her finger stretches along the inside of the bowl, slightly beyond the mid-finger joint. Then she holds her hand up, extending her little finger, and places her thumb's tip on the spot where the bowl's rim had met her finger. 'She is stingy, by God, is she ever stingy', mutters Hamda. 'I gave her this much', moving her thumb upwards to the joint at the end of the finger. Hamda sends her daughter off with the bowl, telling her to say to her neighbour Museilma that it is too little. A few minutes later the girl returns, informing Hamda that Museilma added some flour. Hamda repeats the procedure. She levels the flour in the bowl and measures the distance between its surface and the rim with her little finger. The bowl is fuller and the bowl's rim reaches decidedly below the mid-finger joint, but not near the amount Hamda had indicated. Shaking her head in disapproval and sighing, Hamda pours the flour into her plastic storage bag.

At first, I was puzzled by what Hamda was doing. Without her speaking, I could not make sense of it. Only when she moved her thumb to indicate the difference between where the flour reached in the bowl and where she remembered it reaching, when she lent it to Museilma, did I understand that Hamda was measuring. The little finger with its two joints – the end and mid-finger knuckles – served as a kind of yardstick to indicate the fullness of the bowl. Hamda claimed that the distance to the rim was only from the fingertip to shortly above the end joint when she gave Museilma flour. Museilma was reviled and accused of being stingy, of purposely returning a lesser amount of flour than she received: an amount that when levelled out in the bowl leaves a much greater distance to the rim, reaching below the mid-finger joint. By measuring this distance, Hamda attempted to establish evidence that Museilma reciprocated with too little and by sending her daughter back drew attention to her dissatisfaction. After Museilma added more flour, Hamda was still convinced she had given more, but refrained from pursuing the issue further, probably hesitant to enter into a fight. Whereas I cannot confirm the veracity of Hamda's claim, in view of the bowl's concave form, even slight differences of height amount to a significant difference in volume.

That Hamda measured the flour she lent indicates that she was concerned about a fair and equal exchange. Already when she sent Museilma the flour, she was suspicious about being cheated and perhaps imputed such motives. Instead of trusting the exchange partner, measuring the flour with these simple means implies an attempt to compare two amounts and to generate evidence about their quantity. As an evidentiary practice, measuring thus not only reveals something about the quantity of exchanged items but also allows the person carrying out the measurement to assess the quality of the sender in reciprocating, enabling a moral judgement (stingy, generous, accurate, etc.).

But why this attempt to measure flour accurately, if there are no means to enforce and prove a fair exchange of exactly the same amounts? Hamda felt cheated, but she let the issue rest. She knew she needed Museilma to borrow from her and would have to lend to her again, when she demanded it. Further, retaliating by lending or reciprocating a lesser amount during the next exchange in the long run could lead to a breakdown of much-needed cooperative relations. In view of the many fights surrounding food, its distribution, its scarcity and the need to rely on others to fill gaps, women tend to want exact equivalents of the most urgently required staples. The taken-for-grantedness of the three standard bowls supports this. Hamda's measurement with her little finger bespeaks this search for fair exchanges, something that guarantees the equivalence of exchanged quantities of flour and avoids 'losses' of this precious resource. It provided insurance when all assurance is lacking. Hamda planned ahead and envisioned a certain outcome, namely to prevent the eventuality of one-way flows or one-sided benefits.[32] Hence, I have argued that the exchange of staples is organized by a logic of balanced reciprocity – ideally exact equivalents are exchanged. Yet, this kind of logic was often associated more with market exchanges and distant ties, whereas a leaning towards generalized reciprocity was assumed in small, close-knit communities (Sahlins 1972: 204–206, 211–13; Polanyi 1944: 48).[33]

After observing Hamda's measurements, I paid close attention to what happened when bowls where reshuffled and noticed that Hamda was not the only one measuring what she handed out and received back. On one occasion I saw Umikhras assessing with her thumb how much flour another neighbour had returned to her. Sometime later, I was visiting another neighbour. She measured the amount of flour she lent by filling and counting tea glasses before emptying them into a bowl. Apart from that I did not see any of the other women attempt to measure and compare exchanged quantities. But a situation in Hamda's hut led me to suspect that these practices are more widespread.

Hamda, who would normally measure the amount of flour with her little finger, refrained from doing so in the company of other women. The situation I refer to occurred when Hamda had three women from the neighbourhood over and her daughter returned a small bowl with little flour in it. Observed by the other women, Hamda hesitated, inspected it only from afar while lying on the floor, and commented 'little'. Although she uttered her dissatisfaction about the inferior amount of what was sent back to her, Hamda did not attempt to assess by how much it fell short, compared to how much she remembered sending. She voiced some criticism publicly but eschewed demanding a larger share. Hamda's reactions were patterned after the exchange of sugar, where women publicly comment upon quantities but in a more playful, bargaining spirit. In this case, she tolerated the discrepancy without trying to reclaim what she considered a fairer balance. This indicates that practices to establish accurate equivalents are not highly esteemed socially and run counter to an ethos of generosity upon which I will expand in the next section. Therefore, they are largely practised in private and not exposed to public scrutiny. Extending the above argument, measuring not only enables one to make conclusions about the quantity of the flour and the qualities of the sender, but also subjects the recipient, i.e., the one who measures or not, to an evaluation of her motives. Measuring then more abstractly is a way to gauge social relationships between exchange partners.

Cooked Foods: Giving from Oneself

> Cast your bread upon the waters, for after many days
> you will find it again.
> – The Holy Bible, Ecclesiastes 11:1,
> *New International Version* (1984)

In this section I focus on another form of cooperation, namely the exchange of cooked foods. Women often sent small amounts of prepared dishes to neighbouring women, especially when they had rare ingredients. I noticed this very soon after my arrival in Um Futeima, when I was sitting together with Hamda's daughters on a large mat in front of her house after dinner. Dinner had consisted of a plain ⁣*ᶜabūda* with salt and oil. Then a girl arrived from the direction of the mosque carrying a small metal bowl, issuing a sweet and earthy odour. The metal bowl contained a small portion of food: two and a half loafs of *kisra*, a flat, very thin and slightly sour sorghum bread that is consumed across north-eastern Sudan, covered with a warm sauce containing onions, oil, potatoes and lentils. 'Where is this from?' I asked as the women called me to join them in eating it. 'This is Saliya's *karāma*', one of Hamda's daughters replied. Hamda added, 'Taste it, ya Santara! She wants us to taste her sauce'. After eating the rough, crunchy and dry *ᶜabūda* bread for days, tasting the sauce's creamy texture, the small lumps of potato and the crisp onions in it and the delicate, sour *kisra* was delightful.

Saliya and her co-wife Birkiya are some of Hamda's closest neighbours, but they are not longtime acquaintances. The family hails from another clan and settled in Um Futeima in late 2009. The women regularly cooperated with Hamda and other women in exchanging staples. Yet, Saliya's sending samples of her food to Hamda is called *karāma*. *Karāma* literally means generosity and dignity. Material objects, what was given, the open-handed disposition of which it was given, and the act of giving are critical components of *karāma*. When I enquired about the reasons for this gift of food – why had Saliya sent the food to Hamda? – the women retorted that she did so on her own, she gave it from herself, indicating the incalculable and utterly voluntary aspects of these gifts. Giving food gifts enables women such as Hamda and Saliya, who regularly assess the equivalence of exchanges, to experience themselves as generous in a setting of scarcity. Generosity was one of the most highly esteemed qualities and was needed to build social ties with other women.

A point made famous by Claude Lévi-Strauss (1969b) in *The Raw and the Cooked* is that the transformation of food items in their raw states into cooked foods is by extension the very process of turning nature into culture. Between raw and cooked lie the many transformations of the material through preparation, seasoning and cooking, which give each food item its unique shape, flavour, texture and smell (Lévi-Strauss 1969b: 142–43; Sutton 2010). Although the dualism in Lévi-Strauss's work has been criticized for taking the abstract ideals too literally and missing the many discontinuities (Descola 2009: 113), this perspective does highlight a special property of cooked food: as a cultural artefact it is invested with the work and efforts that women expend in preparing food. Staples, in contrast, figure as raw products, which are not invested with care and diligent effort to transform them into another state, yet they can be exchanged easily.

Thus, cooked foods are invested with other values and higher affective dimensions than staples (Alexeyeff 2004). Homemade food is something that should be tasted and enjoyed; it expresses intimacy and can initiate social ties. Therefore, it is not made the object of direct exchange and calculations in Um Futeima. Another dimension of the food in its natural and raw state is its natural transformation through putrefaction – the rotten (Lévi-Strauss 1969b: 142–43). In view of climatic conditions in Sudan, cooked food especially is easily perishable. Bread will dry out and spoil easily, whereas flour will last much longer. Given that cooked food cannot be stored for a long time and especially in view of the difficult climatic conditions in Sudan, leftovers or surpluses are stored in social relationships by sending cooked foods to other households.

Similar to the exchanges of staples, bowls of cooked food were also reshuffled frequently. Yet only very small portions were given and diverse bowls were employed as vessels. It is usually plain bread leftovers that would harden overnight that are passed on, but at times vegetables and very rarely meat sauces were added. Children often transported these bowls, but in contrast to the exchange of staples, women did not hesitate to carry these bowls themselves to other women. As gifts that reflect positively upon the giver, they are not associated with the delicate deliberations about whom to approach to satisfy an urgent need, who might have some staples to exchange, who can be approached again, who might reject one's request for flour and so on, and thus the women did not necessarily need to rely upon the children's porterage. What is important about these types of food gifts is that only women profit from them. Men, even if present, were not offered any of this food, and children were likewise not invited to share in consuming cooked foods sent by other women.

Women talked of these food gifts as coming from oneself and *karāma*, generous deeds, indicating a desire to please others, to show them goodwill. In the chapter 2 discussion of the charity's distribution, I showed that there is a difference between the principles of generosity and charity for the poor, both of which are called *karāma*. I argued that the latter was invoked mainly as a discursive resource pertaining to the charity's distribution, while in other situations charity involves condescension and people who count as poor are disdained as incapable and weak. Thus, generosity is not charity and women rarely gave cooked foods to their impoverished neighbours, but rather most transfers occurred between the very same households participating in the exchange of staple foods. I argue that this circle of exchanging cooked foods is based upon the principle of generalized reciprocity and represents a way of forging bonds through social obligations among women who find themselves in similar situations. Thereby it figures as a way to soften the deliberate calculations and measurements pertaining to the exchange of staples, while at the same time gifts of food raise the expectation that the recipients give something back whenever they have something to share, generating debts and obligations.

Still, *karāma* is not solely the lubricant of direct exchange; food exchange also entails irreducibly affective dimensions. The concept of *karāma* is not simply a norm of generosity and charity, but also an emotion that women express in action, namely, giving generously. *Karāma* as a disposition stirred the women and motivated the gift of food. Hamda and her daughters described this as a desire to give that arose in people on its own and prompted actions (*min hālha 'arsalat*). The gift then expresses the women's large-heartedness and open-handedness and becomes the *karāma*. It also produces another emotion in the receiving and indebted party, to wit bashfulness (*tahaššud*) (W. Young 1988: 413–14), an eschewing of further favours and an urge to reciprocate. In his study of nomadic Rashaida, Young talks of a 'circle of conassociation', social ties marked by commensality without bashfulness, the ability to accept food and drink without polite reluctance (ibid.: 117–18, 122–23). In this novel situation of settlement, where fights about food often escalated, I could not identify a circle of conassociation, but rather both freely sharing and unrestrained fighting for food from the same hearth was narrowly defined by co-residence and kinship. Yet, there was a similar finding to Young's, namely, that people generally sought to avoid a situation in which they were only at the receiving end, because in that case the giver's condescension mirrors their perceived incapacity and wretchedness. Bashfulness held them back from accepting further favours and gifts, as in Birkiya's case above. Therefore, participation in the exchange circle of cooked food was also guided by the ability to participate in sending, receiving and reciprocating, although the material equivalence and the length between prestation and counterprestation were purposely not defined.

Bashfulness, as the virtue produced by gifts of cooked food and the inability to reciprocate, works against the most destitute. Instead of a principle that encourages charity for the poor, *karāma* constrains people such as Birkiya, who could not reciprocate, from demanding inclusion in the exchange circle.[34] Yet cooked food – returning to Sahlins's point – can also figure as a starting mechanism of social relationships and can be the springboard for inclusion in the exchange circle. Zeinab and her daughters, who due to their poverty did not participate in the lending and borrowing of staples, sent *karāma* of cooked food to Hamda and other women in the neighbourhood whenever they had some special food items. They therewith produced obligations in them to reciprocate at some point in time. During my presence in Um Futeima, after having twice received a gift of cooked food from Zeinab, once even including two or three pieces of meat, Hamda felt compelled to return some cooked food, *kisra* and dried okra sauce, after only a few days.

The Researcher's Food Dealings with Hosts

In view of the scarcity of food, the strictness around its exchange and distribution as well as its affective materiality substantiate the delicate nature of food dealings. Even though I was very frank about my connections solely to the university, Hamda and her daughters believed that something exceptional was due to come their way through me. As a foreigner, I was considered by people to be a powerful and rich gift-giver.[35] I was powerful based on my relative wealth, but I was not powerful in actually implementing my initial ideas on how to transfer some of it by giving food to my host. The way in which I inserted myself into everyday food exchange was not appreciated. A foreigner was not supposed to be there, was not supposed to suffer want and be hungry, and was not supposed to engage in food exchange.

Aware of scarce food supplies in Um Futeima,[36] I pushed my way into the food cycle by what I viewed as a compromise between my desire to study conflicts around food distribution and what I considered a moral imperative to avoid adding to the exhaustion of already scarce food supplies. I paid for food staples that Hamda's household would normally consume from my purse, without actively introducing other edibles. Whereas the women felt obliged to accept the food I gave, they were dissatisfied when I supplied them with what they would normally consume in the quantities that they would normally consume.

After a trip to the market, I overheard one of Hamda's neighbours asking her whether I had bought Hamda a generous gift (*karāma*) from the market, referring to food. To my surprise Hamda told them: 'no, she didn't bring a thing to us'.[37] Flustered, I began to discern a discrepancy between the women's expectations and mine. An obvious problem was that Hamda and her daughters received only the amounts of food they normally would receive from sheikh Tahir, who was in charge of providing for them. There was no benefit, nothing more than the usual for Hamda that resulted from my presence. Tahir saved the money that I had spent on staples; thus he alone benefitted. Hamda was not indifferent to my intervention. She told me in a deep and clear voice, 'Tahir buys the sorghum'. How was this meant? Hamda remained silent.

I had to find a more direct way to compensate her and her daughters for the food I consumed in their home, bypassing male mediation. I thus undertook another effort to shape our food relations: I began to purchase regular food items at the two tiny and more expensive grocery stores on the other side of the village, which I could directly hand over to Hamda, such as oil, tea, sugar or coffee.[38] After two or three weeks neighbours from the other side of the village came over for coffee and again I overheard a conversation among the women, who initially assumed I understood less of their conversation than I actually did.

While Hamda was preparing coffee, the women were talking about meat and one woman asked Hamda, in disbelief, whether I really had not fetched them any. 'She doesn't bring [things]', replied Hamda. 'We are eating just the bread there'. Then one of Hamda's daughters stated that at times I ate bread when she herself was still hungry. Her mother hissed at her to be quiet, telling the neighbours and me not to pay attention to her daughter. I instantly felt very uncomfortable. I had been charged with unsociable behaviour, of taking more food that I was entitled to, eating more than I was supplying.

In this situation my behaviour and contribution to the food system were explicitly evaluated, as it is commonly done among members of Hamda's household. Dropping the rhetoric of hospitality and politeness, in this regard I was treated as an equal, someone who could be directly and openly criticized. On the other hand, I could never be of their 'economic kind': I was continually inserting food into the exchange cycle through my host's household and yet it was not seen as enough. I was considered stingy for providing people with what they normally would eat, in the quantities that they would normally consume, even if it came from my purse. My purchases of everyday food items were not considered as part of a fair exchange. People's expectation was that my presence as a foreigner would lead to something extraordinary, some advancement, something that they could tell other people about. This also reverberated in women's demands (see chapter 2, during the distribution) that I fetch them camel meat because as a foreigner and guest I could claim a privileged access to it for the benefit of 'my family'. Since Hamda and her daughters could never acknowledge our situation as being similar or of a kind, they were closed to the possibility of entering into reciprocal food relations with me and could not appreciate the food I brought as part of a fair deal. Loftsdóttir (2002: 303) recalled that 'you can make friends with people who are so much poorer than you. You will forget the difference of power but they cannot, because the former is a luxury which you can afford but they not'. Whereas I thought in terms of reimbursing Hamda for the costs my presence inflicted upon her household, my hosts thought in terms of gains. I then began to purchase extraordinary and more expensive things from time to time, food items that are considered luxuries, for instance, lentils, rice, pealed sorghum grains, fresh fruits, biscuits and meat. While this settled for a short while the direct accusation levelled against me, it did not quell the overall tensions around food among my host family; often they then fought about what I had brought. Having thus illustrated the delicate nature of food dealings in this setting of scarcity and especially the expectations that my presence raised, I now want to reflect more on the various ways in which equivalences, ideas of fairness and social relationships are connected.

Exchanges and Their Limits in Existential Situations

Given that food, unlike other commodities, is urgent, many authors emphasize that its exchange is viewed as immoral and there is a moral imperative to share it without calculation.[39] The prevalence of the second circle of exchange concerning cooked foods points in a similar direction. Women stressed that generosity motivated them to give and that the gift itself was their generosity. That women made this logic explicit while trying to hide their measurements highlights the fact that giving freely and the norm of generalized reciprocity is still more acceptable in food dealings. I connected womens' desire to establish exact equivalents in their lending and borrowing of staples to the novel situation of suddenly disrupted food supplies in the settlement (related to the boom in gold mining). Women are under pressure to seek predictability concerning their most vital food needs, while relegating generosity and the social ties it engenders to a less essential kind of exchange. This poses thorny questions regarding morality and agency when survival is at stake. How can we conceive of agency at all when a person is hungry and what does the refusal to give food imply? To master these enormous uncertainties of daily life, what understandings of needs and options did women develop in the situation? How did they calculate and plan ahead or conversely which things did they take for granted?

The Ambiguity of Standards

> The push to standardize presumes the ability to constrain a phenomenon within a particular set of dimensions, as well as the ability to dictate behavior to achieve the narrowly defined dimensions that stipulate its outcome.
> – Lampland and Star 2009: 14

Standardization is a measure that women in Um Futeima implement to create a predictable outcome.[40] In a situation of exhausted supplies and frequent episodes of hunger or 'avoiding eating', standards for exchange facilitate cooperation because they enable women to estimate what will be returned in the very near future and further reduce uncertainty by making things ready-to-hand for action. The standard of the vessels for exchanging oil and flour was established successfully. It had become a type of commonsense knowledge, which provided semantic security because it was so obvious that it did not have to be articulated verbally. Although the standard may appear small and unimportant, much energy needs to be expended to establish and to maintain it (Lampland and Star 2009: 13). Thévenot (2007, 2009: 795) stresses the heavy costs or sacrifices such operations inevitably entail, which are always connected to the possibility of doubt about what was sacrificed, i.e., diversity for universality. However, the enormous effort which is required until something is taken for granted as a standard may also explain why some standards endure obstinately or, as asserted by Bowker and Star (1999: 14), can account for their 'inertia'. As a procedure, standardization sifts out the unlimited variation of things and establishes a type that can serve as a reference for qualification of the exchanged good, its vessel, the sender and the receiver, revealing novel things about their properties (see Boltanski 2011: 69).

With regard to lending and borrowing, women had to remember the size of vessels. Whereas the bowls are standards, which aim at creating equivalences, the women were employing different means to assess the quantities of flour in the bowl. I argue that these types of measurement are evidentiary practices that women employed to reflect upon, test and judge the situations in which they interacted with other women, the principles of cooperation, and the qualities of their exchange partners. Thereby, measuring enables women to assess motives, to plan their own actions as well as future engagements with other women. Measuring itself is therefore not a part of standardization, but it is closely linked to the standard of the bowls that is purposely kept flexible and ambiguous, leaving room for trade-offs, tinkering, calculations and subversion. It is in this space between a woman's private measurements of the amounts of flour that she lends and what she measures when it returns that social relations come into play. Here, in this ambiguous and private space surrounding the standard, where women measure, compare, contemplate and evaluate the exchange, they also reflect upon whether to ignore disparities, or to pursue a more equal exchange by making their discomfort public, or even to insist on their understanding of a fair exchange, risking a fight.

In Um Futeima, the attempt to establish equivalences was geared towards establishing a stable relationship between what was borrowed and returned. Standards thereby figure as institutionalized equivalences that have become common sense and are taken for granted, offering predictability or, in the case of deviance, a stable type to which critique can refer. Hamda's measurements suggest that the exchanged staples were compared quantitatively, but without means of assessing or proving their exact equality. Still, Hamda evaluated what Museilma had sent her and perceived the amount as too little. Unable to accept what she understood as an imbalance in exchange, Hamda sent the flour back, renegotiating its quantity. After her neighbour had added more flour, Hamda still viewed herself as the losing party in this exchange. But evidently she evaluated this discrepancy in the exchanged quantities as tolerable, preferring her disadvantage over the damage that persisting in her own understandings of fairness might have inflicted on her relationship with Museilma. Thus, Hamda placed the maintenance of a certain quality of relationship above the pursuit of an exact equivalence in this situation. Importantly then, the exchanges of staples are always subject to evaluation in line with women's ideas of fairness, that is in/tolerable discrepancies in the exchanged quantities. Thereby, the boundary of what is tolerated as a deviance from the ideal of equal, final exchange balances shifts according to the social relations between women.

Thus, the fact that Hamda felt cheated by Museilma but let the issue rest after complaining once and returning the bowl to Museilma allows for speculation over standards and their properties. When standards are somewhat flexible, this can even be advantageous, because they allow creative in-situ adaptations. Timmermans and Epstein (2010: 81), for instance, suggest that 'loose standards' often operate better than overly rigid ones.[41] Concomitantly, standards are also threatened by too much flexibility that would render them ineffective. These authors further (ibid.) note: 'The trick in standardization appears to be to find a balance between flexibility and rigidity and to trust users with the right amount of agency to keep a standard sufficiently uniform for the task at hand'. At times women succeeded and the problem of coordination in uncertain circumstances did not translate into a conflict. At other times, it made more sense to women in the situation to pursue a fight concerning the standard, especially when they felt repeatedly disadvantaged.

Unbalanced Exchanges: Deliberating Options

When staples are exhausted, women are pressed to fill the gaps or to avoid eating, the latter hardly being a sustainable practice. I have described two types of food exchange. To swap staples, women first had to appreciate their own situation and assess which of the women with whom they were cooperating might have the desired staples. Simultaneously, they projected their relationships with their neighbours both into the past and future, reflecting on the equivalence of past exchanges and future engagements with envisioned exchange partners. Crucial questions included whose husband was successful in gold mining, who had recently returned with some money or from the market, and the length of the interval between the last exchange. For example, I described above a situation in which Hamda sought to borrow flour from Umikhras. Hamda sent her daughter to Umikhras's house because her husband Qismallah had returned during the night from gold mining. At breakfast, gathering around the fire, talk had concentrated on the amount of money that Qismallah's mining team had made. Hamda thus rightly anticipated that Umikhras's stocks had been replenished overnight. This explains why she sent her daughter there on this occasion and not, for example, to Museilma, whose husband had been absent for more than two weeks.

Another exchange that I described was when Hamda had lent Museilma flour. Thereby the former felt betrayed but grudgingly accepted an imbalance in exchanges. How did this perceived imbalance on Hamda's part affect her disposition towards further exchanges and how did it then translate into the next situation? I could not observe any differences in Hamda's daily neighbourly dealings with Museilma or attitude towards her. A few weeks later, however, one of Hamda's grown daughters got into a fight with Museilma concerning exchanged quantities of flour, whereby she referred to past transactions – including the one described – between her mother and Museilma. The claim was that Museilma routinely returned less, to Hamda's detriment. In view of Hamda's severe punishment of her daughter for her misbehaviour in her private home, I doubt that she agreed with her daughter's comportment. Yet, the fact that her daughter, who was not present to witness this specific exchange, knew about it shows that Hamda aired her dissatisfaction with this specific exchange and Museilma's alleged niggardliness.

In this particular case the imbalance affected not only Hamda's expectations and wishes for fairer exchanges, but also prompted her daughter's refusal to bear up under what she perceived to be an injustice. The procedure of measuring, the perceived lack of equivalency in exchange, and the verbal articulation of inequivalence affect dispositions for further actions and may narrow the willingness to tolerate discrepancies without protest. However, Museilma did not send back more flour when Hamda's daughter protested, but rather after two days invited her to a special meal of *kisra* and lentils to appease her, mending their personal relationships by offering a sensual experience that can arouse emotions – the taste of palatable food.

I have also reflected on my own engagements with the women in my host household, which they perceived as unfair in view of their heightened expectations of me as an economically powerful foreigner. By means of several critiques, some more subtle, others more direct, the women pointed to a limit in our reciprocal engagements. As I responded reflexively, they used me to bypass the men and gain access to other, rarer food items. We developed a form of cooperation through our interactions, a form that had emancipatory properties in a setting of utter scarcity and female dependence upon established structures of provisioning. In this sense, the way of organizing and adjusting material relations revealed not only the women's interpretations and expectations of me but also their critical abilities and their attempts to negotiate a greater range of manoeuvres in view of existential shortages.

Kinship and Economic Strata

An intuitive approach in anthropology would be to relate the type of exchange to kinship distance, as is done for instance by Sahlins (1972) with regard to this formal principle. This is also supported by other studies that indicate that the closer the kin ties, especially when overlapping with affinal ties, the less the inclination to business and the greater the proclivity to trust in balancing things out in the long run (Rottenburg 1991: 102). Concerning the two types of exchange presented above, kinship in its formalistic sense is, however, not a principle that oriented coordination among cooperating married women in this existential setting in rural Sudan. The logic of balanced reciprocity was the organizing factor in the exchange of staples, whereby women cooperated pragmatically with their neighbours – both kin and non-kin – to fill urgent supply gaps. The exchange of cooked foods, in contrast, followed a logic of generalized reciprocity. Expressed in terms of generosity, an emotion that welled up in the giver and prompted actions, women gave freely to other women – a gift in the Maussian sense. Sahlins (1972: 186) in one astute line proposes an answer to 'transcend the Hobbesian chaos', namely that giving initiates social bonds: 'If gifts make friends, then friends make gifts'. The flow of *karāma* is then oriented towards instigating and strengthening social ties among women and, following the same logic after those bonds have been forged, they prompt further gifts to maintain them. It is not about kinship but about making friends through gifts.

Above I mentioned that women who perceived themselves as somehow 'the same' cooperated in filling supply gaps. This sameness relates to a similar economic situation: Hamda received food gifts, small bowls of cooked items, mainly from women with which she also engaged in lending and borrowing staples but also from four other women, who were considered too poor to participate in the exchange of staples.[42] She sent *karāma* most frequently to four of the six women who cooperated with her. The women with whom Hamda exchanged staples all are married women whose husbands earned more or less regular incomes and replenished their most essential staples. Hamda's closest relative among the six – both through kinship and affinity – is Tahir's wife, who was rarely the beneficiary of Hamda's *karāma*, likely due to the overall tensions. Zeinab, who sent cooked foods to Hamda, was also only seldom considered. Overall, amity or at least the desire for friendly relations between certain women defined this form of prestation, in which cooked food was used to express a tender feeling towards someone, instigating bonds of friendship and obligation. It thus makes sense to differentiate at least two economic strata that have a bearing on the flow of exchanges: women whose husbands earn incomes and manage to restock supplies; and poor women, who do not dispose of their own food regularly. For the women, I was on another economic strata, far beyond their own means. Because I was not of Hamda's economic kind, I could not engage with her as an equal.

Economic standing affects who is considered an appropriate partner for exchange. Poor people could not exchange staples, but they could make gifts and they did so whenever they could to forge supportive relationships. It is thus not kinship distance as an abstract normative principle that determined the relationships of women, but rather bonds created through daily interactions and negotiations, experiencing daily uncertainties and cooperating to delimit them. While women built and invested in social bonds by giving and exchanging food, they discursively stressed the importance of kin ties, claiming that kin were the only source of help in times of adversity. There is a particularly affirmative discourse on the role of father's brothers' sons and the normative expectation that they will help (Miller 2007: 538). I will return to this issue in the next chapter when I discuss health crises. These expectations concern help in cases of emergency, but importantly people did not mention these kinds of supports in relation to overcoming the gruelling uncertainties of dwindling supplies.

Conclusion

I am sitting in the house of one of Hamda's daughter, who is preparing coffee, while I am conversing with her husband. When she serves us the coffee, it is bland without ginger and cloves to spice it. Her husband gets angry and pours out his coffee on the floor, shouting, 'There is no use for this coffee. There is no taste. Don't you have any neighbours, woman?' Thereby, he squarely delegated the responsibility for replenishing supplies to his wife, a responsibility that is customarily considered to be his. His wife remains silent.

When food runs out in Um Futeima, women are expected to develop ways of coping with gaps in their food supplies until their male breadwinners return and/or manage to restock their supplies. Women experienced this as a vexing uncertainty that left them worried and dependent upon others. I outlined two circles of exchange through which women dealt with this difficulty – the exchange of staples and of cooked foods. The staple food circle was marked by women's careful attention that equivalent amounts were exchanged and by their attempts to produce standards. The latter was characterized by a rhetoric of generosity and giving that springs from an inner motivation without calculations. However, because the latter did not predominantly address the neediest but occurred mainly along the same set of relationships through which staples were exchanged, I interpreted this form as a way of taking away the bite of direct exchange. It buffered its calculative features, while offering women a space to experience themselves as generous in spite of the overall scarcity of provisions. Gifts (*karāma*) produced bashfulness (*taḥaššud*) only among the poor in view of their indebtedness and inability to reciprocate. It is this inability to reciprocate in kind and within a certain time span that explains why people such as Birkiya had to resort to other networks in times of need. The community – especially Um Futeima, as a recent conglomerate – did not appear as a locus for aiding the poor. Existential uncertainties and the supply gaps befell most women from time to time, irrespective of whether they were counted among the most economically precarious or not. Although there are wealth differentials in Um Futeima, the standard of living is low and barely suffices to support lives. The general scarcity of resources may explain why generalized reciprocity, which is considered to emerge especially in settings with substantial differentials of wealth, was not the dominant principle of coordination. Instead, balanced reciprocity was the organizing factor in the exchange of staples. None of the women who were in roughly the same economic situation should profit to the detriment of another.

Debates on balanced reciprocity tend to focus on the exchange of equivalents, but pay little or no attention to the social work that lies behind the production of such forms. In this setting of hunger, women regulated their material interactions by selecting some aspects and turning them into standards. Once achieved, as in the case of the three bowls, they facilitated interactions and made them more predictable. The measurement of exchanged flour is a practice which aims at comparing quantities and qualities of engaged entities. The practice of measuring indicates the ambiguity and flexibility of the standards, opening a space for deliberations, negotiations and adjustments.

Gaps in the food supply are problems that have to be overcome in order to satisfy daily food needs. Standardization of exchanges can be read as an attempt to provide a technical solution to a problem of social coordination in existential circumstances. Closing a gap in one's food supply means causing a gap for another woman or at least speeding up the exhaustion of her food supplies, and thus relocates and spreads uncertainty among women. Women improvise with regard to how they make sense of what is at stake in the situation and how they understand prior exchanges and what is expected of them. Thereby they strike a delicate balance between the equivalence of exchanges (quantities), their relations to other women and their actions (expectations, outcomes, motives), and their own emotions (anxiety, desperation, generosity, bashfulness) in perceiving the situation and evaluating its fairness. Women thus have to understand the expectations of others in relation to their own interpretation of the situation; they need to be aware of established principles and the moral understandings expressed in them, and to adapt this to their own often urgent situations. In view of much uncertainty, women frequently fail to do so smoothly. The prevalence of discord and fights about food attests to this failure.

Notes

1. Hamda, for instance, had a small herd of goats until 2009, shortly before she settled at Um Futeima. She remembers herding as 'sweet' – at least she had milk that she could drink or exchange. Some impoverished women have resorted to rain-fed sorghum farming or have supported their husbands in agricultural labour in the past, but this is disdained as shameful and since 2007 a Sahelian drought cycle had foreclosed this option.

2. To borrow food from a store, the man in charge will usually have to establish ties with the shopkeeper, which can be maintained by his children in his absence, but they demand a reliable routine in lending and settling debts. The poor are known, however, and they are unable to draw upon new credit with the grocery stores until their pre-existing debts have been settled.

3. Literature on drought and famine in Sudan suggests that pastoralists in particular resort to wild foods in times of crisis (De Waal 2005 [1989]). Also Rashaida commonly name a number of wild plants that they used to consume while migrating, but to my knowledge none of the women in the settlement collected and consumed these plants. This was partly because they were not in season, but the more frequent reaction was *al-balad da kaʿb* (this land is no good).

4. See De Waal (2005 [1989]) for pastoralists' reaction to the great Sahelian famine of 1984–1985 in Darfur and Spittler (1989) for reactions of Kel Ewey in Niger during the same drought period.

5. As Sahlins (1972: 37–39) suggests, poverty and infinite needs should be understood as the invention of modernizing civilization.

6. See Evans-Pritchard (1969: 85) for an assumption about solidarity in small communities.

7. A proclivity in anthropology has been to emphasize solidarity, gifts and emotions, especially in non-Western, non-capitalist societies, while downplaying people's concomitant calculation, selfishness and profit-seeking. In their volume on *Money and the Morality of Exchange*, Parry and Bloch (1989: 3–6) offer pungent critiques of such dichotomization – the glorification of solidarity and morality in gift economies as well as the demonization of money. A case in point is Parry's own contribution to the volume (1989), in which he shows that among Hindus in India some gifts are associated with sin and evil, whereas the profits from some commercial dealings are interpreted as innocent and morally neutral. A similar but more recent contribution to the debate was made by Daniel Miller (1998) in his study of consumption on a shopping street in North London. He also points out an inverse relationship between commodities and gifts: shopping for consumption is described as a predominantly female act of love for the family. Women express their care and affection by purchasing groceries that match their family members' needs and/or preferences. Simultaneously, Miller shows that shopping for gifts – far from being disinterested and voluntary – involves much forethought and calculation. The status quo of real-life relationships between them and other people is then assessed and materializes as a gift with a certain price tag.

8. Lévi-Strauss (1969a), for instance, speaks of restricted and generalized exchange. Restricted change would be the direct exchange of sisters for marriage, whereas generalized exchange demands trust. For example, 'A surrenders a daughter or a sister to B, who surrenders one to C, who, in turn, will surrender one to A' (ibid.: 265). In the middle of these two extremes, there is delayed exchange, which entails a short cycle of reciprocity. As Mauss (1954) already established, exchange has various dimensions.

9. Another well-known example are three hierarchical spheres (subsistence goods, prestige goods with brass rods as currency, and rights for humans, especially marriageable women) among Tiv in Nigeria, running from market to gift exchange (Bohannon and Bohannon 1968).

10. Since Karl Polanyi's (1944, 1957) critique of assumptions in mainstream economics, which postulates the maximizing rationales of the individual, highlighting the 'embeddedness' of economic institutions in an integrated system of various social institutions has become a penchant in economic anthropology. Polanyi's intellectual heirs dealt in what appeared as clear oppositions between traditional/modern, precapitalist/ capitalist, gift/commodity, and perhaps too uncritically proposed a 'great transformation' based on monetization (Parry and Bloch 1989: 12; cf. Bohannan and Bohannan 1968; Taussig 1980). The moral consequences of mediating exchange by means of money and its gradual, creative introduction into subsistence economies constitutes another important field of anthropological scholarship. Examples taken from such literature are

the payment of bride wealth in cattle and money, sharing farmwork reciprocally and hiring wage labour, investing 'devilish' or 'bitter money' only in certain economic spheres and so on (Taussig 1980; Shipton 1989; for Sudan, see Barth 1967; Duffield 1981; Omer 1985; Rottenburg 1991). Studies, especially in the Marxist tradition, tended to condemn money as a 'radical leverer' and as the root of evil, holding it accountable for the demise of intercommunal solidarity and the rise of individual profit-seeking. This risks developing a blind spot regarding 'the importance of money in many "traditional", pre-capitalist economies' (Parry and Bloch 1989: 4–7, on 7; Fuller 1989).

11. Wendy James contested Barth's view that labour is exchanged for beer, by showing that it is labour that is exchanged for labour. This point is further elaborated by Rottenburg (1991: 84), who discusses exchange patterns and their relation to capital accumulation, specifically Moro strategies to integrate monetary elements into the subsistence economy.

12. Boltanski and Thévenot (2006) not only stress the plurality of principles of coordination that can be used to justify actions, but also their orientation towards other higher common goods, i.e., efficiency in the so-called industrial world, profit in the market world, tradition and hierarchy in the domestic world, and the various compromises that are stabilized among these. An analogous approach is proposed by Daniel Miller (1997) in his study of capitalism in Trinidad. He analyses how commodities emerge through branding, advertising and consumption as complex symbolic formations. Instead of being associated only with profitability issues, commodities are invested with aesthetic values throughout production, distribution and consumption, whereby the aesthetic attributes are reinterpreted in line with broader trends and desires (D. Miller 1997: 4).

13. For an overview of the anthropology of food, see Messer (1984), Shipton (1990) and Mintz and Du Bois (2002). There is an anthropological literature on food related to religious practice, focused around themes such as rituals, feasting, sacrifice, classifications and taboos (Radcliffe-Brown 1971b[1952]; Douglas 1996; Lévi-Strauss 1969b; Goody 1982: 10, 11). Whereas the classification of things as edible or not plays an important role in what is considered as food by Rashaida in Sudan, this chapter does not deal with Islamic prescriptions (halāl) and cultural preferences concerning a wide range of things that could be consumed but rather only looks at the exchange of things already qualified as food.

14. Extending this thought, Mol (2009) asserts that normativity can be embodied in the ability to discern good tastes, which are not only oriented towards pleasure but are shaped in complex socio-material practices with a view to a variety of other common goods as well, i.e., sustainability.

15. Avieli (2009) offers a critique of studies that stress the functions of food or abstract underlying structural patterns without attending to the specific meanings of foods consumed at particular events. He analyses a Christmas breakfast among a Protestant community in Hoi An, central Vietnam. He relates different culinary codes, which establish a reference to the Jewish Maccabees and the French colonizers, to the community's dually marginal position – as Christians in overwhelmingly Buddhist Vietnam and as Protestants in Vietnam's predominantly Catholic Christian minority.

16. Appadurai (1981) draws attention specifically to the immaterial properties of food, that is how food can be used to challenge or preserve social relations.

17. Carsten (1997: 107–28) relates how in Kedah people refer to the provision of food from the same hearth as producing a sort of 'shared substance', transforming the blood in bodies and therewith kinship. The bad taste of food can also be used as a reason to refuse social intimacy; see Sutton (2010: 212–13).

18. The staple I am mainly considering is flour; this is of course not raw but a product which involves much work, but since flour is bought in this context, it is treated like a raw item. Lévi-Strauss (1969b) drew attention to different categorizations of food, famously 'the raw' and 'the cooked'. The former stands for nature and the latter for its transformed state, culture. In this sense, 'cooking brings about the cultural transformation of the raw' (Lévi-Strauss 1969b: 142).

19. Two of Hamda's married daughters live in huts next to hers with their husbands. The third daughter and her son live in Hamda's house. Her husband migrated to Kuwait two years ago with Hamda's husband.

20. Men will not eat with women for fear they might be menstruating, which in their understanding might cause them to become ritually unclean. Women, in turn, refrain from eating with children who are too small to keep themselves clean and to eat cleanly (using the unclean left hand).

21. Men have access to other kinds of foods and fill up on beans and meat when they go the market or work at the gold mines.

22. 'Household' here simply denotes those living in her house (*bait*). When I talk of household or house then I refer to a linguistic convention among Rashaida, whereby upon marriage women receive a tent (or house) which is then named after her (W. Young 1988). Accordingly, I was living in '*bait* Hamda'. I do not mean the extended household, which in Hamda's case numbered twenty people in the settlement, including myself. The twenty people are named after the senior man, sheikh Tahir, 'those of Tahir' (*dhuwī* Tahir). Whereas there is some measure of commensality among *dhuwī* Tahir, only Hamda and three of her married daughters and husbands share all their meals.

23. For instance, Evans-Pritchard (1969: 85) interprets the ways in which Nuer shared food functionally as reinforcing generalized reciprocity: 'This habit of share and share alike is easily understandable in a community where everyone is likely to find himself in difficulties from time to time, for it is scarcity and not sufficiency that makes people generous, since everybody is thereby insured against hunger. He who is in need today receives help from him who may be in need tomorrow'.

24. This observation resonates with Carsten (2004), who posited that kinship needs to be revisited, as many presentations have overemphasized cohesion and solidarity, neglecting conflict.

25. This is again expressed by reference to their material endowments. The poor are those who do not have a thing (*mā ʿindahum ḥāǧa*); see chapter 2.

26. As girls near adolescence they may no longer go near the grocery stores, whereas boys begin to shun female association in the homes as early as the age of six or seven (W. Young 1988) and no longer transport things between women.

27. In households without young girls, or when they are sick, married women transport water and wood; the water canisters are usually head-loaded or transported by donkey cart.

28. William Young describes Rashaidi classifications of maturity and the corresponding garb (1988: 35–37).

29. *Ruṭal* (449.28 g) is a standard weight, but since people cannot usually afford to buy this much, they buy half or a quarter of a *ruṭal*.

30. Lampland and Star (2009: 4, 5) identify some shared properties of standards that they see as proliferating greatly in the contemporary world: standards are increasingly complex, nested in each other, interlocking across fields, systems and nations; they are unevenly distributed, pertain to communities of practice and are charged with normative ideas.

31. Standards are explicitly named as some of the subtypes of forms, which Thévenot (1984) discusses in his seminal article on 'investments of forms'.

32. This search for exact equivalence may also relate to the use of *kela* and *ruṭal* to measure small quantities in markets in this region of Sudan, which are weighed on scales, compared to other measurements based on volume, i.e., *marwa*. However, the sack (*ğ/šawāl*), a hollow measure, is also a standard measure in which grain, sugar and other commodities are sold.

33. While there are many kin ties in Um Futeima and people generally know each other, it is hardly close-knit; the settlement is new and has expanded with the onset of gold production in nearby places, and there is a fluctuation of residents. Sahlins (1972) noted that tribal societies may tend towards balanced reciprocity when they are more complex and a type of currency is instituted. Spittler (1989: 101) likewise noticed a search for equivalence in lending/borrowing millet among camel-herding Kel Ewey in Niger.

34. 'Asking is easily interpreted as begging, and pride forbids stooping low to do this', writes Spittler (1989: 112, my translation) with regard to Kel Ewey, who also sanction behaviour based on ideas of shame and honour.

35. It was noteworthy that many of the people I encountered in the nomadic hinterlands of north-eastern Sudan demanded upon meeting that their names be put down in my book. Introducing me to new people, my hosts often enquired whether I had written them down on my list (*sağğaltīhim?*), and if I had not, that I should do so swiftly. This demand connects to changes in the sociopolitical and economic landscape of Sudan and people's increasing awareness of and experience with the programmes of different aid agencies. Many of the settlement's residents had formerly been mobile with their livestock in Kassala, where development organizations were more strongly engaged. Some told of herding their livestock on distant pastures when *ḥauwāğāt* (foreigners) appeared out of nowhere, as if by chance, distributing blankets and sacks of wheat and sugar. They put their names on a piece of paper and never heard from the agencies again. This imaginary of how aid works connected my presence as a foreigner to the idea of being included through a personal name in something that might come one's way later.

36. I knew that food was scarce and that getting enough food was a critical concern of people in the settlement. Furthermore, I had experienced that financial issues were touchy and could not be addressed directly, but also that paying people for accommodation and food would have been an insult to Rashaidi hospitality. Thus before I returned to my field site I prepared and sought advice on the dilemma of doing research in an existential situation, when the ways in which people process such uncertainties are the main object of study (Calkins 2013).

37. At first, it occurred to me that Hamda might claim to not have received anything to protect herself from envy. But as time passed I realized that Hamda and other women, when receiving presents or favours, communicated freely about these occasions, paying no heed to the possibility of arousing envy. Thus, Hamda purposely criticized me for not bringing things so that I could overhear it. What is more, whether or not I handed over some of the conventional goods of consumption to Hamda did not much matter, because it was Tahir's duty to supply Hamda's household with these basic items in any event.

38. Additionally, on my trips to the market I faced another obstacle: arriving and travelling on my own, having independent financial means and speaking an educated standard Arabic, I initially was more of a social 'male' and my trips to the market were tolerated. Yet, the longer I stayed, the more my identity was perceived to be female. Men gradually refrained from eating with me from one tray and my market trips became inappropriate.

39. See again Sahlins (1972: 215–19) for a summary of such positions.

40. According to Timmermans and Epstein (2010: 71), standardization is 'a process of constructing uniformities across time and space, through the generation of agreed upon rules'.
41. De Laet and Mol (2000) made a similar point concerning the flexibility and fluidity of technologies as opposed to their firmness.
42. These are two of Hamda's married daughters, who only rarely cook for their husbands themselves, the wife of Antar, sheikh Tahir's client and maternal cousin, as well as Zeinab and her daughter, who are from another clan.

Chapter 5

ESTABLISHING URGENT FORMS

Uncertainties of Ill Health

The experience of uncertainties is perhaps most disorienting and troubling when related to issues of health. People are afraid of dying. This existential angst is most outstanding when sickness and poverty coincide. Tracing how care is provided (or not) for sick poor people allows for important insights into uncertainties of health and their management. This chapter investigates how poor people, who are held back by the norm of bashfulness (*taḥaššud*) from demanding support in the community, deal with ill health. To whom can they turn in times of need?

In contrast to earlier chapters, this one does not touch on form or technologies in the sense of lists, plans, devices, standards or measurements. Rather, it concentrates on the less tangible forms of speaking about sickness, shaping it as a social phenomenon, and most importantly, mobilizing people and financial resources to seek treatment. To tease out the uncertainties in making sense of a situation of ill health, I avoid assuming that there exists an unproblematic convergence between normative expectations of sick people and the actual practices of their caregivers. This redirects attention to what happens before the agreement is established that 'this is sickness' and before institutionalized expectations of proper behaviour can be referred to. The discussion shows how Rashaida distinguish among different types of health-related uncertainty: everyday infirmities, chronic illnesses and acute health crises. One finding is that how people interpret such uncertainties and the urgency to act – for instance, as normal travails connected to poverty or as matters of life and death – is crucial when dealing with and processing them individually and collectively.

While I focus here mainly on the uncertainties of assessing a situation of ill health and deliberating options, a large body of work has explored the uncertainties in clinical practices themselves, that is, the burdens and successes of therapies. The rapid development of evidence-based medicine since the 1980s is a direct response to such uncertainties and constitutes a widespread effort to generate predictability, rationality and accountability in medical practices by means of standardization (Timmermans and Berg 2003: 8). Going back to the 1950s, Parsons (1991) was intrigued by the uncertainty of illness and treatment. He drew attention to the institutionalization of normative expectations towards sick people, their associates and medical practitioners as sanctionable social roles in a social system. Certainly in Sudan expectations are raised when people get sick, but I seek to go behind this attribution of 'sickness' to see how it was situationally configured and what kinds of practices it afforded.

The chapter thus enquires into how Rashaida go about determining that something is a sickness. How do they know that it needs treatment? How do they represent this knowledge to others? And, conversely, when is ill health ignored as an unpleasant but minor thorn in one's side, the kind of ailment that poor people simply have to put up with? While the answers to these questions are thoroughly uncertain, there is no doubt about the proper responses to serious sickness: it is taken for granted that it demands medical treatment. 'Life-threatening sickness' denotes an understanding among concerned people that the situation constitutes a clear turning point, resulting either in life or death. Koselleck (2002: 237) recalled that the ancient Hippocratic school referred to such a decisive situation as a crisis, a 'phase of sickness in which the battle between life and death was definitively settled, in which the decision was due but not yet made'. The understanding of Rashaida that a sickness has reached a crossroads between clear alternatives – life or death – implies a certain temporality, an urgent decision-making; as Koselleck (2002: 237, 242) observed, 'the right point in time must be met for successful action'. The compelling issue for me is not the reality of the crisis or the conformance of people's assessments with medical diagnoses but rather when people observe and evaluate a situation as a critical turning point and the consequences that this entails.[1]

A large body of scholarship in medical anthropology has explored the questions of health and the seeking of therapy and how the appropriate treatment is determined. Among Rashaida in the Lower Atbara area the type of therapy was hardly an issue of debate – their concern was mainly about getting medical treatment at all. Poor people in this part of Sudan cannot usually afford medical treatment but need to mobilize money from their social networks in order to pay for travel and medicines. I contend that ill health needs to be represented or established in a certain form in order to pass the threshold of 'sickness' and activate help. Pursuing medical treatments thus not only means deliberating whether the illness is sufficiently serious to approach others for help to pay for treatments versus whether it is too soon to voice a health concern again, or whom to approach at all; it also involves the potential giver's assessment of the situation's seriousness – is it a matter of life and death? – and of their obligations towards the pleader for charity. The fragile knowledge about physical conditions is explored in four steps: the uncertainty of qualifying ill health; the uncertainty of others' evaluations; uncertain boundaries between chronic and urgent cases; and the bracketing of uncertainty when something has been established as a crisis. It is not a question of attributing causality to the misfortune of sickness or the outcomes of therapies, but rather of situations in which there was both a sense of urgency about acting and an uncertainty regarding the proper course of action. How is it possible to act with assurance when there is a lack of knowledge about one's condition, the severity of ill health and the dread of deadly outcomes? What I want to explore is how people project their situation into the future, upon what they rely for acting in the present, with which sense of anticipation they engage in everyday dealings, and which forms they invest in and mobilize to cope with ailments.

Chronic sickness is particularly murky. Care is constantly needed, but when is it necessary to signal for additional support? In contrast, interpretative uncertainties are pushed aside and bracketed in times of crisis. Relying on Roitman (2013), I understand crisis as a device which signifies a state of affairs that calls for urgent life-saving actions. I follow how people applied different techniques to invest in forms, such as establishing certain conditions as self-evident and factual, invoking principles of brotherhood and solidarity, and appealing to rules of behaviour and social categories through which support should be provided. I examine the logic by which 'therapy management groups' (Janzen 1978) were constituted in the marginal and scarcity-afflicted hinterlands of north-eastern Sudan and upon which forms they were based. I assert that the range of predictability within which people operated and processed uncertainties of ill health that challenged the flow of everyday lives in Sudan was underpinned by means of anticipating outcomes, weighing options and moral understandings, as well as asymmetrical capabilities and relationships between people.

Ill Health in the Lower Atbara Area

One of the most chilling moments of my fieldwork occurred when I was sitting with Farah Humeid, a lineage chief, who estimated his age at about seventy-five. He told me about his life and his marriages to nine women, then in a census-like manner asked that I put down the names of his ten sons and nine daughters and their families in my (paper) notebook.[2] After Farah listed his children and who they are married to, I asked him whether I had noted down all of his children. Or were there more? He looked at me and asked, 'You do not want the dead ones too, do you? All of them small children'. Somewhat startled, I said that I did. Farah began:

Abdelrahim, seven months, measles
Farah, two years, measles
Mubarak, three years, infections
Ali, four years, cough
Hamda, five years, fever
Hmouda, six years, injury to teeth
Aisha, forty days, fell into the fire (of the hearth)
Medina, 1.5 years, diarrhoea
Salim, three years, reaction to injections
Hamid, 2.5 months, fell off a camel
Suqri, two years, weakness

In listing his eleven dead children, he did not speak in sentences but rather almost brutally hurled out each name, age, and cause of death. A slight tremor in his voice revealed the pain suddenly evoked by these memories. Farah did not mention the years in which his children died. The list he gave me is not chronological. It is associative, according to whom he remembered, how dear the child and also how close its mother was to him. He started listing sons but then named four daughters who had died. He paused only twice. Once striking the air with his hand, saying that he divorced Aisha's mother after the infant fell into the hearth, because he could no longer bear to see her face. The other time he paused to tell me that Hamid, who slipped from his mother's arms off a camel, was his first child from his very first wife. They thought, 'We would go crazy [from pain]', when he died.

In this list of dead children the cause of death is attributed to various circumstances. Apart from the two horrific accidents, one death is attributed to vaccination, another to an infected tooth from an injury. Measles killed two of his young children. The causes of other deaths are unspectacular and remain underspecified – fever, infections, cough, diarrhoea and weakness (ḍuᶜf). Weakness denotes a condition that results from too little food over a long period of time, a physical condition which biomedicine and nutrition refer to as malnutrition and link to a heightened susceptibility to infectious diseases. Overall, this indicates that either medical treatment was not sought or that it did not lead to a clear diagnosis. I wanted to enquire about this but Farah suddenly became tired, needed to rest and lay down on the cot. He was indisposed, unavailable for further questions.

This list of dead children is not only a gravely disturbing field note but can also teach us about cultural responses to human suffering and death. The dead are counted and remembered. In itself this is nothing significant, but for me this moment was insightful. Prior to this, talk of death and the dead only emerged as brief footnotes in conversations. I had wondered why people talk so little about the dead when so much death abounds and interpreted this as a determination to look ahead, to get on with one's life and to forget about painful losses. Farah's enumeration of his dead children confirms that the death of children is common. At the same time, Farah's reactions indicate that he was still grieving and had not become indifferent to the death of his children. A different and shocking response to the lethal mixture of impoverishment, malnutrition and disease was explored by Nancy Scheper-Hughes (1993: 16) in 1980s north-eastern Brazil, what she described as the horror of 'the routinization of human suffering ... and the "normal" violence of everyday life'. This contrast is relevant for this chapter. As opposed to the maternal neglect for babies thought too weak to survive or the rejoicing over the death of infants (cf. Scheper-Hughes 1993), Rashaida I got to know never fundamentally challenged the understanding that a person with a life-threatening condition had to be treated medically. In most places there seems to be a tendency to treat sickness and in particular to avoid 'premature death' of children (Parsons 1991: 289). Rashaida from the settlement recognized the advantages of biomedicine, its drugs and therapies and often seemed to prefer them to alternative treatments, viewing the former as a potent means of eschewing death. Evading death was a necessary orientation for actions.[3]

But how to make sense of illness? What is it? Fever, diarrhoea, headaches and belly aches, coughs as well as pain when urinating are terms Rashaida employed to describe their maladies. When medical services were sought, problems were often diagnosed as malaria, malnutrition (protein-energy malnutrition, iron deficiency anaemia, etc.), diarrhoeal diseases, urinary tract infections and acute respiratory infections. But how do people know when they have to see a doctor? Rashaida did not talk explicitly about their typologies of illness. I observed how they made sense of their bodily discomforts, how they talked about the physical condition of people, enacting these understandings and the moral sense upon which they leaned when a case was urgent enough to warrant asking for financial support for treatment.

Thereby I discerned the practices through which people reached conclusions about sickness (*marḍ*) and appropriate responses.

In view of the frequent lack of food and the weakness that accompanies chronic hunger, children are particularly vulnerable to sickness and death. In 2009 and 2010, I accompanied my host Hamda several times to comfort mourning kin, who had lost young children to diarrhoea, fever and infectious diseases – causes that are principally preventable and/or curable by the standards of biomedicine. But this requires one to assess when something is a sickness and when it is timely to treat it, and to project the outcomes of treating/not treating and the type of treatment into the future. Farah's list suggests that at times people wait too long. This circumstance connects to the relative difficulty in accessing health services in rural areas.

Accessing Medical Services in Sudan

A lack of access to health services means that considerable effort and costs are involved in pursuing treatment, and therefore it becomes necessary to distinguish between moments of ill health when medical treatment is needed and those when it is not. Overall, the health care situation in Sudan is poor. The World Health Organization in 2007 speaks of 'high mortality and morbidity rates' in Sudan, particularly among children (Decaillet et al. 2003: 5).[4] Thereby 'the main causes of morbidity and mortality are parasitic diseases such as malaria, and tuberculosis, diarrhoeal diseases and respiratory infections', which are aggravated by conflicts, chronic malnutrition, floods and droughts (FMOH 2007a: 9; WHO 2010: 17). A World Bank survey of health facilities from 2003 notes that 'many of the health facilities are either not functioning or not satisfying the minimum requirements. ... The current health facility population ratios of one rural hospital for every 100,000 population and one health centre for every 34,000 of the population in the North are below the acceptable levels' (Decaillet et al. 2003: 12). The same report concluded that the Sudanese government's spending on health was among the lowest in the world, approximately only US $4 per person and 1 per cent of the GDP (ibid.: 7).[5]

The health system in Sudan was overhauled in the 1990s. It was decentralized due to federal administrative reform, leading to budget cuts and the distribution of responsibility for funding health facilities to lower administrative levels (Decaillet et al. 2003: 6; WB 2013), and a market-oriented health care model was implemented, introducing user fees for health services and drugs that had formerly been free of charge (FMOH 2007a: 18; 2007b).[6] The result is a system wherein health services and drugs are provided for paying customers and only minimal services are free of charge, always depending upon the respective funding institution's budget. This complicates the access to services, especially among the rural poor. The financial means to access health services are often not readily available, but have to be mobilized from elsewhere.

Apart from the financial obstacles, regional disparities in health services make access challenging for rural people. The primary health care system is devised hierarchically through a referral system: local health facilities servicing rural areas send patients in need on to more sophisticated levels of care, such as hospitals in urban areas.[7] The organization of the health sector thus amplifies a strong rural-urban divide with regard to the concentration of doctors, health workers and facilities (Gruenbaum 1981: 59, 60; Decaillet et al. 2003: 7; FMOH 2007a: 11, 2007b: 5). Hospitals are concentrated in towns, with the more specialized treatment centres in Khartoum only, whereas vast rural areas are serviced by so-called health centres, dressing stations, dispensaries and primary health care units, which are understaffed, underfunded and often inoperative.[8]

In view of the absence of health services in Um Futeima, villagers have to travel to seek treatment. This is expensive. It calls for a distinction between situations when help is needed to cope with a health concern and when it is not. The question of what a sickness is and how different types of ill health are classified is thus not only a question of interpreting bodily ailments, but the typology interacts with a material situation in which access to medical treatment is problematic and needs to be carefully managed in view of scarce financial resources. To treat minor sicknesses, people who have some funds at their disposal may travel to Seidon, the closest rural town with some low-key administrative functions, to buy their own medicines at the market or to consult the health centre. To treat serious sickness people travelled to hospitals in the city of Atbara.[9] As my neighbour Nafiᶜ noted repeatedly, there are real doctors 'who know anything' and 'who know how to treat'. But Atbara is distant and travel involves much money and effort, particularly in the rainy season due to the absence of tarmac roads. Seidon can be reached in thirty minutes by car but diagnoses tend to be crude. People consulted the health centre for minor or very common illnesses, such as malaria.[10] An additional constraint in accessing treatment is that transportation by car is unavailable when family heads are absent mining for gold. Furthermore, visiting the market town unaccompanied by a close male relation harms a woman's reputation. In view of more limited options, this puts women in a structural situation in which they experience uncertainties of health – their own or their children's – differently and more acutely than men. In view of the extraordinary efforts and high expenses involved in pursuing medical treatment in the city, there is a tendency to wait and reserve this option for the gravest cases, especially among poor people (called *miskīn* of whom it is said they do not have a thing).

The reader might be surprised by this biomedicalization of health in this marginal part of Sudan. Folk Islamic healing practices and beliefs were increasingly under attack and were stigmatized as expressions of false religion and as being full of lies; at least this was the case in the settlement. The sheikhs of Um Futeima, above all Tahir, the urban-educated sheikh and imam, saw the wearing of amulets, the furnishing of other lucky charms and the women's laying out of cowrie shells – technologies to explore and control misfortune – as some of the main causes for the alleged backwardness of Rashaida.[11] Streamlining religious practices of Rashaida in Um Futeima appeared to be the only plausible way to bring them closer to visions of Islamic modernity as propagated by the present regime in Khartoum.[12]

Caring for the Sick

Sick people need care. Care-giving is essential for survival and well-being. It involves doing things with and to bodies. It epitomizes intimate, personal relationships and at the same time is political, reverberating with broader normative understandings. I use the notion of care to denote imperfect activities oriented towards a common value – in this case, the improvement of health (cf. Heuts and Mol 2013). Parsons made a thought-provoking contribution to debates on care by comparing illness to a form of deviant behaviour. An important difference is that the sick person is not held responsible for her condition (Parsons 1991: 320). Put in a situation in which the sick one is prevented from being a 'normal' member of society through no fault of her own, she 'can't help it' and she can't help herself (ibid.: 296). This understanding engenders the obligation that others should assume the sick person's place and act in her stead. It calls others to action, to help in seeking therapy and treatments to normalize the sick person.[13] In Sudan, as I argued in the introduction to this book, the government has not instituted mechanisms to normalize health risks. Among Rashaida in the Lower Atbara area, care for the sick is considered to be the responsibility of kin. But of all kin?

A useful notion to reflect on how therapies are selected and how responsibility is allocated and assumed is the 'therapy management group', a concept Janzen (1978) proposed in an ethnographic study of what is now the Democratic Republic of Congo to understand the organization of healing in African contexts. The therapy management group refers to the collective that is configured temporarily when someone gets ill and needs care (Janzen 1978: 4). It can include concerned kin, friends, neighbours and various health practitioners. I concentrate on the low end of this therapy management group – on how Rashaida (not doctors) know that someone is sick and how they determine whether medical treatment is necessary for survival. What I observed in cases of sickness was not the constitution of therapy management groups in the full sense – people who actually intervened and deliberated treatment options – but rather a sort of therapy financing group, which is to say, people who felt obligated to pay without asking questions. I will explore the logics by which therapy management groups were mobilized around a health concern. I follow how uncertainties of health were processed by the emerging group until resources were made available and medical treatment was pursued. Instead of taking 'sickness' as a starting point, I pay closer attention to the uncertainties people experienced in qualifying the situation and in identifying the right moment to act. Thinking along the lines of an assembling 'therapy management group' directs me to another source of uncertainty: the reliance on others. The sick person's access to health services and practitioners is mediated by a number of people with different interpretations of the situation and of the urgency to act.

During my stay in the settlement it was mostly young children who got seriously sick. In the following, I examine three similar yet different cases of sickness among small children. In these cases their caregivers had to assess the situation, anticipate its course and deliberate treatment options. In order to portray the indeterminacies that people lived and felt, I describe these cases in some detail and then explore what can be learned from these short episodes in 2009 and 2010 about uncertainty, its management and human vulnerability. I untangle connections between people's perception of the situation and curative options deemed appropriate and necessary for recovery. Different individuals had to put up with various indeterminacies when undergoing an illness or taking care of sick ones.

ᶜUbeid

For a number of days, ᶜUbeid has been sick. He no longer eats, has pain in his stomach and has constant bouts of diarrhoea. His mother Muslima, after caring for the child for some days, tells Hamda, the child's grandmother, and me that her two-year-old is sick (*marḍān*). Muslima and ᶜUbeid live and eat in Hamda's house since Muslima's husband is in Kuwait on labour migration. Living under the same roof, Hamda and I observed and knew of his condition all along. Then what was Muslima doing? I suggest she was demanding recognition of a certain state of affairs – that this incident of ill health was a sickness which demanded care. But Muslima not only established this knowledge within her mother's house but also sought to further publicize her son's sickness. When neighbours enquire of her, Muslima no longer responds with the conventional greeting (*ṭayyiba*) but says, 'By God, my son is sick'. Soon everyone around Muslima knows her son is ill.

ᶜUbeid has lost weight and the diarrhoea continues. She is afraid, and tells me, 'His body is hot'. Take him to the doctor, I suggest. 'I don't know these things', she shrugs her shoulders. I tell her I will come with her, but she tells me it is not possible for her to go. What if her husband who works in Kuwait found out that she went alone to the market? What would he say?

The next day, sheikh Tahir, her uncle, returns to Um Futeima after spending several days with his second wife at her parents' campsite. Muslima immediately seeks him out. He asks her about her son. She tells him that ᶜUbeid has been sick for days and is not getting better. Tahir calls Muslima's husband in Kuwait, who promises to send money via a local moneylender to Seidon, where Tahir can fetch it. Muslima's husband tells her on the phone that he will send SDG 200 (€ 61) to cover expenses for treatment. He also tells her to get more substantial food for his son, so that he can fatten up. Tahir goes to the market the next day. He returns and tells Muslima that the money has not arrived yet. He advances her SDG 80 (€ 24) and arranges their transport to Seidon. Early next morning a neighbour picks up Muslima, her mother Hamda and ᶜUbeid to take them to Seidon, where ᶜUbeid is examined. He is diagnosed with malaria and a bacterial bowel infection. Muslima spends most of the money on transportation, food and the treatment.[14] Antar later goes to the money lender's partner in Seidon market and picks up the SDG 200 sent from Kuwait, after which he runs an errand for Tahir. He buys four sacks of cement, each costing SDG 40 (€12), using SDG 120 from Kuwait (and SDG 40 from Tahir's purse) to put cement on the roof of Tahir's shop to protect it from rain.

The case of ᶜUbeid's sickness is important as it draws attention to how a complex and spatially distributed therapy financing group was called into being. When ᶜUbeid's health deteriorated, Muslima wondered whether his condition deserved medical treatment. Worried but uncertain about the severity of his condition, she spread the word that he was sick. This 'investment of forms' could have failed – people could have contested the attribution of 'sickness' to ᶜUbeid's condition, telling Muslima that it is something minor, ᶜUbeid will get well, and so on. But she successfully dealt with her limited options of getting help and the uncertainty regarding ᶜUbeid's condition by telling others about it, calling it a sickness. Tahir's enquiry about ᶜUbeid immediately upon his return suggests that someone had already told him that ᶜUbeid was sick. He thus was already prepared to contact Muslima's husband. Muslima does not even suggest that he call her husband, but Tahir instantly reaches for the phone. Her success was in establishing and spreading knowledge about her son's condition. On this basis, a therapy financing group began to rally for ᶜUbeid. It involved his mother, who played the pivotal role in positing his sickness and a need for treatment; her husband, who had migrated to Kuwait and earned a regular income there; the people with whom she lived under the same roof, such as Hamda and myself, but also Tahir and her extended family as well as neighbours who spread the news of ᶜUbeid's sickness. Money was made available for treatment.

Yet, when a therapy management group begins to take shape, the ideal of providing the best possible care for the sick may have to be compromised by other logics. Sheikh Tahir evidently felt that Muslima needed less money than her husband had sent. ᶜUbeid's sickness was understood as minor by Tahir. He thus used the money to buy cement and reinforce the roof of his shop. I felt that this was unfair and asked Muslima what she thought about it. Muslima was not upset and did not interpret it as something ignoble. She would have liked to buy more food for her son and to share with others, but she explained that Tahir is her father's brother. She would not say anything against him. Did he not give her money when she needed it? Muslima added, 'Sometimes my husband does not send anything, then Tahir gives me money. I got medicine for my son. I am happy'. As in the situation where the charity distributed things, Tahir – by virtue of his know-how and technological means to address labour migrants abroad, to pick up the transferred money and to withhold it – assumes a crucial mediating role in these transnational kin-related transfers and plays a dominant role in ᶜUbeid's therapy financing group by limiting the amount of money available. These long-distance transfers would not work without Tahir. Muslima's position acknowledges this. What is more, she claimed to be disinterested in receiving the exact amount her husband sent her and has higher esteem for the long-standing and reciprocal relationship between herself and Tahir. In contrast to the exchange of flour that was described above where women who understood themselves as equals paid attention to equivalent exchanges, Muslima here acknowledged the opposite – the obviously asymmetrical relationships of generalized reciprocity between herself and her uncle.

Futoum

Futoum, a three-year-old, has been sick with diarrhoea for weeks, which has weakened her. I visited her family frequently during this time. Futoum's bouts of diarrhoea were uncontrollable but were accepted as something normal and common, neither eliciting much concern nor excitement. In view of the fact that most people get sick with diarrhoea from time to time, diarrhoea alone did not unduly distress anyone. But then Futoum catches a cold, coughs, her nose is congested even more than usual and she falls sick with a high fever. After days of high fever, Futoum's grandmother Zeinab tells me that she fears 'death has drawn near her granddaughter'. Futoum looks pale and blueish.

Zeinab, afraid that she waited too long, tells me her plan: Futoum has to see a doctor in Atbara immediately and perhaps – God willing – she will live. Zeinab tells her daughter to pack a few things and to borrow a bag from the neighbours; she asks me to sit and watch over Futoum. Then Zeinab and her daughter disappear. I sit uncomfortably on Zeinab's old cot, suddenly anxious that Futoum, the fragile, heavily breathing bundle on the bed in front of me, would breathe her last and I would be unable to prevent it.

Zeinab and her daughter return in Salim's pick-up truck after what seemed like hours but can have been no more than twenty minutes. The two women carry Futoum and get in the back of the pick-up truck, covering the girl with a thin sheet to protect her from the sun and the dust. Zeinab later tells me that she had no money when she left with Salim to Seidon. She was afraid and anxious but nonetheless determined to save Futoum's life. As Futoum's father was absent mining for gold and Zeinab's own husband was old and confused, she approached Salim, a kinsman and neighbour, and asked him to take them to Seidon with his car, explaining that Futoum was close to death. Salim complies with Zeinab's demand and takes them to Seidon free of charge, well aware of Zeinab's poverty. Salim also gives her SDG 50 (€ 15) to cover some of the costs in Atbara. In Seidon, Zeinab makes her way to the grocery store of someone she calls her *wad ʿaamm* and asks him to lend her some money in this emergency. He does not lend her anything but gives her SDG 20 (€ 5) as a gift (*karāma*). He promises to inform her brothers.

In this situation, presumably of life and death, Zeinab, Futoum's grandmother, is convinced that the child needs to see doctors in a hospital in Atbara. Futoum's mother and Zeinab cared for Futoum, cleaning her behind, consoling her, trying to feed her morsels of bread and give her some water but without publicly discussing her condition as a 'sickness'. But the fear of death suddenly brought about a reclassification of Futoum's condition from what might be seen as 'normal sickness' to 'life-threatening sickness', which had to be treated in a hospital in Atbara. Unlike Muslima, Zeinab moves and acts with urgency alone, before a broader therapy financing group is established to help her and at the same time thereby calls such a collective into being. When her brother Malik hears that Zeinab's granddaughter is seriously sick and that she is travelling to Atbara alone without money, he spreads the news among her kin in the nearby Rashaida camps at al-Hillou and al-Gazira and collects money. One of her brothers contributes SDG 20, another brother adds SDG 30 (€ 9), a sister SDG 10 (€ 3) and one of her cousins (*wad ʿamm*) SDG 20. When sheikh Tahir hears that Zeinab has left, he and a more distant kinsman both agree to send SDG 5 to Malik in Seidon. Malik collects the money, adds SDG 10 from his own purse and takes public transportation to Atbara. He searches for Zeinab in the hospital in Atbara to give her the money (SDG 100 = € 30). In view of her severe malnutrition and amoebic dysentery, Futoum is hospitalized for twelve days and doctors tell Zeinab to fetch her fresh milk and food from the souk every day. She recounts that the treatment for the child was free of charge as was the accommodation, but she had to pay for medicine and spent nearly all her money on food and drink in Atbara during the twelve days. Futoum recovers but doctors tell Zeinab that her weight is still critically low and that she should give her milk every day – a challenging prescription for a poor family.[15]

A motif that already appeared above in the chapter on food exchange was the reluctance of poor people to ask for something because they could not reciprocate. Asking for help is disdained and regarded as shameful (ᶜayb). Zeinab prided herself on the fact that she did not ask others for sugar or groceries; she was too bashful. But she disregarded conventions to preserve Futoum's life. Firstly, she approached Salim to take her to Seidon, and secondly, she demanded of a kinsman who owns a shop in Seidon to lend her some money. Tahir was the only community member, apart from the driver Salim, who gave Zeinab a small amount of money to cover costs. She explained the lack of help from the people in Um Futeima as follows: 'We haven't known the people for a long time. Nobody but your father's brother's children will help you'. This logic was invoked time and again by Rashaida as an integral part of how therapies were managed. This is peculiar since she called her relative in Seidon her father's brother's son (wad ᶜamm) whereas he is a more distant relative. At the same time she received the most significant assistance from her neighbour Salim, likewise a more distant kinsman, and money from her siblings, especially her brother Malik, who travelled to Atbara to give her the collected money.

Zeinab was both anxious and courageous, unable to wait for her son-in-law to return from gold mining. She interpreted the situation as being too serious to waste any more time. Nonetheless, one may ask why Zeinab, the child's grandmother, and not her mother took a leading role in managing Futoum's treatment. Begging is shameful and viewed as indicative of incapacity. It was easier for Zeinab, an old and poor woman married to a near-deaf and demented husband, to ask others for help than for her daughter. Her age put her beyond disrepute and her low social status was even helpful in the situation in moving beyond some of the norms that limit the radius of female activities, such as the designation of marketplaces and towns as male spheres. It was not only Zeinab's energetic spirit but also her relative freedom from male oversight and criticism that provide some clues as to why she was able to take the initiative instead of her daughter. Zeinab's actions shielded her daughter's reputation from harm. This situation had a happy ending. But in 2014, I learned from people who had visited the area that Zeinab, her husband and Futoum had meanwhile died.

The translation of uncertainty about present circumstances into a crisis or turning point between life and death is significant. It establishes a need for urgent curative actions. This often puts the main caregivers in a difficult position: taking urgent actions is demanded of them, but their range of available options is limited by hierarchical relations. In fact, poor caregivers must move and provoke others to act on behalf of the sick person. The agency and money of others have to be mobilized.

Tahir

On meeting the couple Antar and Noura, I wondered why their baby, whom I thought to be about nine or ten months, had so many teeth. Soon I learned that their son Tahir is more than two years old. He was etiolated by the constant diarrhoea from which he suffered, and the little food he and his nursing mother consumed. Seeing Tahir, who instead of toddling, playing or curiously discovering his surroundings only clings lethargically to his mother and is unable to walk, made me concerned. I talked to Noura several times about taking her son to see a doctor to at least stop the diarrhoea. Noura responded: 'It is only diarrhoea'. But then she paused and asked me bluntly whether her son will recover.

Tahir is Noura's only child. She gave birth before, but her first child died three or four years ago from weakness (*ḍuʿf*). Antar and Noura were always struggling and never seemed to have enough to eat. People in the settlement called them 'hungry ones'. Antar depends upon sheikh Tahir for his subsistence. Fittingly Antar's son was named after sheikh Tahir. Antar runs errands for sheikh Tahir, operates his diesel-run grain mill and works in his shop. As Tahir's client, he receives no salary but says that he opens his hand and does not count since Tahir is his *wad ʿamm*. In Um Futeima Antar is sneered at.[16] For instance, he was the only grown man in whose presence Hamda's daughters did not feel bashful – they did not change their bodily posture when he entered the house, and instead sat relaxed and spread out on the floor and beds, talking and laughing loudly. Seen as weak and unable to earn his own living, he was not considered as a complete man.

Later I learned that Antar had already repeatedly asked sheikh Tahir for support to take little Tahir to the doctor, but received no money for his son's treatment. In view of Antar's poverty and the likely recurrence of similar situations, some suffering is accepted as normal, even probable, sickness and hunger being common experiences of the poor. Sheikh Tahir replied he had no money and Antar had to wait. For weeks. There was no help until little Tahir's health deteriorated further, until he only slept or whined, was too weak to sit up and refused to even hold a piece of bread. Would he die like their first son?

Figure 5.1 Noura waiting in her house with her weakened son Tahir

Antar's son has been weak and ill for a long time. But how do Antar and Noura make sense of their situation and how do they deal with the uncertainties of how Tahir's condition will develop? Noura withdraws into her hut with her son, anxious and downhearted about her son's weak condition. She refuses all food herself. Hamda and I urge her to continue eating to at least be able to breastfeed her child. But Noura retorts, how can she continue eating when her child is wasting away? The women in Hamda's house talk about Tahir and Noura in lowered voices. Some say Noura has gone mad. Antar, instead of withdrawing, persists in demanding assistance. One evening while I am discussing a recent fight about land rights with sheikh Tahir, Antar enters Tahir's house. He asks sheikh Tahir again for money, urgently, begging Tahir for help. Tahir states that he has no money to give to Antar. 'What should I do?', he shouts. 'Where should I get it from?' Antar angrily sheds tears and cries out, 'By God, if he does not see a doctor he will die'.

Moved by Antar's desperation and sense of urgency, Tahir calms him and tells him he will try to get money. Tahir draws his mobile phone from his pocket and calls Suleih, Antar's *wad ʿamm* and Noura's brother,[17] who works in Saudi Arabia. Suleih promises to send SDG 100 for Antar's son. Another day passes and nothing happens. In the evening when the women sit together for coffee, Hamda gets upset and claims that Tahir lies when he says he has no money. Antar sits there miserably and is silent. The next morning it is still unclear when Suleih will send the money, so, anxious about the child's condition, I give Antar money to take his family to Atbara. I later learn that the amount of money I had given Antar was too small in view of the uncertainty of how long Antar and his family would have to stay in Atbara and how costly food and medication would be. While Antar accepted my gift, I later learn that he felt hesitant around me and could not ask me to lend him money or to give him more. Tahir was the only person he could approach freely. Apart from the child's main caregivers, his parents and Tahir, the emerging therapy financing group encompassed women in the extended family, such as Hamda and myself, and neighbouring women who likewise expressed concern and visited. But because Antar needed money to access treatment, Tahir also played a central role in rallying a broader therapy management group among kin, which included labour migrants in the Gulf.

Two days later Suleih's money is transferred via moneylenders to Seidon. Two other parallel cousins of Antar also send smaller amounts of money. Antar fetches a total of SDG 210 (€ 64) and takes his son and wife to Atbara. Before he leaves sheikh Tahir also gives him a small amount of money from his purse, Antar relates. Tahir is hospitalized for ten days. In the first

Figure 5.2 Noura and Tahir after their return from Atbara (Tahir's behind is placed on the dirt due to his diarrhoea to avoid soiling the sheets and the carpet)

few days he is supported by parenteral nutrition. Then the family returns with medication for amoebic dysentery, bacterial infections and nausea. The doctors told them that Tahir is not seriously sick, his weakness (*ḍuʿf*) results mainly from his chronic undernutrition. Tahir recovers somewhat but his diarrhoea worsens and he grows feeble again just as I leave the settlement.

The case of Antar and Noura highlights the fact that a contemptuous attitude towards poor people prevails, something that strongly affects how they assess their options with regard to approaching others for help in a situation of crisis. Bashfulness or modesty holds back people who are unable to reciprocate after demanding gifts and favours. For example, Antar felt that he could not approach me and ask me for more money. He was already indebted to me due to my gift of money and this produced shame. Giving to poor people thus is seen as condescension, something that highlights social asymmetries. Antar's reaction underlined his dependency and what many interlocutors interpreted as a lack of manly honour. He was the only man I saw shedding tears in Um Futeima. A man is supposed to bear hardships and discomfort with self-control (see Abu-Lughod 1986: 90 for a related idea among Awlad 'Ali). The poor and miserable are not considered equals. Only Tahir could mobilize help on behalf of Antar and thereby could constitute a group who would not only care but also pay for little Tahir's treatment. Acknowledging the asymmetries between himself and Tahir, Antar explained the bonds of mutual help as given due to father brotherhood. This rhetorical confirmation of the *'auwlād ʿamm* principle in the frame of patron–client relations is peculiar. Firstly, it refers here to non-calculative, long-term exchanges for regular subsistence and not to help in crises. Secondly, although they are from the same clan and can trace their origins to one agnate, the genealogical distance between Antar and Tahir was greater, as people are easily able to point out.[18] I will explore below what this affirmative discourse on *'auwlād ʿamm* relationships may indicate. Before that, however, I investigate what we can learn from these ways of dealing with uncertainties.

Uncertainties between Life and Death

How is one to know whether the outcome of an untreated sickness will be recovery or death? This leads to other complex questions: how to navigate the shifting ground between health and serious sickness? When to decide that urgency is needed to avert death? How to communicate that urgency to others to gain their support? What unites the three presented cases is that some form of help was eventually provided. I visited other families whose children had died from sickness and who did not sound a rallying call for help: they explained that they had no money to take their child to the doctor.

I first address the above questions and then in the remainder of this chapter reflect on what these examples can teach us about notions of uncertainty in Sudan; the ways in which people experience, classify and address such situational unknowns; and how this in turn relates to complicated and reconfiguring relationships between people.

'Sickness' as a Form

The uncertainty of qualifying ill health concerns situations between 'normal' and 'life-threatening' sickness. Antar sought help when he feared that little Tahir was about to die. Antar was long uncertain as to the severity of his son's condition. Had his son Tahir not always been sickly? How sick was he then? Did he need to see a doctor to recover? Would he recover at all? Was his life really in peril? Did this situation deserve the shame and humiliation associated with pleading for support? In view of Tahir's increasing feebleness and the mounting concern voiced by close kin and neighbours, Antar and Noura reached an understanding that their son's precarious condition was between life and death. Little Tahir's sickness was established in a gradual process. 'Normal sickness', where medical treatment is not deemed necessary, and 'serious sickness', where urgent medical therapy is needed to prevent death, are not two clearly delineated states.

Zeinab's example points in a similar direction. It was not Futoum's diarrhoea and fever in itself that mobilized help but Zeinab's understanding that this was a sickness and that her actions in this situation would be decisive for the boy regarding life or death. This knowledge cannot be reduced to observed symptoms, but is also related to a context where resources are scarce and need to be rationed, to prior experiences and anticipation, concerned comments from neighbours, fear of death, regret over having waited too long and hope that recovery is still possible through medical treatment. This understanding of Futoum's sickness prompted her to seek help actively, urgently and self-reliantly. In reflecting on this situation, Zeinab explained later that she cared only about Futoum, nothing else. She had seen other children die, four of her own and only a few years back her daughter's little son. 'A person cannot bear seeing them die', she told me. Futoum was too dear to her. In this situation, she subordinated the evaluation of her own behaviour as a female to the need to preserve Futoum's life – if at all possible. The fear of death can indeed be a powerful motivator.

Defining what is at stake in the situation is difficult. To overcome a paralyzing sense of powerlessness and enable action, semantic work has to be performed, interpreting, qualifying, deliberating on the situation and investing in forms that can serve as shorthand for acting. The form 'sickness' as a condition that deserves to be treated medically engenders certain actions and can mobilize a therapy management group. But 'sickness' is not the same for poor and wealthier people. This leads to the question of when is something noticed and when can it be proclaimed a 'sickness'. I relate this to asymmetrical economic circumstances.

Uncertainty of Others' Assessments

Deciding whether to seek medical help entails a careful assessment of the situation at hand. When a family has no money, the question arises as to when is the right time to ask people who are less poor for money. Finding the right moment involves issues of honour and shame. Poor people have to ask themselves when and whether the illness is sufficiently serious, that is life-threatening, to express a need for urgent help in covering costs for treatment. The situation is aggravated by the social convention that forbids poor people to ask for help directly. Speaking up is therefore vital, but begging for something is disgraceful (see Whyte 1997: 14 for a very different understanding of the importance of speaking out about sickness so as to address it). This was brought home to me in different conversations with Zeinab, Noura, Antar and other people classified as have-nothings, who indicated that they felt ashamed to demand money from most people, because they were known to be poor and unable to return it. They spoke and told other people about their most extreme plights without asking for anything specific; it was always up to the listeners to act upon what they had heard. Poor people can approach only a few people for help directly – their closest kin, companions or patrons – but even such careful deliberation about whom to approach and when to do so does not liberate poor people from shame. Giving entails condescension and results in humiliation.

Tahir's reluctance to respond earlier to little Tahir's condition underscores the potential giver's uncertainties in assessing the situation.[19] Money is not freely available for most people, but has to be allocated with great care. I observed this in a number of other cases in 2009 and 2010; when adults got sick with fevers and pains, this had to be endured for a while. When a poor person has signalled a need, the giver has to answer various issues for himself, such as: is this a normal situation of sickness, with recovery likely, or does it demand medical treatment? How close do I feel to the affected person and how desperate is the need for money? Is it a situation of life and death and will a death be attributed to my failure to help? This is not to say that persons who are first approached and who figure as potential givers bear the sole responsibility for poor people in such situations. But when they are unable to meet a dire need, they are expected to sound a rallying call for help. It is their responsibility to mobilize others. For instance, Hamda reproached Tahir for not responding earlier to little Tahir's sickness, indicating that the reactions of potential givers are evaluated and can likewise lead to shame or honour.

Antar's failure to get money for treatment earlier is somewhat puzzling. What are patron–client relationships for, if not to provide security for the client in times of duress? Tahir is supposed to help Antar, but was it really Tahir who shied away from the responsibility? Or was it Antar who failed to convey enough of a sense of urgency regarding his son's condition? Responsibility is contextual. It cannot be attributed with finality. It is something that emerges from the situation, involving persons and the in/stability of invested forms. I have shown that the situation is rife with various intersecting uncertainties concerning the main caregivers and the people in their networks whom they seek to mobilize. But the situation can be further qualified by reflecting upon existential uncertainty in relation to a scarcity of resources. In this part of Sudan one could charge that an economy of scarcity has emerged: resources are meagre and scarce; they hardly allow one to make a living and there is little predictability for livelihoods (Manger 1996). In view of this scarcity, the need to preserve lives and to reproduce therefore means that resources need to be carefully allocated, never exceeding what is absolutely essential. They cannot be wasted.

This attention to the context in which the exchanges between Antar and Tahir occurred enables further insights. Antar was long uncertain with regard to the severity of little Tahir's condition and irresolute regarding the need for treatment and its urgency. Tahir, in turn, was not a rich patron: he supplied Antar with food and clothing, and he made sure Antar was allotted a house and other things by the charity. But beyond this, he was only ready and able to help Antar in cases of extreme emergency. He also doubted for a while that little Tahir's condition met the criteria for intervention. Clearly, in this economy of scarcity, there is little room for generosity. Life for poor people involves the hardship of experiencing normal sickness for which there is no help and no additional support.

Managing uncertainties of health involves testing equivalences by publically qualifying a health condition, and when the qualification is uncontested by others, it enables acting with assurance. It is not enough that the nuclear family establishes something as a case of sickness; to gain support the form has to hold up to other people's assessments. Whether others will follow the interpretation thus figures as a further source of uncertainty. In her concern for her son Muslima gradually spread the news that he was sick. This was a way of testing how others felt about the situation. It was not only an exercise of gaining clarity for herself and refining her understanding; she also sought to establish ʿUbeid's sickness as unquestioned, common knowledge. Ill health needs to be understood as sickness and this form aims at the greatest generality that is possible (cf. Thévenot 1984). This classification does not impose itself unproblematically, but rather the transition from health to sickness has to be abstracted from observation and discursively marked to have an effect in rallying support. This experiment can always fail.

For poor people the passage between ill health and death is even more troubling. It involves knowing and acting upon a fuzzy distinction between normal and life-threatening sickness and anticipating others' evaluation of the situation. Thus, I am tempted to suggest that the moment when sickness (*mard*) is established as a form to support the coordination of actions depends upon a household's material endowments: the poorer the family, the more serious the illness must become before the category sickness is applied, which usually indicates a near-death condition. *Mard* then means any physical ailment requiring treatment, whereby what is worth treating and who is worth being treated is contingent upon the situation and the (a)symmetrical relationships between the actors involved. Whereas the moment when something is noticed as 'sickness' depends upon economic circumstances the willingness of others to help seems to correlate positively with the signified exceptionality and unpredictability of health concerns. Conversely, the more mundane and everyday the health concern, the less likely and the later help is mobilized. In a setting of scarcity, the form usually has to convey an urgency that exceeds everyday difficulties.

Uncertain Transitions: Sickness and Chronicity

Chronic illness is something that sits uncomfortably between normal and life-threatening sickness. It denotes that some kind of permanent impairment or disability is recognized by others, and in contrast to 'normal' sickness, there are institutionalized patterns through which care is organized. In this section, I analyse the example of Salman, a chronically sick man aged about forty in my hosts' extended family, who became acutely sick. I focus on the difficulties of caregivers to assess the need for medical treatment beyond the long-term care provided and the difficulty of anticipating how actions will be evaluated by others. Responsibilities for everyday care have to be differentiated from sickness, which demands that a broader therapy financing group rallies for help.

From the beginning of my stay in Um Futeima people told me that Salman is sick and deranged. People are afraid of him. Sheikh Tahir refers to his condition as 'mental illness' (*mard nafsi*). Salman is the elder brother of Hamda's husband, sheikh Tahir and Rahala. Tahir is held responsible for caring for his brother Salman. Tahir sees no other way than locking Salman in a clay house, the house the charity gave to Rahala. Before Salman was confined to the house, he caused a stir. Hungry for meat, he twice killed a neighbour's goat, for which Tahir had to provide compensation. Tahir further explains why the room is completely empty – Salman had wrecked everything that was previously there and begun to hurt himself. He is bound with an iron chain around his neck, connected to two heavy weights. He receives food twice a day from either Hamda or Tahir's wife and is given one jug of water for drinking and washing. Salman does not leave the house to relieve himself, but from time to time the house is cleaned of excrement. Salman is filthy, covered with dust, sweat and excrement. Tahir and his helper Antar take him to the river by car to clean him, dipping him into the water every two or three months.[20]

During my stay Salman gets sick. Salman cries and whines in his house for days. Hamda and her daughters discuss what pains him, noticing that he has stopped eating. He has diarrhoea, they tell me. 'Maybe he will die', Hamda's daughter Saliha wonders, afraid to go near him. The women inform sheikh Tahir about his condition. After seeing Salman and talking to him, Tahir returns, confirming that he is sick (*marḍān*). Still, this situation continues unchanged for days until Salman's sisters Rahala and Hakima pay Hamda an overnight visit. At first, they complain to Tahir that Salman has to eat alone and is completely isolated. When the women see that Salman's bowl of food is returned untouched, they go and talk to him through the window. I join them. They are first appalled by the stench, then by how thin and dirty their brother looks. Salman complains to them about aches and pain, crying, begging them to let him out of the house. Then he starts to scream for food and throws excrement at his sisters.

Shocked, Ruha and Hakima run away, pause briefly to consult with each other and then march directly to Tahir's house. They accuse Tahir of neglecting their brother and maltreating him, not even providing him with enough food. He is hungry, they insist. In response to their critique, which implies his cruelty, Tahir goes to the small cafeteria on the other side of the settlement and buys a portion of Sudanese bean stew with bread for Salman. But Salman does not touch it, and instead cries for hours. That same night, Tahir's sisters Rahala and Hakima confront him again and tell him that poor Salman is sick and has to see a doctor. On that occasion, Tahir calls his brother ꞌUbeid and three of their kin (*'awlād 'amm*) who work in the Gulf, asking them to send money for Salman's treatment. Within the next three days, the three migrants in Saudi Arabia each send SDG 100 (€ 30), while Hassan sends SDG 500 (€ 152). Tahir picks the money up, takes another two days to prepare, then embarks on a ten-day trip to Kassala to take Salman to a famous *baṣīr*, a traditional healer.

This situation provides important insight into how care is organized in Um Futeima. As head of the extended family, sheikh Tahir is considered responsible for Salman's everyday needs. He was reproached for not doing his job well. "'I had wanted to speak", he says at the grave', Whyte (1997: 16) wrote, referring to a Nyole proverb that comments on the peril of delaying responses to illness. People fear to ask for help too early, which is considered shameful, but Tahir was accused of not having asked others early enough. There is a danger of asking too early or too late – finding the right moment to act and to mobilize money is a delicate issue. How to know when? People have to do something, but without knowing which collective interpretations will prevail and how their behaviour will be evaluated. This uncertainty points to a struggle for the power to define sickness and the demand for therapy. This semantic struggle ended with Salman's acute sickness being established, thereby putting Tahir on the spot. It had a bearing on his honour, in that he had to justify his behaviour. Yet, once consensus was reached among the emerging therapy management group that Salman needed to see a doctor, the responsibility no longer rested upon Tahir alone. In view of the scarce resources and Tahir's own relative poverty, the burden for extras has to be distributed among kin, since it is too much for one person to shoulder alone. The appeal mobilizes transnational kin ties through which money is sent for Salman's treatment. Three of Tahir's 'awlād ʿamm help, but their elder brother Hassan (Hamda's husband) sends the largest share. Tahir does not mention this, when he recounts the names of those who helped in this situation, stating, 'Of course, my father's brother's sons have to help me'.

Chronic illness sits uncomfortably between two types of illness, normal sickness and life-threatening sickness. It poses interpretative problems. It blurs the rather clear lines, characteristic of this economy of scarcity, between minor illness that poor people have to endure silently and more serious sickness worthy of medical treatment. The struggle for the right interpretation between Tahir and his sisters attests to this. Care for the basic needs of chronically sick people is institutionalized, responsibilities are attributed and people are judged according to how they live up to them. However, when chronically ill persons get seriously sick, it is likely that more extensive therapy management groups will be mobilized. But as with the plight of poor people, a high level of gravity has to be reached before help is offered.[21] The long-term familial structures of support and care for needy ones are central to the survival of poor people, especially the chronically sick and the old. Whereas the extended family plays an important role in the subsistence of poor families, it is not the only source of support. Antar approached his patron first, who provides for his daily needs. 'The family is not always the first resort'; rather one should always assume a more or less 'mixed economy' of care (Horden 1998: 27, 9). The attribution of responsibilities is even clearer in times of crisis, but who will show up and assume them is open (Cooper 2012: 440).

Signifying Crises

This section explores the links between the severity of illness and the willingness to help. The notion of crisis was used by the ancient Hippocratic school as an analytical tool to define a decisive moment in the course of sickness between life and death. Inspired by newer conceptualizations of crisis (Roitman 2013), I understand it here not as an empirical observation but as an invested form in the sense of Thévenot (1984) – that is, as something that holds together and facilitates action by enabling a bracketing of uncertainty. Rashaida I encountered, however, did not usually employ the notion of crisis (*'azma*) but used a variety of other terms, such as accident and event (*ḥādit*), blow (*ḍarba*) or constriction (*ḍīq*), to describe the occurrence of events that are associated with notions of unpredictability, surprise, exception and, importantly, arbitrariness. Harm can strike anyone.

Consider the tragic accident of fifteen-year-old Hamid, who was working in a mine when a shaft collapsed on him (cf. chapter 3). Three buried workers suffocated to death. Hamid was lucky to be saved, even though his foot was severely injured. After nearly four months of pain and agony, consulting and staying with different local healers, Hamid was told that his foot had suffered permanent damage. Hamid returned to his family, devastated. Weeks passed and Hamid feared he would not be able to walk anymore. He recalls, 'In my foot the bone was beginning to stick out in different directions. It took me two, no, four months, and I stayed at home. Then they took me to the hospital in Atbara; when they saw my foot, they transferred me to Khartoum'. In Khartoum Hamid's foot was operated on and an iron implant was put in place to support the realignment of bones. He was hospitalized for more than a month. He gradually learned to walk again and now is able to walk without crutches, but he limps. While he is happy about his recovery, he regrets the excessively high costs of being sent from doctor to doctor. Hamid estimates that his treatment in Khartoum alone cost at least SDG 15,000 (€ 4,560), a high price that exceeds many times what Hamid had earned in gold mining.

The case of Hamid illustrates how money can be mobilized when an injury is understood as a sudden and exceptional crisis. Hamid comes from a poor family. He is the eldest of three sons and his father cannot work due to chronic illness. Unable to furnish the costs for treatment, Hamid stresses that his kin group (*ğamāʿat*) helped to pay for it. 'It was a severe blow', Hamid explains, 'all of the *'awlād ʿamm* and the *'awlād ḫāl* [matrilineal cousins], all of them gave out of their generosity [*karāma*]'. His therapy was managed through his father and a distributed kin network. Financial support for his treatment issued from several sources, among them his maternal and paternal cousins, many of whom are labour migrants in the Gulf States. Several individuals sent him SDG 200–400 (€ 61–122) from Saudi Arabia,

Kuwait and Abu Dhabi. But in his dire situation other people also helped. Hamid continues, 'Who has many sheep or a goat, gives one to you. People that have something, like those with cars, give you an animal or give you money, 200 or 300'.

Hamid received much more money than any of the other sick persons mentioned above, where a persistent uncertainty surrounded the assessment of the health condition. His case can be understood as a crisis, invoking elements of suddenness, urgency and obvious injury. Hamid was a tall, strong young man. Hearing of his severe accident and his foot injury was an exceptional situation that affected people and prompted them to give comparatively large amounts to contribute to his treatment. Importantly, he had already incurred damage, and there was a consensus, without uncertainty, that Hamid had to be treated medically. Crisis as a form is thus juxtaposed to the experience of the exhausting uncertainties of how to qualify ill health and establish some reference for acting. Crises signify a state of affairs, denoting that something has already happened and demands urgent actions, not epistemological reflection on the status of knowledge. As Roitman (2013) points out, crisis is usually posited without inquiring into the claim's foundations, enabling the producing of certain knowledges and histories while constraining others. To mobilize urgent actions, crisis has to take 'reality' – in the sense of Boltanski (2011) – for granted. It therefore does not allow the most radical forms of uncertainty and reflexive interrogation to emerge. Raising a situation to the level of crisis enables one to bracket uncertainties about the best course of action and focuses them on outcomes. Outcomes then become matters of urgent uncertainty.

Because crises of health can establish unchallenged orientations for action, this may explain why larger and more generous therapy management groups are constituted at such moments. Hamid says something important regarding the obligation to help: 'Those who have money give you some, whoever has no money we know they have none'. Crises oblige kin to give money for therapy, particularly the well-off and patrilineal kin. If someone has money and withholds it, this will cause scorn and resentment. Perhaps Hamda's reaction to Tahir's reluctance to give money to Antar is related to this expectation. This supports my argument: help seems to be reserved for the unexpected, the extraordinary, for emergencies and crises. Care for everyday concerns is organized differently with unambiguous personal responsibilities. Uncertainties about when to seek therapy mark the transition between situations that are considered to be in the realm of the everyday and thus beyond the obligation to give, and situations of crisis where needy ones have to be supported. The result is a gruelling type of uncertainty, which poor people live through continually, concerning everyday health problems, their seriousness, and their ability to mobilize money for treatment.

Managing Uncertain Health: Normative References

In dealing with sickness (when established as a category of ill health that deserves treatment), people have certain expectations that affect how therapy financing groups are constituted. I relate obligations to help to the socio-economic setting and cultural meanings, which are invoked in the situation, particularly ideas about responsibility and shame/honour. And I take a closer look at how Rashaida classify kin relationships and connected obligations to help in times of duress. This will aid in making sense of apparent contradictions between the highly normative discourse on father-brotherhood as an exclusive source of assistance, and the enormous support that was offered through other family members. But first I compare how Rashaida view responsibilities for food and health.

Food and Health: Defining Responsibilities

There are differences and similarities in how needs of food and health are met in this setting of scarcity. The comparison indicates that two temporal horizons define responsibilities: an everyday order in which uncertainty about present and future conditions results in the characteristic saving and rationing of scarce resources, and an order of exception or crisis, where uncertainty is bracketed, urgency for acting is signalled and help has to be extended.

Food and health are interwoven. Both concern survival. But people do not normally starve, although many eat less than what they would need. While it is worrisome when food supplies run out, and linked to physical suffering, my interlocutors did not necessarily understand this as hunger (ǧūʿ). Rashaida experience this as a highly unpleasant, painful and troubling period but for most it is only an episode, a short supply gap. Many Rashaida ration their food supplies, planning ahead for when staples run out, and refer to this as 'avoiding eating'. In contrast, there is no choice, no room for manoeuvring, when hunger is chronic. The poor are the miserable and hungry ones (ǧauwʿānīn). Hunger is what befalls people whose agency is limited – they have no food, no money, no means to evade hunger, and they embody it permanently. Their children do not grow and prosper but are sickly and weak.

Food is a daily need. Its provision is the responsibility first and foremost of a nuclear family's head. The practical inability to live up to this normative ideal and the ensuing depletion of food supplies results in a gruelling unpredictability of everyday life, which the nuclear family and also the extended family are responsible for. The search for equivalences in the exchange of staples among women suggests that in this overall existential setting, there is little or no room for generosity concerning daily food needs. Rashaida see a strong connection between eating properly – that is, fatty food – and good health. The lack of adequate food over a longer period of time is a problem of the poor, which undermines their health and makes them vulnerable to sickness. Health then is tied to economic status, where the better-off can eat more regularly and can eat heartier and more diversified foods, while the poorest are mostly severely malnourished and prone to sickness. Health can also be located in the realm of the everyday. It is considered the nuclear family's responsibility. While the better-off may have options to care for everyday problems of ill health, poor families lack the money to treat 'normal sicknesses' and tend to ignore them. Similar to the condition of wasting associated with a lack of food, it is a responsibility they shoulder alone. Thus there is no help to cover daily food needs and health concerns, and instead only a nagging uncertainty.

Death is different. It must be avoided by any and all means. The dread of death can mobilize action. It moves those who are outside the circle of the nuclear family (*bayt*) and even the extended family (*dār*) to help stave off a fatal outcome. It is no longer in the realm of the everyday, but rather a state of affairs accepted as exceptional by a collective, which entails obligations that are sanctioned by causing shame or honour. In view of the overwhelming poverty and scarcity of resources, support for poor people's therapies has to be metered out and reserved for the most outstanding hardships. More complex, spatially distributed therapy financing groups emerge. Yet, in each instance of 'sickness', a collective first has to be formed and mobilized, so that it can notice, interpret, manage and finance the sick person's therapy. These groups can only be identified as the 'sickness' is being established as a form that needs to be acted upon.

Therapy financing groups are not composed of equals; rather, their constitution is based upon a hierarchical principle, mobilizing kin along economic asymmetries. An outstanding characteristic of therapeutic relations is that the knowledge about the exact monetary contributions of different people is remembered and these numbers form a central part of people's conversations. So and so gave five pounds, so and so twenty, thirty, fifty and so on. For instance, Hamda's daughters could exactly recall who had given Zeinab how much money when Futoum got sick. Knowledge of the various monetary donations travels widely in the community; it is commonly known, recited and remembered, and allows one to evaluate the appropriateness of extended help and by extension to measure the quality of social bonds. As Hamid suggests, Rashaida know whether someone has something or not. This exerts pressure on people to give according to their economic circumstances and not to shame themselves by being too stingy. It is an opportunity to build a reputation for being generous, something that brings honour to a (predominantly) male giver. But the circulation of numbers also works the other way around: it inhibits people who have received money and reminds them of their outstanding debts. In conversations people time and again confirmed the 'awlād 'amm logic as the only truly reliable source of help in situations of life and death. But this normative expectation did not converge with actual practices, and I now explore what this might imply.

What Counts: Kinship and Help

Rashaida whom I met define 'awlād 'amm relations (father's brother's sons) as binding and reliable sources: only father's brother's sons are a source of true help and support in critical times. I examined discrepancies between this ideology and the actual ways in which care was provided for poor people. Janet Carsten has contributed substantially to a field of studies termed 'new kinship', which questions premises of an earlier generation of kinship studies. Accordingly, kinship – far from being assigned at birth – is 'a process of becoming ... brought about by a variety of means which include feeding, living together, fostering and marriage' (Carsten 1997: 12). Adopting this sensitivity towards becoming, the affirmative discourse on 'awlād 'amm relations (father's brother's sons) can be read as a means of establishing and maintaining relationships among various people. Therapy financing groups emerge and are recruited through investments of money, time, advice and emotion.

The emphatic focus on patrilineal ties can be related to an enduring principle of kinship ideology among Rashaida, which needs to be qualified. William Young's (1988) study of marriage rituals among nomadic Rashaida emphasized that social organization – as in many pastoral societies – is agnatic, based on the ideal of patrilineal descent, whereby people and livestock are recognized and identified through the name of a family father. People today in the settled circumstances of Um Futeima still conceptualize group membership as being based on patrilineal descent, but affinal ties also play an important role in everyday conversations when people relate themselves to others. Patrilineal brotherhood and cousinhood, however, is one designation among several. *Bayt* literally means habitat, house or tent, but also works as a metaphor for intimate social relationships. It is associated with the conjugal couple and is used to refer to the nuclear family. Young's (1988) analysis of marriage rituals among Rashaida pointed out that the process of building a *bayt* was a central part of the wedding ceremony.[22] On entering the tent for the first time alone with her husband, the bride was expected to initiate the hearth by preparing coffee for her spouse, suggesting intimate links between reproduction through food and sex.[23] In South Asia the hearth stands for the 'commensal unity of close kin', to wit, all people under one roof (Carsten 2004: 40–41, 55). Similarly, among Rashaida in the Lower Atbara area, *bayt* denotes the people who eat from the same hearth and sleep in the same dwelling, relationships marked by the absence of bashfulness (*taḥaššud*). The house is the place where food and care for everyday illness should be provided. It is a space where people eat together, drink together, sleep together, hunger together, get sick together and possibly die together. Togetherness, however, does not imply harmony or the absence of competition and conflicts. Relationships among members of the nuclear family are also wrought with tensions about who is entitled to how much food. This applies to the extended family as well.

Extended households (*dār*) are crucial in supporting weaker nuclear families and ensuring their supply of food. In view of the scarcity of resources in Um Futeima, many young couples cannot get by on their own and are connected to a senior woman's hearth, often the young women's mothers. While the nuclear household (*bayt*) is named after the family head, often a junior man, an extended household (*dār*) is named after its senior man (W. Young 1988: 43), normally denoting the most influential and respected man. For instance, several *buyūt* (pl. of *bayt*) were called *dhuwī* Tahir, literally meaning 'those of' or 'those belonging to' sheikh Tahir: Hamda, her small children (including myself), her married daughters and their husbands, and Antar and his family.[24]

Whereas my Rashaida hosts stressed that there is help (*musāʿada*) from 'awlād ʿamm, or plainly that 'they give you', in the above examples there was no unproblematic conformity to these behavioural expectations. Poor families also garnered much support from their extended families. But an important difference is that this was not classified as help (*musāʿada*). This invites reflection on the quality of relationships among the extended family. As opposed to 'awlād ʿamm, among members of the extended family – children, parents and siblings – there can be no 'help'. There is only the obligation to give support – emotional or material – in terms of monetary gifts or by expressing concern for the sick by visiting and providing them with company. I argued that death and its aversion is considered the responsibility of the patrilineage. Helping thus conceived implies a paradox, an emphasis on economic differences and the normative expectations of solidarity as paternal kin (cf. Carsten 1997: 14), and simultaneously a sort of distance or othering, a standing outside of the nuclear and extended family. Hamid called such help 'generosity', additionally implying an acknowledgement of economic asymmetries. In many cases, help was literally mobilized from great physical distances through technologically mediated ties between migrant kin in the Gulf and residents in Sudan. But not all such transfers were recognized as help. Help (*musāʿada*) implies going out of one's way for another in a situation that deserves urgent attention, such as a severe accident or life-threatening sickness. 'Help' in this sense can also be seen as a specific invested form that implies a set of prescriptive expectations of what ʾawlād ʿamm should be willing to do in critical situations, namely, help; such expectations have to be met in order to avoid sanctions, such as a bad reputation.

Reference to ʾawlād ʿamm can be understood as a convention in the sense of Boltanski and Thévenot (2006) – that is, a widely accepted framework for interpretation and evaluation upon which people can rely in controversial situations. It is a principle of coordination, a logic by which actions can be narrated and justified but also exposed as insufficient. It helps in making sense of a situation and what should count, namely, solidarity among the patrilineage which transcends economic inequalities. At the same time, to actually enable a coordination of actions, it has to be invoked and performed in practice, whereby it has to be adjusted to the situation at hand. Thus, while the ʾawlād ʿamm logic is highly prescriptive, it is at the same time invented, remade and negotiated in dealing with sickness. In mobilizing help to finance therapies, more distant kinship relations – in a performative, postfoundational sense – are asserted and thereby come into being. Biological ideas of kinship are secondary. Reflecting on Futoum's sickness, Zeinab explains that she had known the shopkeeper in Seidon for many years as he used to live in a neighbouring campsite. He is not her wad ʿamm but a more distant kinsman from her lineage, descended from her grandfather's brother. By calling him her father's brother's son, she was referring to his actions, which make him like a father's brother's son to her. It means that somebody, although not literally related in a way that would oblige the person to help, assumes the expectations that accompany this social role and then actually becomes the wad ʿamm.

This supports Carsten's (1997: 23) contention that 'kinship is not a lifeless and pre-given force which in some mysterious way determines the form of people's relations with each other. On the contrary, it consists of the many small actions, exchanges, friendships and enmities that people themselves create in their everyday lives'. Hamid, for instance, also mentioned that he received help to deal with his serious accident from his maternal cousins (ʾawlād ḫāl). In contrast, neither intimate relationships within the family nor asymmetrical relationships between patron and client need to be rhetorically invoked and performed to be a resource in times of need. This underscores that the ʾawlād ʿamm logic is a peculiar, somewhat contradictory, but also pliable invested form when death lurks and a collective beyond the extended family needs to be moved to finance therapies. Both formalistic and experiential, prescriptive and negotiated relationships of patrilineal kinship exemplify the ties that can be activated situationally and that are thereby created to deal with the uncertainties of ill health.

Assistance was provided within nuclear and extended families, by neighbours and patrons. But importantly assistance was also delayed and denied in cases of 'normal sickness'. 'Sickness' mobilized different responses and involved collective therapy management groups of different sizes and shapes. There are no stable and robust networks of care in place; 'there is nothing cosy and readily sustaining' about informal networks (Horden 1998: 34). In a volume on *The Locus of Care*, Horden and Smith (1998: 1, 2, 9) seek to debunk the tenacious myth that household- or kin-based systems of support mark a golden age and ideal state of care, moved by love and concern, which in many Western countries has been replaced with an inferior and rationalized public care provision. This myth has resulted in too broad a generalization of the nuclear family's generous role in caring for poor needy ones and it leaves aside the constraints weighing on care in an economy of scarcity.[25] When my interlocutors in Sudan needed care beyond the realm of the everyday, it was provided through asymmetrical relationships, between wealthier and poorer paternal kin or patrons and clients.

This brings us back to a point made in the introduction of this book: the lack of 'modern' institutions that can address and contain the most outstanding vicissitudes of human existence, such as the perils of suffering and death, and that can normalize the risk for population categories. When we think about 'the locus of care' with Horden and Smith, then in Sudan we have to conclude that the government only to a very limited and highly selective degree cares for its citizens. Among Rashaida in the Lower Atbara area responsibility is assumed by families – nuclear and extended – and when death is near, responsibility is often distributed more widely, mostly among paternal kin. There are strikingly few health-related transfers in the community that are not underwritten by kin ties and/or patron-client relationships. In this connection Horden (1998: 54–57) makes an arresting point: many ancient sources point to co-residence/neighbourhood as an even more binding principle than kinship or family ties in farming communities. But what does this mean for a people who have only known settled life for a few years? Solidarity among Rashaida, who used to be nomadic breeders of camels and small stock, was rooted in an ideal of patrilineage and agnatic descent. The established principle of patrilineal kinship is manifested in the settled context and is still prescriptive to a certain extent. Translating the old ways to the new setting means that the relationships through which support is actually extended tend to be conceived in terms of patrilineal kinship.

Conclusion

This chapter has dealt with the uncertainties of assessing ill health and when to seek a therapy, the uncertain convergences between individual and collective judgements of 'sickness' and the ensuing un/willingness to help, and the uncertainties of classifying sickness as either chronic or urgent. Chronic illness poses interpretative problems, while crises enable the bracketing of uncertainties. The main focus was on how poor people live through uncertainties regarding ill health; how they interpret their situation and deliberate options in dealing with them; and how they voice a health concern; and how this appeal mobilizes emotions and money.

I suggested that 'normal sickness' is common to a specific social category: those who 'do not have a thing' (mā ʿindahum ḥāǧa), encompassing the old, poor, dependent and chronically sick. Normal sickness is associated with poverty, a type of health uncertainty and minor suffering that relates to scant material endowments and little food. Poor families are expected to endure these ailments of everyday life silently. Asking for help is deemed shameful. This raises the threshold for helping such needy ones. Uncertainty pertains exactly to knowing when ill health is severe enough to deserve treatment. It must be reclassified with some degree of exceptionality and urgency. For poor people this uncertainty entails making and enacting a distinction between normal and life-threatening sickness and anticipating whether their evaluation of the situation will be shared by others.

For the giver/provider of care or money, the challenge is to assess and qualify the situation correctly, that is, to anticipate which interpretations will be shared by others, to project the relationship both into the past and into the future, and to know when help is really needed and in which times the sickness is 'normal'. This uncertainty that the potential provider of care experiences in a setting where scarce resources have to be carefully allocated explains the reluctance to voice problems and to give money and why poor people often receive help belatedly. I suggested a strong link between a family's material situation and the moment when 'sickness' is established as a form to generate curative actions: the poorer the family, the later the category 'sickness' is applied. Death needs to be lurking. The more exceptional and surprising the health problem, the more likely it will move people to donate money. Sickness in this understanding emerges as any physical ailment worth treating, but what and who is worthy of treatment is negotiated in asymmetrical relationships between people and according to situational dynamics.

This uncertainty about the condition of people with ill health and the outcomes is a gnawing and debilitating experience. Wondering, waiting, worrying, perhaps regretting. But in the cases discussed the perceived forebodings of death could swiftly transform a paralyzing uncertainty into an urgency for action. To return to a central pillar of my argument, this transition from ill health to sickness is facilitated by investments of forms. To process uncertainties, forms – here categories and labels – were established through tautological expressions. For instance, Muslima established knowledge about her son's sickness and confirmed this time and again. Or in Salman's case, before he received care, consensus was established that he really was sick and needed to be treated by a healer. It is about establishing equivalences, framing certain understandings as facts, as an unquestioned state of affairs that everyone knows is urgent and that invites further actions. The urgency to survive can bracket uncertainty about the situation and the need to act. When something is established as a 'crisis' this form promotes people to assemble a network of concerned allies, money and transport, but it does not suspend uncertainty about outcomes. It rather defines it as a matter of urgent uncertainty.

In an economy of scarcity, as in the marginalized hinterlands of north-eastern Sudan, resources have to be prudently allocated and rationed. There is no room for squandering. There are different responsibilities for the everyday and the exceptional realm. The house is responsible for daily needs – both food and ill health. Poor people – for example, Antar, Zeinab and Birkiya, or the chronically sick Salman – rely heavily on their extended families and patron–client relationships to care for their everyday needs. Money for medical treatment given by parents, brothers and patrons is not considered help. Rather, help means going out of one's way, and is reserved for exceptional crises. In view of the multiple uncertainties and the fear of death, Rashaida attach particular values to 'auwlād ʿamm relations and confirm the obligation to help along the patrilineage lines in times of crises. Yet, in practice, by way of extension of the prescriptive expectations towards patrilineal kin, a discrete collective to finance medical treatment was mobilized from whoever is ready to give for each and every case of sickness that was found to be worth treating. A therapy financing group as a social form was constituted with each case of ill health and is most inclusive and generous financially when ill health is defined as a 'serious sickness' or sudden emergency; after such moments it gradually peters out.

What does it mean when one circumstance is defined as sickness that must be treated for one person and as a 'normal sickness' for another? Are some people worthier than others? People would not think of it in terms of worth but honour. Some are more honourable (ʿazīz), self-sufficient and able than others who are considered weak and unable (miskīn). That the latter need help in shocking and exceptional crises and accidents is taken for granted. These grander uncertainties are more likely to elicit a response. It is the gruelling uncertainties around health problems that poor people live through daily which often go unnoticed or are muted and ignored.

Notes

1. See Roitman (2013) for an enquiry into the concept of crisis and how it is often taken for granted as an a priori in scholarly analyses.
2. I already noted that many people I encountered in the nomadic hinterlands of north-eastern Sudan demanded upon meeting that their names be put down in my book. I suggested that this is partly caused by people's increasing awareness of development aid programmes and their understandings of organizational procedures.
3. This is at least somewhat peculiar in view of public discourses in Sudan, which depict Rashaida as being backwards, recalcitrant in the face of change, and superstitious.
4. This report was released before the secession of South Sudan on 9 July 2011, and thus pertains to both Sudan and South Sudan and to the situation before violent conflicts had reignited in South Kordofan, Blue Nile and Darfur.
5. International NGOs have attempted to fill this large gap left by the government: for instance, in 2005 a total governmental health budget of about US $80–90 million was available for 36 million citizens. In the same year, international NGOs offered health services and humanitarian assistance of US $390 million (FMOH 2007a: 18, 19). In March 2009, after the Sudanese president Omar al-Bashir was indicted by the International Criminal Court, thirteen international organizations were expelled from Sudan, among them Save the Children and Doctors without Borders ('NGO Expelled from Darfur Considered ICC Cooperation' 2009).
6. For example, in 1989 a more capital-oriented medical supply system was inaugurated in Khartoum State, the so-called Revolving Drug Fund (RDF). This medical supply system was put in place through the cooperative efforts of Save the Children, UK, who invested much of the project's initial capital to purchase supplies and start the programme in sixty health centres, and the Ministry of Health (Ali 2009). The RDF was successful in generating the necessary revenues from customers to keep this medical supply system running and was gradually extended to all Sudanese states (ibid.). However, it had trouble in servicing war-torn areas and SPLM/A-controlled areas, being inefficient, slow and irregular, and it did not overcome regional inequalities (Sharif 2015).
7. For instance, dressing stations and primary care units – which are already considered as offering services below the official minimum standard – should refer patients to health care centres, which in turn transfer difficult cases to hospitals in towns, which are funded by the State Ministry of Health (SMOH). The SMOH is also in charge of establishing, administering and financing more specialized health facilities in state capitals (FMOH 2007a: 11). This decentralization of responsibility, in the view of World Bank analysts, has 'led to deterioration of the primary health care system, in particular in rural and peripheral areas' (Decaillet et al. 2003: 7).
8. The Federal Ministry of Health (2007a: 11) states: 'in principle PHC units are staffed by community health workers (CHWs), while dressing stations are staffed by a nurse and/or a medical assistant, and dispensaries are headed by a medical assistant'. Health centres in contrast are supposed to be headed by a physician and the above-mentioned health units should refer difficult cases to these facilities, but due to the preferred location in towns, up to 50 per cent of health centres are inoperative (Decaillet et al. 2003: 6, 7; FMOH 2007a: 11).
9. While in Um Futeima there is a building for the health centre and a house for the physician, erected by the Kuwaiti charity (cf. chapter 2), neither doctor nor nurse had been found to service the village.

10. Alternative medical treatment can also be sought in the Lower Atbara area. People from the settlement occasionally consulted so-called seers or traditional healers (*baṣīr*) and a *ḥaṭāṭa*, a Bishari woman laying out cowrie shells, who promised to treat ailments such as infertility. However, during my stay in Um Futeima these healers were consulted to a much lesser degree. A possible explanation for this is that in view of their poverty people tended to wait and sought treatment only in cases of emergency – and serious cases, as many people mentioned, had to be referred to Atbara.

11. In contrast, to Young (1988), who still mentioned the use of amulets and other lucky charms to prevent misfortunes among Rashaida, I only rarely encountered such objects in the settlement. My interlocutors referred to such changes and linked them to their increasing conversion to a purer Islam. The sheikhs in particular admonished people that such practices cause the backwardness of Rashaida and prevent their integration into the Islamic riverine society of Sudan.

12. Whyte (1997) has shown how divination can provide people with a means of assessing uncertainty about the causes of misfortune and about social relationships, even if these practices remain inconclusive, and how people can protect themselves through magical practices. My interlocutors in the Lower Atbara area knew about such practices, but situated them in a time before they knew about proper Islam and tended to laugh about their own foolishness. However, the chapter on gold mining showed that Rashaida do causally relate wealth/poverty to divine providence. An Islamic God is seen as preordaining all things, allotting shares, but at the same time remains inscrutable and remote from people's daily lives. There is an idea of fate but it does not diminish uncertainty. Rashaida are pragmatic, as highlighted by the gold prospectors – everyone must test empirically what exactly it is that God has ordained.

13. Parsons (1991: 302) wrote: 'Within these limits there is a very important area of uncertainty. As in so many practical situations, some of the factors bearing on this one may be well understood, but others are not. The exact relation of the known to the unknown elements cannot be determined; the unknown may operate at any time to invalidate expectations built up on analysis of the known'.

14. The nurse prescribed medicine for SDG 15 (€ 5) and took another SDG 10 (€ 3) for the examination. Muslima paid SDG 12 (€ 4) for her and her mother's transportation. She invited the other women for breakfast in a cafeteria for another SDG 12. She spent another SDG 25 (€ 8) on cosmetics (hair oil, lotion) and food (bananas, tomatoes, biscuits, milk powder, wheat bread). She lent SDG 5 to Museilma's daughter and SDG 5 to her sister to buy a lotion for her injured feet; Museilma herself asked Muslima to lend her SDG 10. Muslima locked the last SDG 5 in a small box with her personal belongings in Hamda's hut.

15. This explains why Zeinab was so angry and demanded the allocation of a milk goat by the charity.

16. It is not only Antar but also his wife Noura who is treated with disdain. For instance, I once observed a situation in which Hamda and her daughter asked Noura whether she had cooked and what she had cooked. Noura, taken aback, replied, 'What do you know?' She retorted that she ate bread. The women then replied that they had not seen the smoke from her fire. She said she still had leftovers.

17. Noura is Tahir's sister: they have the same mother but different fathers.

18. But there is also an affinal tie: Antar is married to Tahir's half-sister Noura. Noura was born to Tahir's mother, whose first husband had divorced her, after her remarriage.

19. In contrast, any hesitation in 'Ubeid's case relates to Muslima's dependence upon Tahir in mediating the access to money and thereafter treatment.

20. Between October 2009 and May 2010 Salman was taken to the river three times.
21. Salman is but one of several people who need continual care. Zeinab and her husband, who is old and confused, are supported in their daily food needs by her brother and sometimes by her daughter's husband. Although they are not necessarily chronically sick, old people also have to be supported financially by others. Usually older people are provided for by their sons or other close, co-resident family members.
22. In monogamous marriages the house is named after the family head, while in polygamous marriages each house is identified by reference to the woman (W. Young 1988: 41, 42).
23. The new husband is expected to have furnished his bride with kitchen equipment and importantly also foodstuffs. Compare with Carsten (1997: 34ff) for the links between house construction and cooking in Kedah, Malaysia.
24. W. Young (1988: 71ff) pointed out that social relations materialized in terms of spatial residence patterns, whereby a central place in a camp site was reserved for the most senior man. In Um Futeima, Tahir as the senior man occupied the largest house among those of his lineage, the space closest to the village centre, particularly the mosque. The other houses of 'those belonging to him' are dispersed around and behind Tahir's house, as if shielding him from the open and potentially dangerous desert. Hamda's house is behind Tahir's, those of her married daughters to her left and right. Noura and Antar's house is farthest away from the village centre and Tahir's house, as is Salman's house.
25. Horden and Smith (1998: 9) contend that there have always been limitations in kin-based care – this is a historical continuity – and that mostly a mixed economy of care is in place, meshing formal/informal aspects as well as mutually supportive horizontal and vertical ties. Along these lines Horden (1998: 52) observes that there are 'numerous testimonies to the fragility and unpredictability of support networks among the poor; to the calculating, instrumental manner in which transactions are undertaken; to the narrowness of the sphere within which support may be hoped for (whether because of reluctance or unavailability); and finally, crucially, to the frequency with which the "horizontal" world of informal networks is very seldom self-contained but continually intersects with the "vertical" world of patronage and institutions'.

UNCERTAINTY AND FORMS

Asking New Questions

This book has sought to make a step towards a new approach to the anthropology of uncertainty. It claims to have identified tools in other realms of the social sciences to prepare and analyse ethnographic field material in ways which are better able to capture insecurities and unknowns of various kinds. Acknowledging uncertainty at the heart of the human condition is – following pragmatism – crucial to make sense of human efforts to hold things together. I have proposed to look at forms as the temporarily unquestioned props for action, following in particular Thévenot (1984) and Boltanski and Thévenot (2006), and at how they are crafted, confirmed and contested to gain insights into how at least some level of stability, predictability and coherence is achieved. I have outlined the ways in which different uncertainty phenomena are being dealt with by breaking down the indeterminacies into lesser and better known unknowns. In describing this down-scaling of uncertainties, I became aware that the ways in which knowledge about the unknown is engaged – interrogated or posited as real and true – is crucial to differentiating between uncertainties. Risks are model cases because framing something as risk assumes that references are so stable that probablities can be calculated. In other cases, references were taken to be less stable. In the following I will first summarize the analytical and ethnographic insights this book has made regarding the situation of Rashaida in the Lower Atbara area, and then show how these insights contribute to a pragmatic theory of uncertainty.

Ethnographic Contributions

I have taken the reader through various situations. This book has discussed charitable gifts and a controversy surrounding the communal distribution of donated resources; the emergence of new livelihoods from gold mining and the insistence on organizational forms; the scarcity of food and equivalence in exchanges among women; and finally health concerns and challenges in the management of treatment. It is time to return to the questions with which I began. In which particular ways is uncertainty as a human condition experienced in Sudan and how can this be studied? How is uncertainty qualified and processed? Have I found answers?

The experience of uncertainty is both daunting and contextual: the limited predictability of daily life in Sudan is caught up with a national political system that does not protect and insure its citizenry against harm. Such a failure at the national level links to globalizing processes of political and economic ordering that produce black holes, pushing people out towards the margins and producing 'wasted lives' – that is, people excluded from global capitalism (for instance, Rottenburg 2002; Stichweh 2005; Bauman 2007). Such ordering is reinforced by various intersecting sociocultural, economic and political processes of marginalization at work within Sudan, which result in a massive exclusion of rural populations. I have suggested that institutional mechanisms aimed at securing the general population never developed in Sudan. We arrive at a situation in the Lower Atbara area where resources are scarce and survival is often the immediate concern. While the surge in gold mining holds out the promise of new wealth for some, the daily lives of poor people are overshadowed by hunger, sickness and death.

The specific character of uncertainties that Rashaida live through in this part of Sudan relates to an economy of scarcity whose contours I have sketched out in the various chapters. Most people in Um Futeima are poor. Still, some are better-off, mostly due to migrant labour transfers, but apart from one or two households nobody can be considered so wealthy that food and money are always available. In this economy of scarcity, rationing and conserving access to the few central resources underpins survival. Apportioning vital resources is crucial to maintaining some level of control and predictability – essentials of life have to be protected and guarded; they cannot be wasted or put at risk. Getting enough food is an ongoing concern in Um Futeima. 'To avoid eating' is a strategic, episodic hunger as a means of rationing scarce supplies. Similar to the exchange of staples, it is an option for people who have a source of income and have to overcome short-term supply gaps. Food cannot be shared freely but is largely subject to calculation and balanced reciprocity. People 'who do not have a thing' are the hungry ones. Hunger and affliction is accepted as being unavoidable among this group of have-nots. Similarly money for medical treatment has to be allocated with care and restraint. Sickness is often not treated. Some die. People have to deliberate the appropriateness of voicing a need in a setting where needs are greater than the means to accommodate them on a very basic level. When a situation is understood as urgent is not self-evident. Urgency is established in painstaking/laborious investments of forms, interpretations that have to be made by an emerging therapy financing group to hold together and provide clear orientations for acting.

When livelihoods – incomes, food, and health – are at stake, uncertainties are limited by focusing on what can be reasonably assumed and posited. For instance, men refrained from criticizing the distribution of shares from gold mining because this might mean their exclusion from the main source of revenue. In contrast, the items distributed by the charity, while coveted, were not indispensable for life and where anyhow just a drop in an ocean of poverty. People criticized the distribution as unfair because they could afford to do so without suffering immediate existential consequences.

Individuals experience uncertainties differently, but there are still patterns in how unknowns are commonly experienced. Exploring uncertainty through gender, we can learn what enables/limits agency in existential situations. Rashaida women in this part of Sudan tend to experience various uncertainties more severely than men. Perhaps this is not surprising among people who favour boys over girls and base their kinship system on agnatic descent. Rashaida men have a greater range of agency in dealing with unknowns: they are free to move about, they control productive resources and money, they can establish credit at shops and borrow money from kin and friends – unless they are classified as poor. Male agency is perhaps best exemplified by the gold miners I introduced, who may take the risks of working underground or eschew them, calculating and deciding on options. However, men, although being granted more room to navigate, are also expected to shoulder more of the responsibility. Caring for the daily needs of family members is the duty of the family head. There is little help available from kin and neighbours to meet daily needs such as food, or money to treat minor illness. This responsibility adds further nuances to grasping the insistence on forms in artisanal gold mining and why men may avoid challenging organizational forms, even when inconsistencies arise. Men appear to accept the hierarchies and inequalities in the artisanal gold sector because they have few alternatives when it comes to earning an income. For them the issue at stake is not only providing for their families, feeding their children and wives, but also showing that one is able and honourable, a man in the full sense of the word. These more urgent concerns help to explain why reflexively questioning what is going on is not always desirable. Rashaida men focus on the extractive work to be done, not its modalities and conditions. A pragmatic orientation towards doing and achieving something together with others to a certain extent has to rule out questioning the grounds of actions reflexively (see, for instance, Dewey 1929; Rottenburg 2005a; Thévenot 2007; Boltanski 2011). In artisanal gold mining, where the need to earn an income is paramount but utterly unpredictable, the insistence on forms prevents paralyzing complications, which could interrupt this precious source of revenue. The same applies in existential moments, such as a health crisis, when a moral urgency to preserve lives forbids probing the truth and coherence of reality claims, and uncertainty about the situation is rather translated into an uncertainty about outcomes.

Women depend on men for their living. Their actions are more circumscribed by moral understandings, which limit the radius of female activities predominantly to the house and its immediate surroundings. Their options to lend food and money are restricted and sanctioned by the norm of shame ('aib), which denies them the ability to go to shops and marketplaces and to talk to men. To avoid shaming themselves and their male providers, women need to display bashfulness (taḥaššud), a sense of modesty that acknowledges an inferior position in hierarchical relations.[1] In contrast, honour is closely connected to the ideal of autonomy, being free, self-reliant (if not, wealthy) and strong, something only men can fully realize among Rashaida I met.

In contrast to men, the options and also the responsibility of women for subsistence is limited. It is not their fault if they run out of food or if their children need treatment: it is the responsibility of the men to find solutions. But in practice men were frequently absent and women had to cope with hunger and/or limited supplies for an uncertain time. The food exchange system in place underscores how women can situationally negotiate forms that can enhance the predictability of daily life. Or think of Museilma, who gradually achieved a consensus among the people around her that her son was sick and needed to be treated. Zeinab's case was interesting. She acted in a self-reliant way in a case of life-threatening sickness, moving beyond normative constraints that weigh upon the behaviour of women and poor people. Poor men are in a similar situation to that of women. Unlike 'real men', they are dependent and lack honour. They also need to display taḥaššud and cannot freely borrow or ask for things they need, in view of their inability to reciprocate. The options of women and dependent people (clients, poor people) in dealing with the perils of existence hence are constricted but can be transcended by individuals.

The chapters in this book have explored an anxiety about the future, an unease about acting and a loss of orientation in view of various unknowns. Uncertainties can be extreme and can lead to a questioning of the presumptions about what is going on, what is real and what is just. But more often, uncertainties in this part of Sudan appear as nagging, vexing sensations, doubts about renderings of reality related to existential fears in the everyday. My point is that uncertainties have to be processed in some way to enable acting, to overcome the paralysis of not knowing how or where to direct one's actions. I have tacked back and forth between the experience of uncertainty and the semantic work through which forms as temporarily unquestioned props for action are crafted, invoked, confirmed and contested. In a setting where resources constantly have to be apportioned and meted out with care, uncertainties can only partially be controlled. Doubts about what is just and what is tolerable are bound to emerge. Daily life in Um Futeima is infused with reflexivity and criticism. Still, difficulties are not intellectualized. Like most rural people, Rashaida in this area of Sudan have to be pragmatic. The uncertainties I examined caused disconcertment, but more often than not was translated into something manageable of a lesser reflexivity, as attention was directed to an activity or a goal.[2]

Contributions to Pragmatic Theories of Uncertainty

Uncertainty is such a vague and elusive notion that it can slip away from us even when we are in the middle of discussing it. In this book, it sometimes concerned outcomes such as hunger and death, while at other times it related to understanding the situation and developing the means to deal with it appropriately. To structure my argument our journey I explored the links between uncertainty, reflexivity and the forms that people create to make their actions social, i.e., comprehensible and to some degree predictable. Uncertainty in this book is mainly about figuring out what to do and how to do it, and to a lesser extent about problems that cause uncertainties or the outcomes of action. While I focus on forms and thereby on the means to an end, I do not suggest that means and ends can be sensibly pulled apart. Rather, following Dewey, I argue that this compartmentalization emanates from an a posteriori reflectivity. Uncertainty precisely means that the conception of an end, a goal or an option is lacking, since what the situation is about is unclear, as is the course of action that can take us to an end. As people devise ways to address uncertainty, they are beginning to outline what is problematic about the situation and therewith they are beginning to articulate a solution. Deploying Dewey's argument helped me to clarify what uncertainty meant in the settings I studied: I am dealing with uncertainties that relate to acute problems demanding resolution, but in circumstances where knowledge about how to act is in crisis. I am not considering uncertainty as a primarily epistemological problem – the predicament of a loss of foundations for knowledge claims. My concern is with existential problems and actions.

Much of the interest in social theory in uncertainty has been focused on the problem of being unable to determine outcomes and thus the inability to be confident in which direction to move forward (see Zinn 2008 for an overview). While this is an important concern of people in existential circumstances, there is more to consider when one follows pragmatism. Uncertainty can be perceived as a chance people have to change the world they inhabit, to challenge and enrich it. Boltanski and Thévenot attend to this additional dimension of uncertainty that I qualified as constitutive and which is their starting point. It concerns what is, what has value and how we can know it, and thus relates not only to outcomes of action but also to the very conditions under which something like 'purposive action' and 'social coordination' can be conceived at all. The proposed approach enables tracing small movements, investments of forms, through which security in acting can be increased. It refrains from taking stability or continuity as starting point and as the normal modus operandi of ordering practices. If there is stability, this is examined as the outcome of ordering practices; its main focus is on practices in concrete situations and on the elements that are tied together in them. Formulated more generally, this approach offers an account of how knowledge is institutionalized through practices and how institutionalized elements – i.e. the often mentioned forms – are engaged in practices – as unquestioned premises or as stumbling blocks causing critique. It does not outline a way to overcome uncertainty and achieve a final ordering of things – this would anyhow be futile, but rather it is very much attuned to the interplay between continuity and innovation.[3] Emerging knowledge and orderings are always provisional, and how effectively they stabilize in time and space is an empirical question.

My main point was that various kinds of uncertainty can be differentiated based on the degree of confidence in reality with which situations and invested forms in them are engaged. Uncertainties somehow play out between two extremes – a radical doubt about all entrenched knowledges, and a situation premised on consensus where uncertainty is bracketed and critical examination is limited. This argument is supported particularly by two situations analysed in this book, in which my Rashaida hosts dealt very differently with uncertainties. In chapter 2 I discussed how radical uncertainty erupted and challenged the distribution of gifts in the community, and chapter 3, which debated how gold miners turned a blind eye to the exploitive character of their activities, bracketing uncertainties in the social organization of mining to gain a livelihood – if God wills. Continuing the debate on how forms are used to process indeterminacies, chapter 4 showed how a nagging, existential uncertainty of female everyday life was limited. To buffer the exhaustion of food supplies, women engaged in exchange. They invested in standards of exchange to restrain the uncertainty of equivalence. In chapter

5, attention shifted to situations in which urgent action was required. It dealt with the uncertain transitions between ill health and serious sickness. When urgency was signalled and death appeared as a possible outcome, reflexive projects had to be bracketed, while all efforts were expended to save lives. To reiterate a point made in the introduction, radical uncertainty denotes a highly reflexive interrogation of foundations. It does not qualify the affective quality of uncertainty, whether one type is more fear-inspiring or emotionally troubling than another. The dread of death from sickness is undoubtedly more agonizing than the unease that results from doubts about the status of knowledge in the controversy about the charity's gifts, even if the chances for something new to emerge are greater in the latter situation.

The ways in which uncertainties are processed are subject to the values at stake: something was classified as a sickness earlier when a wealthier person was affected, whereas the same condition was not yet registered as such among the poorer. The ways in which uncertainties are processed also depends upon the power relations implicated in shaping the forms of coordination: in gold mining the asymmetrical ability to define the rules of sharing and team composition, social categories, shifts, appointments, etc. is both pronounced and uncontested. Owners set the rules, workers abide by them.[4] The theoretical approach I have chosen captures such asymmetries through the notion of 'semantic domination' (Boltanski 2011: 9). The term 'semantic' denotes a kind of domination pertaining to the creation and imposition of meanings, that is, the establishment of qualifications, which define beings and their worth. Referring to the creation of meaning as 'domination' highlights the coerciveness of all forms and points to their fragility. Establishing forms means shaping a reality, thereby forfeiting alternatives at least temporarily, although doubts may arise at any time (Thévenot 2007: 412–14; Blokker and Brighenti 2011: 384–85). Therefore forms may only appear to be neutral and technical on the surface; enquiry reveals that they are profoundly normative. This frailty of all forms easily leads to charges of injustice, oppression and arbitrariness. It threatens cooperation, but in other cases it is liberating by challenging taken-for-granted normativities.

But why were some forms more stable than others? I have related this to the reflexivity with which situations and the material surroundings that give shape to them are addressed. Reflexivity – or more precisely, 'reflexive enquiry' – is central to the stability of forms. It means testing, trying, examining and validating forms, the premises and grounds of convictions about what is accepted as reality. When contested, forms and their foundations have to be explained and have to be connected to widely-held moral ideas and/or materialities that tend to be taken for granted (lists, standardized vessels, detectors, etc.). The hedging in of uncertainties appeared to be more successful when founded on well-known representations, collective and learned experiential patterns as well as widely shared moral ideas, such as the imaginary of divine ordination in artisanal gold mining. The God-givenness of wealth and livelihood is an understanding that probably all Rashaida are familiar with; it cannot be contested publicly without deviating from religious doctrine. In contrast, forms seem to be less stable when they draw upon less widely shared moral ideas.[5]

I repeat one point for emphasis: meanings are crucial in this approach to uncertainty but so is materiality. Forms and the reality constructions they support are more stable when they are underwritten by material objects. Some forms (lists, appointments, rules of sharing profits, etc.) hinged on bureaucratic procedure, but their stability was contingent upon materialization: for example, having an authentication paper to support a claim to an artisanal gold mine or keeping written accounts of profits and calculated shares. Conversely, during the distribution organized by the charitable foundation, the failure to produce any evidence of the list's existence led to its disintegration. This finding resonates with scholarship in science and technology studies, which stresses the obstinate character of objects and their ability to stabilize social arrangements.

My contribution was to focus on forms, a recent pragmatist revision of what classical sociology and anthropology called 'institution', and to flesh out ways to make this useful for empirical work, particularly outside of Europe and North America. Institutions are central to the in/stability of social orders and they can create regularity and predictability; uncertainty thus is a problem of low predictability. The pragmatist take on institutions is that they are mainly semantic devices to bestow meaning on the world and order it. In this they follow an established tradition represented in anthropology, for instance, by Evans-Pritchard or Mary Douglas. Yet, arguing in a practice theoretical and pragmatist idiom, social action was seen as being neither determined by institutions, as Evans-Pritchard and Douglas would have had it, nor by interests and cost-benefit calculations. Rather, French neopragmatism identified the dialectics of confirmation and critique as being at the core of institutions and the emergence of social orders. People's everyday practices thus draw on manifold forms and institutions on different scales of ordering and thereby confirm them, but inconsistencies and incoherences are bound to emerge and, with them, uncertainties. In such moments, individuals can and will get beneath the surface to 'dig up dirt' on institutions and expose them, if need be. All forms involve coercion and thus are also fragile, because the exclusion of some elements can always be pointed out. Thus, the central work of institutions is to establish equivalence and commonality between positions, which are invariably heterogeneous and dissenting.

While my focus has been on forms on a more or less micro level, this approach can also offer valuable inputs to the discussion about problems of statecraft in Sudan (see also Calkins et al. 2015a). Firstly, the heterogeneity of the population in Sudan should not necessarily be considered as an obstacle to peace (to be solved through coerced homogenization, i.e., Islamization and Arabization policies). The problem is the absence of institutional mechanisms, which can peacefully format and negotiate different interests.

Secondly, institutions – especially so-called traditional institutions – are often depicted as timeless regulative constructs, clearly delineated and immutable, which are related to predefined groups such as tribes or cultures, pitted against modern institutions. A pragmatist stance does not reproduce a binary between modern and traditional institutions but is attentive to situational sense-making and the interlacing of the old and the new on different scales of ordering, i.e., from the establishment of small local agreements, as I outlined, to state law.

Thirdly, in postcolonial Sudan Studies there has been comparatively scant interest in social theory. Instead a main focus has been on ethnographies that explored the specificities of various places and ethnic groups, overall highlighting the historical-cultural uniqueness of Sudan (see Assal and Abdul-Jalil 2015 for an overview of the past 50 years of anthropology in Sudan). Adopting a pragmatist stance allows us to connect the un/making of social orders in Sudan to broader theoretical debates about knowledge production and institutions, and enables us to connect everyday understandings of what should be the case in Sudan to debates about global justice and governance.

Fourthly, while I have deployed a particular analytics taken from French pragmatist thought, I do not wish to imply that the ethnographic exploration of uncertainty can be guided only by this. Rather, I have selected an approach that is particularly good at capturing people's struggles in coming to grips with intolerable material conditions and whatever limits them in realizing new forms of being. There surely are other useful approaches. However, in contrast to earlier approaches that saw people constrained by their modes of thought and their institutions, a focus on becoming 'has the potential of art: to invoke neglected human potentials and to expand the limits of understanding and imagination – a people yet to come' (Biehl and Locke 2010: 337).

I have joined the chorus of those who argue that something can be gained from disbanding a tendency towards closure and fixation in ethnographic narrations. This book was written as an attempt to capture the subtleties of experience and indeterminacies and to open up to the unexpected, even the improbable. It is likely to raise many questions and only offers tentative responses to some of them. Yet, I contend that this approach enables insights into how knowledge is made and solidified in the management of uncertainties. I tracked how people in north-eastern Sudan, ethnically classified as Rashaida, create meanings in different situations by drawing on old forms and inventing new ones, and how they align them, adjust them coherently and test them in situations. I deployed the notion of forms and traced the stabilization of forms in circumstances with different senses of urgency and need for coordination. Forms are material-semiotic things that can hold action together. In my ethnography, classifications, social categories, and rules of behaviour were forms that were most frequently called upon in situations to clear up some aspects of uncertainty. I traced how such forms were established, reinterpreted or criticized, the latter depending mainly on a reflexive exploration of the hiatus between present and desired circumstances. Forms, when institutionalized, figure as elements of reality. At the same time they not only define what is real but importantly they embody normative ideas about what should be. Hunting for forms in different situations was productive. These analytical devices helped me to explore how different ways of engaging them reflexively test realities and enact different versions of what could and/or should be. 'Investments of forms' are practices of anticipating certain futures, and this type of anticipatory knowledge production is a means of enhancing security in acting; it establishes anchors for doing. These practices and forms may give way to new uncertainties.

The Rashaida in the Lower Atbara area who were my hosts live through existential uncertainties. They process them in ways that are attuned to their specific situations and in view of multiple processes of marginalization, which attempt to keep them constrained, to make their future more calculable. Theirs is often a struggle for survival, not due to war and forced displacement as in other parts of Sudan but rather because they have to get by on scarce resources, relying on their own efforts to deal with everyday hardships such as hunger, sickness and dwindling incomes. But not all is gloominess. Uncertainty is a part of the human condition and experience and also opens a space for hope, a space to renegotiate social inequalities. With uncertainty something new can arise.

Notes

1. Although derived from another Arabic root, this *taḥaššud* resembles the code of modesty (*ḥaššam*) that Abu-Lughod (1986) analyses among Egyptian Bedouins; it is the only way for the weak and dependent to gain some respect and a measure of honour in their situation of dependency. There is a linguistic irregularity: *taḥaššud* is derived from the fifth stem of the Arabic root *ḥašada* (lit. to amass, mobilize, collect) whereas the adjective commonly used (*muḥtašida*) is derived from the eighth stem, the noun being *iḥtišād*. Both, however, denote a state of being densely packed and cramped. Above I suggested that the notion is used in situations when people describe a feeling of bashfulness that

inhibits actions. (For the information in this note, I consulted the Arabic-German version of *The Hans Wehr Dictionary of Modern Written Arabic* [1985].)

2. For example, in gold mining, uncertainties were delegated to technological devices (metal detectors), seen as executors of providence, and were translated into more calculable unknowns through an elaborate system of rules that redistributed risks and benefits among team members.

3. In this way 'structural' conditions of action or moral grammars, if you like, are sometimes taken for granted in anthropology, which tends to focus on how people muddle through, without planning, tossed hither and tither (Johnson-Hanks 2005).

4. An additional example was the prominent role of one sheikh and the charitable foundation's representatives in defining forms of coordination in the distribution campaign.

5. A case in point is the democratic logic that the charity sought to implement during the distribution of camel meat in chapter 3, which did not withstand the test of practice.

References

Abdel Ati, Hassan. 1985. *Lower River Atbara Area (Nile Province)*. Final Report for USAID, Institute of Environmental Studies, University of Khartoum.

Abu-Lughod, Lila. 1986. *Veiled Sentiments: Honor and Poetry in a Beduin Society*. Berkeley, CA: University of California Press.

Ahmed, Abdel Ghaffar M. 1980. 'Planning and the Neglect of Pastoral Nomads in the Sudan', in Gunnar Haaland (ed.), *Problems of Savannah Development: The Sudan Case*. Bergen: Department of Social Anthropology, University of Bergen, 39–54.

Akrich, Madleine. 1992. 'The De-scription of Technological Objects', in Wiebe Bijker and John Law (eds), *Shaping Technology/Building Society*. Cambridge, MA: MIT Press, 205–24.

Alexeyeff, Kalissa. 2004. 'Love Food: Exchange and Sustenance in the Cook Islands Diaspora', *Australian Journal of Anthropology* 15(1), 68–79.

Ali, Gamal K.M. 2009. 'How to Establish a Successful Revolving Drug Fund: The Experience of Khartoum State in the Sudan', *Bulletin of the World Health Organization* 87, 139–42.

Appadurai, Arjun. 1981. 'Gastro-Politics in Hindu South Asia', *American Ethnologist* 8(3), 494–511.

———. 1986. *The Social Life of Things: Commodities in Cultural Perspective*. Cambridge: Cambridge University Press.

Asad, Talal. 1970. *The Kababish Arabs: Power, Authority and Consent in a Nomadic Tribe*. London: Hurst.

———. (ed.) 1973. *Anthropology and the Colonial Encounter*. London: Ithaca.

Assal, Munzoul and Musa Adam Abdul-Jalil. 2015. *Fifty years of Anthropology in the Sudan: Past, Present, and Future*. Bergen: CMI.

Avieli, Nir. 2009. 'At Christmas We Don't Like Pork. Just Like the Maccabees: Festive Food and Religious Identity at the Protestant Christmas Picnic in Hoi An', *Journal of Material Culture* 14(2), 219–41.

Azarya, Victor. 1996. *Nomads and the State in Africa: The Political Roots of Marginality*. Aldershot: Avebury.

Ballard, Chris and Glenn Banks. 2003. 'Resource Wars: The Anthropology of Mining', *Annual Review of Anthropology* 32, 287–313.

Barnett, Tony. 1977. *The Gezira Scheme: An Illusion of Development*. London: Frank Cass.

Barth, Frederik. 1967. 'Economic Spheres in Darfur', in Raymond Firth (ed.), *Themes in Economic Anthropology*. London: Tavistock, 149–74.

Battahani, Atta el. 2000. 'Economic Liberalisation and Civil Society in Sudan, 1989–1995', in K.L. Prah and A.G.M. Ahmed (eds), *Africa in Transformation*. Vol. 2: *Political and Economic Reforms, Transformations and Gender issues*. Addis Ababa: OSSREA, 145–60.

Bauman, Zygmunt. 2007. *Liquid Times: Living in Age of Uncertainty*. Malden: Polity Press.

Bayart, Jean-Francois. 2010. *The State in Africa. The Politics of the Belly*, trans. S. Ellis. 2nd edn. Malden: Polity Press.

Beck, Ulrich. 1986. *Risikogesellschaft: Auf dem Weg in eine andere Moderne*. Frankfurt: Suhrkamp.

———. 1999. *World Risk Society*. Cambridge: Polity Press.

Beck, Ulrich, Wolfgang Bonss and Christoph Lau. 2003. 'The Theory of Reflexive Modernization: Problematic, Hypothesis and Research Programme', *Theory, Culture & Society* 20(2), 1–33.

Biehl, João and Peter Locke. 2010. 'Deleuze and the Anthropology of Becoming', *Current Anthropology* 51(3), 317–51.

Bierschenk, Thomas. 2002. 'Hans-Dieter Evers und die "Bielefelder Schule" der Entwicklungssoziologie'. Working Papers 1, Department of Anthropology and African Studies, Johannes-Guttenberg Universität Mainz.

Bierschenk, Thomas and Olivier de Sardan (eds). 2013. *States at Work: Dynamics of African Bureaucracies*. Leiden: Brill.

Blokker, Paul and Andrea Brighenti. 2011. 'An Interview with Laurent Thévenot: On Engagement, Critique, Commonality and Power', *European Journal of Social Theory* 14(3), 383–400.

Bloor, David. 1991 [1978]. *Knowledge and Social Imagery*. 2nd edn. Chicago: University of Chicago Press.

———. 1999. 'Anti-Latour', *Studies in History and Philosophy of Science* 30(1), 81–112.

Bogusz, Tanja. 2010. *Zur Aktualität von Luc Boltanski: Einleitung in sein Werk*. Wiesbaden: VS Verlag.

Bohannan, Paul and Laura Bohannan. 1968. *Tiv Economy*. Evanston, IL: Northwestern University Press.

Boholm, Åsa. 2003. 'The Cultural Nature of Risk: Can There Be an Anthropology of Uncertainty?', *Ethnos: Journal of Anthropology* 68(2), 159–78.

Boltanski, Luc. 1999. *Distant Suffering: Morality, Media and Politics*, trans. G. Burchell. Cambridge: Cambridge University Press.

———. 2011. *On Critique: A Sociology of Emancipation*, trans. G. Elliot. Malden: Polity Press.

———. 2012. *Love and Justice as Competences*, trans. C. Porter. Malden: Polity Press.

Boltanski, Luc and Laurent Thévenot. 2006. *On Justification: The Economies of Worth*, trans. C. Porter. Princeton, NJ: Princeton University Press.

Bormann, C. v., W. Franzen, A. Krapiec and L. Oeing-Hanoff. 1972. 'Form und Materie', *Historisches Wörterbuch der Philosophie* 2, 977–1029. Basel: Schwabe.

Bourdieu, Pierre. 1983. 'Ökonomisches Kapital, kulturelles Kapital, soziales Kapital', in Reinhard Kreckel (ed.), *Soziale Ungleichheiten. Soziale Welt*. Göttingen: O. Schwarz, 183–98.

———. 1984. *Distinction: A Social Critique of the Judgment of Taste*, trans. R. Nice. Cambridge, MA: Harvard University Press.

———. 1990. *The Logic of Practice*, trans. R. Nice. Cambridge: Polity Press.

Bowker, Geoffry and Susan Leigh Star. 1999. *Sorting Things Out*. Cambridge, MA: MIT Press.

Bryceson, Deborah F. and Jesper B. Jønsson. 2010. 'Gold Digging Careers in Rural East Africa: Small-Scale Miners' Livelihood Choices', *World Development* 38(3), 379–92.

Bryceson, Deborah F., Jesper B. Jønsson and Richard Sherrington. 2010. 'Miners' Magic: Artisanal Mining, the Albino Fetish and Murder in Tanzania', *Journal of Modern African Studies* 48(3), 353–82.

Burawoy, Michael. 1998. 'The Extended Case Method', *Sociological Theory* 16(1), 4–33.

Burr, Millard and Robert O. Collins. 2003. *Revolutionary Sudan: Hasan al-Turabi and the Islamist State, 1989–2000*. Leiden: Brill.

Busch, Lawrence. 2011. *Standards: Recipes for Reality*. Cambridge, MA: MIT Press.

Bushra, Eman. 2005. 'Local-Level Political Dynamics in Kassala State: The Rashayda', in Catherine Miller (ed.), *Land, Ethnicity and Political Legitimacy in Eastern Sudan, Kassala and Gedaref State*. Cairo: CEDEJ, 277–307.

Calkins, Sandra. 2009. 'Transformed Livelihoods in the Lower Atbara Area: Pastoral Rashayda. Responses to Crisis', *Nomadic Peoples* 13(1), 45–68.

———. 2013. 'Translating Research Techniques in Sudan: Professional Ethics and Distributive Justice'. Paper presented at *How to Put Models into Practice? African Perspectives on Technologies of Ordering in Legal, Organisational and Medical Contexts*. MLU Halle, 8–9 February 2013.

———. 2014. 'Gaining an Access to Land: Everyday Negotiations and Ethnic Politics in Northeastern Sudan', in Jörg Gertel, Richard Rottenburg and Sandra Calkins (eds), *Disrupting Territories: Land, Commodification and Conflict in Sudan*. Woodbridge: James Currey, 180–205.

Calkins, Sandra and Enrico Ille. 2014. 'Territories of Gold Mining: International Investments and Artisanal Extraction in Sudan', in Jörg Gertel, Richard Rottenburg and Sandra Calkins (eds), *Disrupting Territories: Land, Commodification and Conflict in Sudan*. Woodbridge: James Currey, 52–76.

Calkins, Sandra, Enrico Ille, Siri Lamoureaux and Richard Rottenburg. 2015a. 'Rethinking Institutional Orders in Sudan Studies: The Case of Land Access in Kordofan, Blue Nile and Darfur', *Canadian Journal for African Studies* 49(1), 175–95.

Calkins, Sandra, Enrico Ille and Richard Rottenburg. 2015b. 'Emergence and Contestation of Orders in the Sudans', in Sandra Calkins, Enrico Ille and Richard Rottenburg (eds), *Emerging Orders in the Sudans*. Bamenda: Langaa, 1–22.

Calkins, Sandra and Guma Kunda Komey. 2011. 'Umkämpfte Weiden: Landzugang und Überleben im Sudan', *Geographische Rundschau* 63(7/8), 28–35.

Callon, Michel. 1986. 'Some Elements of a Sociology of Translation: Domestication of the Scallops and the Fisherman of St. Brieuc Bay', in John Law (ed.), *Power, Action and Belief: A New Sociology of Knowledge?* London: Routledge, 196–233.

Callon, Michel, Pierre Lascoumes and Yannick Barthe. 2009. *Acting in an Uncertain World: An Essay on Technical Democracy, Inside Technology*. Cambridge, MA: MIT Press.

Carney, Diana (ed.). 1998. *Sustainable Rural Livelihoods: What Contribution Can We Make?* London: DFID.

———. 2002. *Sustainable Livelihoods Approaches: Progress and Possibilities for Change*. London: DFID.

Carsten, Janet. 1997. *The Heat of the Hearth: The Process of Kinship in a Malay Fishing Community*. Oxford: Clarendon Press.

———. 2004. *After Kinship*. Cambridge: Cambridge University Press.

Cartier, Laurent and Michael Bürge. 2011. 'Agriculture and Artisanal Gold Mining in Sierra Leone: Alternatives or Complements?', *Journal of International Development* 23, 1080–99.

Casciarri, Barbara and Abdel Ghaffar M. Ahmed. 2009. 'Pastoralists under Pressure in Present-Day Sudan: An Introduction', *Nomadic Peoples* 13(1), 10–22.

Castells, Manuell (ed.). 2004. *The Network Society: A Cross-Cultural Perspective*. Cheltenham: Elgar.

Castoriadis, Cornelius. 1987. *The Imaginary Institution of Society*, trans. K. Blamey. Oxford: Polity Press.

Chambers, Robert and Gordon Conway. 1991. 'Sustainable Rural Livelihoods: Practical Concepts for the 21st Century'. IDS Discussion Paper 296, Brighton: IDS, UK.

Clarke, Adele and Susan Leigh Star. 2008. 'The Social World Framework: A Theory/Methods Package', in Edward Hackett, Olga Amsterdamska, Michael Lynch and Judy Wacjman (eds), *The Handbook of Science and Technology Studies*. Cambridge, MA: MIT Press, 113–37.

Clifford, James and George Marcus (eds). 1986. *Writing Culture: Poetics and Politics of Ethnography*. Berkeley, CA: University of California Press.

Comaroff, Jean and John Comaroff. 2001. 'Millennial Capitalism: First Thoughts on a Second Coming', in *Millennial Capitalism and the Culture of Neoliberalism*. Durham, NC: Duke University Press, 1–56.

———. 2003. 'Ethnography on an Awkward Scale. Postcolonial Anthropology and the Violence of Abstraction', *Ethnography* 4, 147–79.

———. 2012. 'Figuring Democracy. An Anthropological Take on African Political Modernities', in *Theory from the South: Or, How Euro-America Is Evolving toward Africa*. Boulder, CO: Paradigm, 109–31.

Conrad, Sebastian and Shalini Randeria (eds). 2002. *Jenseits des Eurozentrismus: Postkoloniale Perspektiven in den Geschichts- und Kulturwissenschaften*. Frankfurt a.M.: Campus.

Cooper, Elizabeth. 2012. 'Sitting and Standing: How Families Are Fixing Trust in Uncertain Times', *Africa* 82(3), 437–56.

Das, Veena and Deborah Poole. 2004. 'State and Its Margins: Comparative Ethnographies', in Veena Das and Deborah Poole (ed.), *Anthropology in the Margins of the State*. Santa Fe, NM: School of American Research Press, 3–33.

Dean, Mitchell. 1999. *Governmentality: Power and Rule in Modern Society*. London: Sage.

Decaillet, François, Patrick D. Mullen and Moncef Guen. 2003. 'Sudan Health Status Report'. World Bank/AFTH3.

Deleuze, Gilles. 1991. 'Was ist ein Dispositiv?', in François Ewald and Bernhard Waldenfels (eds), *Spiele der Wahrheit: Michel Foucaults Denken*. Frankfurt a.M.: Suhrkamp, 153–62.

Deleuze, Gilles and Félix Guattari. 1987. *A Thousand Plateaus: Capitalism and Schizophrenia*, trans. Massumi. Minneapolis: University of Minnesota Press.

Delmet, Christian. 2005. 'The Native Administration System in Eastern Sudan: From Its Liquidation to Its Revival', in Catherine Miller (ed.), *Land, Ethnicity and Political Legitimacy in Eastern Sudan, Kassala and Gedaref State*. Cairo: CEDEJ, 145–72.

Deng, David K., Paul Mertenskoettter and Luuk van de Vondervoort. 2013. 'Establishing a Mining Sector in Postwar South Sudan. Report. United States Institute of Peace'. Retrieved 9 January 2015 from www.usip.org/sites/default/files/SR330-Establishing%20a%20Mining%20Sector-%20in%20Postwar-%20South%20Sudan.pdf.

Descola, Phillippe. 2009. 'The Two Natures of Lévi-Strauss', in Boris Wiseman (ed.), *The Cambridge Companion to Lévi-Srauss*. Cambridge: Cambridge University Press, 103–17.

Dewey, John. 1896. 'The Reflex Arc Concept in Psychology', *Psychological Review* 3(4), 357–70.

———. 1929. *The Quest for Certainty*. New York: Minton, Balch.

Diaz-Bone, Rainer. 2011. 'The Methodological Standpoint of the 'économies des conventions': The Economics of Conventions and Statistics', *Historical Social Research* 36(4), 43–63.

Diaz-Bone, Rainer and Robert Salais. 2011. 'Economics of Conventions and the History of Economics: Towards a Transdisciplinary Approach in Economic History', *Historical Social Research* 36(4), 7–39.

Diaz-Bone, Rainer and Laurent Thévenot. 2010. 'Die Soziologie der Konventionen: Die Theorie der Konventionen als zentraler Bestandteil der neuen französischen Sozialwissenschaft', *Trivium* 5, 2–15.

Dodier, Nicolas. 2011. 'Konventionen als Stützen der Handlung: Elemente der soziologischen Pragmatik', in Rainer Diaz-Bone (ed.), *Soziologie der Konventionen: Grundlagen einer pragmatischen Anthropologie*. Frankfurt a.M.: Campus, 69–97.

Douglas, Mary. 1986. *How Institutions Think*. London: Routledge.

———. 1990. 'Risk as a Forensic Resource', *Daedalus* 119(4), 1–16.

———. 1996 [1966]. *Purity and Danger: An Analysis of the Concepts of Pollution and Taboo*. London: Routledge.

Douglas, Mary and Aron Wildavsky. 1982. *Risk and Culture: An Essay on the Selection of Technical and Environmental Dangers*. Berkeley, CA: University of California Press.

Duffield, Mark R. 1981. *Maiurno: Capitalism and Rural Life in Sudan*. London: Ithaca Press.

———. 1990. 'Absolute Distress: Structural Causes of Hunger in Sudan', *Middle East Report* 166, 4–11.

———. 2002. 'Social Reconstruction and the Radicalization of Development: Aid as a Relation of Global Liberal Governance', *Development and Change* 33(5), 1049–71.

Eisenstadt, Shmuel (ed.). 2002. *Multiple Modernities*. New Brunswick, NJ: Transactions.

Eisenstadt, Shmuel and Luis Roniger. 1981. 'The Study of Patron-Client Relations and Recent Developments in Sociological Theory', in Shmuel Eisenstadt and Réne Lemarchand (eds), *Political Clientelism, Patronage and Development*. London: Sage, 271–95.

Elden, Stuart. 2005. 'Missing the Point: Globalization, Deterritorialization and the Space of the World'. Transactions of the Institute of British Geographers. *New Series* 30, 8–19.

Elwert, Georg, Hans-Dieter Evers and W. Wilkens. 1983. 'Die Such nach Sicherheit: kombinierte Produktionsformen im sogenannten informellen Sektor', *Zeitschrift für Soziologie* 12(4), 281–96.

Enzyklopädie Philosophie und Wissenschaftstheorie (EPuW). 2005. 'Form (logische)'. Vol. 2, Letters C-F. Stuttgart: J.B. Metzler, 521–22.

Eriksen, Thomas H. 2001. *Small Places, Large Issues: An Introduction to Social and Cultural Anthropology*. Sterling: Pluto Press.

Evans-Pritchard, Edward E. 1968 [1937]. *Witchcraft, Oracles and Magic among the Azande*, 6th edn. Oxford: Oxford University Press.

———. 1969 [1940]. *The Nuer: A Description of the Modes of Livelihood and Political Institutions of a Nilotic People*. Oxford: Oxford University Press.

Evens, T.M.S. and Don Handelman. 2005. 'Introduction: The Ethnographic Praxis of the Theory of Practice', *Social Analysis* 49(3), 1–11.

Evers, Hans-Dieter. 1986. *Subsistenzwirtschaft, Markt und Staat: Der sogenannte Bielefelder Ansatz*. Bielefeld: Universität Bielefeld.

Ewald, Francois. 1991. 'Insurance and Risks', in Graham Burchell, Colin Gordon and Peter Miller (eds), *The Foucault Effect: Studies in Governmentality*. London: Harvesters Wheatsheaf, 197–210.

Fabian, Johannes. 1983. *Time and the Other: How Anthropology Makes it Object*. New York: Columbia University Press.

Fardon, Richard. 1987. 'The Faithful Disciple: On Mary Douglas and Durkheim', *Anthropology Today* 3(5), 4–6.

Federal Ministry of Health (FMOH). 2004. 'Sudan's National Policy towards Voluntary Sector in Health. Republic of Sudan'. Retrieved 9 January 2015 from www.fmoh.gov.sd/English/Health-policy/doc/National%20Policy.pdf.

————. 2006. 'Nutrition Policy for Sudan and Strategy for Implementation'. Retrieved 9 January 2015 from www.fmoh.gov.sd/English/Health-policy/doc/Nutrition%20Policy_final.pdf.

————. 2007a. '5-year Health Sector Strategy: Investing in Health and Achieving the MDGs. Republic of Sudan': 2007–2011. Retrieved 30 September 2013 from www.fmoh.gov.sd/English/St_Plan/doc/Health%20Five-year-strategy%201.5.2007.pdf.

————. 2007b. 'Policy for Market Based Private Health Care Sector. Republic of Sudan. Draft Policy Statement'. Retrieved 9 January 2015 from www.fmoh.gov.sd/English/Health-policy/Private%20sector%20policy-%20statements%20v%5b1%5d%5b1%5d.5.pdf.

Ferguson, James. 2006. *Global Shadows: Africa in the Neoliberal World Order.* Durham, NC: Duke University Press.

Ferguson, James and Akhil Gupta. 2005. 'Spatializing States: Towards an Ethnography of Neoliberal Governmentality', in Jonathan X. Inda (ed.), *Anthropologies of Modernity: Foucault, Governmentality, and Life Politics.* Malden, MA: Blackwell, 105–31.

Fischler, Claude. 1988. 'Food, Self and Identity', *Social Science Information* 27(2), 275–92.

Fisher, Eleonor. 2007. 'Occupying the Margins: Labour Integration and Social Exclusion in Artisanal Mining in Tanzania', *Development and Change* 38(4): 735–60.

————. 2008. 'Artisanal Gold Mining at the Margins of Mineral Resource Governance: A case from Tanzania', *Development Southern Africa* 25(2), 199–213.

Flint, Julie and Alex De Waal. 2005. *Darfur: A Short History of a Long War.* New York: Zed Books.

Foucault, Michel. 1980. *The History of Sexuality.* Vol. 1: *An Introduction*, trans. R. Hurley. New York: Vintage.

————. 1991. 'Governmentality', in Graham Burchell, Colin Gordon and Peter Miller (eds), *The Foucault Effect: Studies in Governmentality.* London: Harvesters Wheatsheaf, 87–104.

————. 2007. *Security, Territory, Population: Lectures at the Collège de France 1977–1978*, trans. G. Burchell. New York: Picador.

————. 2008. *The Birth of Biopolitics: Lectures at the Collège de France 1978–1979*, trans. M. Senellart. Basingstoke: Palgrave Macmillan.

Frisby, David. 1992. *Simmel and Since: Essays on Georg Simmel's Social Theory.* New York: Routledge.

Fuller, C.J. 1989. 'Misconceiving the Grain Heap: A Critique of the Concept of the Indian Jajmani System', in Jonathan Parry and Maurice Bloch (eds), *Money and the Morality of Exchange.* Cambridge: Cambridge University Press, 33–63.

Gaonkar, Dilip P. (ed.). 2001. *Alternative Modernities.* Durham, NC: Duke University Press.

Geissler, Paul Wenzel. 2005. 'Blood-stealing Rumours in Western Kenya: A Local Critique of Medical Research in Its Global Context', in Vibeke Steffen, Richard Jenkins and Hanne Jessen (eds), *Managing Uncertainty: Ethnographic Studies of Illness, Risk and the Struggle for Control.* Copenhagen: Museum Tusculanum Press, 123–48.

Geissler, Wenzel and Ruth Prince. 2010. *The Land Is Dying: Contingency, Creativity and Conflict in Western Kenya.* New York: Berghahn Books.

Geissler, Wenzel, Richard Rottenburg and Julia Zenker. 2012. '21st-Century African Biopolitics: Fuzzy Fringes, Cracks and Undersides, Neglected Backwaters, and Returning Politics', in Wenzel Geissler, Richard Rottenburg and Julia Zenker (eds), *Rethinking Biomedicine and Governance in Africa Contributions from Anthropology.* Bielefeld: Transcript, 11–19.

Gellner, Ernest. 1977. 'Patrons and Clients', in Ernest Gellner and John Waterbury (eds), *Patrons and Clients in Mediterranean Societies.* London: Duckworth, 1–6.

Gertel, Jörg. 2007. 'Mobility and Insecurity: The Significance of Resources', in Jörg Gertel and Ingo Breuer (eds), *Pastoral Morocco: Globalizing Scapes of Mobility and Insecurity*. Wiesbaden: Reichert Verlag, 11–30.

Gertel, Jörg, Sandra Calkins and Richard Rottenburg. 2014. 'Commodification and Its Consequences', in Jörg Gertel, Richard Rottenburg and Sandra Calkins (eds), *Disrupting Territories: Land, Commodification and Conflict*. Woodbridge: James Currey, 1–30.

Gluckman, Max. 1958 [1940]. 'Analysis of Social Situation in Modern Zululand', *Rhodes-Livingstone Papers 28*. Manchester: Manchester University Press.

———. 1968. 'The Utility of the Equilibrium Model in the Study of Social Change', *American Anthropologist* 70(2), 219–37.

Godoy, Ricardo. 1985. 'Mining: Anthropological Perspectives', *Annual Review of Anthropology* 14, 199–217.

'Gold Last Hope for Sudan to Avert Economic Collapse'. 2012. *Reuters*, 18 July 2012. Retrieved 9 January 2015 from www.reuters.com/article/2012/07/18/us-sudan-gold-idUSBRE86H0SX20120718.

'Gold – Sudan: Output Has Soared Nearly Twentyfold in Two Years as Gold Fever Strikes'. 2011. *Africa Research Bulletin* 16 April–15 May, 19104-105.

'Gold – Sudan: A Series of Contracts Are Signed with International Private Companies'. 2011. *Africa Research Bulletin* 16 November–15 December, 19320.

Goody, Jack. 1982. *Cooking, Cuisine and Class: A Study in Comparative Sociology*. Cambridge: Cambridge University Press.

GRAS. n.d. 'Gold in the Sudan'. Leaflet.

Grätz, Tilo. 2002. 'Gold Mining Communities in Northern Benin as Semi-Autonomous Social Fields'. Max Planck Institute for Social Anthropology. Working Paper 36, Halle.

———. 2010. *Goldgräber in Westafrika*. Berlin: Reimer Verlag.

Gregory, C.A. 1994. 'Exchange and Reciprocity', in Tim Ingold (ed.), *Companion Encyclopedia of Anthropology: Humanity, Culture and Social Life*. London: Routledge.

Gruenbaum, Ellen. 1981. 'Medical Anthropology, Health Policy and the State: A Case Study of Sudan', *Review of Policy Research* 1(1), 47–65.

Gupta, Akhil. 2012. *Red Tape: Bureaucracy, Structural Violence, and Poverty in India*. Durham, NC: Duke University Press.

Gupta, Akhil and James Ferguson. 1997. 'Discipline and Practice: "The Field" as Site, Method, and Location in Anthropology', in Akhil Gupta and James Ferguson (eds), *Anthropological Locations: Boundaries and Grounds of a Field Science*. Berkeley, CA: University of California Press, 1–46.

Hacking, Ian 1990. *The Taming of Chance*. Cambridge, UK: Cambridge University Press.

Hansen, Thomas Blom, and Finn Stepputat. 2006. 'Sovereignty Revisited', *Annual Review of Anthropology* 35, 295–315.

Haraway, Donna. 1991. 'Situated Knowledges: The Science Question in Feminism and the Privilege of Partial Perspective', in *Simians, Cyborgs and Women: The Reinvention of Nature*. New York: Routledge, 183–202.

Harding, Sandra. 1993. 'Rethinking Standpoint Epistemology. What is "Strong Objectivity"?', in Linda Alcoff and Elisabeth Potter (eds), *Feminist Epistemologies: Thinking Gender*. New York: Routledge, 59–82.

Harir, Sharif and T. Tvedt (eds). 1994. *Short-cut to Decay: The Case of the Sudan*. Uppsala: Nordisaka Afrikaninstitutet.

Harvey, David. 2005. *A Brief History of Neoliberalism*. New York: Oxford University Press.

'Heavy Fighting over Gold Mine in Sudan'. 2013. *News24*. 1 January 2013.Retrieved 9 January 2015 from www.news24.com/Africa/News/Heavy-fighting-over-gold-mine-in-Sudan-20130109.

Hasan, Yusuf Fadl. 2005. *The Arabs and the Sudan from the Seventh to the Early Sixteenth Century*. Khartoum: SUDATeK.

Heuts, Frank and Annemarie Mol. 2013. 'What Is a Good Tomato? A Case of Valuing in Practice', *Valuation Studies* 1(2), 125–46.

Hilson, Gavin. 2002. 'Small-scale Mining and Its Socioeconomic Impact in Developing Countries', *Natural Resources Forum* 28, 3–13.

———. 2007. 'Championing the Rhetoric? "Corporate Social Responsibility" in Ghana's Mining Sector', *Greener Management International* 53, 43–56.

———. 2010. 'Child Labour in African Artisanal Mining Communities: Experiences from Northern Ghana', *Development and Change* 41(3), 445–73.

Hilson, Gavin and S.M. Banchirigah. 2009. 'Are Alternative Livelihood Projects Alleviating Poverty in Mining Communities? Experiences from Ghana', *Journal of Development Studies* 45(2), 172–96.

Hilson, Gavin and M. Clifford. 2010. 'Tackling Mercury Pollution in African Small-Scale Gold Mining Communities: Challenges and Progress', *International Journal of Environment and Pollution* 41(3–4), 185–94.

Holt, P. M. and M.W. Daly. 2000. *A History of the Sudan: From the Coming of Islam to the Present Day*. 5th edn. Harlow, UK: Pearson Education.

Honkasalo, Marja-Liisa. 2006. 'Fragilities in Life and Death: Engaging in Uncertainty in Modern Society', *Health, Risk & Society* 8(1), 27–41.

Horden, Perigrine. 1998. 'Household Care and Informal Networks: Comparisons and Continuities from Antiquity to the Present', in Perigrine Horden and Richard Smith (eds), *The Locus of Care: Families, Communities, Institutions, and the Provision of Welfare since Antiquity*. New York: Routledge, 21–67.

Horden, Perigrine and Richard Smith. 1998. 'Introduction', in Perigrine Horden and Richard Smith (eds), *The Locus of Care: Families, Communities, Institutions, and the Provision of Welfare since Antiquity*. New York: Routledge, 1–20.

Hubig, Christoph. 2000. 'Dispositiv als Kategorie', *Internationale Zeitschrift für Philosophie* 1, 34–47.

Hutchinson, Sharon. 1996. *Nuer Dilemmas*. Berkeley, CA: University of California Press.

Ibrahim, Mohamed S. 2003. 'Information about Ingessana Hills Artisanal Gold Mining Sites Chosen for the Environmental and Health Assessment'. Global Mercury Project.

Ibrahim, Mohamed S. and M.A. Abdel Baqi. 2010. '*Raṣd wa taqaīym anšāṭ taʿdīn aḏ-ḏahab al-ʿašwāʾī – 2010. Wilāyāt nahr an-nīl – al-bahr al-ahmar – aš-šamālīya.*' (Briefing and Assessment of Artisanal Mining Activities, 2010, River Nile State—Red Sea State—Northern). Ministry of Energy and Mining. Geological Research Authority of Sudan. Preliminary Report March 2010.

Ille, Enrico. 2011. *Tracing a Golden Past: Historical Narratives about Shaybun and Shawabna in the Nuba Mountains, Sudan*. Leipzig: Ille & Riemer.

———. 2013. *Projections, Plans and Projects: Development as the Extension of Organizing Principles and Its Consequences in the Rural Nuba Mountains / South Kordofan, Sudan (2005–2011)*. Leipzig: Ille & Riemer. Dissertation (2012). University of Halle. Retrieved 9 January 2015 from http://wcms.uzi.uni-halle.de/download.php?down=27894&elem=2642839.

Ille, Enrico and Sandra Calkins. 2013. 'Gold Mining Concessions in Northern Sudan's Written Laws and Political Practices: The Case of South Kordofan', in Elke Grawert (ed.),

Identity, Economy, Power Relations and External Interest: Old and New Challenges for Sudan and South Sudan. Addis Abeba: OSSREA, 112–26.

James, Wendy. 2007. *War and Survival in Sudan's Frontierlands: Voices from the Blue Nile.* Oxford: Oxford University Press.

Janzen, John. 1978. *The Quest for Therapy: Medical Pluralism in Lower Zaire.* Berkeley, CA: University of California Press.

Japp, Klaus and Isabel Kusche. 2008. 'System Theory and Risk', in Jens Zinn (ed.), *Social Theories of Risk and Uncertainty: An Introduction.* Oxford: Blackwell, 76–105.

Jenkins, Richard, Hanne Jessen and Viebeke Steffen. 2005. 'Matters of Life and Death', in Viebeke Steffen, Viebeke, Richard Jenkins and Hanne Jessen (eds), *Managing Uncertainty: Ethnographic Studies of Illness, Risk and Struggle for Control.* Copenhagen: Museum Tusculanum Press, 9–30.

Joas, Hans. 1989. 'Institutionalisierung als kreativer Prozeß: Zur politischen Philosophie von Cornelius Castoriadis', *Politische Vierteljahresschrift* 30(4), 585–602.

Johnson, Douglas H. 2003. *The Root Causes of Sudan's Civil Wars.* Oxford: James Currey.

———. 2007. 'Why Abyei Matters. The Breaking Point of Sudan's Peace Agreement?', *African Affairs* 107(426), 1–19.

———. 2010. *When Boundaries Become Borders: The Impact of Boundary-Making in Southern Sudan's Frontier Zones.* London: Rift Valley Institute.

———. 2011. 'Abyei: Sudan's West Bank'. The Enough Project. 4 April. Retrieved 9 January 2015 from www.enoughproject.org/files/abyei_west_bank.pdf.

Johnson-Hanks, Jennifer. 2005. 'When the Future Decides: Uncertainty and Intentional Action in Contemporary Cameroon', *Current Anthropology* 46, 363–85.

Jok, Jok Madut. 2007. *Sudan: Race, Religion and Violence.* Oxford: Oneworld.

Jønesson, Jesper B. and Niels Fold. 2009. 'Handling Uncertainty: Policy and Organizational Practices in Tanzania's Small-Scale Mining Sector', *Natural Resources Forum* 33, 211–20.

Jorgensen, Dan. 1998. 'Whose Nature? Invading Bush Spirits, Travelling Ancestors, and Mining in Telefolmin', *Social Analysis* 42(3), 100–16.

Kapferer, Bruce. 2005. 'Situations, Crisis and the Anthropology of the Concrete: The Contribution of Max Gluckman', *Social Analysis* 49(3), 85–122.

Kibreab, Gaim. 2002. *State Intervention and the Environment in Sudan, 1889–1989: The Demise of Communal Resource Management.* Lewiston, ME.: Edwin Mellen Press.

Kleinman, Arthur. 1999. 'From One Human Nature to Many Human Conditions: An Anthropological Inquiry into Suffering as Moral Experience in a Disordering Age', *Suomen Antropologi—Finnish Anthropologist* 14, 23–36.

Kleinman, Arthur, Veena Das and Margaret Lock (eds). 2003. *Social Suffering.* Berkeley, CA: University of California Press.

Knöbl, Walter. 2007. *Die Kontingenz der Moderne: Wege in Europa, Asien und Amerika.* Frankfurt a.M.: Campus.

Komey, Guma Kunda. 2010. *Land, Governance, Conflict and the Nuba of Sudan.* Woodbridge: James Currey.

Kopytoff, Igor. 1986. 'The Cultural Biography of Things: Commoditization as Process', in Arjun Appadurai (ed.), *The Social Life of Things: Commodities in Cultural Perspective.* Cambridge: Cambridge University Press, 64–91.

Koselleck, Reinhart. 2002. *The Practice of Conceptual History: Timing History, Spacing Concepts. Cultural Memory in the Present.* Stanford: Stanford University Press.

Laet, Marianne de and Annemarie Mol. 2000. 'The Zimbabwe Bush Pump: Mechanics of a Fluid Technology', *Social Studies of Science* 30(2), 225–63.

Lampland, Martha and Susan Leigh Star. 2009. *Standards and Their Stories: How Quantifying, Classifying, and Formalizing Practices Shape Everyday Life.* Ithaca, NY: Cornell University Press.

Large, Daniel and Luke Patey (eds). 2011. *Sudan Looks East: China, India and the Politics of Asian Alternatives.* Woodbridge: James Currey.

Latour, Bruno. 1993. *We Have Never Been Modern*, trans. C. Porter. Cambridge, MA: Harvard University Press.

———. 1999. 'For David Bloor… and Beyond: A Reply to David Bloor's "Anti-Latour"', *Studies in History and Philosophy of Science* 30(1), 113–29.

———. 2003. 'Is Re-modernization Occurring? And If So, How to Prove It?: A Commentary on Ulrich Beck', *Theory, Culture and Society* 20(2), 35–48.

———. 2005. *Re-assembling the Social: An Introduction to Actor-Network-Theory.* Oxford: Oxford University Press.

Launay, Luis. 2010 [1908]. *The World's Gold, Its Geology, Extraction, and Political Economy.* Milton Keynes, UK: Bibliolife Reproduction Series.

Law, John. 2004. *After Method: Mess in Social Science Research.* New York: Routledge.

Lemke, Thomas. 2011. *Foucault, Governmentality, and Critique.* London: Paradigm.

Lesch, Ann Moseley. 1996. 'The Destruction of Civil Society in the Sudan', in A.A. Norton (ed.), *Civil Society in the Middle East.* 2nd edn. Leiden: Brill, 153–91.

———. 1998. *Sudan: Contested National Identities.* Oxford: James Currey.

Lévi-Strauss, Claude. 1969a [1949]. *The Elementary Structures of Kinship*, trans. J.H. Bell, J.R. Von Sturmer and R. Needham. Boston: Beacon Press.

———. 1969b [1964]. *The Raw and the Cooked: Introduction to a Science of Mythology.* Vol. 1., trans. J. and D. Weightman. New York: Harper and Row.

Lienhardt, Geoffry. 1954. 'Modes of Thought', in Edward E. Evans-Pritchard, Raymond Firth and E. R. LeachOxford (eds), *The Institutions of Primitive Society: A Series of Broadcast Talks.* Oxford: Basil Blackwell, 95–107.

Linke, Janka. 2014. 'Oil, Water, and Land: Chinese Impact on Sudanese Land Use', in Jörg, Gertel, Richard Rottenburg and Sandra Calkins (eds), *Disrupting Territories: Land, Commodification and Conflict in Sudan.* Woodbridge: James Currey, 77–101.

Livingstone, Julie. 2012. *Improvising Medicine: An African Oncology Ward in an Emerging Cancer Epidemic.* Durham, NC: Duke University Press.

Lock, Margaret. 1998. 'Breast Cancer: Reading the Omens', *Anthropology Today* 14(4), 7–16.

Locke, Karen, Karen Golden-Biddle and Martha Feldman. 2008. 'Making Doubt Generative: Rethinking the Role of Doubt in the Research Process', *Organization Science* 19(6), 907–18.

Loftsdóttir, Kirstìn. 2002. 'Never Forgetting? Gender and Racial-Ethnic Identity During Fieldwork', *Social Anthropology* 10(3), 303–17.

Luhmann, Niklas. 1984. *Soziale Systeme: Grundriß einer allgemeinen Theorie.* Frankfurt a.M.: Suhrkamp.

———. 2005 [1990]. 'Risiko und Gefahr', in *Soziologische Aufklärung* 5. Konstruktivistische Perspektiven. Wiesbaden: VS Verlag, 126–62.

———. 2011 [2002]. *Einführung in die Systemtheorie.* 6th edn. Heidelberg: Carl-Auer.

Luning, Sabine. 2008. 'Liberalisation of the Gold Mining Sector in Burkina Faso', *Review of African Political Economy* 117, 25–39.

———. 2012. 'Corporate Social Responsibility (CSR) for Exploration: Consultants, Companies and Communities in Processes of Engagements', *Resources Policy* 37(2), 205–11.

MacMichael, H.A. 1922. *A History of the Arabs in the Sudan and Some Account of the People Who Preceded Them and of the Tribes Inhabiting Dàrfûr*. Cambridge: Cambridge University Press.

Malinowski, Bronislaw. 1922. *Argonauts of the Western Pacific*. London: Routledge and Kegan Paul.

Mamdani, Mahmood. 1996. *Citizen and Subject: Contemporary Africa and the Legacy of Late Colonialsm*. Princeton: Princeton University Press.

———. 2009. *Saviors and Survivors: Darfur, Politics, and the War on Terror*. New York: Doubleday.

Manger, Leif. 1996. 'General Introduction', in Leif Manger, Hassan Abd el Ati, Sharif Harir, Knut Krzywinski and Ole Veetas (eds), *Survival on Meagre Resources: Hadendowa Pastoralism in the Red Sea Hills*. Uppsala: Nordiska Afrikainstitutet, 18–36.

Marcus, George E. 1995. 'Ethnography in/of the World System: The Emergence of Multi-Sited Ethnography', *Annual Review of Anthropology* 24, 95–117.

Massey, Doreen. 2005. *For Space*. London: Sage.

Mauss, Marcel. 1954 [1924]. *The Gift: Forms and Functions of Exchange in Archaic Societies*, trans. I. Cunnison. London: Routledge and Kegan Paul.

Mbembe, Achille. 2002. 'African Modes of Self-Writing', *Public Culture* 14(1), 239–73.

Medani, Khalil A. Al. 2003. 'Socio-economic Sample Study of the Ingessana hills Artisanal Gold Mining Community, Blue Nile State, Sudan. Global Mercury Project'. Retrieved 9 January 2015 from http://archive.iwlearn.net/www.globalmercuryproject.org/countries/sudan/docs/Sudan_Sociological_Report.pdf.

Merton, Robert K. 1995. 'The Thomas Theorem and the Matthew Effect', *Social Forces* 74(2), 379–422.

Messer, E. 1984. 'Anthropological Perspectives on Diet', *Annual Review of Anthropology* 13, 205–49.

Meyer, John and Brian Rowan. 1977. 'Institutionalized Organizations: Formal Structure as Myth and Ceremony', *American Journal of Sociology* 83(2), 340–62.

Miller, Catherine (ed). 2005. *Land, Ethnicity and Political Legitimacy in Eastern Sudan*. Cairo: CEDEJ.

Miller, Daniel. 1997. *Capitalism: An Ethnographic Approach*. New York: Berg.

———. 1998. *A Theory of Shopping*. Cambridge: Polity Press.

———. 2007. 'What Is a Relationship? Is Kinship Negotiated Experience?', *Ethnos* 72(5), 535–54.

Minelab. n.d. Instruction Manual GPX 4500. Retrieved 9 January 2015 from www.minelab.com/__files/f/3965/4901-0063-1.1%20Instruction%20Manual%20GPX-4500_screen.pdf.

Mintz, Sidney and Christine Du Bois. 2002. 'The Anthropology of Food and Eating', *Annual Review of Anthropology* 31, 99–119.

Mol, Annemarie. 2009. 'Good Food: The Embodied Normativity of the Consumer-Citizen', *Journal of Cultural Economy* 2(3), 269–83.

Morton, James. 1989. 'Ethnicity and Politics in Red Sea Province, Sudan', *African Affairs* 88(35), 63–76.

Mühlmann, Wilhelm E. and J.R. Llaryora. 1968. *Klientschaft, Klientel und Klientelsystem in einer sizilianischen Agro-Stadt*. Heidelberger Sociologica 6. Tübingen: J.C.B. Mohr.

Nash, June. 1979. *We Eat the Mines and the Mines Eat Us: Dependency and Exploitation in Bolivian Tin Mines*. New York: Columbia University Press.

'NGO Expelled from Darfur Considered ICC Cooperation'. 2009. *Reuters*, 16 March 2009. Retrieved 9 January 2015 from www.reuters.com/article/2009/03/16/us-sudan-warcrimes-ngo-idUSTRE52F6SX20090316.

Nguyen, Vinh-Kim. 2010. *The Republic of Therapy: Triage and Sovereignty in West Africa's Time of AIDS*. Durham, NC: Duke University Press.

'North Sudan Expands Its Gold Mining Sector'. 2012. *Trade Precious Metals*, 24 January 2012. Retrieved 9 January 2015 from www.tradepreciousmetals.com/north-sudan-expands-its-gold-mining-sector/.

Notermans, Catrien. 2008. 'The Emotional Work of Kinship: Children's Experience of Fosterage in East Cameroon', *Childhood* 15, 355–77.

O'Brien, Jay. 1986. 'Toward a Reconstitution of Ethnicity: Capitalist Expansion and Cultural Dynamics in Sudan', *American Anthropologist* 88(4), 898–907.

O'Malley, Pat. 2004. *Risk, Uncertainty and Government*. London: Glasshouse Press.

———. 2008. 'Governmentality and Risk', in Jens Zinn (ed.), *Social Theories of Risk and Uncertainty: An Introduction*. Oxford: Blackwell, 52–75.

Omer, El Haj Bilal. 1985. *The Dangala Traders of Northern Sudan: Rural Capitalism and Agricultural Development*. London: Ithaca.

Osman, Elhadi and Günther Schlee. 2014. 'Hausa and Fulbe on the Blue Nile: Land Conflicts between Farmers and Herders', in Jörg Gertel, Richard Rottenburg and Sandra Calkins (eds), *Disrupting Territories: Land, Commodification and Conflict in Sudan*. Woodbridge: James Currey, 206–25.

Pantuliano, Sara. 2005. 'Comprehensive Peace? Causes and Consequences of Underdevelopment and Instability in Eastern Sudan'. Report, Save the Children, UK. September.

Pardie, Sandra and Gavin Hilson. 2006. 'Mercury: An Agent of Poverty in West Africa's Small Scale Gold-Mining Industry', in Gavin Hilson (ed.), *Small-scale Mining, Rural Subsistence and Poverty in West Africa*. Rugby: Practical Action, 55–65.

Parry, Jonathan. 1989. 'On the Moral Perils of Exchange', in Jonathan Parry and Maurice Bloch (eds), *Money and the Morality of Exchange*. Cambridge: Cambridge University Press, 64–93.

Parry, Jonathan and Maurice Bloch. 1989. 'Introduction: Money and the Morality of Exchange', in Jonathan Parry and Maurice Bloch (eds), *Money and the Morality of Exchange*. Cambridge: Cambridge University Press, 1–32.

Parsons, Talcott. 1991 [1951]. *The Social System*. London: Routledge.

Pfaffenberger, Bryan. 1992a. 'Social Anthropology of Technology', *Annual Review of Anthropology* 21, 491–516.

———. 1992b. 'Technological Dramas', *Science, Technology & Human Values* 17(3), 282–312.

Pinch, Trevor. 2008. 'Technology and Institutions: Living in a Material World', *Theory and Society* 37(5), 461–83.

Polanyi, Karl. 1944. *The Great Transformation*. New York: Rinehart.

———. 1957. 'The Economy as Instituted Process', in Stuart Plattner (ed.), *Economic Anthropology*. Stanford: Stanford University Press, 243–70.

Polier, Nicole. 1996. 'Of Mines and Min: Modernity and Its Malcontents in Papua New Guinea', *Ethnology* 35(1), 1–16.

Porter, Gina, Kate Hampshire, Albert Abane, Alister Munthali, Elsbeth Robson and Mac Mashiri. 2012. 'Child Porterage and Africa's Transport Gap: Evidence from Ghana, Malawi and South Africa', *World Development* 40(10), 2136–54.

Powdermaker, Hortense. 1966. *Stranger and Friend: The Way of an Anthropologist*. London: Norton.

Prowse, Martin. 2010. 'Integrating Reflexivity into Livelihoods Research', *Progress in Development Studies* 10, 211–31.

Radcliffe-Brown, Alfred R. 1971a [1952]. 'On Social Structure', in *Structure and Function in Primitive Society. Essays and Addresses*. London: Cohen & West, 188–204.

———. 1971b [1952]. 'Taboo', in *Structure and Function in Primitive Society: Essays and Adresses*. London: Cohen & West, 133–52.

Rao, Aparna and Michael Casimir. 2002. 'Nomadism in South Asia: An Introduction', in Aparna Rao and Michael Casimir (eds), *Nomadism in South Asia*. Delhi: Oxford University Press, 1–38.

Rasborg, Klaus. 2012. '"(World) Risk Society" or "New Rationalities of Risk"? A Critical Discussion of Ulrich Beck's Theory of Reflexive Modernity', *Thesis Eleven* 108, 3–25.

Renn, Ortwin. 2008. *Risk Governance: Coping with Uncertainty in a Complex World*. London & Sterling: Earthscan.

Rickford, Viera. 2006. 'Mercury-Free Gold Mining Technologies: Possibilities for Adoption in the Guianas', *Journal of Cleaner Production* 14(3–4), 448–54.

Roitman, Janet. 2013. *Anti-Crisis*. Durham, NC: Duke University Press.

Rottenburg, Richard. 1991. *Ndemwareng: Wirtschaft und Gesellschaft in den Morobergen*. Munich: Trickster.

———. 1995. 'OPP. Geschichten zwischen Europa und Afrika', *Kursbuch* 120, 90–106.

———. 2002. 'Das Inferno am Gazellenfluss: Ein afrikanisches Problem oder ein "schwarzes Loch" der Weltgesellschaft?', *Leviathan* 30(1), 3–33.

———. 2005a. 'Code-Switching, or Why a Metacode Is Good to Have', in Barbara Czarniawska and Guje Sevon (eds), *Global Ideas: How Ideas, Objects and Practices Travel in the Global Economy*. Malmö: Författarna och Liber AB, 259–74.

———. 2005b. 'The Figure of the Third in the Field', *Folk: Journal of the Danish Ethnographic Society* 46/47, 41–53.

———. 2008a. 'Übersetzung und ihre Dementierung', in Georg Kneer, Markus Schroer and Erhard Schüttpelz (eds), *Bruno Latours Kollektive: Kontroversen zur Entgrenzung des Sozialen*. Frankfurt: Suhrkamp, 401–25.

———. 2008b. 'Introduction', in Richard Rottenburg (ed.), *Nomadic-Sedentary Relations and Failing State Institutions in Darfur and Kordofan (Sudan)*. Martin-Luther-Universität Halle-Wittenberg. *Orientwissenschaftliche Hefte* 26: VII–IX.

———. 2009a. *Far-Fetched Facts: A Parable of Development Aid*, trans. A. Brown and T. Lampert. Cambridge, MA: MIT Press.

———. 2009b. 'Social and Public Experiments and New Figurations of Science and Politics in Postcolonial Africa', *Postcolonial Studies* 12(4), 423–40.

———. 2013. 'Ethnologie und Kritik', in Thomas Bierschenk, Matthias Krings and Carola Lentz (eds), *Ethnologie im 21. Jahrhundert*. Berlin: Reimer, 55–76.

Rottenburg, Richard, Guma Kunda Komey and Enrico Ille. 2011. 'The Genesis of Recurring Wars in Sudan: Rethinking the Violent Conflicts in the Nuba Mountains/ South Kordofan'. Working Paper, University of Halle, Germany.

Sahlins, Marschall. 1972. *Stone Age Economics*. London: Tavistock.

Salais, Robert. 2011. 'Labour-Related Conventions and Configurations of Meaning: France, Germany and Great Britain Prior to the Second World War', *Historical Social Research* 36(4), 218–47.

Samimian-Darash, Limor. 2013. 'Governing Future Potential Biothreats: Toward an Anthropology of Uncertainty', *Current Anthropology* 54(1), 1–22.

Schatzki, Theodore. 2001. 'Practice Mind-ed Orders', in Theodore Schatzki, Karin Knorr Cetina and Eike von Savigny (eds), *The Practice Turn in Contemporary Theory*. New York: Routledge, 42–55.

Scheper-Hughes, Nancy. 1993. *Death without Weeping: The Violence of Everyday Life in Brazil*. Berkeley, CA: University of California Press.

Schmieder, Falko. 2012. *Überleben: Historische und aktuelle Konstellationen*. Munich: Wilhelm Fink.

Scoones, Ian. 1998. 'Sustainable Rural Livelihood: A Framework for Analysis'. Working Paper 72. Brighton: Institute for Development Studies.

Sharif, Mariam. 2015. 'Institutionalisation and Regulation of Medical Kits in an Emergency Situation in the Nuba Mountains / South Kordofan', in Sandra Calkins, Enrico Ille and Richard Rottenburg (eds), *Emerging Orders in the Sudans*. Bamenda: Langaa, 241–50.

Sharkey, Heather. 2008. 'Arab Identity and Ideology in Sudan: The Politics of Language, Ethnicity and Race', *African Affairs* 107(426), 21–43.

Sharkey, Heather, Elena Vezzadini and Iris Seri-Hersch. 2015. 'Rethinking Sudan Studies: A Post-2011 Manifesto'. *Canadian Journal for African Studies* 49(1), 1–18.

Shipton, Parker. 1989. *Bitter Money: Cultural Economy and Some African Meanings of Forbidden Commodities*. Washington, DC: American Ethnological Society Monograph Series 1.

———. 1990. 'African Famines and Food Security: Anthropological Perspectives', *Annual Review of Anthropology* 19(1), 353–94.

Simmel, Georg. 1992. 'Soziologie: Untersuchungen über die Formen der Vergesellschaftung', in Otthain Rammstedt (ed.), *Georg Simmel: Gesamtausgabe*. 11th edn. Frankfurt a.M.: Suhrkamp.

Spiegel, S.J. and M.M. Veiga. 2005. 'Building Capacity in Small-Scale Mining Communities: Health, Ecosystem Sustainability, and the Global Mercury Project', *Eco-Health* 2, 361–69.

———. 2010. 'International Guidelines on Mercury Management in Small-Scale Gold Mining', *Journal of Cleaner Production* 18, 375–85.

Spittler, Gerd. 1989. *Handeln in einer Hungerkrise: Tuaregnomaden und die große Hungerkrise von 1984*. Opladen: Westdeutscher Verlag.

Star, Susan and James Griesemer. 1989. 'Institutional Ecology, Translations and Boundary Objects: Amateurs and Professionals in Berkeley's Museum of Vertebrate Zoology, 1907–39', *Social Studies of Science* 19(3), 387–420.

Steffen, Vibeke, Richard Jenkins and Hanne Jessen (eds). 2005. *Managing Uncertainty: Ethnographic Studies of Illness, Risk and the Struggle for Control*. Copenhagen: Museum Tusculanum Press.

Stichweh, Rudolf. 2005. 'Inklusion/Exklusion, funktionale Differenzierung und die Theorie der Weltgesellschaft', in *Die Weltgesellschaft: soziologische Analysen*. Frankfurt a.M.: Suhrkamp, 45–63.

'Sudan Airstrike Mystery'. 2009. *New York Times*, 26 March 2009. Retrieved 9 January 2015 from http://thelede.blogs.nytimes.com–/2009/03/26/sudan-airstrike-mystery/.

'Sudan Pins Economic Hopes on Gold Prospects'. 2012. *Sudan Tribune*, 26 July 2012. Retrieved 9 January 2015 from www.sudantribune.com/spip.php?article43373.

'Sudan Predicted to be Africa's Largest Gold Producer by 2018'. 2014. *Sudan Tribune*, 7 July 2014. Retrieved 9 January 2015 from www.sudantribune.com/spip.php?article51609.

'Sudan Signs 10 Gold, Iron Mining Exploration Agreements, Minister Says'. 2010. *Bloomberg*. 7 November 2010. Retrieved 9 January 2015 from www.bloomberg.com/news/2010-11-07/sudan-signs-10-gold-iron-mining-exploration-agreements-minister-says.html.

Sutton, David. 2010. 'Food and the Senses', *Annual Review of Anthropology* 39, 209–23.

Taussig, Michael T. 1980. *The Devil and Commodity Fetishism in South America*. Chapel Hill: University of North Carolina Press.

Tetzlaff, Rainer and Karl Wohlmuth (eds). 1980. *Der Sudan: Probleme und Perspektiven der Entwicklung eines weltmarktabhängigen Agrarstaates*. Frankfurt a.M.: Metzner.

Thévenot, Laurent. 1984. 'Rules and Implements: Investment in Forms', *Social Science Information* 23(1), 1–45.

———. 2001. 'Pragmatic Regimes Governing the Engagement with the World', in Theodore Schatzki, Karin Knorr Cetina and Eike von Savigny (eds), *The Practice Turn in Contemporary Theory*. New York: Routledge, 56–73.

———. 2006. *L'action au pluriel: Sociologie des régimes d'engagement*. Paris: La Découverte.

———. 2007. 'The Plurality of Cognitive Formats and Engagements. Moving between the Familiar and the Public', *European Journal of Social Theory* 10(3), 409–23.

———. 2009. 'Governing Life by Standards: A View from Engagements', *Social Studies of Science* 39(5), 793–813.

Timmermans, Stefan and Marc Berg. 2003. *The Gold Standard: The Challenge of Evidence-Based Medicine and Standardization in Health Care*. Philadelphia: Temple University Press.

Timmermans, Stefan and Steven Epstein. 2010. 'A World of Standards but Not a Standard of World: Towards a Sociology of Standards and Standardization', *Annual Revue of Sociology* 36, 69–89.

'Tribal Clashes Kill Dozens near Gold Mine in Sudan's Darfur'. 2013. *Reuters*, 27 June 2013. Retrieved 9 January 2015 from www.reuters.com/article/2013/06/27/us-sudan-darfur-idUSBRE95Q0D720130627.

Tschakert, Petra. 2009. 'Digging Deep for Justice: A Radical Re-Imagination of the Artisanal Gold Mining Sector in Ghana', *Antipode* 41(4), 706–40.

Tschakert, Petra and Kamini Singha. 2007. 'Contaminated Identities: Mercury and Marginalization in Ghana's Artisanal Mining Sector', *Geoforum* 38, 1304–21.

Tsing, Anna Lownhaupt. 1993. *In the Realm of the Diamond Queen: Marginality in an Out-of-the-way Place*. Princeton, NJ: Princeton University Press.

Tulloch, John. 2008. 'Culture and Risk', in Jens Zinn (ed.), *Social Theories of Risk and Uncertainty: An Introduction*. Oxford: Blackwell, 138–67.

Turabi, Hasan Al-. 1987. 'Principles of Governance, Freedom, and Responsibility in Islam', *American Journal of Islamic Social Sciences* 4(1), 1–11.

Umbadda, Siddig. 2014. 'Agricultural Investment through Land Grabbing in Sudan', in Jörg Gertel, Richard Rottenburg and Sandra Calkins (eds), *Disrupting Territories: Land, Commodification & Conflict in Sudan*. Suffolk: James Currey, 31–51.

United Nations (UN). 2012. *Sudan/ South Sudan*. Retrieved 25 June 2013 from www.un.org/depts/Cartographic/english/htmain.htm.

United Nations Environment Programme (UNEP). 2011a. *Analysis for Stakeholders on Formalization in the Artisanal and Small-Scale Gold Mining Sector Based on Experiences in Latin America, Africa, and Asia*. A compendium of case studies. Geneva: United Nations Environment Programme.

———. 2011b. *Reducing Mercury Use in Artisanal and Small-scale Gold Mining*. A practical guide. Geneva: United Nations Environment Programme.

United Nations Industrial Development Organization (UNIDO). 2007. *Removal of Barriers to the Introduction of Cleaner Artisanal Gold Mining and Extraction Technologies*. GMP in Sudan. Final summary report. Vienna: Global Mercury Project, United Nations Industrial Development Organization.

Van Dongen, Els. 2008. 'Keeping the Feet of the Gods and the Saints Warm: Mundane Pragmatics in Times of Suffering and Uncertainty', *Anthropology & Medicine* 15(3), 263–69.

Veiga, M.M. and R. Baker. 2004. *Protocols for Environmental and Health Assessment of Mercury Released by Artisanal and Small-Scale Miners.* Report to the Global Mercury Project. Removal of Barriers to Introduction of Cleaner Artisanal Gold Mining and Extraction Technologies.

Verhoeven, Harry. 2011. '"Dams Are Development": China, the Al-Ingaz Regime and the Political Economy of the Sudanese Nile', in Daniel Large and Luke Patey (eds), *Sudan Looks East: China, India and the Politics of Asian Alternative.* Woodbridge: James Currey, 120–38.

———. 2012. 'Sudan and Its Agricultural Revival. A Regional Breadbasket at Last or Another Mirage in the Desert?', in J. Allen (ed.), *Handbook of Land and Water Grabs in Africa.* London: Routledge, 132–66.

Waal, Alexander De. 1997. *Famine Crimes: Politics and the Disaster Relief Industry in Africa.* Oxford: James Currey.

———. 2005 [1989]. *Famine that Kills: Darfur, Sudan.* Rev. edn. New York: Oxford University Press.

Wagner, Peter. 1993. 'Die Soziologie der Genese sozialer Institutionen: Theoretische Perspektiven der neuen Sozialwissenschaften in Frankreich', *Zeitschrift für Soziologie* 22(6), 464–76.

Wallerstein, Immanuel. 1974. *The Modern World System: Capitalist Agriculture and the Origins of the European World Economy in the Sixteenth Century.* New York: Academic Press.

Warburg, Gabriel. 1988. *Islam, Sectarianism and Politics in Sudan since the Mahdiyya.* London: Hurst.

Weber, Max. 1922 [1904]. 'The Objektivität sozialwissenschaftlicher und sozialpolitischer Erkenntnis', in *Gesammelte Ausätze zur Wissenschaftstheorie.* Tübingen: J.C.B. Mohr, 146–214.

Werthmann, Katja. 2006. 'Gold Diggers, Earth Priests, and Districts Heads: Land Rights and Gold Mining in Southwestern Burkina Faso', in Richard Kuba and Carola Lenth (eds), *Land and the Politics of Belonging in West Africa.* Leiden: Brill, 119–36.

———. 2009. *Bitteres Gold: Bergbau, Land und Geld in Westafrika.* Cologne: Rüdiger Köppe Verlag.

Winch, Peter. 1997 [1968]. 'Understanding a Primitive Society', in Roy R. Grinker and Christoff B. Steiner (eds), *Perspectives on Africa: A Reader in Culture, History and Representation.* Oxford: Blackwell, 312–26.

Wittgenstein, Ludwig. 1977. *Philosophische Untersuchungen.* Frankfurt: Suhrkamp.

Whyte, Susan Reynolds. 1997. *Questioning Misfortune: The Pragmatics of Uncertainty in Eastern Uganda.* Cambridge: Cambridge University Press.

———. 2005. 'Uncertain Undertaking: Practicing Health Care in the Subjunctive Mood', in Vibeke Steffen, Richard Jenkins and Hanne Jessen (eds), *Managing Uncertainty: Ethnographic Studies of Illness, Risk and the Struggle for Control.* Copenhagen: Museum Tusculanum Press, 245–64.

Woolgar, Steve. 1988. 'Reflexivity Is the Ethnographer of the Text', in Steve Woolgar (ed.), *Knowledge and Reflexivity: New Frontiers in the Sociology of Knowledge.* London: Sage, 14–34.

World Bank (WB). 2013. *Sudan Overview.* Retrieved 9 January 2015 from www.worldbank. org/en/country/-sudan/overview.

World Health Organization (WHO). 2010. *Country Cooperation Strategy for WHO and Sudan 2008–2013*. Retrieved 10 January 2015 from http://applications.emro.who.int/docs/CCS_Sudan_2010_EN_14477.pdf.

Wynne, Brian. 2001. 'Creating Public Alienation: Expert Cultures of Risk and Ethics on GMOs', *Science as Culture* 10(4), 445–81.

Young, John. 2007a. *The Eastern Front and Its Struggle Against Marginalization*. Small Arms Survey, Geneva. Retrieved 9 January 2015 from www.smallarmssurveysudan.org/pdfs/HSBA-SWP-3-Eastern-Front.pdf.

———. 2007b. *Armed Groups along Sudan's Eastern Frontier: An Overview and Analysis*. Small Arms Survey, Geneva. Retrieved 8 October 2010 from www.smallarmssurveysudan.org/pdfs/HSBA-SWP-9-Eastern-Frontier.pdf.

Young, William. 1988. 'The Days of Joy: a Structuralist Analysis of Weddings among the Rashaayda Arabs of Sudan'. PhD dissertation, University of California, Los Angeles.

———. 1996. *The Rashaayda Bedouin: Arab Pastoralists of Eastern Sudan: Case Studies in Cultural Anthropology Series*. Orlando, FL: Harcourt Brace.

———. 2008. 'The Rashaayida Arabs vs. the State: The Impact of European Colonialism on a Small-Scale Society in Sudan and Eritrea', *Journal of Colonialism and Colonial History* 9(2). Project MUSE.

Zinn, Jens. 2008a. 'Introduction: the Contribution of Sociology to the Discourse on Risk and Uncertainty', in Jens Zinn (ed.), *Social Theories of Risk and Uncertainty: An Introduction*. Malden, MA: Blackwell, 1–17.

———. 2008b. 'A Comparison of Sociological Theorizing on Risk and Uncertainty', in Jens Zinn (ed.), *Social Theories of Risk and Uncertainty: An Introduction*. Malden, MA: Blackwell, 168–210.

INDEX

A

Abyei, 15, 41

agency, 3–4, 38–39, 52, 55, 59, 63, 66, 69, 145, 161–62, 184, 186, 210, 222, 235

Akrich, Madeleine, 127–29, 133

Alexeyeff, Kalissa, 168

ambiguity, 148, 150, 174, 185–86, 191

Appadurai, Arjun, 193n16

anticipation, 32, 34, 62, 86, 199

  anticipatory knowledge, 51, 242

Arabization, 13–15, 241

arbitrariness, 4, 32, 52, 70–71, 96, 101, 145, 220, 239

Avieli, Nir, 193n15, 167

ʿawlād ʿamm, x, 90, 100, 218–20, 224–26

ʿawlād ḫāl, 108n11, 220, 226

ʿayb, 88, 108n17, 164, 209

Azande, 47–49, 70n3

Azarya, Victor, 40n5, 40n7

B

Barth, Frederik, 166, 167, 193n11

Bashir, Omar al-, 26, 230n5

Bauman, Zygmunt, 41n19, 54–55

Bayart, Jean-Francois, 92

bayt, x, 95, 99, 223–25

Beck, Ulrich, 39n1, 51, 55–57, 71nn9–10

Beja Congress, 15–16, 40n11, 41n15

biopolitics, 11, 24–26, 39n3, 57

Bishariyn, 16, 75–76, 80–81, 84, 91, 126, 158n29

blessing, 120, 127, 133, 150–51

Bloor, David, 49, 50

Blue Nile State, 17, 23, 32, 117, 119, 123, 156n5, 157n16

Boltanski, Luc, 21, 58–63, 68–69, 71n14, 98, 238

  on dialectics of confirmation and critique, 50, 60, 240

  on institutions, 46, 37, 50, 52

  on reality and world, 59–60, 63, 71nn11–12, 153–54

  on semantic domination

  on uncertainty, 58–61

Bourdieu, Pierre, 69, 75, 90, 172

Bowker, Geoffry, 185

Breadbasket strategies, 27

Burkina Faso, 138, 156n8, 157n18

Bush, Lawrence, 175–76

Butana, 157n19

C

calculation, 10–11, 52, 58–59, 62, 87, 134–35, 142, 144, 146, 148, 152, 165, 169, 180–81, 184, 192n7, 234, 240

Callon, Michel, 95

camel, 17, 37, 73, 75, 77, 81–82, 84, 115, 127, 200, 227

  camel meat, 82, 88, 91, 95, 115, 184

capitalism, 21, 27, 160n38, 234

  millenial capitalism, 148–49

  peripheral capitalism, 21

care, 172, 197, 199, 203–5, 217, 219, 221, 223–25, 227–29

Carsten, Janet, 168, 193n17, 194n24, 224–26

Castells, Manuel, 20, 22

Castoriadis, Cornelius, 113, 149, 160n39, 160n41

classification, 11, 15, 56–57, 70n5, 145,